Japan

IN

China

Japan

IN

China

By T. A. BISSON

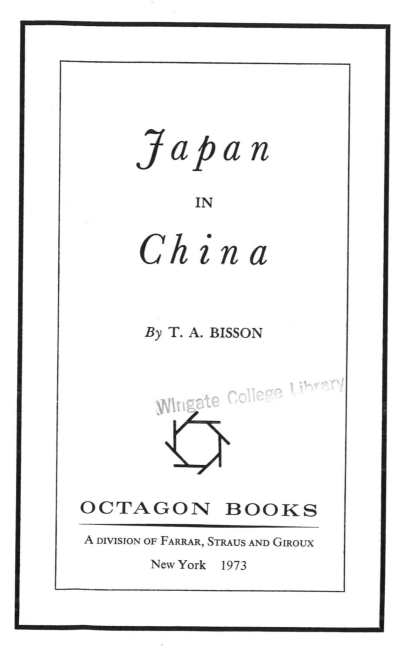

OCTAGON BOOKS

A DIVISION OF FARRAR, STRAUS AND GIROUX

New York   1973

Reprinted 1973
by special arrangement with T. A. Bisson

OCTAGON BOOKS
A Division of Farrar, Straus & Giroux, Inc.
19 Union Square West
New York, N. Y. 10003

Library of Congress Cataloging in Publication Data

Bisson, Thomas Arthur, 1900-
   Japan in China

   Reprint of the ed. published by Macmillan, New York.
   1. Sino-Japanese Conflict, 1937-1945—Causes. 2. Japan—
Armed Forces—China. 3. China—Politics and government—
1912-1949. 4. Japan—Politics and government—1912-1945.
5. Manchuria—History—1931-1945. I. Title.   10-17-74
DS777.53.B5   1973   952.03'3   73-4546
ISBN 0-374-90640-8

Manufactured by Braun-Brumfield, Inc.
Ann Arbor, Michigan

Printed in the United States of America

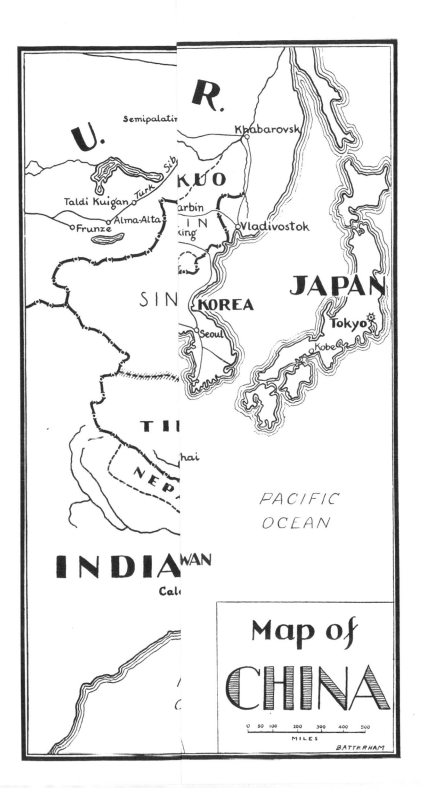

Map of

CHINA

0 50 100 200 300 400 500
MILES

BATTERHAM

PREFACE

THIS book is the outgrowth of travel and investigation in the Far East during 1937, made possible by a fellowship from the Rockefeller Foundation. Its content and emphases were necessarily affected by the outbreak of Sino-Japanese hostilities during that period. In addition to presenting the more immediate background of the conflict, I have sought to deal briefly with what will probably constitute merely its first stages.

I take this opportunity to express my appreciation to the many individuals, both in China and Japan, who have freely volunteered information, placed materials at my disposal, or otherwise assisted me in the preparation of the manuscript. To the Foreign Policy Association, which generously enabled me to devote a full year to this research project, my thanks are due in special measure.

My greatest obligation is to my wife. Without her unfailing optimism and encouragement, the task would never have been completed. To her the book is dedicated.

T. A. BISSON.

Port Washington, L. I.,
April 12, 1938.

CONTENTS

ILLUSTRATIONS

Japan

IN

China

CHAPTER ONE

THE OUTBREAK OF WAR

THE spring of 1937 was the quietest that China had experienced for more than a decade. Internal peace seemed assured; while external relations, save for disquieting undercurrents in the north, were marked by a degree of tranquillity unusual for some years past. The transfer of Chang Hsueh-liang's Northeastern troops to Honan, Anhwei and Kiangsu provinces, and their reorganization by the Central Government, had been peacefully effected by the end of May. Agreement on a similar reorganization of the Szechuan provincial armies was reached during June. Mr. Lin Sen, Chairman of the National Government, had visited Kwangsi province in April, conferred with its erstwhile antagonistic chiefs, and passed in review the soldiers of the Fifth Route Army. Government leaders and the Communists were quietly working out the details of a political rapprochement. The officials of the Hopei-Chahar Political Council were drawing closer to Nanking, notably in arrangements concluded for the election of northern delegates to the National People's Congress scheduled for November. Economic indices were no less favorable. Foreign trade was growing rapidly, the currency reform was being extended, railway construction was actively progressing, agreements to refund old foreign loans were being made, and new foreign loans secured. Encouraged by these concrete evidences of political unification and economic advance, the whole nation was buoyed up by a new feeling of self-confidence and self-respect.

There was perhaps too little apprehension that China's domestic progress might be interrupted by outside intervention. Relations with Japan, it was true, had been characterized by a diplomatic *détente* since the beginning of the year, and overt Japanese aggression had been discontinued. On the whole the visit of the Kodama Economic Mission to Shanghai in March, carrying the olive branch of "economic cooperation," was viewed skeptically, yet Foreign Minister Sato's policy seemed to represent a new attitude on the part of Japanese business and political circles toward China. More attention should possibly have been paid to the address delivered by General Sugiyama, Japanese Minister of War, to the conference of prefectural governors at Tokyo on May 19, when he declared: "As for China, we find that it is concentrating on centralization, replenishment of armaments, and other defensive undertakings based on anti-Japanese slogans. As a result, it has come to overestimate its national strength, and this in turn has served to encourage the anti-Japanese sentiments of its people. We fear that China may ultimately resort to sundry steps to obstruct Japan's peaceful advance at its very foundation." [1] Under the conditions prevailing at the time, however, such a statement was dismissed as ordinary home propaganda by the War Ministry. With the formation on June 3 of the Konoye Cabinet, generally held to be liberal despite the predominance of reactionary members, the prospects for continued peace were thought to have still further improved.

In North China disturbing political undercurrents partially belied the surface calm. Mutinies among the pro-

[1] *The Japan Advertiser,* Tokyo, May 20, 1937.

Manchoukuo irregulars controlling north Chahar, and the activities of armed Chinese volunteers, were raising a barrier against further Japanese encroachment on the Inner Mongolian provinces. Following a visit made to Jehol and north Chahar early in May by General Uyeda, Commander-in-Chief of the Kwantung Army, reports of Japanese plans for a renewed invasion of Suiyuan became current. During this period, also, the leaders of the Hopei-Chahar Political Council were proving hesitant about carrying through a series of economic projects involving the exploitation of North China under Japanese auspices. On May 11 General Sung Che-yuan went into a prolonged retreat at Loling, his birthplace in northern Shantung; it was rumored that his continued retirement was due to a desire to avoid Japanese pressure. The growing authority of the Central Government was evidently reacting on events in the north. To the Japanese military, it seemed that the Hopei-Chahar Political Council was becoming something less than a pliant tool through which Japan's purposes in North China could be accomplished. Japanese newspapers at home and in China's port cities sounded warnings against "over-confidence," "provocations," and the "obstructions placed in Japan's path."

The members of the Hopei-Chahar Political Council, some two dozen in number, were not all of one mind. Nanking had deliberately placed many of them on the Council by reason of their recognized pro-Japanese orientation. None of them, however, was wholly immune to the national consciousness that was spreading over China; some were strongly affected by it. The important leaders of the Council were commanding officers of the 29th Route Army, and also held the chief government posts in the two provinces. General Sung Che-yuan, Chairman of the Council, was Commander-in-Chief of the 29th

Army. General Chang Tzu-chung, commander of the 38th Division, was Mayor of Tientsin. General Feng Chih-an, commanding the 37th Division, was the acting governor of Hopei province. These two Divisions, which were stationed in the Peiping-Tientsin area, played the leading role in the July events. Several other figures also deserve mention: General Chin Te-chun, Mayor of Peiping; General Chao Teng-yu, commander of the 132nd Division, located between Peiping and Paotingfu; and General Liu Ju-ming, Governor of Chahar and commander of the 143rd Division, with headquarters at Kalgan. In the spring of 1937 the four divisions of the 29th Army and several other attached brigades probably exceeded 100,-000 troops, although less than half of these were in the Peiping-Tientsin area. Several thousand *Paoantui* (Peace Preservation Corps), well armed but used mainly for policing purposes, were also under the jurisdiction of the Hopei-Chahar Political Council. Eight Japanese civilian advisers were attached to the Council, and three Japanese military advisers to the 29th Army. These advisers exerted but nominal influence over the 29th Army and the *Paoantui* units in Peiping and Tientsin; a few miles east of Peiping at Tungchow, however, the East Hopei *Paoantui* corps were puppet Chinese forces under direct Japanese control.

During the spring the underlying uneasiness in the north never took on tangible form. Through most of June no hint of the approaching storm was let fall in Peiping. A sudden change of atmosphere occurred at the end of the month. Rumors of an impending upset began to fill the air, and were multiplied during the first week of July. They were discussed over luncheon and dinner tables, and bandied about in hotels and clubs. The correspondents were alert to know when the Japanese were "going to

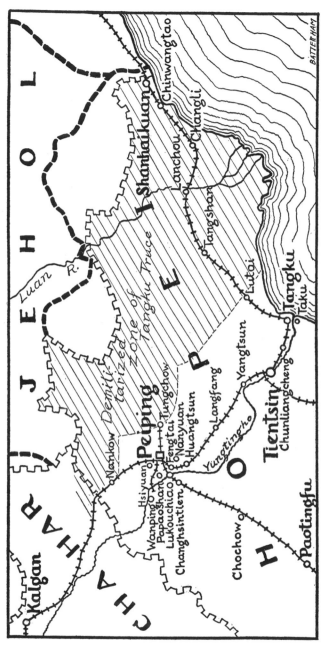

THE PEIPING-TIENTSIN AREA, SHOWING LINE MARKED BY THE TANGKU TRUCE.

strike." The following *Reuter* despatch shows that this
state of mind was the product of something more than
unsubstantial fancy.

"Peiping, June 30. Precautionary measures have been
strengthened by the local defence authorities during the
last two days as the result of rumors that plain clothes
men have smuggled themselves into the city for the purpose of creating disturbances. Semi-martial law was enforced on Monday and Tuesday nights when pedestrians
were subject to search. It is reported that four suspicious
characters were arrested at the Chien Men Station on
Monday night and that they have confessed that they are
in the pay of a certain disgruntled politician. The continuance of field exercises by Japanese troops at Marco
Polo Bridge and vicinity has given rise to considerable
anxiety in Chinese circles. It is stated that at first the
Chinese authorities were given to understand that these
exercises would last only one day, but they have since
continued for three days." [2]

Two possible sources of future trouble are noted in this
despatch: the activities of plain clothes men, and Japanese
troop maneuvers at Marco Polo Bridge. It is significant
that, despite the assurances reportedly given the Chinese
authorities, these maneuvers continued in the same locality for another week and eventually gave rise to the
incident which precipitated Sino-Japanese hostilities.
Meanwhile, throughout the first week of July, the North
China officials were forced to deal with a continuous
incursion of plain clothes agents. The following chrono-
logical summary of events, taken from the local press,[3]
indicates that the Chinese authorities were thoroughly
aware of the danger which confronted them.

[2] *The Peiping Chronicle,* July 1, 1937.
[3] *The Peiping Chronicle, The Peiping News,* July 2-7, 1937.

July 1st. Unscrupulous elements reported attempting to stir up disturbances in Tientsin, Peiping, and Paotingfu. The Peiping police begin to enforce "summer defence" regulations. General Chang Tzu-chung, Mayor of Tientsin, arrives in Peiping to confer with his associates on the Hopei-Chahar Political Council.

July 2nd. Two suspicious characters, loitering in vicinity of Hopei-Chahar Political Council's quarters, arrested yesterday in Peiping; reported to have confessed that they were in the pay of certain quarters to create disturbances during the forthcoming election of local delegates to the National People's Congress; admitted having confederates in various parts of the city, and also in Paotingfu and Kalgan.

Scores of plain clothes agents reported to have been arrested in Peiping by detectives and police during last few days. As precautionary measure, the local defence force has been reinforced by troops from the 29th Army stationed in the suburbs.

July 3rd. Defence measures discussed yesterday afternoon in Peiping at a conference attended by General Chang Tzu-chung, Mayor of Tientsin; General Chin Te-chun, Mayor of Peiping; General Feng Chih-an, Governor of Hopei province; and General Liu Ju-ming, Governor of Chahar province. These officials decided to cooperate in the maintenance of peace and order in the two provinces and two special municipalities under jurisdiction of the Hopei-Chahar Political Council. General Chang Tzu-chung returned to Tientsin shortly after the meeting.

High Chinese official in Peiping quoted as saying that the authorities have the situation well in hand and that no anxiety need be felt by the public.

July 4th. General Chang Tzu-chung, Mayor of Tientsin, reappears in Peiping at 6:30 P.M.

July 5th. Colonel Matsui, Chief of the Japanese Special Service Mission in Peiping, leaves for Tientsin to confer with Lieutenant-General Tashiro, Commander of the North China Garrison.

General Feng Chih-an, the Hopei governor, having returned to Paotingfu, declares that all is quiet in Peiping and Tientsin.

July 6th. Two plain clothes men captured by police after gun chase in western suburbs of Peiping. More than forty shots exchanged; one policeman and one plain clothes man wounded. Latter admits to being a member of the East Hopei *Paoantui* (Peace Preservation Corps).

General Chang Tzu-chung inspects the 29th Route Army troops in the Nanyuan barracks outside Peiping.

Wild rumors circulating in Peiping and Tientsin during the last few days reported to have gradually died down as a result of the precautionary measures taken by the authorities.

If the plain clothes agents had planned to create disturbances that would serve as a pretext for Japanese intervention, their object was evidently frustrated by the determined actions of the North China officials. Escape from this danger did not prevent the outbreak of conflict. The exact details of the Lukouchiao, or Marco Polo Bridge, incident will probably never be known. As at Mukden on September 18, 1931, the event which gave rise to the armed clash took place under cover of darkness, and contradictory versions as to what actually happened were immediately put into circulation.

According to the Japanese version,[4] Chinese soldiers about 1,000 metres north of Lukouchiao fired several tens of rifle shots, some time before midnight [5] on July 7, at a body of Japanese troops holding maneuvers in that

[4] *The Peiping Chronicle,* July 9, 1937; *The Japan Advertiser,* July 9 and 10, 1937.

[5] The time is given as "about ten o'clock" by the Japanese Military Attaché at Peiping (*Chronicle,* July 9), and as "shortly after eleven o'clock" in the Tokyo Foreign Office statement (*Advertiser,* July 10).

vicinity. The maneuvers were immediately halted and the troops concentrated to watch developments. With only one live cartridge for each soldier in his force, the Japanese commander was obliged to hold fire and summon reinforcements from Fengtai.[6] Meanwhile, arrangements were made for a joint Sino-Japanese investigation committee to be despatched to the scene from Peiping. This committee reached the spot between four and five o'clock on the morning of July 8. The Japanese reinforcements reached Lukouchiao at five o'clock in the morning; about half-past five, in consequence of renewed firing by the Chinese troops, fighting was resumed and lasted until half-past nine, when a temporary truce was effected.

The official Chinese version [7] claims that shortly after midnight Colonel Matsui, Chief of the Japanese Special Service Mission at Peiping, telephoned to the Hopei-Chahar Political Council, stating that while a company of Japanese troops was engaged in field maneuvers near Lukouchiao rifle shots were suddenly heard.[8] The exer-

[6] This point is stressed in the Foreign Office statement. It is contradicted by the testimony of a Japanese private, who was wounded in the fighting at Lukouchiao, given during the course of an interview with an *Asahi* correspondent. The interview reads in part as follows: "An intense sham battle was carried out Wednesday night. Just as the bugle call concluded the activities, rifle fire was heard. Bullets whistled over the heads of the Japanese. The officers ordered the men to fall flat on the ground, but the bullets began to fall fast. Orders were given to return the fire and the men began shooting in the direction from which the bullets came. They continued to fire until their live ammunition was all gone, 'before they realized what they were doing.' At last the unseen enemy stopped firing and fled. It was dawn when the battle was resumed." *The Japan Advertiser*, July 12, 1937.

[7] *The Peiping Chronicle*, July 9, 1937.

[8] Chinese newspaper reports suggested that these shots might have been fired by plain clothes men under Japanese direction. There are indications that certain "young officers" planned the whole affair in emulation of the Mukden incident of September 18, 1931. The names usually mentioned include Major-General Torashiro Kawabe, Lieut.-Col. Wachi, and Colonel Matsui. See *China Weekly Review*, July 31, 1937, p. 324.

cises were then stopped, declared Colonel Matsui, the number of men checked, and one man found to be missing. He concluded by saying that the Japanese had demanded the right to enter Wanping to search for the missing soldier, but that this demand had been rejected. Later Colonel Matsui again telephoned the Council, saying that the Japanese troops would enter Wanping by force unless permission for entry was granted. Since the missing soldier had now turned up, the Chinese claimed that there was no further necessity for the Japanese to enter the town. Colonel Matsui, however, replied that it was difficult to check up on all the troops that were mobilized, and pressed the need for sending representatives into Wanping for an investigation. At this time the Hopei-Chahar Council authorities learned that the Japanese troops were closing in on Wanping; hoping to prevent the outbreak of hostilities, they agreed to have a joint delegation sent to the scene.

The Japanese delegates were Captain Teradaira, vice-chief of the Special Service Mission, and Colonel Sakurai, adviser to the 29th Route Army. The Chinese delegation comprised Mr. Wang Lei-chai, magistrate of the Wanping district; Mr. Lin Keng-yu, an expert of the Foreign Relations Commission of the Hopei-Chahar Political Council; and Colonel Chow Yung-nien, vice-chief of the communications staff of the Hopei-Chahar Pacification Commissioner's office. These delegates reached Wanping at four o'clock on the morning of July 8. The Japanese officers again insisted that their troops be permitted to enter and search the town, but the Chinese officials declined to entertain the demand. The delegates entered the town, however, and about five o'clock, while negotiations for a settlement were proceeding, the Japanese troops outside the east gate opened fire. Soon afterwards heavy artillery fire was heard coming from outside the west gate of the town. Up to this point the Chinese troops had not replied to the attack, but under the bombardment they were compelled to open fire in self-defence. The statement concluded by declaring that the Chinese authorities hoped to reach a peaceful settlement, but that if the Japanese continued the attack on Wanping the Chinese troops would not hesitate to resist to the best of their ability and means.

The fighting at Wanping ended at half-past nine on the morning of July 8, with several score Chinese soldiers and about ten Chinese civilians killed or wounded; Japanese casualties were officially announced as ten, including two non-commissioned officers and one sub-lieutenant. A one-hour armistice was declared at ten o'clock, later extended to noon—the first of several truces made only to be broken on this and subsequent days.

Several aspects of the Lukouchiao incident deserve further consideration. In the first place, as noted in the *Reuter* despatch quoted previously, the Japanese troop maneuvers at Marco Polo Bridge had already been proceeding for three days as early as June 30. Yet field exercises were still continuing there on the night of July 7, when the incident occurred. What made it necessary for the Japanese maneuvers to be prolonged over a ten-day period? In the second place, the Lukouchiao-Wanping area is of extreme strategic importance. This region lies athwart the Peiping-Hankow Railway which, in view of the Japanese occupation of the Fengtai railway junction in September 1936, afforded the last unobstructed access to Peiping from the south for Chinese troops. Could the Japanese army have been designedly aiming to secure military control of Lukouchiao and Wanping, thus completing the isolation of Peiping?

There is, finally, the technical point that the Japanese military forces had no legal justification for conducting maneuvers in the Lukouchiao area. Since the Japanese authorities, on a number of occasions in recent years, have referred rather loosely to the Boxer Protocol as justifying the exercise of certain military rights in North China which they have in fact arbitrarily assumed, it is necessary to examine at some length the relevant sections of this protocol and the later exchanges of notes between China and the powers. Article IX of the Final Protocol, signed on September 7, 1901 and commonly known as the Boxer Protocol, reads as follows:

"The Chinese Government has conceded the right to the Powers in the protocol annexed to the letter of the 16th of January, 1901, to occupy certain points, to be determined by an agreement between them, for the maintenance of open communications between the capital and the sea. The points occupied by the powers are: Huangtsun, Langfang, Yangtsun, Tientsin, Chunliangcheng, Tangku, Lutai, Tangshan, Lanchou, Changli, Chinwangtao, and Shanhaikuan." [9]

Two points arise in connection with this article of the protocol. The right to station foreign troops at the places specified rests on the declaration that they are located "between the capital and the sea." Peiping ceased to be the capital of China in 1928; since then, it may be questioned whether any of the powers has a legal right to continue the maintenance of its armed forces at these places. An adviser to the Chinese Ministry of Foreign Affairs, in a recent brochure, notes that the powers entering into formal treaty relations with the National Government since 1928 did so "with the knowledge that

[9] John V. A. MacMurray, *Treaties and Agreements with and concerning China, 1894-1919*, Volume I, p. 282-283.

Nanking had been chosen as the new capital and without making reservation in favor of Peking." He therefore maintains that Article IX of the main protocol, as well as the provisions of the treaty instruments of 1901-1902 relating to it, "should all be considered as obsolete and subject to termination when and if the Chinese Government chooses to raise the question with the Protocol Powers." [10]

Aside from this general issue, it should be noted that the Article under consideration permits the occupation of only twelve specified points. In actual practice, up to 1933, all the powers including Japan had restricted their troops to Peiping and Tientsin, except for small contingents despatched in rotation to summer camps at Chinwangtao and Shanhaikuan. Only Japan, since 1933, had exercised the right of stationing troops at most of the twelve places specified in Article IX. In addition, from the end of 1935 Japan arbitrarily assumed the right of stationing a military force at Tungchow, and from September 1936 at Fengtai. The maintenance of Japanese troops at these two towns was clearly contrary to the provisions of the Boxer Protocol.

During the first week of July 1937, the issue at Lukouchiao was not one of military occupation but whether Japan had treaty sanction for holding troop maneuvers in that area. The provisions relating to this question are found in the identical notes addressed to China by five

[10] Shuhsi Hsu, "The Boxer Protocol and Japanese Aggression," *Information Bulletin*, Council of International Affairs, Nanking, Volume IV, No. 8, August 18, 1937. In support of the same position, the editor of *The Peiping Chronicle* cites the precedent of Turkey. He states: "When the capital of Turkey was removed from Stambul (Constantinople) to Ankara practically all the accumulated and accreted privileges that foreign Powers had obtained in Constantinople under the old régime were swept away, and there seems to be no reason why special privileges should persist here." "The Documents in the Case," *The Peiping Chronicle*, July 27, 1937.

powers, including Japan, under date of July 15, 1902, and are supplementary to Article IX of the Boxer Protocol. They read as follows:

"By Article IX of the same Protocol it is provided that the powers shall have the right of occupying certain points between Peking and the sea, of which the whole town of Tientsin is one. Consequently, after the dissolution of the Tientsin provisional government, foreign troops will continue as hitherto to be stationed there, in the places actually occupied by them, and their supplies of all sorts continuing, as at present, to be exempt from all taxes or dues whatsoever. They will have the right of carrying on field exercises and rifle practice, etc., without informing the Chinese authorities, except in the case of *feux de guerre.*

"It is desirable, however, to avoid as far as possible occasions of collision between the foreign troops and those of China. I propose, therefore, that with this object the Chinese Government shall undertake not to station or march any troops within 20 Chinese *li* (6⅔ English miles) of the city or of the troops stationed at Tientsin; further . . . it was agreed that the jurisdiction of the commanders of the posts to be established along the line of communications should extend to a distance of 2 miles on either side of the railway, and this arrangement ought to be maintained as long as the line of posts specified in Article IX of the protocol continues to be occupied." [11]

These provisions confined the right to carry on "field exercises and rifle practice, etc." exclusively to the foreign troops stationed in Tientsin. By no possible interpretation can they be stretched to cover troop maneuvers farther than 6⅔ miles from Tientsin or beyond the two-mile zone on either side of the railway. Nor does the

[11] MacMurray, cited, Volume I, p. 317.

article of the main protocol which sanctioned the maintenance of Legation Guards in Peiping make provision for their deployment beyond the limits of the Legation Quarter. Article VII of the main protocol, relevant to this point, reads as follows:

"The Chinese Government has agreed that the quarter occupied by the legations shall be considered as one specially reserved for their use and placed under their exclusive control, in which Chinese shall not have the right to reside and which may be made defensible. . . . In the protocol annexed to the letter of the 16th of January, 1901, China recognized the right of each Power to maintain a permanent guard in the said quarter for the defence of its legation." [12]

By a later arrangement, the various Legation Guards secured the privilege of using an international rifle range which was laid out to the east of Peiping.[13] This privilege, however, did not carry with it the right to hold troop maneuvers in the neighborhood of Peiping. Yet the Japanese military forces, from 1935 to 1937, arbitrarily assumed the right to conduct field exercises on an extended scale throughout the Peiping-Tientsin area. It was by virtue of this assumed right, wholly unsanctioned by treaty provision, that the Japanese troops were holding maneuvers at Lukouchiao in July 1937.[14]

Following the Lukouchiao incident, events in North China—with deceptive interludes of calm—marched to the appointed climax of July 28. In retrospect, these three weeks call up a confused picture of sporadic clashes between Chinese and Japanese troops in the environs of

[12] MacMurray, cited, Volume I, p. 282.

[13] "The Documents in the Case," cited.

[14] Some authorities refer to a note of November 15, 1913, sent to the powers by the Chinese Foreign Minister, as conferring such a right. The exact degree of validity to be attached to this note is in doubt.

Peiping; reported settlements, alternately confirmed and denied, the details of which were only verified much later; the rapid breakdown of normal railway passenger schedules; and the steady influx of Japanese troops and war supplies. Less tangible was the unremitting tension created by a prolonged, severe political struggle, in the course of which resort to force is continually threatened. The disparity in the attitudes assumed by the opponents was marked: irresolution, partial compromise, and differences of opinion on the part of the leading officials of the Hopei-Chahar Political Council; on the side of the Japanese military, unity, determination, and a grim certainty of objective.

Early on the morning of July 9, the War Office at Tokyo sent urgent orders to the commanders of certain divisions in Japan to postpone disbandment of privates whose service terms were expiring. Even more significant measures were taken by the Japanese government on July 11.[15] Consular officials in China were ordered to instruct Japanese nationals to prepare for evacuation "in the event of serious developments." The Foreign Office announced that the Cabinet had decided "to take all necessary measures for despatching military forces to North China," in pursuit of "its fixed and immovable policy." At a specially summoned meeting of Japan's political and financial notables, the Premier explained the government's policy and elicited pledges of support. On the same day 2,200 Japanese troops arrived in Tientsin from Manchuria. With these forces came large quantities of supplies and military equipment, including field guns, armored cars, motor trucks, and airplanes.

On July 11, also, the first settlement of the Lukouchiao incident was reached. General Chang Tzu-chung, Mayor

[15] *The Japan Advertiser*, July 12, 1937.

of Tientsin, provisionally accepted the following terms: apology by a representative of the 29th Army, and punishment of responsible Chinese officers; replacement of 29th Army troops in the Lukouchiao-Wanping area with *Paoantui* units; and suppression of anti-Japanese and Communist activities in North China. Denied at first by Chinese officials in Peiping, the validity of this agreement was later confirmed. Its terms could not be upheld; eventual breakdown was ensured by the forces at work in both camps.

Throughout the period of crisis, a sharp internal struggle was taking place among the highest ranks of the North China officials. The compromisers were mainly located in Tientsin; at Peiping, a more militant mood prevailed. Strongest of all was the feeling among the lower Chinese officers and the private soldiers, who were especially determined that the Lukouchiao-Wanping area should not be turned over to occupation by Japanese troops, as had occurred at Fengtai in the previous September. On the other hand, the Japanese forces in the Lukouchiao area were at no time wholly withdrawn to Fengtai—a factor which led to continued skirmishing, since the 29th Army troops were unwilling, under such circumstances, to retire in favor of the *Paoantui* units. The position of the Chinese officials, who were at the same time responsible military commanders, was most unenviable. In line with official policy, sanctioned by Nanking, they sought to avoid a frontal clash by complying so far as possible with the Japanese demands. In contrast with previous years, however, their yielding stopped short of an outright surrender of national rights, and thus failed to satisfy the requirements of determined Japanese aggression. The corollary to this policy, which should have been definite, planned resistance on the military side in case of a show-down, was never drawn. No straightforward lead was given to the militant spirit of the Chinese troops.

Despite the agreement of July 11, Japanese military reinforcements continued to pour into North China. Foreign military observers estimated that 10,000 Japanese troops had crossed the Great Wall by July 13 and occupied positions between Shanhaikuan and Tientsin. The majority of these troops, which lacked the distinctive badge of the Kwantung Army, had evidently been mobilized in Japan. During the succeeding week the bulk of this force, liberally supplied with war equipment of all kinds, was disposed at various points in the Peiping-Tientsin area, thus doubling the local Japanese garrison. A new commander of the North China Garrison, Lieutenant-General Katsuki, had arrived in Tientsin and assumed office by July 14.[16] On arrival, he had declared that his "mission in North China was to lead the Japanese army to justice and righteousness and to chastise the outrageous Chinese, and simultaneously to protect Japanese residents and Japanese rights and interests in North China on the basis of the immutable decisions adopted by the Cabinet." [17]

General Sung Che-yuan had meanwhile broken off his two months' retreat at Loling and reappeared in Tientsin. On July 18 he called upon Lieutenant-General Katsuki and accepted in principle the terms of the July 11 agreement. This action was reported to Nanking on July 22 and approved by the central authorities on July 24.[18] General Chang Tzu-chung, Mayor of Tientsin, had meanwhile discussed further details of this accord with Jap-

[16] His predecessor, Lieutenant-General Tashiro, was seriously ill and died a few weeks later.

[17] *The Peiping Chronicle*, July 15, 1937.

[18] Shuhsi Hsu, "The North China Crisis," *The China Quarterly* (Shanghai), Vol. 2, No. 4, Special Fall Number, 1937, p. 592.

anese representatives on July 19. Fulfilment of the terms began on July 21, when a detachment of the Peace Preservation Corps arrived at Lukouchiao. During the next two days both Chinese and Japanese troops began a gradual withdrawal from this area, with the former being replaced by *Paoantui* units. Three Chinese and three Japanese representatives supervised the withdrawal. Simultaneously the Chinese garrison in Peiping, comprising a section of the 37th Division, was retiring south to Chochow. Two thousand men were estimated to have left Peiping by July 23; they were replaced by contingents from the 132nd Division under General Chao Teng-yu.

The tension in North China had considerably eased by July 25. Sand-bag barricades had been removed from the streets of Peiping; martial law, still nominally in force, had been greatly relaxed. For the first time since July 7 passenger trains were reaching Peiping from the south along the Ping-Han line. Other aspects were less reassuring. Relatively few Japanese troops had withdrawn from the Lukouchiao area, and these for but a short distance. The 29th Army troops were also slowing down their retirement; some of them, it appears, had merely exchanged their uniforms for those of the *Paoantui*. Most ominous of all, an uninterrupted stream of Japanese troops and equipment was still pouring into North China. On July 25 the first of a fleet of Japanese ships began to unload 100,000 tons of military supplies at Tangku. That night another incident, occurring at Langfang, proved to be the signal for the outbreak of general hostilities.

During these weeks, the central authorities at Nanking cautiously watched developments in the north. Routine protests and reservations of rights were exchanged with the Japanese government between July 9 and 12. The Chinese government, from the beginning, was mainly concerned over the influx of Japanese troops. As a counter measure, several Chinese divisions were mobilized in Honan and later sent into southern Hopei. Dr. Wang Chung-hui, Chinese Foreign Minister, proposed on July 12 to Mr. Hidaka, Counsellor of the Japanese Embassy, that there should be mutual cessation of military movements and withdrawal of both sides to their original positions, but Tokyo paid no attention to this proposal. On July 16 a Chinese note outlining the circumstances of the conflict was transmitted to the signatories of the Nine-Power Treaty, Japan excepted, as well as to the U.S.S.R. and Germany. A Japanese memorandum, presented at Nanking on the following day, warned China to suspend all hostile acts and not to obstruct a local settlement in the north. These were the central points in the diplomatic debate. In effect Japan was demanding, first, that the Chinese government refrain from sending troops into Hopei province, while offering no check on the despatch of its own forces; and, second, that the Hopei-Chahar Political Council should be considered an independent government, in no way amenable to Nanking's jurisdiction. In reply to these demands the Chinese Foreign Office presented an aide-mémoire to the Japanese Embassy on July 19, containing the following counter-proposals: (1) joint fixing of a definite date on which both sides should simultaneously cease all military movements and withdraw their respective armed forces to the positions occupied prior to the incident; (2) settlement of the Lukouchiao incident through regular diplomatic channels; (3) questions of a local nature susceptible of adjustment on the spot should be subject to sanction of the National Government.[19]

At Kuling, on the same day, Generalissimo Chiang Kai-

[19] For text of the aide-mémoire, see *The Peiping Chronicle*, July 21, 1937.

Times Wide World

GENERALISSIMO CHIANG KAI-SHEK.

shek issued his ringing proclamation to the nation, declaring that "China's sovereign rights cannot be sacrificed, even at the expense of war, and once war has begun there is no looking back." In this address the Generalissimo laid down four points as the "minimum conditions" for a basis of negotiation: "first, any kind of settlement must not infringe upon the territorial integrity and the sovereign rights of our nation; second, as the status of the Hopei-Chahar Political Council is fixed by the Central Government, we will not allow any illegal alterations; third, we will not agree to the removal by outside pressure of those local officials appointed by the Central Government, such as the Chairman of the Hopei-Chahar Political Council; fourth, we will not allow any restriction being placed upon the positions now held by the 29th Army." [20]

Japan's diplomatic pressure at Nanking was immediately intensified. The Japanese Military Attaché, Major-General Seiichi Kita, in the course of a talk with General Ho Ying-chin, Chinese War Minister, on the late afternoon of July 19, intimated that failure to remove the central troops from Hopei might aggravate the Sino-Japanese crisis, which was "rapidly approaching the final stage." [21] Other reports described this interview as the Japanese army's "last warning" to China.[22] On July 20, at an early morning session with the Chinese Foreign Minister, Mr. Hidaka stressed the demands previously raised by his government. Dr. Wang Chung-hui firmly countered both demands. If the legality of central troop movements in Hopei should be questioned,[23] he declared,

[20] For text, see *North-China Daily News,* July 20, 1921.
[21] *The Peiping Chronicle,* July 21, 1937.
[22] *North-China Daily News,* July 20, 1937.
[23] An allusion to the Japanese claim that the terms of the Ho-Umetsu agreement barred central government troops from Hopei province. For discussion of this agreement, see Chapter II.

then it must be equally recognized that the presence there of a large Japanese army was an undoubted violation of the territorial and sovereign rights of China. As to the issue of local negotiations, he stated that in every country the conduct of foreign relations was reserved exclusively to the central government.[24] Since Mr. Hidaka refused to consider the proposals of the Chinese aide-mémoire, which Dr. Wang renewed in this conversation, the deadlock seemed complete.

To the very end, however, the Central Government kept open the possibility of a diplomatic settlement. The presence of central troops in Hopei was played up in Japan in order to rally popular support behind the militarists' aggressive plans. The *Domei* reports sent to Japan greatly exaggerated the number of these troops, which never exceeded two divisions during the month of July. Neither in Hopei nor Honan, moreover, did the mobilized divisions consist of first-class troops; the crack divisions were all kept at Nanking. The sequel showed that there was no intention even for these troops to enter the Peiping-Tientsin area. Nor did the central authorities prejudice the attempts to reach a local settlement. Hsiung Pin, Vice-Chief of Staff, went north and conferred with the 29th Army commanders at Peiping on July 23-25, but there is no evidence that he counselled military resistance. The Nanking government, as already noted, had ratified General Sung Che-yuan's acceptance of the July 11 agreement with the Japanese military; in so doing, it came perilously close to violating the four-point minimum enunciated by the Generalissimo. This, too, was of no avail; the blow fell with unrelenting vigor.

Left mainly to its own resources, the leadership of the 29th Route Army proved wholly unable to measure up to

[24] *The China Press*, July 21, 1937.

its task. To the end, it hoped to stave off general hostilities by a compromise settlement; against the day when negotiations might collapse and fighting begin, it prepared no scheme of military defence. A month earlier Chu Teh, then Commander-in-Chief of the Chinese Communist armies,[25] had given a prophetic forecast of the events that were now about to take place in North China. Asked to state the position and prospects of General Sung Che-yuan and the 29th Army, he made the following reply:

"The northern troops are under Japanese pressure and are influenced by the national salvation movement. The lower officers are very anti-Japanese, but they have no plan of action for a crisis. Once war comes, they are likely to be destroyed one after another. So it is necessary to consolidate these forces under one command, and work out a general plan for resisting Japan. We are trying to have these troops coordinated with the central command." [26]

The key to the sudden collapse in the north at the end of July lies in the concluding sentences of this brief commentary. The leaders of the 29th Route Army had formulated no plan of action of their own; much less was there a coordinated scheme of military operations between this army and the central forces. Japan's military command was enabled to complete its preparations at leisure, and then to choose the moment to strike a paralyzing blow.

The interlude of comparative peace that had followed the agreement of July 18-19 was rudely broken on the morning of July 26 by a sanguinary clash at Langfang.

[25] Now commander of the Eighth Route Army, under authority of the National Government.

[26] Interview by author at Yenan in north Shensi on June 23, 1937.

As usual, the incident which precipitated hostilities occurred during the previous night, and the details as published were presented in two contradictory versions.[27] According to the spokesman of the Japanese Military Headquarters at Tientsin, two unsuccessful attempts had been made to repair the Japanese military telephone line at Langfang, which—he alleged—had been cut by Chinese troops. On the night of July 25, he claimed, an arrangement had been reached with General Chang Tzu-chung, senior commander of the Chinese troops stationed at Langfang, to send a third repair corps accompanied, this time, by a detachment of 300 Japanese troops. The party arrived at Langfang—this being a fact not mentioned in the official Japanese statement—at about half-past eleven on the night of July 25. As they approached the station to effect repairs, they were suddenly fired upon by Chinese troops. The Japanese force immediately returned the fire, occupied the station, and summoned reinforcements.[28]

According to the Chinese version,[29] the commander of the Japanese force, after the repair corps reached Langfang, had demanded that his troops be permitted to establish themselves at the railway station. The local Chinese officer had refused the request, on the ground that in the dead of night such an occupation might create trouble with the Chinese troops, whose barracks were located only a few hundred yards distant. Thereupon, shortly after midnight, the Japanese force had attacked

[27] In the case of an incident that takes place late at night, it should be observed that, aside from the difficulty of checking up on the facts, the news does not reach the public until the second day after the event.

[28] For text of the Japanese statement, see *Peking & Tientsin Times,* July 27, 1937.

[29] There was no official Chinese statement; these details are pieced together from various unofficial Chinese sources.

the Chinese troops and occupied the station, using machine-guns, artillery, and an armored train.

Hostilities ceased for a brief period; they were resumed at 3 a.m., when 1,300 Japanese reinforcements rushed from Tientsin launched an attack on the Chinese positions. At dawn seventeen Japanese airplanes reached Langfang and bombed the Chinese barracks severely, forcing the Chinese troops to withdraw. The Japanese forces completed their occupation of the town at eight o'clock on July 26. During the morning the Chinese continued their retreat towards Huangtsun, a few miles south of Fengtai, with the Japanese forces in pursuit. Japanese casualties were thirteen; the Chinese casualties, including civilians, were much heavier—one report placed them at several hundred.

This incident, the "challenging attitude" of the Chinese troops, and the delay in carrying out the terms of the agreement accepted by the 29th Army were made the grounds for an ultimatum addressed to General Sung Che-yuan by the Japanese Garrison Headquarters on July 26. The ultimatum was delivered to General Sung in Peiping at three o'clock in the afternoon and read to the press correspondents in Tientsin at half-past three, only a few hours after fighting had ceased at Langfang. Its terms were embraced in the following sentence: "If your army should have the intention not to make the situation more serious, the 37th Division stationed near Lukouchiao and Papaoshan should, first of all, be withdrawn as soon as possible before the noon of the 27th inst. to Changhsintien, and the 37th Division in Peiping, inclusive of the troops of the same Division at Hsiyuan, should be evacuated from the Peiping wall to the westward of the Yungtingho, through the area north of the Pinghan

Railway, before the noon of the 28th inst., and the transportation of these troops to Paotingfu should be commenced immediately afterwards." In case of failure to carry out these demands, the ultimatum concluded, "the Japanese Army must, to its greatest regret, take its own decisive measures. Every responsibility incurred in this case ought to be taken by your army." [30]

The Japanese command at once proceeded to effect certain changes in the disposition of its forces, in order to strengthen its military position in the Peiping-Tientsin area. Additional Japanese reinforcements were despatched to Langfang from Tientsin during the morning of July 26. The Japanese troops in the Lukouchiao area were greatly increased. Special efforts were made to reinforce the Japanese Embassy Guard at Peiping. About 300 Japanese troops sought to enter the Chao Yang Men shortly after noon, but finding the gate closed marched around the city toward Fengtai. A similar effort in the evening led to a serious clash. Shortly before seven o'clock, about 500 Japanese troops arrived at the Kwang An Men from Lukouchiao in motor lorries and demanded admittance to the city. This force was accompanied by a Japanese adviser of the 29th Army, who explained to the Chinese guards that these Japanese soldiers belonged to the Embassy Guard. After a lengthy parley, about 120 of these troops were allowed to enter, but as soon as they had passed through the gate, the Japanese forces outside opened fire with machine-guns and field artillery. The guards immediately closed the gate, and soon a brisk exchange of fire developed. The Chinese soldiers on the wall rained hand grenades on the Japanese inside the city, who had meanwhile alighted from their lorries and deployed for action. Firing continued until nearly mid-

[30] For text, see *Peking & Tientsin Times*, July 27, 1937.

night, when an agreement was effected which permitted the Japanese troops inside the city to proceed to the Embassy barracks.

The crisis precipitated by the clashes at Langfang and Peiping, and by the Japanese ultimatum, found the leaders of the 29th Route Army still unprepared for resolute action. July 27, the day on which the first clause of the ultimatum expired, saw General Sung Che-yuan attempting to arrange a compromise with the Japanese military authorities. He apparently offered to withdraw the troops of the 37th Division, as demanded, but sought to have these replaced with the 132nd Division. This offer the Japanese rejected, since the ultimatum clearly aimed at evacuation of all Chinese troops, i.e., demilitarization of the Peiping area. When convinced that the Japanese would brook nothing less, General Sung finally broke off negotiations. In the evening he issued a circular telegram to the country expressing his determination to defend national territory against aggression. Fighting had already begun that afternoon south of the Nanyuan barracks, where Japanese troops had opened an attack on the Chinese positions at Tuan Ho. There could be no further doubt that a major struggle was impending. At this zero hour, the Chinese commanders contented themselves with bringing a few of the Chinese troops at Nanyuan into the city. No offensive operations were ordered by the higher command; the bulk of the Chinese troops were not even deployed for action in the surrounding territory, but were left in their barracks at Nanyuan, Peiyuan, and to a lesser extent at Hsiyuan.

Large-scale operations began on the morning of July 28. A proclamation issued by Lieutenant-General Katsuki, commander of the North China Garrison, and distributed by military aircraft at dawn, stated that the Japanese

Army had decided "to launch a punitive expedition against the Chinese troops, who have been taking acts derogatory to the prestige of the Empire of Japan." [31] Bringing aircraft and heavy artillery into action, the Japanese forces attacked the 29th Army troops at all points in the Peiping sector, except the city itself. At dawn fleets of airplanes bombed Hsiyuan, Peiyuan, and Nanyuan; other places were also shelled and bombed in the course of the day. Most of the Chinese troops had evacuated the Hsiyuan barracks, where relatively small casualties were reported. Concentrations of Chinese troops were dispersed at Peiyuan. The most severe attack was directed against Nanyuan, which contained the largest concentration of Chinese troops in the neighborhood of Peiping. Here the debacle was complete. Driven from their barracks by a severe bombardment, the Chinese troops withdrew down the nearby roads in mass formation—strafed by the Japanese airplanes. Press correspondents later found the bodies of the Chinese soldiers heaped along the roads leading from the Nanyuan barracks, where they had been slaughtered by machine-gun fire from the air. Chinese casualties in this sector numbered several thousand, including the deaths of General Chao Teng-yu, commander of the 132nd Division, and his vice-commander, General Tung Lin-kuo. For days afterward hundreds of wounded Chinese soldiers straggled into Peiping.

That night Generals Sung Che-yuan, Chin Teh-chun, and Feng Chih-an departed for Paotingfu, leaving the reins of government in the hands of General Chang Tzu-chung.[32] Following the departure of their leaders, the

[31] *Peking & Tientsin Times,* July 29, 1937.
[32] The latter held his post for a week, and then escaped in disguise and made his way south. In March 1938 he commanded a Chinese force fighting on the Hsuchow front.

troops of the 37th and 38th Divisions within Peiping also evacuated. From midnight of July 28 until four o'clock the next morning, a continuous stream of motor lorries and trucks laden with Chinese soldiers passed out of the city gates. Many of these troops had been manning the defences in various parts of the city throughout the preceding day and night, and "when word was passed round to them that they had been ordered to leave their defences and evacuate the city, they cried bitterly." [33]

Up to this point, the Japanese operations had proceeded entirely according to schedule. Two surprises were in store, one at Tungchow and the other at Tientsin. Reference to the background and origins [34] of the East Hopei *Paoantui* throws considerable light on the macabre features of the mutiny at Tungchow. In April and May 1933, the Japanese troops which invaded Hopei province were assisted by semi-bandit Chinese renegades. The Tangku Truce of May 31, 1933 had specified that a Chinese gendarmerie should police the demilitarized zone of East Hopei. For some months the Japanese military prevented the organization or functioning of such a Chinese police force. During this period the demilitarized zone was overrun by the semi-bandit renegades, whose depredations kept the area in turmoil. On Japanese insistence, these irregulars were incorporated in the Chinese gendarmerie eventually organized to police the demilitarized zone. After formation of the East Hopei Autonomous Government under Yin Ju-keng in November 1935, four *Paoantui* corps, the basic stock of which was still the former semi-bandit elements, were created. For more than a year the resident Japanese Military Mission at Tungchow had devoted careful efforts to the training of the

[33] *The Peiping Chronicle*, July 30, 1937.
[34] See Chapter II.

East Hopei *Paoantui* and apparently had implicit confidence in the loyalty of this Chinese force, despite its questionable background. Of the four corps only the 1st and 2nd, numbering several thousand men, were at Tungchow when the mutiny occurred.

A characteristic incident supplied the prelude to the revolt. Tungchow was located on the extreme southern edge of the East Hopei régime's territory. A battalion of the 38th Division of the 29th Army was stationed at the south gate of the city. Despite its precarious position, this battalion had received no orders to evacuate when the Lukouchiao incident developed. It kept its post even after the East Hopei *Paoantui* were ordered to surround it in a semi-circle, hemming it in against the city wall. On the morning of July 27, before the ultimatum expired, the Japanese troops opened fire on the battalion from the gate and wall with trench mortars and machine-guns. Facing complete annihilation, this Chinese force escaped only because the *Paoantui* seem to have let it through; total casualties, so far as could be discovered, were 18 killed and 18 wounded. The main body withdrew safely, but was later pursued by the bulk of the Japanese garrison at Tungchow, of which only forty-three officers and men were left behind. The resulting situation proved too great a temptation for the *Paoantui,* who mutinied on the morning of July 29.[35]

No extra precautions seem to have been taken by the small Japanese force left at Tungchow. Awakened by the sound of rifle fire at three o'clock, the garrison found that the mutineers had completely surrounded the mud walls of the barracks. This attack was never pushed home,

---

[35] The details of this paragraph are taken from an eye-witness account, summarized editorially in the *Peking & Tientsin Times* for August 14, 1937.

despite the overwhelming disparity of numbers. Japanese planes bombed the city in the afternoon; the bombardment started a stream of Chinese refugees, numbering nearly ten thousand, flowing into the mission compounds. Seven more planes appeared over Tungchow on the following morning and engaged in a two hours' bombardment. At four o'clock that afternoon a relief detachment of Japanese troops reached the scene; by dark this force had mopped up most of the *Paoantui* still in the city and gained control of the gates. Twenty of the Japanese garrison were killed and thirteen wounded. Five officers and associates of the Japanese Military Mission escaped; eleven were killed. Of some 385 Japanese and Korean residents, there were only 135 survivors. Chinese casualties, including civilians killed or wounded during the bombardments, were estimated at approximately one thousand. The remaining *Paoantui* groups were relentlessly hunted across the countryside in the neighborhood of Peiping. Yin Ju-keng, who had been captured during the revolt, was brought by one of these groups to the gates of the city. Unaware of the change of régime in Peiping, this group was apparently intending to surrender him to the 29th Army as a pledge of their loyalty. At the gate Yin Ju-keng was rescued, set at liberty, and escorted to the Japanese Embassy.

The outbreak at Tientsin, which exactly paralleled the Tungchow mutiny in point of time, was wholly different in character. Again the Chinese forces consisted of a few thousand *Paoantui*, but they fought against heavy odds in equipment if not in numbers. They struck hard at a vital Japanese military center and for some hours the issue was in doubt. A similar attack, carried through with equal spirit by a well equipped division of Chinese troops, might well have resulted in a Japanese catastrophe.

Reports of Chinese military victories at Fengtai and Langfang, which gave rise to enthusiastic celebrations at Shanghai and Nanking, were current in North China during the afternoon of July 28. Although these reports seem to have been greatly exaggerated, they were given full credence in Tientsin, where there was no means of verifying the actual results of the hostilities in the Peiping area, and may possibly have supplied the spark which set off the attack by the local *Paoantui*. Leadership of this Chinese military operation, the most effective conducted in the north during these early days, is attributed to the deputy commander of the Tientsin *Paoantui*, who insisted on resistance and virtually forced his senior officer to abdicate before he had his way. The Japanese forces were taken unawares, and the initial successes owed much to the factor of surprise.

At two o'clock on the morning of July 29, the *Paoantui* opened vigorous attack on a series of carefully chosen military objectives. They captured the Peitsang station north of Tientsin; occupied the West and Central Stations in the city, overcoming small Japanese garrisons in each case; and laid siege to the East Station. Here they surrounded a fairly strong Japanese garrison, which was forced to defend itself against Chinese troops in the railway sidings, snipers posted on the rooftops of buildings, and a major concentration based on the nearby branch headquarters of the *Paoantui*. Another Chinese detachment moved rapidly against one of the Japanese airfields, where some forty planes were resting on the ground. Warned in time, the Japanese guards made good their defences, while the planes took to the air and bombed and machine-gunned the Chinese troops as they approached the field. Success in this enterprise, despite the fact that other Japanese planes were within striking distance, might have prolonged the struggle in Tientsin. Failure sealed the fate of the attack.

During the morning, nevertheless, the Japanese position was extremely critical. The *Paoantui* commanded the International Bridge and its approaches, concentrating a heavy fire on all Japanese military traffic attempting to proceed to the East Station. Two of the three main stations were occupied, and a struggle of serious proportions was occurring at the third. The Japanese garrison at East Station was cut off, and the Japanese Concession was isolated. All ground connections between the airfield under attack and the East Arsenal were broken. River communications were severed by Chinese forces on the south bank; the railway to Tangku was blocked by a serious train wreck; and fighting was taking place at Tangku and Taku. Many Japanese nationals were isolated in the industrial section down-river below the city; the military forces could neither afford them protection nor escort them in through the Concessions. The bulk of the Japanese troops had gone inland toward Peiping, where they were thoroughly occupied. Resort was had to the air force.

Bombing planes, sent up in the early afternoon, loosed destruction on the city. Japanese headquarters announced that certain carefully mapped areas had to be wiped out to meet the military necessities of the situation. Circled in red on the map of Tientsin landmarks, which allegedly harbored "anti-Japanese elements", was Nankai University. Systematically and unhurriedly, the heaviest bombers of Japan's North China air force set about their task. "For four hours," in the words of the editor of the *Peking & Tientsin Times*, they "rained bombs upon the Municipal Government building, the old Administration building of the Peining Railway, the Central Station, Peining Park,

Paoantui Headquarters, the villages in the Palitai area, and Nankai University. They went up in regular formation, and as soon as one squadron had dropped its bombs and returned to the airfield three miles from the city another squadron went up, so that the bombing, with periodical bursts of machine-gun fire from the planes, was almost continuous. . . . The incendiary bombs soon started fires and the main hall of Nankai University, the Peining Railway office at the Central Station, and the various Government buildings were enveloped in columns of smoke and flames." [36] By nightfall many of the principal Chinese public buildings were smoldering ruins; at Nankai University the concrete-and-steel Library and Science Building withstood destruction but the Administration Building, with its wooden floors, windows and seats, was burned to the ground. East Station, which was held by the Japanese garrison until relief arrived late on the night of July 29, was carefully spared. Against the bombing attack, the *Paoantui* were able to offer only scattered and ineffectual bursts of machine-gun and rifle fire.

Through the night of July 29, the remaining *Paoantui* were blasted from their positions by rifle fire, machineguns and trench mortars, operating in concerted offensive. The hiding quarters of the snipers, as they were discovered, were subjected to a ceaseless fire, and gradually the Japanese forces reestablished control. On the next morning there was a lull, broken only by an occasional shot. The critical period had already passed. The main forces of the *Paoantui* were evacuating the city, although scattered groups still remained near the East Station, in the section of the Chinese Bund adjoining the Japanese Concession, and in the Chinese city. At Tangku and Taku, following withdrawal of the Chinese troops, the threat to

[36] *Peking & Tientsin Times,* August 1, 1937.

the main line of Japanese military communications had been removed. Japanese patrols began to move about more freely in Tientsin. Thousands of Chinese refugees thronged the entrances to the foreign Concessions. Shops and residences in the Chinese city, especially near the Courts and the Municipal Government quarters, were badly damaged; the streets were littered with debris and the bodies of dead and wounded, many of whom were children.

Tension was renewed in the afternoon when another intensive bombing operation, chiefly affecting Chinese institutions, was carried out. Incendiary bombs, dropped in the area of the Hui Wen Academy and the Nankai Middle and Girls' Schools, started a fire which was fanned by a stiff breeze and spread rapidly. Fires of the previous day were re-started at the Chinese Court and the Municipal Government buildings, and in the Palitai villages. The destruction of Nankai University, including the Science Building with its valuable equipment and the irreplaceable Library, was completed. Parties of Japanese troops, sent out in trucks carrying supplies of oil, "set fire to the trees and brushwood all round the campus. The wind took the flames in the direction of the build-ings. Then artillery opened up on the concrete buildings which had escaped the fire from the incendiary bombs. The campus was soon a mass of flames and the surround-ing countryside, together with the adjoining premises, were involved in the conflagration." [37]

Clouds and occasional heavy rains on the morning of July 31 promised an end to the anarchy and destruction that had ruled Tientsin for forty-eight hours. All signs of Chinese opposition, save for infrequent sniping, had virtually ceased. Japanese armored cars made patrols dur-

[37] *Peking & Tientsin Times,* July 31, 1937.

ing the morning, but the bombers did not take the air. The severest measure of the punitive campaign was reserved for that afternoon. A heavy artillery bombardment of several districts in the Chinese city began soon after three o'clock, and lasted continuously until nightfall. The shelling virtually wiped out the old Boxer villages near the Central Station; until well into the night, the huts of the Chinese villagers in this area blazed fiercely. By the time the bombardment ended, an area of approximately one square mile was ablaze, and columns of smoke were rising from various other sections of the Chinese city. Panic-stricken residents made a wholesale exodus from many areas, particularly the mud-hut villages, which were almost completely destroyed. Since thirty thousand refugees were already crowded into the British Concession, it proved necessary to direct this new stream along the British Bund into the First Special Area; it was estimated that nearly forty thousand refugees passed along the British Bund on the afternoon and evening of this day. Crowds of onlookers along the Bund were deeply moved by the long line of refugees, which consisted largely of careworn and exhausted women and children. The Japanese military spokesman later claimed that the bombardment was necessitated by the presence of anti-Japanese elements in the Chinese districts, which could not be driven out by other means. To many, however, it appeared that this measure could not be justified by any military objective; its chief effect was to terrorize the Chinese civilian population of Tientsin.

The events at Tientsin were rounded out by a final act of vandalism. On the night of August 1, shortly before nine o'clock, a band of some twenty-six White Russians surrounded the Soviet Consulate, threw hand grenades into the grounds, scaled the walls, and broke into the official residence. Mr. M. Smirnoff, acting Soviet Consul-General and his staff, forewarned of the raid, had vacated the premises an hour earlier. Besides notifying the Consular Corps of the expected raid, Mr. Smirnoff had approached the Japanese Consulate-General with a request for protection. He was informed that efforts would be made, but an hour before the attack no policemen were in sight, although Japanese troops had taken over the nearby police headquarters. The few Chinese guards at the Consulate grounds scattered when the raiders appeared, and for six hours the White Russians had systematically looted the building. Soon after their arrival a motor truck drove up and was loaded with valuables; four more trucks, or possibly the same truck successively, followed at intervals. The office safe, the archives and other documents, personal belongings, the silver, and much of the furniture was carried away. Every room in the spacious house had been systematically pillaged, and virtually nothing breakable left intact. Drawers had been wrenched open and their contents strewn over the floors. Heavy tables and chairs were smashed, the telephone line cut and the instrument broken, paintings of Soviet leaders were slashed, phonograph records and the electrola destroyed, and articles of clothing torn to ribbons. In the dining room, where the men had feasted, bottles, ash trays, glasses and cups were thrown at the walls, cabinets and pictures. The names of several of the White Russians who participated in this affair were known to the Soviet Consul-General. According to Mr. Smirnoff's statement, the ringleaders of the attack were in the employ of the Japanese secret service. An official Soviet protest was later presented at Tokyo, but the Japanese Foreign Office disclaimed all responsibility.

With the defeat of the *Paoantui* at Tientsin, the curtain

was drawn over the last act of hostilities in the Peiping-Tientsin area. For some days Japanese "mopping-up" operations, disturbing chiefly to the Chinese citizenry, continued in this vicinity. No reliable estimates of Chinese casualties, or of the property losses, were made. Japanese casualties at Tientsin, up to eleven o'clock on July 30, were officially listed at twenty-two, including nine killed. In the short space of four days, the bulk of the Chinese troops had been cleared out of the most populous region of North China. Except for unexpected reverses, notably at Tungchow, the operation had been carried out with relatively slight Japanese losses. The fighting at Tientsin, however, had demonstrated what might have been accomplished by the Chinese troops under more determined leadership. At the end of July there were some forty or forty-five thousand Chinese soldiers in the Peiping-Tientsin area; the total Japanese force amounted to approximately thirty-two thousand men. Given the superior mechanical equipment, especially the air power, of the latter, the ultimate issue could hardly be in doubt. Yet it is certain that coordinated military action by the Chinese forces, especially in the form of well-conceived offensive operations, would have made the whole enterprise vastly more costly for the Japanese. Even if the various units of the 29th Army had merely been ordered to attack the nearest Japanese detachment at will, they would have given a very different account of themselves, in the opinion of most informed observers in North China. That order was never given.

In this fact lies the clearest evidence of Japanese aggression. The mind of the 29th Army's high command was an open book to the Japanese military. They knew well that there was no real military threat to Japanese interests in North China, save of their own making. They chose to create such a threat. The line thus thrown out from China was immediately caught and held in Japan. The speed with which the Toyko authorities expanded the Lukou-chiao incident into a *casus belli* admits of but one inter-pretation. Three days after the early morning hostilities at Wanping, the Cabinet had taken all necessary steps to secure mobilization of the army, evacuation of Japanese nationals from China, and regimentation of public opin-ion at home. The scope of these measures, no less than the rapidity with which they were put into effect, sug-gests the operation of a well-oiled machine which needed only to be thrown into gear at a given signal.

By the beginning of August ominous clouds were al-ready gathering over Shanghai, and a general exodus of Japanese nationals was well under way. Two weeks later the last dam had broken; with the opening clashes at Shanghai, the second Sino-Japanese War had fairly begun. This war, so far as its immediate origins are concerned, had been maturing since the renewal of Japanese pressure on North China in the spring and fall of 1935. The events of that year reacted decisively on the internal political evolution both of China and Japan. They form the natu-ral starting-point for an analysis of the background of the present conflict.

CHAPTER TWO

AGGRESSION IN NORTH CHINA

FROM the signing of the Tangku Truce on May 31, 1933 to the Lukouchiao incident of July 7-8, 1937, four years elapsed. The full extent of Japanese aggression in North China during this period is little realized. Japan's encroachments were carried out by gradual stages, and the exact details of the successive agreements forced upon the Chinese authorities were often not revealed until months or years later. The attention of the outside world was caught only at times of crisis, as during the hostilities in the spring of 1933 or when the complete loss of the northern provinces was threatened in 1935. Between these crises Japanese military-political pressure was equally unremitting. A multitude of agents, official and unofficial, was actively engaged at the task of filling in the outlines of Japan's new *imperium* south of the Wall. By the spring of 1937 this process had gone so far that any effort by the local officials to safeguard China's few remaining rights in the north was treated as a challenge to Japan's "peaceful advance" and cause for military intervention.

Japan's military command inaugurated the first stage of the advance into North China when the League of Nations was completing its consideration of the Manchurian question. The coincidence in time was so striking that it could hardly be thought accidental; it was generally taken as a warning to Western nations against "meddling" in Far Eastern affairs. On January 1, 1933 fighting had broken out at Shanhaikuan, the main gateway to North China; on the third, Japanese troops took possession of the city. For nearly two months thereafter the Kwantung Army continued preparations for a military thrust into Jehol province, working up its case through such incidents as the alleged kidnapping of Gonshiro Ishimoto, a Japanese captain.[1] An ultimatum, claiming provocations from anti-Manchoukuo forces in Jehol, was presented on February 23 to Dr. Lo Wen-kan, Chinese Foreign Minister. On February 25, the day after the League Assembly had adopted its Manchurian report, the Japanese military invaded the province in full force. Despite the difficult character of Jehol's mountainous terrain, which afforded every advantage to defensive operations, the ill-captained northern troops speedily gave way. On March 4 the Japanese vanguard entered Chengteh, capital of the province. Less than a week later all efforts at organized Chinese resistance in Jehol had collapsed.

At this juncture the Chinese government, concerned lest hostilities should spread south of the Wall, made a determined attempt to remove any pretext for further Japanese aggression. On March 8 Generalissimo Chiang Kai-shek arrived at Paotingfu, where he assumed personal charge of affairs in the north. Marshal Chang Hsuehliang, against whom the Japanese displayed an unrelenting animus, was dismissed on March 13. His post as northern commander was taken by General Ho Yingchin, the Chinese Minister of War, who was made chair-

---

[1] For this and other details of the military campaign in Jehol and Hopei, see Edgar Snow, *Far Eastern Front*, Smith & Haas, 1933, Chapter 16.

man of the newly established Peiping Branch Military
Council. The northern troops were reorganized, a trench
system was constructed south of Kupeikou pass, and several additional divisions were brought up from the south.
Orders were issued to the Chinese military commanders
to keep strictly on the defensive; as a pacific gesture, the
troops stationed before Shanhaikuan were withdrawn to
the Luan River. On March 25 the Generalissimo returned
to the south; his departure was the signal for a renewal
of Japan's advance into North China.

Early in April, on the ground of alleged provocative
Chinese counter-attacks, the Japanese military forces
launched a general invasion of Hopei province. Along
the coast they moved forward to the Luan River; inland
at the Great Wall passes, they were held up by a stubborn
Chinese defence. For some reason, possibly an inadequacy
of forces, the Japanese commanders soon called a halt to
this initial advance and withdrew their troops behind the
Great Wall. At Nanking the breathing spell was utilized
to make another gesture of pacific intention toward
Japan. On May 3 a "political readjustment council",
under the chairmanship of General Huang Fu, was created for North China. Most of the members of this organ,
later known as the Peiping Political Council, were if not
sympathetic at least *persona grata* to Japan. Generals Ho
Ying-chin and Huang Fu, the respective military and
political heads of the new North China régime, were both
educated in Japan and had many Japanese connections.
The way was now cleared for a general diplomatic settlement of Sino-Japanese issues in the north.

Such assurance, it was immediately made clear, was not
at all what Japan required. On May 8 a strong Japanese
expeditionary force opened a second and much more
determined assault on northern Hopei. Bitter fighting

occurred at Kupeikou, Hsifengkou, and other passes along the Great Wall, where the Chinese defenders made a stand reminiscent of that at Shanghai early in 1932. At the Luan River in the open plain, however, the Chinese front collapsed, forcing a general retreat. By May 20 the Japanese forces had advanced to within thirty-five miles of Tientsin and thirteen miles of Peiping, and the occupation of both cities seemed imminent. The Chinese troops which had withdrawn from the northern passes were hurriedly reformed at the walls of Peiping, and preparations were made for a last stand in defence of the city.

General Huang Fu had meanwhile hastened north to assume his new post. On May 22 he secretly opened preliminary armistice negotiations with Mr. Shoichi Nakayama, Japanese Chargé d'Affaires at Peiping. Fighting had slackened in obvious anticipation of a settlement, but any intimation that truce parleys were actually progressing was jealously withheld up to the last moment. "The absurd expedients adopted to conceal the place and time of the negotiations," states the *New York Times* correspondent, "were inspired by the terror of the Chinese delegates, who fear assassination by their enraged countrymen." On May 30 he was able to assert: "After many days of evasions, mystifications and forthright denials that any plan was afoot for early signing of a specific armistice, a group of China's negotiators were actually housed tonight with Japanese delegates at Tangku." On the morning of May 31 the town bristled with Chinese troops and gendarmerie, standing at many points with drawn weapons to ensure the delegates' safety, while the guns of Japanese war vessels in the harbor pointed menacingly toward shore. All details had been settled beforehand; only the ceremonial signature was reserved for

Tangku. It was fittingly staged: "The Japanese, evidently grimly determined to impose humiliations upon the vanquished, sent a Major General to countersign with a Chinese Lieutenant General and also arranged the venue forcing the Chinese delegates to leave their luxurious special trains and proceed afoot across the narrow, dusty roadway to enter the Japanese barracks to sign the final terms of capitulation." [2] This famous truce, the charter of Japan's later aggressions in North China, reads as follows:

"Having accepted on the Twenty-fifth Day of May, 1933 the proposal for the termination of hostilities made by Lieutenant-General Hsiung Pin, Chief of Staff to the Peiping Branch Military Council, under authorization from General Ho Ying-chin, Chairman of the said Council, General Muto, Commander-in-Chief of the Kwantung Army, has authorized Major-General Neiji Okamura, Chief of Staff of the Kwantung Army, to sign as representative of the Kwantung Army, with Lieutenant-General Hsiung Pin, the representative of the Chinese Army in North China duly authorized by General Ho Ying-chin, the following truce agreement:

1. The Chinese Army shall immediately withdraw to the regions west and south of the line from Yenching to Changping, Kaoliying, Sunyi, Tungchow, Hsiangho, Paoti, Lintingkow, Ningho and Lutai and undertakes not to advance beyond that line and to avoid any provocation of hostilities.

2. The Japanese Army may at any time use aeroplanes or other means to verify the carrying out of the above article. The Chinese authorities shall afford them protection and facilities for such a purpose.

3. The Japanese Army, after ascertaining the with-

2 *New York Times*, May 31 and June 1, 1933.

drawal of the Chinese Army to the line stated in Article 1, undertakes not to cross the said line and not to continue to attack the Chinese troops and shall voluntarily withdraw to the Great Wall.

4. In the regions to the south of the Great Wall and to the north and east of the line as defined in Article 1, the maintenance of peace and order shall be undertaken by a Chinese police force. The said police force shall not be constituted by armed units hostile to Japanese feelings.

5. The present agreement shall come into effect upon its signature. In faith whereof the two representatives have signed the present agreement and affixed thereto their seals.

(Signed) Neiji Okamura, Representative of the Kwantung Army.
(Signed) Hsiung Pin, Representative of the Chinese Army in North China.

Declaration: In case there shall be in the Demilitarized Zone armed units disturbing peace and order which the police force shall be unable to cope with, the situation will be dealt with by common accord between the two parties.

(Signed) Neiji Okamura, Representative of the Kwantung Army.
(Signed) Hsiung Pin, Representative of the Chinese Army in North China.
May 31st, 1933." [3]

Neither the preamble nor the accompanying declaration of this complete text was revealed at first publication;

[3] *The Chinese Year Book, 1936-37,* Shanghai, The Commercial Press, 1937, p. 431.

much more important, the second sentence of Article 4 was completely suppressed until 1937.[4] To the significance of this seemingly harmless sentence, which in fact constituted the pivot of Japanese pressure in North China up to 1935, it will be necessary to return later. Taken merely at their face value, the provisions of the Tangku Truce placed Japan in a dominating position south of the Wall. The line fixed by Article 1 started at Yenching, in Chahar province, touched the Peiping-Suiyuan Railway at Changping, passed through Tungchow within twelve miles of Peiping, and ended at Lutai about thirty-five miles north of Tientsin. Virtually all of Hopei province north of the Peiping-Tientsin area was thus included in the "demilitarized" zone. No Chinese troops could enter this zone; the Japanese army, even after withdrawing to the Great Wall, was by virtue of the Boxer Protocol free to maintain garrisons at Shanhaikuan, Chinwangtao, Changli, Lanchou, Tangshan and Lutai, all of which were located within the zone. No specific time limit was set for the Japanese withdrawal. When evacuation was effected it would be "to the Great Wall", not to the Jehol boundary. Since the Great Wall dips well into northern Hopei, an area of several thousand square miles was thus added to the territory of Manchoukuo.

An aura of defensive necessity was imparted to the truce by Japanese pleas that it was required in order to put a stop to China's provocative activities against Manchoukuo. Three months earlier Japan's armed forces had occupied Jehol province on the same plea. A pragmatic observer might be inclined to determine the real aggressor by the new boundary lines successively established by

[4] *The Chinese Year Book, 1935-1936,* p. 376, still gives only the "gist of the armistice agreement", i.e., articles 1-5, omitting the preamble, the annexed declaration, and the second sentence of Article 4.

Japanese arms. In actual operation, the *cordon sanitaire* of the "demilitarized" zone was far from reciprocal. Under the terms of the Tangku Truce, Chinese armed opposition to Manchoukuo was clearly prevented. There was no similar guarantee that Japanese pressure would not continue to operate against North China. The Great Wall passes, which constituted the natural defence line of the Peiping-Tientsin area, were wrested from China's control. All Chinese troops were forced out of the intervening region, while Japanese garrisons were left to command the sole line of railway communications through the zone. The clearest evidence of aggressive intent, however, was supplied by the truce provisions relative to policing the "demilitarized" zone, which were deliberately drawn so as to further Japan's general political aims in North China.

When the Japanese army invaded northern Hopei, it had utilized the services of certain Chinese renegade forces which were not far removed from the status of bandits. The terms of the Tangku Truce, as first published, apparently neglected to provide for the disposition of these Chinese irregulars. "It is significant," wrote the *New York Times* correspondent on May 31, "that the truce fails to mention the future treatment of various renegade Chinese forces now operating in the Luan River triangle, flying the old five-barred Chinese flag." [5] The complete text of the truce shows that the Japanese who drafted it had understood and provided for the use to which these forces would be put. After June 10 the Japanese troops gradually effected their withdrawal to the Great Wall; the Chinese irregulars, however, were left behind in the "demilitarized" zone. In accordance with the declaration annexed to the truce, the authorities of

[5] *New York Times*, June 1, 1933.

the Peiping Political Council were compelled to seek an agreement with the Japanese for the removal of these irregulars. In reply to this request, the Japanese suggested that a conference be held at Dairen. On July 3, when the Chinese delegates reached Dairen, they were immediately confronted with the following demands:

" (a) Employment of part of the irregulars in police service in the demilitarized zone;

(b) Establishment in the evacuated area of agencies to handle matters relating to communications and economics along the Great Wall;

(c) Permission to lease land and residences in the evacuated area for the use of the Japanese troops still stationed there;

(d) Restoration of trade, communications and postal service between the territory on either side of the Great Wall." [6]

These proposals contained the essential items of what were long surmised to be "secret protocols" attached to the Tangku Truce. No such formal protocols, it now appears, actually existed, although the Japanese demands presented at Dairen owed their persuasive force directly to the provisions of the truce. The Chinese delegates were in no position to object to the first of these demands, since Article 4 had specified that the police force should "not be constituted by armed units hostile to Japanese feelings." This item was apparently accepted at the Dairen conference. No agreement was reached on the other three items, which raised wholly new issues of far-reaching political and economic significance. As a result, the Japanese military authorities continued to turn the

[6] Shuhsi Hsu, *The North China Problem*, Shanghai, Kelly & Walsh, 1937, p. 11. The author, an adviser to the Chinese Ministry of Foreign Affairs, had access to official sources.

screws on the North China officials during the summer and autumn of 1933. The Japanese troops had begun to withdraw on June 10, but not so their Chinese auxiliaries. Traffic on the Peiping-Mukden Railway was not restored until late July; even then Japanese control was retained up to Tangshan, subjecting passengers to the inconvenience of a change at this point. Lawlessness reigned supreme in the demilitarized area, which was preyed upon by a variety of Chinese irregular troops. Some of these had been incorporated in the Chinese force that was supposed to police the zone, thus rendering its activities ineffectual. The Chinese authorities made several attempts to send in troops from Tientsin to put down the marauding bands that were terrorizing districts in northern Hopei; in each case the Japanese military forces disarmed the Chinese detachments and turned them back.[7]

In the autumn of 1933 the Japanese government initiated a general diplomatic offensive in China. Mr. Koki Hirota, newly appointed Japanese Foreign Minister, declared on September 29 that he placed at the forefront of his policy the gradual opening of regular negotiations with China looking to "a practical solution" of Sino-Japanese issues. His ultimate aim was "to establish an Asiatic union comprising China, Japan and Manchoukuo, pledging, through a definite protocol, close economic and political collaboration."[8] Throughout China a host of Japanese diplomatic, consular and military officials sought with renewed energy to give effect to the Hirota program. For some months a continuous round of official conversations was held at Shanghai, Nanking and Peiping. At

[7] *China Weekly Review*, Shanghai, September 16, 1933, p. 82-83; November 11, 1933, p. 428-429.
[8] *Osaka Mainichi*, English-language edition, September 29, 1933.

Nanking this pressure was directed toward a reduction of Chinese tariffs and elimination of the boycott, which was still proving effective on a voluntary basis despite the absence of organized support or official encouragement. The Japanese diplomatic campaign registered one major achievement in the south. On October 29 Dr. T. V. Soong, who had just returned from abroad after successfully enlisting American and European aid in China's reconstruction activities, was forced to resign from the Finance Ministry.[9]

The main pressure was exerted in the north, where the Chinese officials were again faced with the demands presented earlier at Dairen. At a three-day conference, held in Peiping on November 7-9, negotiations concerning these issues reached a climax. Dealing directly with Huang Fu at this time were Akira Ariyoshi, Japanese Minister to China, and Major-General Neiji Okamura, Chief-of-Staff of the Kwantung Army, who had signed the Tangku Truce as Japan's representative less than six months previously. Successful efforts were made to conceal the decisive outcome of this conference. The foreign press correspondents were led to believe that the Japanese demands had been rejected, while the local press suggested that their acceptance had been forestalled by a revolt of the Kuomintang political leaders in the Central Executive Committee at Nanking.[10] In reality Huang Fu,

[9] For further details of Japan's pressure at Nanking during this period, see "The New Status in the Pacific", *Foreign Policy Reports*, January 17, 1934, p. 261-262.

[10] This revolt took three forms: an interrogation of Premier Wang Ching-wei in the Legislative Yuan concerning the Sino-Japanese negotiations at Peiping, a resolution passed by the Central Political Council which vested in that body a more complete and effective control over the conduct of foreign relations, and a proposal to the government executive for reorganization of the Peiping Political Council. *China Weekly Review*, November 25, 1933, p. 518.

Premier Wang Ching-wei, it might be noted, had declared at Nanking

acting for the Nanking government, secretly accepted *in toto* the Japanese proposals originally presented at Dairen. The agencies "referred to in (b) were to be established in Shanhaikuan, Kupeikou, Hsifengkou, Lengkou, Panchiakou and Chiehlingkou, all being passes along the Great Wall. The leasing of land and residences referred to in (c) was to be restricted to Shanhaikuan, Shihmengyen, Chienchangying, Taitouying, Hsifengkou, Lengkou, Malanyu, and Kupeikou. It was also understood that in case resort was made to the use of the Luan River for the transportation of military supplies protective measures could be adopted in addition. In the matter of restoring trade, communications and postal service, which formed Japanese condition (d), it was understood that air service was to be included." [11] It is a significant fact that Japanese military officials constantly referred to these political and economic concessions, the surcharges imposed on the Tangku Truce, as part of the truce itself. Some doubt may, perhaps, still be permitted to exist as to whether these surcharges were not raised for consideration at some time during the preliminary conversations which led up to the original military truce signed on May 31, 1933.

Several years elapsed before all of these additional concessions became fully operative, a factor which enhanced the success attending efforts to maintain secrecy over the outcome of the November conversations at Peiping. Special Sino-Japanese agreements, effected for each of the concessions, were gradually reached during the three-year period from 1934 to 1936. In order to avoid *de facto* recognition of Manchoukuo, the Nanking government

on May 31, 1933 that the Tangku Truce was "purely military and does not affect the nation's territorial rights or international position." *New York Times,* June 1, 1933.

[11] Shuhsi Hsu, *The North China Problem,* cited, p. 11-12.

adopted the expedient of authorizing the establishment of joint Sino-Japanese organs, ostensibly private and unofficial in character, where the administration of business enterprises was concerned. The restoration of trade between China and Manchoukuo occurred during the spring and summer of 1934. On June 20 of that year the Chinese government established a Customs Station at Shanhaikuan, and on August 16 five sub-stations at Kupeikou, Hsifengkou, Lengkou, Chiehlingkou, and Yiyuankou. Thirty-six specified products were allowed to pass through these stations from Manchoukuo without paying duty, on the ground that Manchuria and Jehol were still parts of China. This exemption was an expensive means of asserting China's sovereignty; in fact, it first whetted the appetites of Japan's merchants for that "special trade" which later assumed such large proportions. Through traffic was next restored on the Peiping-Mukden Railway on July 1, 1934 by an agreement which established a special joint railway administration. Postal services between China and Manchoukuo were restored on January 10, 1935 by an agreement signed four days previously.[12] The Chinese government took meticulous care in this case to avoid *de facto* recognition of the Manchoukuo régime. Postal communication was restored "between China Proper inside the Great Wall and the Northeastern Provinces." Mail matter was handled by a joint Sino-Japanese agency with transmitting offices at Shanhaikuan and Kupeikou. Postal stamps and mail covers were not allowed to bear the mark of Manchoukuo, and the Japanese side was required to use a special stamp. The Western calendar was used, and charges collected in accordance with the existing postal regulations of the two

[12] Ordinary mails were restored on January 10; postal money orders and parcel post on February 1.

parties.[13] Air communication was not established until much later. A Sino-Japanese concern, the Hui Tung Company, was organized in October 1936; service was inaugurated on November 17 over four routes between various cities in Manchuria and North China, the latter comprising Peiping, Tientsin, Kalgan, Changpei and Shanhaikuan.

The year 1934, during which the restoration of trade, railway traffic and postal services across the Great Wall was largely accomplished, witnessed a marked decline in Japan's direct military encroachments on China. There was good reason for this state of affairs. Foreign Minister Hirota was achieving progress in all phases of his China policy, later summed up in three points: establishment of a Japan-China-Manchoukuo bloc, suppression of anti-Japanese activities in China, and organization of a joint Sino-Japanese front against Communism. Reestablishment of normal relations between China and its provinces north of the Wall was obviously contributing to the realization of the first point. The Japanese officers of the Kwantung Army, enjoying these fruits of the Tangku Truce, were content to rest on their laurels. Another fillip to the idea of an Asiatic bloc was given in July 1934, when Japan's long-continued pressure at Nanking finally secured a revision of the Chinese tariff, which greatly favored Japanese importers. The injunctions of Mr. Hirota's third point were also being fulfilled, especially in the north. Anti-Japanese students and teachers in the Peiping-Tientsin area were jailed, anti-Japanese officials weeded out, and outspokenly nationalist Chinese newspapers were suppressed—all under the ægis of the Peiping Political Council.[14] With regard to the third point, no

[13] For the texts of these several agreements, see Shuhsi Hsu, *The North China Problem*, cited, p. 12-15.

[14] *New York Times*, June 9, 1935.

formal Sino-Japanese front against Communism had been established. During the closing months of 1934, however, Nanking's five-year campaign against the Chinese Communist forces had culminated in a struggle of large proportions, marked in November by the withdrawal of the Communist armies from Kiangsi and Fukien provinces.[15] The Japanese authorities were satisfied to watch this fratricidal conflict from the sidelines.

By the spring of 1935, the Japanese military were ready for a second forward move in the north. Various reasons counselled this step. The gains of the Tangku Truce, for one thing, had been fully assimilated and the officers were anxious for fresh fields to conquer. It was necessary, again, to strike a blow at the Japanese moderates, who were threatening to reassert their political supremacy at home.[16] The international auspices were also favorable. Europe was preoccupied with the complications attending Chancellor Hitler's reintroduction of military conscription, and Japan's relations with the Soviet Union had been improved by the signing of the sale agreement for the Chinese Eastern Railway on March 23 at Tokyo. Once the decision to advance was taken, the Japanese military rudely brushed aside the conciliatory policy long followed by the Peiping Political Council. The crisis was manipulated by the officers of the North China Garrison, who brought forward a long list of anti-Japanese provocations, some of which went back to 1932.[17] General Ho Ying-chin, War Minister in the Nanking government and head of the Peiping Military Council, bore the brunt

[15] This retreat initiated the "Long March" to Shensi and Kansu via Szechuan. See Edgar Snow, *Red Star Over China*, New York, Random House, 1938, Part Five.

[16] For a discussion of this factor, see below, Chapter VI.

[17] For these alleged provocations, see Hugh Byas, *New York Times*, May 31, 1935.

of the attack. Preliminary Japanese agitation was supported by menacing troop movements and airplane flights over Peiping. On June 9 Lieutenant-General Yoshijiro Umetsu, commander of the garrison forces, transmitted to General Ho Ying-chin a memorandum of nine items accompanied by a "final warning". This memorandum, which had been verbally accepted some days previously by General Ho, reads as follows:

"The items which China has accepted and carried out towards the Japanese Army are as follows:

1. Dismissal of Yu Hsueh-chung, Chang Ting-e and their followers;

2. Dismissal of Chiang Hsiao-hsien, Ting Chang, Tseng Kuang-ching, Ho I-fei;

3. Withdrawal of the Third Regiment of Military Police;

4. Dissolution of the Political Training Corps of the Peiping Military Council and the Military Magazine Club of Peiping;

5. Restriction and suppression of the Blue Shirts, the Fu-hsing Club, and other secret organizations inimical to Sino-Japanese relations;

6. Withdrawal of Kuomintang headquarters from the province of Hopei and abolition of the Peiping branch of the Officers' Moral Endeavor Association;

7. Withdrawal of the Fifty-first Army from the province of Hopei;

8. Withdrawal of the Second and Twenty-fifth Divisions from the province of Hopei and dissolution of the Students' Training Corps of the Twenty-fifth Division;

9. Prohibition of anti-foreign and anti-Japanese agitation in general in China.

For your reference I have specially put the foregoing in writing to be sent to you.

H.E. Ho Ying-ching,
June 6th, the Tenth Year of Showa.
(Signed) Yoshijiro Umetsu,
Commander of the North China Garrison." [18]

This memorandum merely lists a set of Japanese demands; it does not contain General Ho Ying-chin's written acceptance. On and before June 9, however, General Ho Ying-chin had discussed these demands with Colonel Takashi Sakai and verbally accepted them. Later, on June 11, Major Takahashi submitted for Ho Ying-chin's signature a document which, in addition to the above nine items, contained three others, reading as follows:

"Concerning the carrying out of the foregoing [China] also accepts the following:

1. What has been agreed upon with Japan shall be carried out within the time specified. Any parties or organizations that have caused strain in Sino-Japanese relations shall not be permitted to re-enter [Hopei];

2. In the appointment of provincial and municipal officials it is hoped that Japan's wish that selection be confined to those who will not be likely to cause strain in Sino-Japanese relations will be taken into consideration;

3. Concerning the carrying out of what has been agreed upon Japan will adopt measures of supervision and examination." [19]

General Ho Ying-chin refused to have anything to do with this document for several reasons: the feeling "that he had done enough to placate the Japanese"; unwillingness "to leave anything in writing in their hands"; and displeasure "at seeing a set of three items which had

[18] For texts, see *The China Weekly Review,* March 14, 1936, p. 38; *China Today,* New York, May 1936, p. 150; Shuhsi Hsu, *The North China Problem,* cited, p. 18-19.
[19] Shuhsi Hsu, cited, p. 22; also p. 22-26 for general discussion of the agreement.

never been brought up and discussed before." [20] On June 13 he left for Nanking. Up to this point, General Ho Ying-chin had given no written assurances of any kind to the Japanese authorities, although he had verbally accepted the nine items first presented and had already substantially executed them. On June 21, therefore, the Japanese again approached General Ho with the request that he should record his acceptance of the demands in writing. This he did on July 6 in the following terms:

"Please be informed: [We] accept all items submitted by Colonel Takashi Sakai on June 9th and shall by our free will see that they are carried out.

H.E. Commander Umetsu,
(Signed) Ho Ying-ching.
July 6th, the Twenty-fourth Year of the Chinese Republic." [21]

The Japanese military authorities afterwards claimed that this acceptance referred to all twelve items; on the Chinese side, it was maintained that only the original nine items were covered by General Ho's note. It is clear that, in contrast to the extreme precision which marked the arrangements connected with the Tangku Truce, the circumstances surrounding the consummation of the "Ho-Umetsu agreement" were highly irregular. Be that as it may, the actual political effects of this later agreement were hardly if any less momentous than those of the first. Before the middle of June the first nine items had been substantially carried into effect. At one stroke General Yu Hsueh-chung, governor of Hopei province, his Fifty-first Army, and all central government divisions had been driven from North China, and all Kuomintang and ancil-

[20] Shuhsi Hsu, cited, p. 24.
[21] Shuhsi Hsu, cited, p. 23.

lary political organs in the province suppressed. Finally, in accordance with the last item of the agreement, the Chinese government felt itself compelled to promulgate on June 10, 1935 the following "Goodwill Mandate":

"The task before our country today, in its efforts to maintain national independence, is, internally, to improve government administration and promote culture so as to consolidate the strength of the nation; and, externally, to preserve international good faith and maintain international peace.

"The cultivation of goodwill with our neighbors being of prime importance, the Central Government has repeatedly ordered that all citizens should observe the proper amenities towards friendly nations; and not indulge in discriminatory or provocative speeches or acts. In this connection, especially, no organizations whatsoever must be formed which might be detrimental to international relations.

"It is hereby again specially ordered that this injunction be fully observed. Persons violating this order will be severely punished." [22]

The demand for the suppression of anti-Japanese activities in China had thus reached the point where the Chinese government was forced to take official steps for the regulation of the speeches, acts and organizations of Chinese citizens. The Goodwill Mandate, however, was defective in one respect. Since it was expressed in general terms, it might not be taken to refer clearly enough to Japan. This matter was cleared up on July 8 when, as part of the settlement of the *New Life Weekly* incident, the Central Publicity Council at Nanking was obliged to issue the following instruction to all provincial and municipal Kuomintang organs:

[22] *The Chinese Year Book, 1936-37*, cited, p. 428.

"In one of its May issues, the *New Life Weekly* magazine in Shanghai published an article containing some remarks considered to be insulting to the Japanese Emperor which has aroused the displeasure of the Japanese community. Be it remembered that the constitution of the Japanese Empire is such that the Emperor of Japan is held in higher esteem, respect, affection and reverence by the Japanese people than the chief executive of any other country in the world is by his respective citizens. The slightest carelessness in editorial comment or news reports concerning the Emperor of Japan would cause ill-feeling between the people of the two countries.

"During the past year, this Central Publicity Council has repeatedly warned against indiscreet comments on the part of the press, and so far no case has been found for reproach. Unfortunately, the *New Life Weekly* has made an exception. The responsible officials of the Shanghai Censorship Bureau and the publisher of the weekly in question have been given due punishment, but in order to avoid recurrence of similar incidents, this order is hereby issued, warning you against carelessness.

"With regard to the anti-Japanese movement, it is hereby urged that the press circles in China conform to the mandate as issued by the National Government on June 10, calling for the promotion of friendly relations with all neighboring countries." [23]

The drastic terms of the Ho-Umetsu agreement, which were restricted mainly to Hopei province, constituted only one phase of the North China crisis of June 1935. During this month Japan's military agents exacted a similar set of concessions, almost equally far-reaching, with regard to Chahar. The terms imposed in the case of Chahar province, however, were related to a wholly dif-

[23] *The China Year Book, 1936-37*, cited, p. 428-429.

ferent geographical and racial setting. This province, along with Jehol, Suiyuan and Ninghsia, occupied the same status in the Chinese administrative system as any of the other North China provinces. As sections of the region commonly termed Inner Mongolia, on the other hand, these four provinces have characteristics which set them apart from Shansi, Hopei or Shantung. Japanese penetration of this region has been studiously adapted to its local peculiarities, and must therefore be treated in relation to a special historical background.

The Mongolian people are chiefly located in three territorial centers: western Manchuria, or "Eastern Inner Mongolia"; western Inner Mongolia; and Outer Mongolia. Some four million Mongols are fairly equally divided among these three regions. Following Japan's occupation of Jehol in 1933, the three remaining western Inner Mongolian provinces of Chahar, Suiyuan and Ninghsia were at once converted into a buffer area of great strategic importance. One notable factor favored the spread of Japanese influence into this area. Since the Revolution of 1911, the relations of the Mongol princes of both Manchuria and western Inner Mongolia with the Chinese Republic had not disposed them toward friendship with China. In the early years of the republic they had tried vainly to win their independence, despite preliminary successes in driving out the Chinese troops.[24] Far better able to obtain foreign arms, the Chinese military forces eventually established a decided superiority over the Mongols. Railway construction, both in Manchuria and North China, led to an influx of Chinese agricultural settlers which steadily dispossessed the Mongols of their best grazing lands. Political and economic

[24] Owen Lattimore, "Mongolia Enters World Affairs", *Pacific Affairs*, March 1934, p. 17-18.

impacts coalesced in the persons of the local Chinese officials, who were heavily interested in the land deals attending the colonization movement.[25] Under pressure from the Chinese officials, many of the princes had connived at alienation of their lands to the incoming settlers. Since the early beginnings of Chinese colonization at the end of the last century, the Mongols had lost about two-thirds of their territory in Jehol, about a third in Manchuria, and large portions of Chahar and Suiyuan provinces. The crowning blow came in 1928, when Inner Mongolia was divided into the four provinces of Jehol, Chahar, Suiyuan and Ninghsia. The new provincial boundary lines cut ruthlessly across the Mongol tribal and league frontiers, contributing still further to the Mongols' disunity and facilitating their ultimate absorption by the Chinese. The ambitious schemes of Japan's empire builders, playing against this background, had long taken into account and assiduously prepared to utilize the support of the Mongolian princes.

The first stage of Japan's advance into Mongolian territory took place early in 1932, when the western section of Manchuria came under Japanese control. The next step followed in March 1933, when Jehol was occupied by Japanese military forces. Soon afterward western Manchuria and the northern portion of Jehol were reconstituted as the Mongolian province of Hsingan—one of the five provinces of Manchoukuo. Later, when the total number of Manchoukuo provinces was increased to fourteen, Hsingan was divided into four sub-provinces. The Japanese authorities sought to apply a liberal policy in this province, including a guarantee against encroachments on Mongol grazing lands by agricultural settlers,

[25] For an analysis of the Chinese official as entrepreneur in the colonization movement, see Owen Lattimore, *Manchuria: Cradle of Conflict*, Macmillan, 1935, rev. ed., Chapter VI.

some measure of local autonomy, and extension of support to the Lama priesthood. Thus constituted, Hsingan province was clearly designed to win the support of the neighboring Inner Mongolian princes, as well as the remnant conservative elements in Outer Mongolia. The same purpose was served by Pu Yi's enthronement as Emperor of Manchoukuo on March 1, 1934, which held out the possibility of national reunification of the Mongols on the traditional basis of allegiance to a Manchu emperor. So long as the Chahar and Suiyuan princes still retained freedom of action, they made no response to these overtures from Manchoukuo. Their initial reservations were strengthened by the course of events in this Japanese-sponsored kingdom. The promised autonomy in Hsingan province was restricted by the rigid control exercised over the Mongols, the refusal to allow them to bear arms unless actually enlisted in military service, and "the fact that none of the Mongols holding office under Manchoukuo" was "considered a really capable potential leader by either conservatives or progressives." [26] Nor were matters helped by the execution of several high Mongol officials of Hsingan province, on the charge of conspiring with Outer Mongolia, in the spring of 1936.

In the first instance, then, the Inner Mongolian princes of Chahar and Suiyuan turned a deaf ear to the blandishments of Japan's agents. Instead they made capital of Japanese pressure by seeking political concessions at Nanking. During 1933-1934 an autonomy movement, led by Te Wang (Prince Te) of Chahar, forced the Nanking government to deal with the princes' demands. On April 23, 1934, after protracted negotiations, an Autonomous Government of Inner Mongolia was established at Pai-

[26] Owen Lattimore, "On the Wickedness of Being Nomads", *Asia*, October 1935, p. 601; also "The Eclipse of Inner Mongolian Nationalism", *Journal of the Royal Central Asian Society*, London, June 1937.

lingmiao in Suiyuan province.[27] The ruling organ was a Mongolian Political Council of twenty-eight members, assisted by two Chinese councillors. Prince Te, the moving spirit in this genuine autonomy movement, was made secretary-general of the Council. The basic Mongol demand for unification of the Mongolian sections of Chahar and Suiyuan provinces into a separate Chinese province, however, was not realized.[28] In any case, the scope for Mongol maneuvering was limited to the brief time during which Japan stayed its advance. By 1934 Japan was already knocking insistently at the door; thereafter, until the definitive occupation of 1937, Chahar and Suiyuan provinces were subjected to progressive encroachment from Manchoukuo, directed by officers of the Kwantung Army.

Shortly after the occupation of Jehol province in March 1933, a body of Japanese troops crossed the border into Chahar. This force took Dolonor early in May; turning south, it then occupied the strip of Chahar-Jehol border territory, including Kuyuan, Paochang and Kangpao. Meanwhile General Feng Yu-hsiang, with headquarters at Kalgan, had organized an Anti-Japanese People's Army with the object of rousing a popular campaign against Japanese aggression and the compromise policy embodied in the Tangku Truce. This force took the field in July, under the command of Generals Chi Hung-chang and Fang Chen-wu, and rapidly reconquered the Chahar territory occupied by the Japanese. With the reoccupation of Dolonor in the middle of July, the whole of Chahar province was restored to Chinese control. At this point the Nanking government stepped in and ordered Gen-

[27] New York Times, May 27, June 17, and July 29, 1934.
[28] See statement by Prince Te, Christian Science Monitor, June 1, 1935; also Edgar Snow, "War Brews in Mongolia", New York Herald Tribune, October 28, 1934.

eral Feng to disband his army and leave the province. To enforce this order Nanking's troops in the north were mobilized in preparation for operations against Feng Yu-hsiang's army; at the same time, additional Japanese forces returned to the attack in Chahar. Faced with this combined opposition, General Feng abandoned his campaign and left Kalgan in the middle of August. Generals Chi and Fang continued the struggle for some weeks, but were soon defeated and scattered by their combined opponents. In the end, Japanese forces withdrew from the Kuyuan area but continued to occupy Dolonor. During the following year the Dolonor region, embracing a territory of some 5,600 square miles, was organized as a "special district" under the jurisdiction of Manchoukuo.[29] Resident Japanese officials consisted of the chief of police and a military mission of Kwantung Army officers. The area was garrisoned by Manchurian forces, comprising one infantry and one cavalry regiment, which drew high rates of pay supplied in part by the Manchoukuo government. Police, currency, and the postal and telegraph services of this district were also controlled by the Manchoukuo régime. Throughout 1934 the Dolonor region was the scene of active preparations for the next phase of the advance into the Chinese section of Chahar, while similar preparations were being made further north at Peisiemiao for an advance into the Mongol regions of the province. Roads were built, airfields laid out, and a constant stream of Japanese emissaries sent into Chahar and Suiyuan to court the support of the princes.[30] The latter still refused to accept these advances, and the Japanese were forced to resort to overt military operations in order to renew their drive into Chahar.

[29] *New York Times*, February 6, 1935.
[30] *New York Times*, March 28, April 4, 19, 1934.

In January 1935 an incident which developed on the Jehol-Chahar border south of Dolonor rapidly precipitated hostilities. Charging that the troops under General Sung Che-yuan, the Chahar governor, had invaded Jehol province in this area, the Kwantung Army headquarters announced on January 18 that it was "forced to take military action." [31] An ultimatum addressed to General Sung on the same day apparently led to a preliminary settlement arranged by joint representatives in Peiping. These negotiations proved unable to ward off the clash. At six o'clock on the evening of January 22 a force of some two thousand Japanese and Manchoukuo troops, using airplanes, armored cars and artillery, launched an attack which speedily carried them into the southeastern corner of Chahar province. Kuyuan, Tungchatze and Tushihkow, all well within the Chahar boundaries, were bombed by seven Japanese planes. Chinese troops, which offered some resistance, were driven back from the Jehol border to the Kuyuan-Tushihkow line. When fighting ended on the night of January 23, the Japanese forces were left in possession of an area in Chahar province totalling approximately seven hundred square miles, which lay between the Great Wall's northernmost spur and the commonly accepted Jehol border line. The Japanese authorities claimed that this region belonged to Jehol province, and that their military action thus merely amounted to a "rectification" of the boundary.

At Nanking on January 29 Premier Wang Ching-wei and Mr. Ariyoshi, the Japanese Minister, agreed to settle this issue locally. The Central Government instructed the Chahar provincial authorities to give way, and the terms were arranged in advance. On February 2 General Sung Che-yuan's delegates signed the formal settlement with the

[31] *The Trans-Pacific*, Tokyo, January 24, 1935, p. 8.

Kwantung Army's representatives in a fifteen-minute session at Tatan, a small town on the western edge of Jehol; by this agreement, the territory in dispute was recognized as belonging to Jehol and so added to the Manchoukuo realm.[32] One of the North China correspondents later summed up this dispute in the following terms: "Actually, the affair of last January amounted simply to an enforcement by the Japanese army of its arbitrary designation of the Great Wall at this point as the southeastern boundary of Jehol province. The effect of this action has been to add to Manchoukuo a slice of territory which most maps show as belonging to the Chinese province of Chahar."[33]

Five months later the Japanese demands which led to the Ho-Umetsu agreement were presented at Peiping. On May 30, 1935, at the outset of this crisis, a group of Japanese officers, some of whom were members of the Special Service Mission resident at Dolonor, set out on a trip through Chahar province in the direction of Kalgan. This party, either through carelessness or purposeful design, carried no passports. At Changpei on June 5 they were detained overnight for questioning by the local Chinese authorities. When word of this affair reached the Chinese provincial officials at Kalgan, an order for their release was immediately issued. They were detained for less than twenty-four hours, and apparently suffered no indignities. On the basis of this "Changpei incident," the Kwantung Army presented a series of far-reaching demands both locally and at Nanking, backed by menacing troop movements on the Chahar border.[34] The Nanking government on June 23 empowered General Chin Te-chun, at that

[32] Shuhsi Hsu, cited, p. 20; also *New York Herald Tribune*, February 4, 1935.
[33] H. J. Timperley, *Christian Science Monitor*, June 17, 1935.
[34] *New York Times*, June 13, 1935; *New York Herald Tribune*, June 14, 1935.

time head of a bureau in the Chahar provincial government, to arrange a settlement with Major-General Doihara [35] at Peiping. Four days later these men exchanged notes embodying terms of settlement. The texts of these notes have never been published, but the essential items of what has since become known as the Chin-Doihara agreement are fairly well established.[36] Terms which might actually be construed as connected with the incident called for an apology, dismissal of the responsible Chinese officers, a pledge that such incidents would not recur, and a guarantee of free and safe travel for all Japanese in Chahar. Other terms, which by no stretch of the imagination could be related to the incident, included dissolution of Kuomintang organs in Chahar, cessation of Chinese immigration into the province, removal of the 132nd Division from Changpei, and demilitarization of a broad area of eastern Chahar. This area, much larger than originally suspected, included all the territory "east of a line drawn from Changping in Hopei to the Wall in East Chahar *via* Yenching and Talinpao, and south of another line drawn from a point north of Tushihkou to a point south of Changpei." [37] The forces of the 29th Route Army were to be withdrawn from this area, within which order was to be maintained by a police force. In addition, though apparently not as part of the settlement, the Nanking government dismissed General Sung Che-yuan from his post as Chahar governor. His place was taken by General Chin Te-chun.

During the course of this affair, Japanese military

[35] Now Lieutenant-General. Doihara, then Chief of Kwantung Army's Special Service Section, had been active in every forward move in China since September 18, 1931.

[36] See official statement by Colonel Takahashi, Japanese assistant military attaché in Peiping, *China Weekly Review*, July 6, 1935, p. 183; also Shuhsi Hsu, cited, p. 21.

[37] Shuhsi Hsu, cited, p. 21.

agents began to exert much stronger pressure on the Chahar-Suiyuan Mongols. Prince Te stated in an interview at Peiping on June 1 that Japanese military officers periodically visited Inner Mongolia, suggesting the advisability of Manchurian and Mongol unity.[38] He declared that a Japanese airplane, bearing a Japanese military representative, had recently landed at Pangchiang, near his own headquarters in western Chahar situated on the northerly route to Urga. This envoy informed Prince Te that the Japanese desired to build an airdrome near Pangchiang, establish a branch of the Kwantung Army's Special Service Mission there, and erect a wireless station; he also submitted a request that the Mongolian Political Council should transfer its capital from Pailingmiao in Suiyuan province to Peisiemiao, north of Dolonor. In his statement Prince Te insisted that the Mongolian Council did not intend to join Manchoukuo but aimed to establish a unified Mongolian province within China. Following settlement of the Changpei incident, direct Japanese influence on the Chahar administration rapidly increased. Kalgan, the provincial capital, had for some time been the seat of a Japanese military mission headed by Colonel Gennosuke Matsui. Most of the dozen or more staff officers of the mission, according to a visiting correspondent, spoke the Russian and Mongolian languages.[39]

On July 5 a spokesman for the Japanese Embassy at Shanghai revealed that Colonel Matsui had been appointed military adviser to the Chahar government; on July 22 the same source announced the appointment of a Japanese ad-

[38] *New York Times*, June 2, 1935; *Christian Science Monitor*, June 1, 1935. Japanese agents were also striving to win the confidence of the Lama priesthood in Chahar and Suiyuan provinces. See Hugh Byas, *New York Times*, April 19, 1935.
[39] *China Weekly Review*, July 27, 1935, p. 282.

viser on civil affairs.[40] Located at Kalgan, which dominates the arteries of communication in Chahar and Suiyuan provinces, Japan's military agents could lay their plans for completion of their conquest of Inner Mongolia.

During September and October of 1935, signs of the approach of a new and more ominous crisis in North China rapidly multiplied. The summer months had been an important transitional period in Hopei province. Despite the enforced withdrawal of the central troops in June, the local northern leaders had smoothly taken over provincial administrative and police functions. General Shang Chen, commander of the 32nd Army, had successfully handled the problems arising during the evacuation period; on June 25 he was appointed governor of Hopei, in addition to his post as commander of the Tientsin-Tangku Peace Preservation Headquarters. On June 28-29 some two thousand Chinese troops, led by one Pai Chien-wu and stimulated by Japanese *ronin*,[41] had mutinied at Fengtai and engaged in an abortive attack on Peiping. Following this affair, part of the 29th Army was transferred from Chahar to assist in policing the Peiping area. On August 28 General Sung Che-yuan, former Chahar governor, was appointed Garrison Commander of the Peiping-Tientsin area, and additional units of the 29th Army were brought in from Chahar. The seat of the Hopei provincial government was removed from Peiping to Paotingfu, which became Shang Chen's military headquarters. Appointments to the various posts were all made by Nanking, and the new North China authorities quickly demonstrated their ability to maintain an effective and orderly government. If the Japanese military leaders had

[40] *New York Times,* July 6, 23, 1935.

[41] Admitted by Colonel Takahashi, Japanese assistant military attaché at Peiping, in an interview with foreign correspondents on July 5. *China Weekly Review,* July 13, 1935, p. 219.

thought that, under the changed political status in the north, separatist tendencies would become dominant, they were disappointed. By September it was evident that any such result would require external stimulus.

Tentative feelers put out during the summer indicated that Japan's military circles were already toying with the idea of an "autonomous" North China. At the end of July several Japanese officers sought to induce Yen Hsi-shan, the Shansi overlord, to take the lead in organizing the government of a bloc of the five North China provinces.[42] A week later, on August 5, Colonel Takashi Sakai, chief-of-staff of the North China Garrison, suggested to Wang Keh-min, acting chairman of the Peiping Political Council, the necessity for a complete reorganization of China's five northern provinces.[43] The Central Government made two further concessions: on August 28 it ordered the abolition of the Peiping Political Council, and on the next day the dissolution of the Kuomintang organs in Suiyuan province. On September 24 a bombshell was exploded in the form of a statement by Major-General Hayao Tada, commander of the North China Garrison, to Japanese correspondents at Tientsin, later distributed as a pamphlet. Seldom has such a proclamation of aggressive aims been made by a responsible military official stationed in a country with which his government was ostensibly on peaceful terms. Its irony was not lessened by Japan's earnest efforts to place a curb on provocative speeches and acts of Chinese citizens. In unqualified language, Major-General Tada demanded the elimination of Western interests in China, and called for the overthrow of the Nanking government, the Kuomintang, and Chiang Kai-shek. His references to North China, nonetheless spe-

---

[42] *The Japan Advertiser*, July 28, 1935.
[43] *China Weekly Review*, August 10, 1935, p. 363.

cific for their glowing phraseology, were expressed in the following terms:

"It has been stated previously that as long as Chiang Kai-shek and his clique continue to dominate China, there can be no hope of the adoption of a friendly policy toward Japan. . . . Therefore the Japanese Empire should act independently . . . by starting to create a paradise for co-existence and mutual prosperity between the two countries out of a zone where the China policy will be adopted. That paradise will be extended by degrees to such an extent that China will have to change her attitude sincerely or even they [Chiang and his clique] will not be permitted to exist.

"North China at present is the district where the above-mentioned policy can be most easily and quickly carried out. . . . So the first step to enforce the national policy is to make North China a land of peace where the Chinese and Japanese can live in peace and enlightenment, a market where Chinese and Japanese commodities and capital will not be subject to jeopardy but circulated freely —a paradise for co-existence and mutual prosperity of the two nations. Such a step will help the healthy growth of Manchoukuo in the north and demonstrate to that part of China lying to the south that . . . cooperation among Japan, China and Manchoukuo with the Empire as the center of gravity can warrant peace in Eastern Asia. Such is the importance of the North China question, upon which depends the success of the outward expansion of the Japanese Empire." [44]

The Tada statement was closely linked to the consultations then proceeding at Tokyo between the Ministries of War, Navy, and Foreign Affairs, which formulated a

[44] For complete text of this illuminating document, see *China Weekly Review*, November 2, 1935, p. 306-312.

so-called "new China policy" eventually adopted by the
Cabinet on October 8. During these two weeks the Tokyo
newspapers referred almost daily to the new policy which
was under consideration by the three Ministries. On September 24 the *Asahi* printed a declaration, attributed to a
War Office spokesman, which was similar in tenor to the
Tada statement but even more specific. It advocated a
three-point program for North China, comprising suppression of anti-Japanese elements, severance of financial connections with Nanking, and military cooperation of the
five northern provinces to prevent sovietization. As the
"first step" in this program, it concluded, "a guiding hand
has to be extended for organization of a united self-governing body among the five provinces in North China." [45]
These two simultaneous declarations from military quarters, one in Tientsin and the other in Tokyo, were calculated indiscretions, designed to bring pressure on the
Foreign Office to accept the army's program. During the
first week of October, both Chiang Tso-pin, the Chinese
Ambassador, and the foreign correspondents made inquiry
as to whether the Foreign Office concurred in press statements to the effect that Japan intended to foster an independence movement in North China. Foreign Minister
Hirota at first avoided a direct reply by declaring that his
only knowledge of the Tada pamphlet was derived from
newspaper reports; on October 7, however, he openly "dis-
sociated" himself from the views of Major-General Tada
in a Foreign Office statement which was cabled abroad.
On the following day, the Cabinet formally approved
Japan's new policy toward China. At the same time, it was
decided to send to China special representatives of the
War, Navy and Foreign Ministries, who should inform

[45] Quoted in *China Weekly Review*, October 12, 1935, p. 184.

Japanese officials in that country on the details of the new policy.

This latter decision led to an extraordinary series of conferences among Japanese military, naval and consular officials at Dairen, Shanghai and Tientsin during the last two weeks of October. The first of these meetings, attended by officers of the Kwantung Army and the North China Garrison, convened at Dairen on October 13. The War Office was represented by Major-General Yasuji Okamura, of the Imperial General Staff. Other participants included Major-General Tada; Major-General Seishiro Itagaki, assistant chief-of-staff of the Kwantung Army; and Major-General Rensuke Isogai, military attaché at Shanghai. The conference opened with a statement by Major-General Okamura, who explained the Cabinet's new China policy and stressed the bearing of the Italo-Ethiopian dispute on the Far East. Sessions ended on the next day, according to press reports, "in complete understanding and accord." Among the reported decisions was one that plans should be pushed for the conversion of North China into "a Sino-Japanese cooperation area." In addition, the conferees felt that the Chinese government should be presented with a demand that all causes of trouble in the north be uprooted. Failing satisfaction of this demand, the Japanese Army should insist on the "divorce of North China from Nanking." [46]

The most elaborate of these conferences occurred a week later at Shanghai. Japanese diplomatic and consular officials assembled on October 19-20 to meet with the Foreign Office representative, Mr. Goro Morishima, chief of the First Section of the Bureau of Oriental Affairs. The military and naval parleys were held separately on October

[46] *China Weekly Review*, October 19, 1935, p. 221, 224.

20-21, with Major-General Okamura and Captain Tadao Honda, chief of the China Section of the Naval General Staff, as the central figures. Though separate, these conferences "were bound together by a unity of mission carried out by Mr. Goro Morishima, Major-General Okamura and Captain Honda, representing the Japanese Foreign, War and Naval Ministries. At the parleys, they had the identic mission of conveying to the officials in the China field of the ministries they respectively represent the new China policy recently agreed upon by the three ministries at Tokyo." [47]

Toward the end of October these official conferences, then continuing at Tientsin, were punctuated by serious disturbances in North China. At Hsiangho, on the edge of the demilitarized zone northeast of Peiping, Chinese farmers seized control of the city, overthrew the district government, and set up an autonomous administration under an official of their own choice. Legitimate tax grievances seem to have underlaid this affair; at the same time, there was clear evidence of assistance from Japanese sources.[48] Unsuccessful efforts were made to spread the riots into the neighboring district of Sanho. When General Shang Chen sought to put down the disturbances with Chinese troops, the Japanese military intervened against such action on the ground that it would infringe the provisions of the Tangku Truce, though actually Hsiangho was just outside the demilitarized zone. Efforts to settle this affair were still proceeding on October 28, when it was overshadowed by much more momentous issues raised by a series of comprehensive Japanese demands addressed to the North China authorities.

At this time General Chiang Tso-pin, Chinese Ambas-

[47] *China Weekly Review*, October 26, 1935, p. 262.

[48] See report of a group of American newspaper correspondents who visited Hsiangho, *China Weekly Review*, November 16, 1935, p. 381-383.

sador to Japan, was making his final round of calls on Cabinet officials at Tokyo preparatory to leaving for China to participate in the Kuomintang sessions scheduled for early November. On October 28 Foreign Minister Hirota chose the occasion of his last interview with the Chinese Ambassador to offer a three-point proposal for Sino-Japanese rapprochement. The "three principles" of Hirota's China policy were thus formally launched. As reported at the time, they were expressed in the following terms: (1) positive aid by the Nanking government to a scheme designed to place Sino-Japanese relations on a firm, friendly basis; (2) a formula for cooperation between China, Japan and Manchoukuo in the development of North China; (3) a program for a common front between China, Japan and Manchoukuo to prevent the spread of Communism.[49] General Kawashima, Japanese Minister of War, urged the Chinese Ambassador to give "serious consideration" to the Hirota proposals. He stressed the necessity for a definite statement of attitude toward the plan from the Nanking government, especially with regard to the last two points, and asked the Ambassador to transmit his views to the officials at Nanking.[50] On the morning of October 29 General Chiang Tso-pin was received in audience by Emperor Hirohito, and on the following day he left for China.

Meanwhile the first steps to enforce Foreign Minister Hirota's proposals for Sino-Japanese cooperation were being taken in North China. On October 29 Shigeru Kawagoe, Japanese Consul-General at Tientsin, had presented a note to the North China authorities embracing a set of five demands. These included abolition of the Pei-

[49] "Hirota's Three Principles vis-a-vis China", *Information Bulletin*, Council of International Affairs, Nanking, Volume I, Number 7, July 11, 1936, p. 5.
[50] *China Weekly Review*, November 2, 1935, p. 299.

ping Branch Military Council within three days; dismissal
of Colonel Yuan Liang, Mayor of Peiping; formal apology
from General Shang Chen for the Luanchow incident, a
long-standing affair that had occurred during the summer
in the demilitarized zone; immediate arrest of active anti-
Japanese elements and Blue Shirts; and extension of the
demilitarized zone to five more *hsien,* or counties, namely,
Hsiangho, Changping, Wuching, Paoti and Ningho.[51] The
note was delivered to the four leading Chinese officials in
the north: General Shang Chen, governor of Hopei; General Sung Che-yuan, garrison commander of the Peiping-
Tientsin area; Cheng Ke, Mayor of Tientsin; and Colonel
Yuan Liang, Mayor of Peiping. In his accompanying representations, the Japanese Consul-General charged that the
Chinese authorities had not complied with the terms of
the Ho-Umetsu agreement, especially on the issue of
suppressing anti-Japanese groups and agents. The fact that
the Consul-General, and not the military officers, presented
these demands may be taken to indicate the measure of
coordination achieved by the preliminary conferences of
Japanese civilian and military officials in China. Nevertheless, Major-General Tada saw fit to notify the same Chinese
officials simultaneously that the Japanese army intended
to put an end to the North China complications, that deep-
seated intrigue and terrorism were being carried on in the
north, and that Japan could not overlook China's efforts
to "sovietize" the northern provinces. Additional evidence
of military-civilian correlation on the new China policy
was supplied by a statement issued at Shanghai on October
29 by Akira Ariyoshi, the Japanese Ambassador, which
deplored the "present unsettled conditions" in "the five
northern provinces" and called for the establishment in

[51] *China Weekly Review,* November 2, 1935, p. 291-292; November 9,
1935, p. 338.

North China "of a stable and reliable government of genuine permanency." [52]

The presentation of these demands ushered in a new era in North China, marked by a determined Japanese effort to sever the five northern provinces from Nanking's jurisdiction. Immediate prosecution of this aim, however, was halted by startling developments at the Kuomintang sessions inaugurated on November 1 in Nanking. From these events, despite further initial losses in the north, emerged a nationalist movement which was destined to forge a united China in the short space of eighteen months.

[52] *New York Times,* October 30, 1935.

CHAPTER THREE

"AUTONOMY" FOR NORTH CHINA

AT the beginning of November 1935 a set of threatening political and economic difficulties, which had slowly gathered force over a period of several years, confronted the Nanking government with a critical emergency. General Ho Ying-chin's surrender in North China during the month of June had strengthened popular opposition to Nanking's foreign policy, which had been nominally controlled since early 1932 by Premier Wang Ching-wei, with Generalissimo Chiang Kai-shek in the background. This question was now raised in even more burning form by the open Japanese preparations to detach the five northern provinces from the rest of China. Equally pressing economic and financial problems had been created by the long-continued trade decline and the increasing outflow of silver. The storm broke on November 1, when Wang Ching-wei was shot and seriously wounded by an assassin at the opening assembly of the Sixth Plenary Session of the Kuomintang. Two days later the government suddenly announced a new monetary program, involving substitution of a managed currency for China's traditional silver standard. The first of these events led to the most thoroughgoing shake-up in government and party offices in nearly four years; the second gave an added stimulus to Japan's activities in the north.

Since the reorganization of the National Government

in January 1932, which brought Wang Ching-wei's group into the ruling circle, Chiang Kai-shek had been continuously occupied with two major political problems: the Communist opposition and Japanese aggression. In November 1934 Nanking's anti-Communist operations finally succeeded in ousting the main Red armies from their Kiangsi and Fukien provincial strongholds, which had been maintained for six years. Despite a vast concentration of nearly half a million government troops, aided by the new airplane bombers purchased abroad, Chiang Kai-shek failed in his main objective of surrounding and annihilating the Communist armies. Under Mao Tse-tung and Chu Teh these forces escaped from the net, marched westward across sections of five provinces, and entered Szechuan province in the early spring of 1935. In June they effected a junction in western Szechuan with the second largest Communist army. Several months later these combined Red armies began a northward movement designed to clear a path for their forces into China's northwest. In November a bitter military struggle to prevent the successful completion of this movement was still continuing in the western provinces.[1]

In dealing with the successive Japanese encroachments, Chiang Kai-shek had consistently sought to achieve compromise settlements on the best terms possible. Nanking's military forces had never been mobilized in full strength against Japan, even in the crises which led to the Tangku Truce and the Ho-Umetsu agreement. This policy was defended on the ground that political unity had to be established under the aegis of the Central Government before effective resistance could be offered Japan. In pursuit of this policy, Chiang Kai-shek had suppressed all anti-Japanese protest movements within China, whether of

[1] For details, see Edgar Snow, *Red Star Over China*, cited, Part Five.

a military or civilian character. The treatment meted out to Feng Yu-hsiang's military operations against Japan in Chahar province in the summer of 1933 has already been noted. Toward the end of that year a second revolt, which also represented a protest against the government's non-resistance policy, broke out in Fukien province. The Fukien rebellion was headed by the 19th Route Army, the Cantonese force which had defended Shanghai against Japan two years earlier. After a swift campaign, however, it was crushed early in 1934. Since that period the government had pursued its temporizing foreign policy without effective political opposition, despite an annoying verbal assault from the Southwest Political Council, which comprised the leaders of Kwangtung and Kwangsi provinces. The threatening emergency in the north had now finally aroused the Chinese public, and its voice was to be heard in more and more powerful tones during the coming months. The first direct expression of this spirit took an unfortunate turn, which may be at least partially attributed to the rigidly enforced patience which the government had imposed on the Chinese people.

At nine o'clock on the morning of November 1 the inaugural ceremony of the Sixth Plenary Session of the Fourth Central Executive Committee of the Kuomintang took place in the auditorium of the Central Party Headquarters at Nanking. A total of one hundred and twelve members of the Central Executive and Central Supervisory Committees was in attendance, and the gallery was filled with over a thousand representatives of various party and government organs and civic bodies. The ceremony was begun by the singing of the party anthem, followed by three bows to the party and national flags and the portrait of Dr. Sun Yat-sen. The last will of Dr. Sun was then read, and a three-minute silence observed. Wang Ching-wei, president of the Executive Yuan, delivered a brief opening address. Immediately afterwards, as the delegates left the auditorium and gathered to pose for a group picture, Wang Ching-wei was shot by a Chinese reporter.[2] The repercussions of this incident were of first-rate political significance. Although dominated by Chiang Kai-shek, the Nanking government had functioned through a number of titular leaders, of whom Wang Ching-wei was the most prominent. As Premier and Foreign Minister, he had for several years been forced to shoulder responsibility for Nanking's policy of non-resistance to Japanese aggression. The attack on his life, particularly under the circumstances prevailing in the north, sharply raised the whole Japanese issue before the Kuomintang sessions, and dramatized it before the country at large. In Japan the reaction was one of ill-concealed dismay. Under military inspiration, the Japanese press generally asserted that no change in China's foreign policy was conceivable, but an undercurrent of uneasiness was equally apparent. "The motive for the attack," declared a Japanese report from Nanking, "is believed to be resentment at the Japan policy of Mr. Wang and the incident is regarded here as likely to mark a turning point in the Government's Japan policy." [3]

The impression created among Japan's official circles by the attempted assassination of Wang Ching-wei was as nothing compared to the outcry which greeted the promulgation of Nanking's new monetary program on November 3. Without Tokyo's consent or foreknowledge, the Chinese government had boldly plunged ahead on a major stroke of policy. Some such effort as this might well have

---

[2] The assassin, Sun Feng-min, subsequently died of gun wounds inflicted by the bodyguards. He had been a member of the 19th Route Army, and later commander of a company of machine-gunners in the 12th Division of the Fukien Army.

[3] *The Japan Advertiser,* November 2, 1935.

been expected, had Japan not felt so certain of the strength
of its influence at Nanking. It had long been realized that
drastic measures were required to support China's shaky
economic and financial structure, which had been seriously
undermined by the conditions prevailing since 1933. So
long as China maintained a silver standard, the nation's
trade and business status was intimately affected by the
price of that metal. During the first two years of the world
depression, when the price of silver fell to low levels,
China experienced an increasing degree of prosperity.
Business activity was well maintained, the price index was
rising, and foreign trade reached new high totals. At the
end of 1931, with successive devaluations of the pound,
rupee and yen, this process was reversed. In 1933 the dollar
was also devalued, and in June 1934 the American government inaugurated the silver purchase policy. With the
consequent rapid rise in the world price of silver, China's
stocks of this metal began to leave the country in large
amounts. From an importer of silver, which was the
normal state of affairs, China turned into a large net ex-
porter. Silver was smuggled out of the country, especially
through North China, in alarming proportions. Travelers
in the demilitarized zone during the summer of 1935 witnessed numbers of Japanese nationals, who were wearing
special vests filled with silver coins, crossing the border
into Manchuria. Japan's exports of silver, which totalled
14 million yen in 1934, amounted to 225 million yen in
1935, and then fell to 36 million in 1936.[4] Under these
conditions, silver stocks in Shanghai declined by at least
one half in the two years prior to November 1935.

Exodus of silver led to a contraction of China's currency supply, which in turn brought on severe deflation.

[4] *Monthly Return of the Foreign Trade of Japan*, Tokyo, Department
of Finance, December 1936, p. 113.

Commodity prices fell, business stagnated, exports were stifled, and overseas remittances dwindled. By 1935 the country was in the throes of a serious depression, marked by widespread bankruptcies and large unemployment in the port cities. Although the Chinese economic crisis was not originally caused by the American silver purchase policy, the "rising price of silver was the principal factor responsible for China's grave economic troubles after early 1932." [5] Repeated Chinese diplomatic approaches at Washington during 1934 failed to secure relief. In October of that year the Chinese government imposed a levy of 10 per cent on silver exports, plus an equalization fee that varied with the price of silver. The salutary effects of this measure on exchange stability were counteracted by the excessive advance in silver quotations, which rose above 80 cents an ounce in May 1935 and markedly stimulated smuggling operations. The collapse of several Chinese native banks in Shanghai and the bankruptcy of the American-owned Raven Trust Company, occurring during the spring and summer of 1935, warned of an imminent financial panic.

Foreign interests in China were seriously affected by these developments. The continued decline in China's foreign trade after 1933, when world trade in general was on the upgrade, was a disturbing phenomenon. Total Chinese foreign trade in 1935, as calculated by the *Monthly Bulletin* of the League of Nations, was only 66 per cent of the 1931 figure. The resulting loss to Chinese government revenues, which depended largely on customs duties, jeopardized the security of foreign loans. In this respect, Great Britain, owing to its leading investment position in China, stood to lose the most should a general

[5] John Parke Young, "The United States Silver Policy," *Foreign Policy Reports*, July 1, 1936, p. 102-103.

economic debacle be precipitated. On the basis of a Chinese appeal to London in March 1935 for a loan of 20 million pounds, Britain had attempted to arrange joint consideration of China's finances with the United States, Japan and France. This proposal, which might possibly have led to a revival of the China international banking consortium, was rejected outright by Japan and coolly received in Washington. As the next step Sir Frederick Leith-Ross, British treasury expert, was sent out to the Far East. In September Sir Frederick had visited Tokyo in a final effort to secure Japanese assistance in stabilizing China's financial situation, which had become a source of acute anxiety to British investors and bondholders. Although a loan project to maintain Chinese exchange at a fixed ratio to the pound was apparently broached at these conferences, Leith-Ross left Japan on September 18 without having obtained Japanese cooperation.[6] He then went on to China, where he had discussed questions related to currency reform with Nanking government officials prior to November 3.[7] On that evening, at one hour before midnight, Dr. H. H. Kung, the Chinese Finance Minister, announced a series of drastic financial reforms.

As summarized in Dr. Kung's announcement, the Currency Mandate decreed, with effect from November 4, 1935, as follows: "(1) The banknotes issued by the three Government banks, *i.e.*, The Central Bank of China, The Bank of China, and The Bank of Communications, shall be full legal tender, and the banknote reserves of the three banks shall be placed under a unified control. The notes of all other issuing banks will continue in circulation, but will gradually be withdrawn and replaced by notes of The Central Bank. No new notes are to be issued by these

---

[6] *New York Times*, September 18, 1935.
[7] *North-China Herald*, November 13, 1935.

banks and all their unissued notes as well as their banknote reserves are to be deposited with the Central Bank.
(2) All debts expressed in terms of silver shall be dis-
charged by the payment in legal tender notes of the nominal amount due. (3) All holders of silver are required to
exchange their silver for legal tender notes. (4) The exchange value of the Chinese dollar will be kept stable at
its present level, and for this purpose the Government
banks will buy and sell foreign exchange in unlimited
quantities." In addition, the "Government-owned Central
Bank is to be reorganized as the Central Reserve Bank
of China and will be owned principally by the banks and
the general public, thus becoming an independent institution, devoting itself chiefly to maintaining the stability
of the nation's currency. The Central Reserve Bank of
China will hold the reserves of the banking system and
act as depository of all public funds and will provide centralized re-discount facilities for the other banks. The Central Reserve Bank of China will not undertake general
commercial business, and after a period of two years will
enjoy the sole right of note issue." [8]

The impounding of China's silver stocks, provided for
under this program, supplied the means by which the exchange stability of the new managed currency could be
maintained. By the sale of these silver stocks large foreign
reserves were acquired, particularly in London and New
York. Acquisition of the dollar reserve was made possible
through a special agreement with the United States,
reached in May 1936, by which the Treasury agreed to
make "substantial purchases" of silver from China.[9] The
extraordinary confidence in the reform displayed by the

[8] *China Weekly Review*, November 9, 1935, p. 335-336.
[9] *New York Times*, May 19, 1935. On two previous occasions the United
States had helped China by purchasing considerable amounts of silver,
once of 19 million and again of 50 million ounces.

Chinese people, who immediately gave up their long-standing allegiance to silver coins, cleared away the second major difficulty confronting the change to a managed currency. From the beginning it functioned smoothly, and led rapidly to a general revival of business and trade. The last difficulty—the reaction from Japan—proved more difficult to handle.

Announcement of the new monetary program was greeted with a chorus of denunciation in Tokyo, centering on the alleged role played by Leith-Ross.[10] The latter maintained, in later declarations, that the reform was an independent move by Nanking, for which he "had no responsibility." [11] In private conversation, Chinese officials who were associated with the launching of the new program asserted that its principles had been worked out months before at Nanking. Certain Japanese circles charged that a British loan had underwritten the currency reform program, but these statements were categorically denied by Leith-Ross.[12] There was no doubt, however, that Nanking's action was thoroughly approved by Sir Frederick. It was followed on November 4 by regulations issued by the British Ambassador, under authority of an Order in Council, which backed up the reform by prohibiting British persons and corporations from making payments in silver on pain of fine or imprisonment.[13] The British colony of Hongkong, moreover, proceeded to institute a managed currency along lines similar to those taken by China. It might seem that in the efforts put forth to assist China in solving its financial difficulties, Great Britain was merely exercising a normal inter-

[10] *New York Times, New York Herald Tribune,* November 5, 1935.
[11] "Statement made by Sir Frederick Leith-Ross at Shanghai on Monday, June 22, 1936," press release.
[12] *North-China Herald,* November 13, 1935.
[13] *North-China Herald,* November 13, 1935.

national right, especially in view of the attempts previously made to secure Japanese cooperation. The opposition raised by Japan was, in fact, a further application of the Amau doctrine enunciated on April 17, 1934, advising Western powers to keep their hands off China.

Statements emanating from official sources in Tokyo during the second week in November left no room for doubt in this regard. An informal declaration by the Foreign Office spokesman on November 8 deplored the suddenness of the reforms. In taking action on a matter of such importance, he suggested, the Chinese government should have consulted the Japanese authorities and secured assurances of their cooperation, in view of the close relations existing between the two nations. The Japanese government, he concluded, felt that any reforms of a general character in China had to be carried out through China's independent efforts.[14] The views of the War Office were expressed much more bluntly. "China's long history," declared the spokesman on November 8, "shows that her economic rehabilitation must come of her own efforts. Foreign attempts to establish control over the financial and economic structure of the country through the grant of loans will, in our opinion, not only affect the welfare of China's four hundred million people, but will also menace the peace of the Orient. Japan may be compelled to take appropriate steps in this connection." [15] This warning was speedily fulfilled by measures adopted in North China.

The stir at Nanking had effectually distracted attention from the results of the demands presented in the north by Consul-General Shigeru Kawagoe. With the resignation on November 3 of Colonel Yuan Liang, Mayor of Peiping,

[14] *China Weekly Review*, November 16, 1935, p. 377.
[15] *China Weekly Review*, November 16, 1935, p. 377.

the first demand was met. Three days later the National Government formally appointed General Chin Te-chun to this post. Hsiangho, Paoti, Changping and Ningho— four of the five *hsien* specified by the Consul-General— were arbitrarily added to the demilitarized zone. The other demands were either left in abeyance or only partially satisfied. General Shang Chen seems not to have apologized for the Luanchow incident, and the Peiping Branch Military Council was not dissolved. On the other hand, the Military Council seems to have made efforts to suppress so-called anti-Japanese elements. The Japanese authorities concentrated their main attention on this latter issue.

When the purge failed to proceed as fast as desired, the Japanese military took matters into their own hands by effecting arbitrary arrests of Chinese citizens and detaining them for examination in the Japanese barracks at Tientsin and Peiping. These arrests began on October 30 and continued for nearly two weeks. During this period Japanese gendarmes arrested four Chinese officials: Li Ming and Wang Chia-chi of the Tientsin Social Affairs Bureau; Wang Yi-fan, deputy director of the Tientsin Press Censorship Bureau; and Colonel Hsuan Chieh-hsi, staff officer of the 29th Army in Peiping. Four Chinese educational leaders were arrested: Professor Yang Yi-chow, dean of the College of Commerce and Law in Tientsin, and Professor Lo Yu-wen, chairman of the department of commerce of the same institution; Liu Hai-hsun, physical director of the elementary school attached to the Tientsin Women's Normal College; and Yao Chin-shen, director of the Tientsin Municipal Library. Among Chinese business circles Nien Kwang-yao, committee member of the Tientsin Chamber of Commerce, and Fu Hung-chin, son of the chairman of one of the merchant guilds, were arrested. The latter managed to effect his escape, and reported that the Japanese military had compiled a list of about one hundred well-known people in North China who were to be arrested and accused of anti-Japanese activities. On November 11 the Chinese Foreign Ministry charged, in a strong protest transmitted to Tokyo through the Japanese Ambassador, that these arrests of Chinese officials and citizens on Chinese territory "constituted grave violations of Chinese sovereignty as well as infringements of international law," and demanded that steps be taken to prevent the recurrence of similar incidents. The arrests were then discontinued, but reportedly on condition that the North China officials would arrest all persons whose names were submitted by the Japanese military authorities.[16]

Much more important moves were already taking place in North China. Major-General Doihara, Chief of the Kwantung Army's Special Service Section, had arrived at Tientsin on November 6 and immediately plunged into a series of conferences with Chinese and Japanese officials both there and in Peiping. In these meetings Doihara was dealing mainly with the leaders of the 29th Army, including Generals Sung Che-yuan and Chin Te-chun, and Mr. Hsiao Chen-ying, newly appointed Chahar governor. These men, with the gradual withdrawal of General Shang Chen's 32nd Army units from Tientsin to Paolingfu, had now come to occupy the key positions in Hopei and Chahar provinces. In addition, Doihara was conferring with the chairman of Shansi province, General Hsu Yung-chang, and with representatives of the Shantung and

[16] For the facts detailed in this paragraph, see *China Weekly Review*, November 16, 1935, p. 369, 375. On November 18 the Foreign Office spokesman said that Japanese gendarmes had arrested a total of 42 lesser Chinese officials in North China. *North China Star*, Tientsin, November 19, 1935.

Suiyuan provincial governments. The Central Government was also in direct touch with the developing situation in the north. General Hsiung Pin, vice-chief of the General Staff and signer of the Tangku Truce, who had been sent north to investigate and report back to Generalissimo Chiang Kai-shek, had several meetings with General Sung Che-yuan at this time. The lines of political pressure reaching into North China crossed on November 12, when Doihara talked with General Hsiung Pin. This day also marked the convening at Nanking of the Fifth National Kuomintang Congress, which had followed upon the sessions of the Kuomintang plenum. The Kuomintang Congress was greeted by a telegraphed appeal from General Sung Che-yuan, the terms of which created a mild sensation. "The period of tutelage has already ended," the telegram stated, "and the time has arrived to introduce and enforce constitutional government. The Legislative Yuan should submit the draft constitution to the Congress for discussion, promulgating it immediately afterwards. Simultaneously, the administrative authority should be returned to the people, to secure their collaboration in national rehabilitation." [17] With its overtones of challenge to the Nanking dictatorship, and its undertones of autonomy consciousness, the telegram seemed to mark Sung Che-yuan as one of the logical choices of the Japanese to work out their purposes in North China. This appeal was echoed by General Han Fu-chu, governor of Shantung, and by the Chamber of Commerce in Tientsin.[18] Yin Ju-keng, administrative commissioner of the demilitarized zone, registered his support of the appeals by Generals Sung and Han.

These declarations carried much greater weight than

[17] *China Weekly Review*, November 16, 1935, p. 375.
[18] Shuhsi Hsu, *The North China Problem*, cited, p. 32.

the independence hand-bills spread broadcast in the north at this time, or than the spurious autonomy organizations, fostered by Japanese agents, that were now cropping up in the Peiping-Tientsin area. Everything seemed prepared for the *coup de main* that was to deliver the five northern provinces into the hands of Japan. To ensure against any last-minute wavering on the part of the North China officials, the threat of military force was invoked at this point. On November 15 the Kwantung Army despatched four divisions from Chinchow, in Manchuria, to Shanhai-kuan, and that night the headquarters of the North China Garrison demanded barrack accommodations for 15,000 troops from the Tientsin authorities. The general public looked for an immediate Japanese occupation, but the threat was not carried out. On November 18 Major-General Doihara delivered a verbal ultimatum to Mr. Hsiao Chen-ying, chief negotiator on the Chinese side. If a North China Autonomous Council was not announced on or before November 20, Doihara stated, five divisions would be moved into Hopei and four into Shantung. Hsiao Chen-ying, in a two-hour interview with the foreign correspondents that afternoon, declared that the autonomy scheme laid down by Doihara had not yet been formally accepted. He said, however, that "a meeting would take place in Peiping on or before November 20, when the chairmen of each of the five provinces, or their representatives, would be present to pass final approval on the plan and announce the formation of the new autonomous régime." General Han Fu-chu, he continued, was expected to arrive in Peiping before that date; General Hsu Yung-chang, the Shansi chairman, had been in Peiping for the past several weeks; General Shang Chen was expected on the following day; Hsiao Chen-ying himself was governor of Chahar; and General Fu Tso-yi, chairman of Suiyuan, had a representative in Peiping. Hsiao Chen-ying stated, further, that he and his colleagues "constantly informed the Central Government of what was going on and asked for instructions." Up to that afternoon, he complained, "not a single concrete suggestion or plan of assistance had been offered by Nanking. Marshal Chiang Kai-shek yesterday sent six telegrams to Mr. Hsiao and his colleagues, but all were vague and indeterminate, such as insisting that spiritual unity between Nanking and General Sung Che-yuan must continue." [19]

At Nanking, meanwhile, the last session of the old Kuomintang plenum had ended on November 6 after taking certain routine actions, such as referring the draft Constitution to the forthcoming National Congress and approving the monetary reforms. The Fifth National Kuomintang Congress, which convened on November 12, was marked by the presence of Generals Feng Yu-hsiang and Yen Hsi-shan. Although Generals Chen Chi-tang of Kwangtung and Li Tsung-jen and Pai Tsung-hsi of Kwangsi did not attend, the Southwest Political Council sent a large and representative group to participate in the sessions. Tsou Lu, Chancellor of the Chung Shan University of Canton and leader of the Southwest delegation, addressing the Congress on November 18, declared: "Kuomintang comrades, whether from the South or the North, have gathered here with a firm belief in the necessity of internal cohesion. Such unity cannot be achieved by means of force, but of a spontaneous common desire to stand together and face the present crisis." [20] On the fol-

[19] For this significant interview, see *North China Star*, November 19, 1935.

[20] *China Weekly Review*, November 23, 1935, p. 419; see also "Special Kuomintang Sessions Supplement", *The China Press Weekly*, December 1, 1935, p. 46.

lowing day, General Chiang Kai-shek delivered an important address on China's foreign relations. After stressing
the need for "balanced progress", involving "the completion of the groundwork of nation building" as well as
the achievement of "equality and independence among
nations", he concluded: ". . . if international developments do not menace our national existence or block the
way of our national regeneration, we should, in view of
the interest of the whole nation, practice forbearance in
facing issues not of a fundamental nature. At the same
time we should seek harmonious international relations
provided there is no violation of our sovereignty. We
should seek economic cooperation based upon the principle of equality and reciprocity. Otherwise, we should
abide by the decision of the Party and the Nation and
reach a resolute determination. As far as I am concerned,
I will not evade my responsibility. We shall not forsake
peace until there is no hope for peace. We shall not talk
lightly of sacrifice until we are driven to the last extremity
which makes sacrifice inevitable. The sacrifice of an individual is insignificant, but the sacrifice of a nation is a
mighty thing, for the life of an individual is finite while
the life of a nation is infinite. Granted a limit to conditions for peace and a determination to make the supreme
sacrifice, we should exert our best efforts to preserve
peace. . . ." [21] Despite its minor refrain, this declaration
left open the possibility of treating with Japan on the
basis of the Hirota three principles which were then being
pressed upon Nanking, not excluding the issues raised by
the North China situation. Nanking's temporizing policy
was still to continue. The task of reorganizing the Central
Government, necessitated by the attack on Wang Ching-

[21] *The Chinese Year Book*, 1936-37, cited, p. 433-434.

wei, was postponed for the first plenary session of the new Central Executive and Central Supervisory Committees, scheduled to meet on December 2.

On November 19, a day charged with tension in North China, the first phase of the autonomy movement reached its climax. In the afternoon Major-General Doihara told the Japanese pressmen in Peiping that the Chinese plans for an Autonomous Council had been completed and he expected formal announcement shortly. The Chinese officials were non-committal, stating that they were waiting until noon of the 20th, when, if no plan was forthcoming from Nanking, they would take responsibility and make the decision. Throughout the day Doihara was in constant touch with Mr. Hsiao Chen-ying, urging upon him the necessity for a definite announcement on the 20th.[22] That evening the long-awaited instructions from Nanking arrived. General Chiang Kai-shek wired the North China officials to drop the negotiations with Doihara, since the whole problem of Sino-Japanese relations was being taken up in Nanking. Mr. Hsiao Chen-ying at once notified Major-General Doihara, adding that under the circumstances the North China officials would not be in a position to act without express instructions from the Central Government. As a further result of Chiang Kai-shek's telegram, General Han Fu-chu decided to remain in Shantung, while General Shang Chen cancelled his proposed visit to Peiping from Paotingfu. On the morning of November 20, Doihara quietly left Peiping for Tientsin. Interviewed by Japanese pressmen, he indicated that postponement of the autonomy announcement would no doubt be necessary owing to the non-arrival of Generals Han Fu-chu and Shang Chen.

[22] For this and other details of the paragraph, see *North China Star*, November 20-21, 1935.

The causes leading to this temporary collapse of the five-province autonomy movement resided in developments at the capital. As the result of approaches from the Japanese Foreign Office, the Chinese government had indicated its willingness to deal with the proposals advanced in Hirota's three-point program. On November 19, after receipt of these assurances, Ambassador Ariyoshi had entrained from Shanghai for Nanking to open formal negotiations. During these preliminary exchanges, the Nanking government was apparently informed that Major-General Doihara possessed no credentials empowering him to negotiate with the North China officials. Japanese officials in Nanking, it was reported, informed the Central Government that Tokyo had no desire to bring either political or military pressure to bear in North China.[23] Acting on this information, instructions to discontinue negotiations had been wired north.[24] Doihara's anomalous position was confirmed in statements made at this time by Colonel Tan Takahashi, military attaché of the Japanese Embassy in Peiping.[25] At eleven o'clock on the night of November 20, Colonel Takahashi informed a *United Press* correspondent that "Doihara was in North China in a private capacity only, and not on any official mission." On the following afternoon, he categorically declared: "Major-General Doihara has no authority to negotiate with Chinese officials." There had never been any formal negotiations in Peiping, he asserted, since such negotiations would have to take place either with him or the appropriate secretary of the Japanese Embassy. As this did not occur, he concluded, there were—properly speaking— no negotiations whatsoever. Ironically enough, this as-

[23] *North China Star*, November 21, 1935.
[24] These instructions were confirmed on the 21st, the day after General Chiang had held a three-hour interview with Ariyoshi.
[25] *North China Star*, November 21-22, 1935.

tounding example of an outright clash between the civilian
and military branches of the Japanese government came
one month after the elaborate October conferences, designed to coordinate policy with respect to China questions.

Though his larger scheme was thus brought to a halt,
Doihara was as yet by no means defeated. He fell back on
an alternative plan, much less ambitious in scope, but
destined to have far-reaching political and economic consequences. Since the signing of the Tangku Truce on May
31, 1933, as already noted, the East Hopei demilitarized
zone had been a thorn in the flesh of China's body politic.
The turbulent motley of Shih Yu-san, which had at first
"policed" the area, had effectively served Japan's purposes
during 1933. Gradually, however, the Peace Preservation
Corps (Paoantui) of the zone had increased to two divisions, and, while still containing large semi-bandit elements, had come more nearly to perform the functions
which its name indicated. In December 1933 the Chinese
authorities had been enabled to establish an administrative
system for the zone. For this purpose the whole area was
divided into two districts, each of which was placed under
an administrative commissioner. The eastern half of the
zone, called the Luanchow-Shanhaikuan district, was controlled by Commissioner Yin Ju-keng, with headquarters
at Tungchow; the western half of the zone, the Chihsien-
Miyun district, was administered by Tao Shang-ming, with
headquarters at Tangshan. Both men spoke the Japanese
language, and both knew Japan well; Yin Ju-keng had the
additional advantage of a Japanese wife. Tao Shang-ming
proved difficult for Japan to handle. His troubles came to
a head in the summer of 1935, when he was lured into
the Japanese Embassy in Peiping by a telephone call from
Colonel Takahashi, the military attaché, and illegally de-

tained there for nearly two weeks, from August 5 to 17. The Chinese press censors forbade publication of this incident, and the news only leaked out gradually.[26] Tao Shangming's usefulness thus came to an end. By order of the Peiping Branch Military Council, Yin Ju-keng was appointed to act concurrently in Tao's place, and so assumed administrative control of the entire demilitarized zone.[27] Following this appointment, Japan's influence in the East Hopei area had steadily increased. On November 8 the Japanese military authorities announced that Yin Ju-keng had concluded an agreement with Lieutenant-Colonel Yoshiharu Takeshita, member of the Kwantung Army's Special Service Section, for the appointment of Japanese advisers to twelve of the *hsien*, or counties, in the zone. The advisers had been appointed, it was said, for the purpose of "strengthening the projected Japanese collaboration in North China." [28]

In the demilitarized zone, at least, Doihara was able to move toward the realization of his plans. On November 24 Yin Ju-keng issued a proclamation of autonomy for the East Hopei area. Simultaneously, he sent a circular telegram to the leaders of the five northern provinces, urging them to join with him in setting up an autonomous government for North China. On November 25 the "East Hopei Autonomous Council" was unceremoniously inaugurated in a small building which formed part of

[26] The *Ta Kung Pao*, a leading Chinese vernacular newspaper, published the following editorial paragraph anent this incident: "The news of the detention of Tao Shang-ming at the Japanese Embassy was not published until ten days after it reached our office. We feel most regretful over this. However, there was nothing else we could do as we were carrying out the orders of the Government. We sincerely hope that our readers will understand this and show us consideration accordingly." Quoted in *China Weekly Review*, October 19, 1935, p. 216.

[27] Shuhsi Hsu, cited, p. 31.

[28] *China Weekly Review*, November 16, 1935, p. 369.

Tungchow's ancient Confucian temple. "No flag was hoisted," wrote *Reuter's* correspondent, "no salute of guns was fired—for the simple reason that the new régime has no flag, while its heaviest armament is a Peace Preservation Corps rifle. No cheering crowds—or crowds of any sort— gathered outside the temple where 'history' was being made. In a long, narrow room with paper windows, and heated by a small, primitive coal stove, nine men sat down without fuss or ado to take office as the 'East Hopei Autonomous Council', while outside stood six members of the Peace Preservation Corps on guard and a handful of Chinese and foreign press correspondents from Peiping. Complete quiet reigned throughout the ramshackle old town, formerly Peking's port at the end of the Grand Canal which housed the vast Imperial rice granaries. The Council of Nine, which controls the whole of the demili- tarized zone together with four nearby hsien (districts) — Hsiangho, Paoti, Changping and Ningho—consists of Yin Ju-keng (Chairman), Chih Tsung-mo (vice-Chairman), Wang Hsia-tsai, Chang Ching-yu, Chang Yen-tien, Li Hai- tien, Chow Lei, Li Yuan-cheng and Yin Ti-hsin. Five of them are commanders of units of the Peace Preservation Corps." [29]

The Executive Yuan, meeting at Nanking on the morn- ing of November 26, ordered abolition of the special ad- ministrators' offices in the demilitarized zone and issued a mandate calling for the arrest of Yin Ju-keng. Neither Shang Chen nor Sung Che-yuan dared enforce the Central Government's ukase, especially after the North China Garrison had despatched two hundred Japanese troops to Tungchow and served notice that any move against Yin Ju-keng would be regarded as an infringement of the

Tangku Truce. A spurious autonomy demonstration by several hundred rioters kept Tientsin in turmoil throughout the day of November 25. Popular opinion in North China, however, was beginning to express its real attitude toward the autonomy movement. The leading Chinese educators of Peiping met on November 24 and unanimously adopted the following resolution: "Since there have appeared statements in the press purporting to represent public opinion in this region as favoring the so-called autonomy movement, we, members of universities and other cultural institutions in Peiping, do solemnly declare that we are utterly opposed to any movement tending to detach any region of China from the jurisdiction of the Central Government, or to set up special political organs for such region. We urge the Central Government to use the energies of the entire nation to maintain the territorial and administrative integrity of China." [30] After the meeting, this resolution—signed by Chiang Mon-lin, Chancellor of Peiping National University; Hu Shih, well-known philosopher and educator; the Chancellors of Yenching and Tsinghua Universities; and other cultural leaders of the north—was issued to the country in the form of a circular telegram. The student organizations in the Peiping-Tientsin area published a similar manifesto on November 26. Another interesting reflection of public sentiment was the resignation, and withdrawal from the East Hopei demilitarized zone, of a number of the *hsien* magistrates.

General Chiang Kai-shek had meanwhile formally initiated negotiations with Japan at Nanking on November 20, in the course of a three-hour interview with the Japanese Ambassador. Reports as to what transpired during

[30] *North China Star*, November 25, 1935; also "Special Kuomintang Sessions Supplement", cited, p. 61.

this conversation differed widely. Chiang apparently told Mr. Ariyoshi that China desired to maintain friendly relations with Japan but refrained from any commitment on Hirota's three-point program, aside from agreeing to continue discussion of the proposals. Regarding the situation in the north, he seems to have said that the Central Government had already decided on appropriate steps which would soon be put into effect. The interview was attended by three of the local Japanese officials, and also by General Chang Chun, chairman of the Hupeh provincial government, and Tang Yu-jen, vice-minister of Foreign Affairs, who interpreted. These two Chinese officials continued negotiations at Shanghai after November 26 with Mr. Ariyoshi and Major-General Rensuke Isogai, senior Japanese military attaché. During this period reports from Chinese sources, bearing an authentic stamp, claimed that the central authorities were approaching the discussions of Sino-Japanese issues in the light of three principles: integration of all Chinese territory, non-impairment of China's sovereignty, and negotiations on a basis of equality. Recognizing that special problems obtained in North China, the Central Government was "considering the eventual establishment of some sort of political council in this area comparable to the Southwest Political Council at Canton." [31] The Executive Yuan, at its meeting of November 26, took the first steps in this direction, three in number: abolition of the Peiping Branch Military Council and the transfer of its functions to the Military Affairs Commission, of which Chiang Kai-shek was chairman: appointment of General Ho Ying-chin, the War Minister, as resident representative of the Executive Yuan at Peiping; and appointment of General

[31] *North China Star*, November 24, 1935.

Sung Che-yuan, garrison commander of Peiping and Tientsin, to the new office of Pacification Commissioner for Hopei and Chahar provinces.

By the end of November tension in North China had again reached the breaking point. Continuing his efforts to force the northern leaders into line, Doihara had visited General Han Fu-chu of Shantung and General Fu Tso-yi, chairman of Suiyuan. Japanese forces effected a temporary occupation of the Fengtai railway junction on November 27, ostensibly to prevent removal of rolling stock to the south. On the following day the Chinese Ministry of Foreign Affairs lodged a strong protest at Tokyo against the occupation of Fengtai and promotion of the autonomy movement by Japanese officers, while identic notes were sent to the foreign powers. Extensive Japanese troop movements in the Peiping-Tientsin area, and the threat that a full division would be sent in from Manchuria, contributed to the general uneasiness. Frequent Japanese airplane flights were made over North China cities, and Japanese troops with full war equipment marched provocatively through the streets. Construction work on a large Japanese airdrome near the International Race Course at Tientsin, which later came to be occupied permanently, was feverishly pushed forward. On the afternoon of November 30 General Sung Che-yuan telegraphed Nanking that he could no longer control the growing "demand of the people" for autonomy.

That night General Ho Ying-chin, the War Minister, and Mr. Chen Yi, chairman of the Fukien government, with several other leaders, entrained for the north from Nanking. The visit of these delegates from the Central Government, bringing plans for a solution of the crisis worked out at the capital, was greeted with ill-concealed hostility by the Japanese military authorities.[32] At Tsinan, in Shantung, General Ho Ying-chin talked with Han Fu-chu; he then crossed over to the Peiping-Hankow Railway and traveled up to Paotingfu, reaching there on the evening of December 2. Interviewed at Tsinan on December 1, General Han Fu-chu declared: "No matter how hard other persons may press, I will remain steadfast to my own policy. . . . The autonomy movement does not express the will of the people. A few persons in Shantung approve of the movement, but they are bad characters who seek to disturb the situation for their own interest and cannot make serious trouble." [33] While General Ho Ying-chin delayed at Tsinan and Paotingfu, Chen Yi went on up to Tientsin, where he immediately entered into conferences with Chinese and Japanese officials, including Major-General Doihara. If the plan broached by Chen Yi proved acceptable, then General Ho, as the representative of the Executive Yuan in North China, was prepared to come up and stamp it with his official approval.

Chen Yi's negotiations in Tientsin apparently went off smoothly, as General Ho Ying-chin arrived at Peiping on the evening of December 3 from Paotingfu. A round of conferences with Sung Che-yuan and the other leaders of the 29th Army, as well as with Japanese officials, followed. By the 7th it was known that a Political Affairs Council for Hopei and Chahar provinces, with General Sung Che-yuan as chairman, was to be set up in Peiping. At this

[32] Major-General Tada, commander of the North China Garrison, according to a *Rengo* despatch, upbraided the Nanking authorities for sending General Ho northward and declared that "the situation would not be cleared up" by the latter's presence. Had General Ho come "to apologize for his past misdeeds," the commandant said, "his presence could have been tolerated. But his return to North China to engage in new subversive activities is inconceivable."

[33] Quoted in "The Bogus East Hopei Régime", *Information Bulletin*, Council of International Affairs, Nanking, March 21, 1937, p. 163-164.

point, the center of the stage was taken by the students of Peiping. During the autumn of 1935 a skeleton union had been organized, and this body now brought the students into the streets in mammoth protests against an "autonomous" North China. In midwinter, and facing brutal police assaults, the Peiping students rallied to mass parades and demonstrations which surpassed those of 1919 and 1925 in numbers and determination. The first demonstration, directed as much against Ho Ying-chin as against the Japanese, took place on December 9. In the face of this elemental protest, the formal launching of the Political Affairs Council was measurably retarded. All appointments necessary to bring the new North China régime into being, however, were quietly gazetted. On December 11 the National Government appointed General Sung Che-yuan to the posts of chairman of the Hopei-Chahar Political Council, and chairman of the Hopei provincial government. General Shang Chen, the retiring Hopei governor, was transferred, along with his 32nd Army, to Honan. The 29th Route Army was left as the sole military force in Hopei and Chahar provinces, except for a few thousand Peace Preservation Corps militiamen. General Sung Che-yuan, commander of this army, also held, in addition to his two new offices, the post of garrison commandant for the Peiping-Tientsin area. His military subordinates or civilian associates monopolized the other chief positions in the two provinces. For some months General Chin Te-chun had been Mayor of Peiping; Hsiao Chen-ying was now appointed Mayor of Tientsin; while in Chahar, the acting governor was General Chang Tzu-chung. A new dynasty, revolving around the 29th Route Army, had been installed in the north. General Ho Ying-chin had carried out his assignment; on the 12th he left quietly for the south. It was announced that he had decided not to take up his post as resident representative of the Executive Yuan in Peiping.

Changes of no less importance had been simultaneously taking place in party and government offices at Nanking. The Fifth Kuomintang Congress had come and gone in November; the first plenum of the Fifth Central Executive and Supervisory Committees was held on December 2-7. On the last day of the sessions, the personnel of the new party and government organs was elected. For many years Chiang Kai-shek's all-pervading influence on the National Government had been exerted indirectly, from the vantage point of his party offices and his position as Chairman of the Military Affairs Commission. Now, on December 7, he was chosen President of the Executive Yuan, or Premier, in succession to Wang Ching-wei. Of the high party offices, Chiang Kai-shek was made vice-chairman of the standing committee of the Central Executive Committee and also of the Central Political Council, the two governing organs between sessions of the Kuomintang plenum. He retained his post of Chairman of the Military Affairs Commission. Feng Yu-hsiang, new vice-chairman of the Military Affairs Commission, reappeared after five years' retirement as an active adherent of the Central Government. Two of Feng's old commanders, Generals Sung Che-yuan and Han Fu-chu, now controlled three of the northern provinces: Hopei, Chahar, and Shantung. Yen Hsi-shan, who exerted controlling influence in Shansi and Suiyuan provinces, was made a member of the Central Political Council. No similar progress in knitting the country together could be noted with regard to the Southwest. Tsou Lu, leader of the delegation from the Southwest Political Council to the Kuomintang sessions, was elected member of the standing committee of the Central Executive Committee. The military leaders of the Southwest—Generals Chen Chi-tang of Kwangtung, and Generals Li Tsung-jen and Pai Tsung-hsi of Kwangsi —occupied none of the leading positions, either in party or government organs.

Anticipating reorganization of the Executive Yuan, consequent upon Chiang Kai-shek's assumption of the presidency, Wang Ching-wei's cabinet resigned *en bloc* on December 9. The new cabinet, appointed on December 12, virtually eliminated Wang's following. Ku Meng-yu, chosen Minister of Communications, shortly resigned; there was left only Tang Yu-jen, one of the vice-ministers. Both Ku Meng-yu and Chen Kung-po withdrew into the background as members of the Central Political Council, important political organ, of which Wang Ching-wei was made chairman. The new Foreign Minister, succeeding Wang Ching-wei, was General Chang Chun, former chairman of the Hupeh provincial government. Wu Ting-chang, Tientsin banker who had just headed a Chinese Economic Mission to Japan, became Minister of Industry. The Shanghai banker, Chang Kia-ngau, became Minister of Railways. Chiang Tso-pin, for three years Chinese Ambassador at Tokyo, assumed charge of the Ministry of Interior. Each of the four new Ministers was educated wholly or partly in Japan. In the country at large, these cabinet choices, as well as the newly established Hopei-Chahar Political Council, were greeted as evidences of truckling to Japan. The *Shanghai Mainichi* admitted on December 14 that the composition of the new cabinet left "no room for fear that Nanking will continue its double-faced policy towards Japan." [34] Tang Yu-jen, newly appointed vice-minister of Communications, was assassinated in the French Concession at Shanghai on December 25; the event was regarded as a witness to Chinese popular dis-

[34] Quoted in *China Weekly Review*, December 21, 1935, p. 82.

trust of government policy. Tang Yu-jen had previously been Wang Ching-wei's assistant in the Foreign Ministry, serving as chief go-between in the negotiations with Japan. At the time of his death he was conferring with Major-General Rensuke Isogai, Japanese military attaché, in Shanghai. Chiang Kai-shek had meanwhile summoned his cabinet to an informal conference at the Executive Yuan on December 16, immediately after they had been sworn into office. In concluding an address to his new associates on this occasion, he had declared: "In respect of problems detrimental to the freedom and equality of the state, the government will make no compromise. For the consolidation of international peace, we shall make a supreme effort. For the maintenance of the life of the nation, we are not afraid to make the final sacrifice. I hope that all my colleagues will fully understand this viewpoint, and that we shall perform our duties to the best of our ability." [35]

Formal inauguration of the Hopei-Chahar Political Council at Peiping had been arranged, after some delay, for December 16. The ceremony did not take place as scheduled. That day Peiping was the scene of a monster student demonstration, which dwarfed the first protest of a week earlier. From early dawn until long after dark nearly ten thousand students paraded the streets in disciplined order, save when the marching lines were broken up by police assaults, and assembled at various points in huge protest meetings. Their movement, despite rigorous press censorship, had already reached nation-wide proportions. Chinese students were marching in all the great port cities along the coast, as well as in the interior centers. Wherever they marched, they broke the government's restrictions on anti-Japanese activities, and stirred up a

[35] *China Weekly Review*, December 21, 1935, p. 82.

new and powerful national consciousness. Despite its strength, the student movement did not prevent formal inauguration of the Hopei-Chahar Political Council, which was quietly effected on December 18.[36] The nucleus of the Council's seventeen members consisted of the leaders of the 29th Army, including Sung Che-yuan, Chin Te-chun and Chang Tzu-chung. Several members of the former pro-Japanese Anfu clique, which the Chinese students had driven from office in 1919, were appointed members of the Council, notably Wang Yi-tang and Liu Chieh. The Japanese authorities ventured the claim that the new Council would be completely autonomous. While the abolition of the Peiping Branch Military Council, and the elimination of all direct representatives of the National Government in the north, supported this view, there were not a few indications to the contrary. The term "autonomy" or "autonomous" did not appear in the title of the Hopei-Chahar Political Council, which was strictly analogous to that used in the case of the Southwest. All appointments to the Council had been made by the central authorities, and continued so to be made. The conduct of foreign and military affairs, finance, and the judiciary continued to be formally vested in the Central Government. Actually, the full validity of these jurisdictional rights depended on the extent to which General Sung Che-yuan accepted the orders of the central authorities rather than the dictates of Japanese officials in North China. There was still another noteworthy aspect to this affair. Unlike the Tangku Truce and the Ho-Umetsu agreement, the arrangements made with the Japanese authorities in connection with the establishment of the Hopei-Chahar Politi-

---

[36] The new governing body for the north was "launched in semi-secrecy. No official announcement of the hour of the ceremony was given in advance and the inauguration started at the unexpectedly early hour of eight o'clock in the morning." *The New York Sun*, Dec. 18, 1935.

cal Council were purely verbal. There was no agreement in writing and no document was signed. Paradoxically enough, it may be fairly asserted that the strength mustered by the student demonstrations contributed materially to the successful launching of the new Council, despite evident Japanese reservations as to the extent to which it might serve their purposes. From December 9 Doihara's five-province autonomy scheme, in so far as voluntary adherence to it by the northern military leaders was concerned, was definitely set at rest. Henceforth it could be achieved only by outright military conquest.

This period, nevertheless, was utilized by the Japanese military to extend and consolidate the positions they had already won in North China. On December 9 a force of Manchoukuo irregulars, commanded by Li Shou-hsin, a former colonel in the Jehol provincial army, launched an attack from Dolonor on districts of north-central Chahar. The invaders were assisted by a squadron of airplanes, as well as tanks. Part of the area under attack was included in the extension of the demilitarized zone effected in June 1935 by the Chin-Doihara agreement. Few of the units of the 29th Army were in this region, which was defended mainly by several thousand Peace Preservation Corps militiamen. Meeting with relatively slight resistance, Li Shou-hsin's forces marched rapidly across the six *hsien* of North Chahar, comprising Kuyuan, Paochang, Kangpao, Huateh, Shangtu and Changpei. By December 24 they had reached Changpei, not far north of Kalgan, and established their control over the whole of the occupied territory. From this enlarged base, these forces began preparations for the invasion of Suiyuan, which occurred a year later.

Yin Ju-keng also made efforts at this time to extend the territory of the demilitarized zone. On December 15 a force of the East Hopei *Paoantui,* taking advantage of the moment when the 29th Army was replacing General Shang Chen's troops in the Tientsin area, occupied the port of Tangku. The withdrawal of the East Hopei militiamen from this strategic North China port was not effected until two months later. General Sung Che-yuan had meanwhile instituted negotiations with Major-General Doihara and other Japanese military officials for the merging of the East Hopei régime with the Hopei-Chahar Political Council and for restoration of the six North Chahar *hsien*. General Sung's energies, however, were distracted by a succession of Sino-Japanese incidents, and the East Hopei and North Chahar territories gradually assumed the status of permanent puppet régimes. On December 25 the "East Hopei Autonomous Council" gave way to the "East Hopei Anti-Communist Autonomous Government." The revenues of the twenty-two *hsien* under Yin Ju-keng's control were appropriated by the new government, circulation of the notes of the Central Bank of China in the area was prohibited, and exportation of silver banned. These were merely the first steps in a program which culminated some months later, when the East Hopei area became the source of entrance for a vast illicit trade in Japanese goods that seriously affected the revenues of the Central Government.

The closing months of 1935 marked an historical turning point in the balance of political forces within China. From that time forward a nationalist resurgence, born of the Peiping student demonstrations in December, rapidly knit the country together on the basis of resistance to Japan's encroachments. Less than a year later the National Government was already taking a stand on foreign policy which brought it measurably closer to the demands of an aroused Chinese nationalism.

CHAPTER FOUR

THE REVIVAL OF CHINESE NATIONALISM

THE year 1935 had witnessed a long succession of encroachments on China's northern provinces. It had opened in January with the Kwantung Army's attack on southeastern Chahar, which had added a strip of that province to the domains of Manchoukuo. Six months later had come the enforced signature of the Ho-Umetsu and Chin-Doihara agreements, which had ousted all central troops and political organizations from Hopei and Chahar provinces. The climax had been reached in November and December, with the threatened alienation of the five northern provinces. Although this threat had been staved off, the actual results of the Japanese drive were by no means inconsiderable. An independent régime sponsored by Japan had been set up in the strategic region of East Hopei; a base of operations for conquest of the sections of Inner Mongolia still under Chinese control had been established in North Chahar; while the newly appointed Hopei-Chahar Political Council, under the chairmanship of General Sung Che-yuan, occupied a status little short of semi-autonomous. Against these losses could be set only one outstanding gain: the revival of the Chinese student movement. This was a not inconsiderable factor. The forces unleashed by the student movement were destined to exert a unifying influence which speedily overcame political cleavages that had existed for ten years and still seemed unbridgeable at the end of 1935. No observer of the Chinese political scene, especially after noting the course of events since the seizure of Manchuria, would have dared predict that China's military leaders would shortly sink their private differences and interests in a common effort to defend the country. The following description of conditions as they existed in the early months of 1933 throws light on the obstacles which confronted political unification:

"Observe for a moment the strategy of the military chieftains everywhere in China. General Chiang Kai-shek was not alone in the policy of feint and withdrawal, of perennial shadow-boxing. Various provinces had their militarists, each regionally supreme, each jealously eyeing his neighbor's armaments, squeezing his peasants to buy more foreign guns, increasing his investments in foreign concessions, each uttering verbiage about 'national resistance' against Japan, each hoping that the other might take it seriously, wreck his power, narrow the circle of rivals for supremacy.

"Thus sat General Pai Chung-hsi and Li Tsung-jen in the southwest, waiting for the missteps of General Chen Chi-tang in Canton; thus sat General Chen, waiting for an opportunity to strike at Nanking, with a sidelong glance at General Tsai Ting-kai whose power increased in Fukien; thus in western China squatted the pair of Lius and Yang Sen, urging Nanking to resist, increasing their own rabble armies for incessant civil wars; thus in the northwest crouched Generals Yen Hsi-shan and Feng Yu-hsiang, ready to pounce on a careless neighbor. And thus, from Nanking, Chiang Kai-shek urged the Young Marshal on toward disaster, and thereby eliminated one more rival in his struggle for effective military mastery in China.

"Each regional militarist thought in his regional way, concerned himself with augmenting his wealth and power and troops, regarded Manchuria as the personal misfortune of Marshal Chang Hsueh-liang. None made the gesture of sacrifice of personal power for the national good. None conceived of the national good except in terms of his personal power. To none, apparently, was the loss of Chinese territory to Japan so grave a matter as the possible loss of his regional control. The concept of nationhood and unity was not in them." [1]

In its first phase, the student movement seemed to dig a deep gulf between the Chinese people and the Central Government. The demonstrations constituted an open declaration of war against the prohibitions on anti-Japanese speeches and acts contained in the government's "good-will mandate" of June 10, 1935. They were equally opposed to the government's coolly calculated, temporizing policy in relation to Japan's aggressions. Both issues were sharply drawn in the December 9 and 16 demonstrations, despite the absence of overt anti-government slogans. Although the first of these demonstrations was largely spontaneous, with many schools as yet unorganized throwing themselves rapidly into action, signs of a developing movement had been apparent for at least two months. There were at this time in Peiping 19 universities and 77 middle schools, with respective enrollments of 13,517 and 24,537 students. Some of the institutions, in Tientsin as well as in Peiping, had Students' Self-Government Associations. Contacts formed between several of these organizations during October had resulted in the submission of an outspoken petition, signed by eleven universities and middle schools in Peiping and Tientsin under date of November 1, to the Kuomintang

[1] Edgar Snow, *Far Eastern Front,* cited, p. 302-303.

plenary session. Decrying Kuomintang absolutism, this petition demanded freedom of press, speech, organization and public assembly, as well as guarantees against arrest of students without due process of law. These demands were supported by an impressive indictment: university discussion groups closed down, and their members arrested; student dormitories raided by the police; publications suppressed and burned. The appeal concluded: ". . . we submit our petition . . . because our country is in danger and all citizens must bear the responsibility of saving our country. The sooner these restrictions are done away with, the sooner can we fulfill our responsibilities." [2]

By early December a Peiping Students' Union, still embracing only a minority of the local schools and universities, had been formed. This skeleton organization planned the details of the first demonstration—marking out the line of march, preparing handbills, and seeking to mobilize the student bodies of the various institutions. On December 7 the students in the universities six miles outside the Peiping walls failed to gain entrance into the city. "Over one thousand students from Yenching and Tsinghua Universities outside the city," writes an observer,[3] "broke through side-gates and left their campuses at seven o'clock to join the demonstration in the town. With banners flying and slogans shouted in high spirits, they marched cross-country, as the main road was effectively cordoned by the police. Nevertheless, they had several skirmishes en route. Armed police tried to beat the leaders back with their leather belts at various times, tore the standards into pieces, and threatened the students generally, but to no avail." Arrived at the west gate, the

[2] *Christian Science Monitor*, December 24, 1935; also *China Today*, New York, January 1936, p. 77.

[3] All quotations from eye-witness accounts in the *China Weekly Review*, December 28, 1935, p. 127-133.

students found it closed against them; late in the afternoon they returned in formation to their schools, making
speeches in the market-places along the way. Meanwhile
"their colleagues in the city were gathering. In some
schools, especially the municipal middle schools, the students climbed over the walls to escape the police guards,
and in others student masses rushed the gates." The first
serious clash with the police occurred in the West City,
where "twenty-seven students were arrested and many injured, two of them severely. Dispersed, they proceeded in
small groups to join the demonstration which was scheduled for eleven o'clock in front of General Ho Ying-chin's
headquarters." Here the students asked to send a delegation of twelve to wait on General Ho, but were informed
that he was out of town. After long parleys they finally
drew up a petition, which was left for the General's consideration, containing the following points: (1) that the
students are unanimously opposed to any form of so-
called "autonomous organizations" in North China; (2)
that the students are opposed to the policy of secret
diplomacy in Sino-Japanese relations, and demand that
the government make known publicly its foreign policy
and publish all previous negotiations; (3) that the people
be granted real freedom of speech, press, right of organization and assembly; (4) that all civil war be stopped
immediately to fight the common enemy; (5) that all
illegal arrests be stopped; (6) that all students arrested
during the demonstration be released immediately.

A decision was now reached to march to the west gate,
in an effort to secure entrance for the students outside
the city. "Half-frozen by the long wait in the bitter wind,
the students warmed up as they marched along shouting
their slogans. At Hsi Tan Pailou some eighty or ninety
police and a squad of big-swords tried to block the way,

waving their guns and swords menacingly in the air and striking the students. Several arrests were made and the line was partly split, but the students poured over the intersection at the sides and quickly reformed. The leaders never hesitated and took the blows without flinching, arguing peaceably with the police and filling their pockets with propaganda." Deciding that efforts to open the west gate would be futile, the student leaders next turned the line of march toward Tien An Men, the historic meeting-place for Chinese student demonstrations. The police gave determined opposition as the parade approached the Legation Quarter. In this sector the "fire department had been called out with a hose . . . good strategy in zero weather upon children who had been waiting or marching since six o'clock in the morning, it being then four o'clock. The leaders ran right into the spray and were mercilessly beaten by the police with leather belts, revolver ends and fists. . . . The retreat was quite orderly, with the victims being dragged away and petted by their comrades."

The demonstration was carried through with admirable self-control, and effectively struck home to the general public. Special efforts were made to win the sympathies of the police. The students "first handed them small handbills that could be read at a glance, addressed 'To the Police and Gendarmes, to our Dear Countrymen Bearing Arms.' " As they approached street intersections, the leaders raised their arms and "began begging the police not to interfere: 'We are all Chinese together. Do not strike your countrymen. Help us to save the country. Don't fight us, fight the Japanese.' The leaders, however, did not stop the marching rhythm for a second, which would have spread confusion in the line. Those who were struck down were marched over, and picked up later in the line.

The girls engaged the police in debate to deflect their attention, and by various means no small number of the police were 'disarmed.' " It was evident that "many of the rank and file police did not seem to enjoy their role in silencing the only anti-Japanese sentiment that has been publicly expressed throughout the many months of the present crisis here. . . . Coming suddenly during the silence and tenseness which has prevailed in the city, the movement has aroused tremendous popular enthusiasm already. Groups of shopkeepers sometimes applauded as the students went past, and everyone ran out and grabbed for handbills which were eagerly read by little knots of rickshamen, apprentices and people in the streets generally. Tens of thousands of handbills were distributed all over the city." There were at least seven different kinds of handbills, the essence of which was summed up in fifteen or twenty slogans, "printed on small slips of paper to coordinate group action. There were no anti-Kuomintang nor anti-Chiang Kai-shek slogans shouted. The most popular slogans shouted were 'Down with Japanese Imperialism', and 'The Whole Nation in Arms for the Defense of North China.' "

The week which intervened between the first and second demonstrations was a period of feverish organizational activity. In virtually every school mass meetings were held or else small committees were formed, and delegates sent to join the Peiping Students' Union. Within a few days "the strike to enforce the granting of the demands made on the 9th was city-wide. In every important school, the newly organized Students' Self-Government Associations took over control and defied efforts of any variety of authority to compel them to resume class schedules. Schools were surrounded on the outside by police and gendarmes and patrolled on the inside by the Students' Self-Protection Corps, unarmed but stern of countenance. Study groups were organized to replace academic class work with research into the serious social, economic and political questions of the day. Girls took up first-aid, wartime dietetics, and athletics in preparation for demonstrations. . . . Information and courier services were installed, wall-newspapers posted throughout the campuses, translators kept busy supplying the school papers and magazines with the world's news . . . delegates were sent to other cities to help organize a nation-wide movement. 'Foreign' and 'Domestic' Publicity Committees sent news to correspondents and Chinese publications abroad, as well as to whatever local press would receive it. A complete administration under severe discipline was installed" in the schools of Peiping. "By Monday, the 16th, the interschool organization was so well formed that the vast demonstration which took place—one of the largest and most impressive ever held in Peiping—seemed to have outwitted the police all along the line."

This time the Yenching and Tsinghua students, aided by the efforts of about one hundred of their number who had spent the previous night in the city, battered their way—under a barrage of bricks thrown by the police—through one of the more decrepit gates. The whole city was aroused, as various "contingents paraded the streets, struggling through police cordons on every important corner, previous to converging together for a big mass meeting at Tien Chiao, the poor workers' district outside the main city, and distributed their handbills over all their appointed territory." The police were enraged early in the day by the complete rout of their fire-hose technique at the hands of the students, who wrested away the nozzle, cut the hose with their pocketknives, turned off the hy-

drant, and smashed the fire engine. This episode was soon
followed by a furious mêlée, in which the "leaders were
singled out by the police and beaten furiously as they
lay on the ground, several being dragged off under arrest.
. . . The Peking National University leader, who was especially intelligent and courageous in marshaling his forces,
received a terrific mauling. . . . Seventeen Peking National
University students were arrested, according to their report, the largest number taken from any school; and of
the twenty-two treated at the Peking Union Medical College nearly all were from the Peking National University,
Northeastern, and the Normal University."

The mass meeting at Tien Chiao was successfully carried through, and aroused the "attention of thousands
of people gathered nearby." At the conclusion of the
meeting, the leaders decided to hold a "demonstration
before the Waichiaopu, where the inauguration of the
Hopei-Chahar Political Council had been set (but was
later postponed) for nine o'clock. Formed into neat
ranks, with a cordon of student bicycle police on either
side and under the most extraordinary discipline, the long
line of about five thousand students began the march
from Tien Chiao to the big Chien Men gate." As the
parade reached the gate and the leaders went forward to
confer with the police, the latter "crouched into position
with their rifles and fired three volleys of blank shots
directly into the mass of students, not over their heads,
as has been reported. If shots were fired overhead they
were from the gendarmes' revolvers." After a momentary
scattering the students surged back, and then "waited in
formation for about an hour and a half, while the leaders
talked with the Chief of Police. . . . At least half a dozen
Japanese were blatantly present in the foreground. . . .
They took notes on the names of the schools represented

on the banners, and seemed very interested in the proceeding, especially when a contingent bearing the banner of a Mongol and Tibetan School appeared on the scene, and I observed them scanning the faces of these students very closely."

After a long parley, the students were promised entrance if they went round to another gate. Reaching this gate, they were still refused admittance. Here Lo Tsei, the famous girl leader from Tsinghua, crawled under the gate, only to be roughly handled by the police and then carried off as a hostage. After some hours she was released, and the police promised to permit the city contingents to enter if the Tsinghua and Yenching students would return to their campuses without reentering the city. The latter then "began the long, weary march through the dark countryside to their campuses, where they arrived at eleven-thirty." Meanwhile, the police had again refused entry to the city students. Some two or three thousand of them at first sat down back to back on the cold ground and chanted their slogans. Finally deciding to return, they managed to enter the city in small contingents. One of these was trapped in a blind alley and brutally set upon in the darkness by policemen and big-swords; the results of this affray accounted for most of the serious casualties of the day. According to figures tabulated by the Self-Government Associations of some 25 universities and middle schools, approximately 6,500 students took part in this demonstration. Forty-six students were arrested or missing by the end of the day. There were 275 casualties, of which 75 represented serious injuries.

Overnight this movement was projected on a nationwide scale. The same scenes were repeated in all the larger cities of the country during the last two weeks of December. Besides the port cities of Tientsin, Shanghai,

Hankow and Canton, student protest meetings and parades were held at Taiyuan, Chengchow, Kaifeng, Nanchang, Chengtu, Hsuchow and many other interior towns. At Taiyuan, while the students were demonstrating in the streets, a mass meeting of various public organizations mapped out plans for a publicity campaign to arouse the public to the seriousness of the North China situation. From Nankai University, following the demonstrations in Tientsin, two hundred students, who had vainly sought free railway accommodation to Nanking, set out on foot in an effort to reach the capital but were eventually turned back. Five thousand students marched at Nanking on December 18 and over eight thousand on the following day; at the national capital the student petitions were tabled with the Executive Yuan, the president of which was Chiang Kai-shek. In the Wuhan cities the provincial authorities suspended ferry services for three days but were finally forced to rescind the order, and a vast demonstration by well over ten thousand students held the streets of Hankow on December 21. A mass protest which began at Shanghai on the 19th eventually tied up all railway traffic, as thousands of students took possession of North Station and demanded transportation to Nanking. One group of Shanghai students commandeered a train and proceeded nearly to Changchow, about seventy-five miles short of Nanking; at meetings held in the towns and villages along the railway, they urged the people to resist Japanese aggression and force suppression of the autonomy movements in North China. The sympathetic response evoked by the students alarmed Nanking, and the military authorities destroyed a bridge in order to block the students' approach to the capital. The assassination of Tang Yu-jen, coming at this juncture, added to the uneasiness of the authorities. In an effort to bring the student agitation under control, the National Government ordered enforcement of martial law on December 25 in Nanking, Shanghai and Hankow.

Despite all prohibitions, the student movement continued into the new year. In most of the larger cities of the country the students' efforts to arouse mass resistance to Japanese aggression proceeded with unabated vigor. On January 8 the students mauled a gendarme caught tearing down anti-Japanese posters at the University of Nanking. The character of the movement, however, was now changing, and the number of such incidents grew more infrequent. Serious efforts of a fundamental kind were being undertaken in many centers to undermine Japan's advance and win the ear of the people. At Canton and elsewhere the students encouraged a revival of the boycott of Japanese goods, which official circles had frowned upon for some years. In Peiping, at the heart of the movement, student brigades were sent out into the North China villages during the New Year vacation on lecture tours, carrying with them thousands of pounds of leaflets, cartoons and posters loaded on wooden carts.

Early in the new year the government organized a conference with students and educators, at which it sought to make clear its foreign policy. The assembly convened at Nanking on January 15, when Chiang Kai-shek met with 89 university presidents and 78 high school principals in a lengthy discussion, while the secretary-general of the Executive Yuan received some 130 students' representatives. On the afternoon of the next day Chiang Kai-shek delivered an address to a combined gathering of the delegates. At this meeting he took an oath that he "would never sign any treaty deleterious to Chinese territorial and administrative integrity, nor any secret agreement." [4] The student movement in general looked askance at this elaborate performance, and boycotted many of the student representatives who attended. Several such delegates, on returning to Peiping, were expelled from their respective student associations.

By the middle of February fifty-two universities and middle schools, represented by duly elected Students' Self-Government Association officers, were members of the Peiping Students' Union; while twelve other schools were represented by the chairmen of special National Salvation Committees. With all the important schools of Peiping enrolled, the Union had become the general staff for nearly 40,000 students in the city. Twenty-eight Tientsin schools were also included in the federated Peiping-Tientsin Students' Union. Every member school was pledged to support the seven Principles of the Union: (1) we are against the Japanese-fostered Autonomy Movement, which is intended to split the territory of China; (2) we are against the surrendering and yielding of secret diplomacy; (3) we struggle for the absolute freedom of speech, press, assembly and organization in order to start a movement to save the country; (4) we are against domestic strife and favor mobilizing the sea, air and land forces of the whole of China to fight with Japanese imperialism; (5) we want to mobilize and arm the people of all China to protect North China and drive the enemy out of China; (6) we want to form an organization of armed people to lead the Chinese national movement; (7) we want to confiscate the goods of our enemy and the property of traitors for the use of our anti-Japanese campaign.[5] Virtually the same program was supported by the overwhelming majority of students throughout China,

[4] *China Weekly Review*, January 25, 1936, p. 272.
[5] *China Weekly Review*, February 22, 1936, p. 403-404.

despite efforts by the school and other authorities to guide the movement into safer channels.

Police suppression, both in Peiping and other cities, was rigorously at work. Some ten thousand Peiping police were mobilized day and night to deal with the activities of the local students' organization. From the end of January all students caught propagandizing in the parks, theaters or public places of Peiping were arrested. Strong Japanese pressure on the Hopei-Chahar Political Council stimulated a continual search for Communist proclivities among the students and their leaders. Secret night raids on the dormitories, usually upon information supplied by the Japanese military, were accompanied by searches of the premises for incriminating documents. Arrested leaders were normally subjected to gruelling examination for a week or ten days, in an effort to force them to implicate their classmates in Communist activities, and then released. As a rule, during this period, there were about twenty students being held for investigation at the headquarters prison of the Peiping Bureau of Public Safety. Special precautions were taken to quarantine the units of the 29th Army against the student approaches, but "fraternization" between the troops and students could not be prevented, especially as the latter took advantage of every Sino-Japanese incident in the north to impress the troops with their mission of defending the country. Unable to stem the general growth of the protest movement, the National Government issued an emergency law on February 20, 1936, authorizing Chinese troops and police to use "force or other effective means" in suppressing meetings, parades and propaganda activities "which aim to violate peace and order." [6] This law placed the

[6] For text, see *News Bulletin*, Society of Friends of China, Shanghai, March 1, 1936, p. 1-2.

central authorities in direct opposition to a widespread popular demand for firmer action against Japan. A deep chasm had opened up between the government and the people on this issue.

During these months a series of inconclusive diplomatic exchanges was taking place between Nanking and Tokyo. Mr. Ariyoshi, the Japanese Ambassador, who was soon to retire under fire from the military, had a second interview with General Chiang Kai-shek on December 19, but without any reported advance in the negotiations on Hirota's three-point program. On December 27 General Chang Chun, new Chinese Foreign Minister, submitted a proposal to Tokyo for a "fundamental readjustment" of Sino-Japanese relations, suggesting that negotiations to that end be conducted through regular diplomatic channels. Foreign Minister Hirota, in the annual address to the Diet on January 21, 1936, defined his three principles more exactly and referred to the new Chinese proposal in the following terms:

"The first point is concerned with the basic readjustment of Sino-Japanese relations, by which we aim to bring about the cessation by China of all unfriendly acts and measures, such as have been hitherto adopted. . . . It would be most regrettable should China resort to unfriendly actions or to her habitual policy of playing off a third Power against this country, thus undermining the stability of East Asia . . . it is plain that no stability can ever be attained without the adjustment of relations between Japan, Manchoukuo and China. In the fulfilment of this purpose lies the second point of our programme. We are convinced that as the first step to a complete and final adjustment of the relations between Japan, Manchoukuo and China, the Chinese Government should recognize Manchoukuo, and the two countries should open diplomatic intercourse and harmonize their interests. . . . The greatest of all difficulties confronting China today is, I believe, Communism. . . . Herein lies the third point. It is the desire of the Japanese Government to cooperate with China in various ways for the eradication of Communism. These, then, are the three points of our programme. . . . The Chinese Government not only has indicated its concurrence with our views, but has proposed recently to open negotiations on Sino-Japanese rapprochement along these lines stated above. Although, much to our regret, there are at this moment student agitations in China which contravene the very spirit of our programme, it is expected that the present situation will soon be rectified by the Chinese authorities and an auspicious atmosphere for the opening of the said negotiations will prevail. The Japanese Government have communicated their acceptance of the Chinese proposal, and are awaiting the notice from the Chinese Government of the completion of its preparations. With the progress of these negotiations we shall be able, I am confident, to lay the foundation for a thorough readjustment of Sino-Japanese relations." [7]

This explanation of the Hirota program, especially in its explicit demand for recognition of Manchoukuo, went far beyond any definition of the three points thus far published. As one Chinese writer expressed it, "Summed up, the three Hirota principles meant practically this: that China shall recognize the *fait accompli* in Manchuria, Jehol, Hopei and Chahar, forsake the world, and

[7] For complete text, see *Contemporary Japan*, Tokyo, March 1936, p. 636-642.

make common cause with Japan against Soviet Russia." [8]
Hirota's address was also notable for its assertion that the
Chinese government had agreed to enter into negotiations
with Japan for the readjustment of Sino-Japanese relations along the lines of the three principles as he defined
them before the Diet. This assertion resulted in an immediate disclaimer by a Foreign Office statement issued
on January 22 at Nanking. After recapitulating the course
of previous negotiations, the statement noted that the
three principles originally presented by Mr. Hirota were
defined as follows: " (1) China must abandon her policy
of playing off one foreign country against another; (2)
China must respect the fact of the existence of Manchoukuo; (3) China and Japan must jointly devise effective
measures for preventing the spread of Communism in
regions in the northern part of China." The statement
then continued:

"However, these three points were considered by the
Chinese Government as being too vague in their phraseology to serve as a subject for useful discussion. So the
Japanese Government was requested to state the concrete
terms embodied in these points. But up to the present the
Japanese Government have not yet done so. Mr. Hirota's
statement to the effect that China had indicated her
concurrence to these points is therefore entirely without
foundation. On the other hand, General Chang Chun,
shortly after assuming his duties as Minister of Foreign
Affairs, proposed that Sino-Japanese negotiations should
be conducted according to regular procedure and through
diplomatic channels with a view to the fundamental readjustment of the relations between the two countries.
Now in his speech on Tuesday, Mr. Hirota not only expressed concurrence with General Chang Chun's proposal

[8] Shuhsi Hsu, *The North China Problem,* cited, p. 82.

but also reiterated Japan's fundamental policy of non-menace and non-aggression against neighboring countries in the hope of restoring the relations of the two countries to normalcy as well as to adjusting their mutual interests. From this standpoint there seems to be no divergence of views between the two sides. With this as a starting point in the negotiations between China and Japan there can be no doubt that the relations between the two countries will be greatly improved." [9]

In certain Japanese circles, especially among the military, this contradiction of Hirota's address to the Diet was considered to have cast gloom over the future of Sino-Japanese relations. As apparent reassurance, a semi-official statement emanating from Nanking on January 26 said that "concerning Mr. Hirota's three points for the settlement of the Sino-Japanese diplomatic situation, it is indicated in Chinese diplomatic circles today that while the Chinese Government has not accepted them, it has not completely rejected them either." [10] At the end of January Mr. Ariyoshi and Major-General Rensuke Isogai, senior Japanese military attaché, made separate visits to Nanking. They interviewed many officials of the National Government, including President Lin Sen, General Chiang Kai-shek and Foreign Minister Chang Chun, but no concrete results emerged from their talks. There seemed to be considerable divergence of opinion between the two Japanese officials as to the status of affairs at Nanking, and shortly thereafter Mr. Ariyoshi retired from his Ambassadorial post. The military uprising at Tokyo on February 26 put a temporary stop to the Sino-Japanese negotiations. These were resumed in the middle of March,

[9] For complete text, see *Kuo Min* despatch, *China Weekly Review*, February 1, 1936, p. 297.
[10] Quoted in "Hirota's Three Principles vis-à-vis China," cited, p. 12.

when Mr. Hachiro Arita, new Japanese Ambassador, had a series of discussions with General Chang Chun. The progress achieved by these talks may be judged from the following joint communiqué issued on March 19:

"With reference to the question of readjusting Sino-Japanese relations General Chang Chun, Minister for Foreign Affairs, and Mr. Hachiro Arita, Japanese Ambassador to China, had a series of four talks at the Foreign Office between March 16 and 19. Each conversation lasted from two and a half to three hours, nobody else being present besides the two diplomats. The conversations were in the nature of an informal exchange of opinions, both expressing their frank views in a free and sincere manner. As the object of the parleys was to facilitate satisfactory progress of future negotiation for readjusting Sino-Japanese relations, no definite procedure had been arranged nor was the scope of discussion limited to any particular subjects. All questions concerning the relations between the two countries were discussed, and no attempt was made to reach any conclusions. The talks were conducted in a most friendly atmosphere throughout the four days and ended at four o'clock this afternoon as previously arranged. Although a complete agreement on all points has not yet been achieved, the parleys may be considered to be very helpful towards producing a better appreciation of each other's viewpoints." [11]

A further delay in the negotiations ensued when Mr. Arita, after a final interview with General Chiang Kai-shek on March 20, left for Tokyo to take up the post of Foreign Minister in the newly formed Hirota Cabinet. If Japan's diplomats were finding their path strewn with certain difficulties, not so the Japanese military in the north. The center of the stage, in the spring of 1936, had

[11] "Hirota's Three Principles vis-à-vis China," cited, p. 14.

been taken by a specially fashioned technique of Japanese penetration—smuggling operations organized on a mass scale. Its advantages were manifold, since it was profitable, robbed Nanking of much-needed revenue, and struck a blow at the Western powers. From the beginning, the demilitarized zone had been the seat of smuggling enterprises of various kinds. Through this area had flowed the precious stocks of silver coin and bullion in a stream that was at flood in the middle of 1935. An extensive traffic in narcotic drugs fostered by Japanese nationals, especially Koreans, had developed since 1933 in the railway towns of the zone. Opium and other more deadly narcotic drugs from Manchoukuo, entering *via* East Hopei territory, had spread widely through all the North China provinces. The Japanese Concession in Tientsin, particularly after the establishment of Yin Ju-keng's régime, became perhaps the largest manufacturing and distribution center for opium and its derivatives in the Far East.[12] Traffic in narcotic drugs had traditionally enjoyed the benevolent protection of the Kwantung Army in Manchuria, where it had early sprung up in the Kwantung Leased Territory and the railway towns within the South Manchuria Railway zone. The transition to protection of a smuggling traffic which embraced Japanese commodities in general, especially with the facilities afforded by East Hopei and out-of-work silver smugglers, was relatively easy.

To clear the road for wholesale entrance of smuggled goods, it was first necessary to destroy the effectiveness of the Chinese Customs Preventive Service.[13] The Japanese military achieved this end as the result of a series of steps,

[12] For details, see "Japanese Concession in Tientsin and the Narcotic Drug Trade", *Information Bulletin,* Council of International Affairs, Nanking, February 11, 1937.

[13] For the complete picture, see *The Chinese Year Book, 1936-37,* cited, p. 891-945.

the first of which was taken in June 1935 when the Customs officers along the Great Wall were disarmed. Some silver smugglers had suffered injuries in jumping from a city wall to escape arrest, so the Japanese army authorities took the logical step of disarming the Customs men; this prohibition was soon enforced throughout the demilitarized zone. On September 9, 1935 the Japanese Garrison Commander at Chinwangtao informed the local Commissioner of Customs that machine-guns should be removed from Customs Preventive Vessels; some days later the same Japanese Commander demanded that all vessels, irrespective of armament, should cease to operate within the three-mile zone along the East Hopei coast. Still later when the Customs vessels sought to apply the right of search within the twelve-mile limit, though outside the three-mile zone, the Japanese military advised the Customs officers that continuance of such action would be considered an act of piracy and treated accordingly. With Customs officers disarmed on land and sea, in virtually the whole area between Tientsin and the Wall, the smuggling operations could go on unchallenged. The capstone to the arch was laid in the spring of 1936, when the East Hopei régime began levying dues on the smuggled goods at rates approximately one-fourth the Chinese national tariff duties. By this stroke, the illicit goods acquired a spurious legality, and new revenues flowed into Yin Jukeng's coffers at Tungchow. The measured words of the annual Customs Report,[14] covering the year 1936, thus describe the resulting smuggling situation:

"In the report for 1935 reference was made to the

[14] *The Trade of China, 1936, Introductory Survey*, Shanghai, The Maritime Customs, 1937, p. 7-8. For figures from actual Customs returns for 1936 illustrating the decline over 1935 in imports at northern ports of cotton piece goods, artificial silk floss and yarn, sugar and kerosene, the principal articles favored by the smugglers, see p. 9-11.

licence afforded smugglers and the impetus given to smuggling in the eastern part of Hopei, owing to the Customs having been compelled to comply with demands from the Japanese military authorities that Customs officers functioning within the 'demilitarized zone' should not be permitted to carry fire-arms and that Customs armed vessels should cease to operate within three miles of the coast included in the 'zone'. These unprecedented restrictions on normal preventive activities having continued throughout the year under review, it is not surprising that the smuggling situation in that area has shown no signs of improvement. Nanlichuang, some two miles from Chinwangtao, and other places on the coast not open to foreign trade but near to the railway stations of Nantasze, Peitaiho, Liushowying, and Changli became veritable hives of smuggling activities, vessels of all kinds, mostly from Dairen, arriving daily and discharging their illicit cargoes under the guard of numerous Koreans armed with iron bars, sticks, stones, etc., and ready to attack any Customs officers who appeared in the vicinity. The position was aggravated during the early part of the year by the action of the so-called 'autonomous régime in Eastern Hopei'—which claims jurisdiction over the whole so-called demilitarized zone—in enforcing their own taxation on the illicit goods landed at rates representing only a small percentage of those of the National Tariff, thus creating a false impression that the importations were regular, an argument which those concerned were not slow to use in defense of their illegal activities. During the earlier stages smuggling was confined to articles paying high duty rates, such as artificial silk yarn and sugar, but with the accumulation of stocks of these commodities attention was turned to other varieties until finally every conceivable kind of sundry, irrespective of the duty rates, was finding its way to Tientsin through the open door created in East Hopei; moreover, arms and ammunition in comparatively small lots were not excluded from the list. The volume of illicit goods arriving at Tientsin from the east attained its peak towards the middle of the year, when it is estimated that some $2,000,000 per week were escaping the duty account.

"In May there was inaugurated a Customs Chief Inspection Bureau for the Prevention of Smuggling by Rail, and while the situation in the North did not permit of the Customs functioning effectively on the Peiping-Liaoning Railway and thus checking the transport of illicit goods from East Hopei to the neighborhoods of Tientsin and Peiping, the establishment of some 17 customs inspection posts on the Tientsin-Pukow, Peiping-Hankow, Nanking-Shanghai, and Shanghai-Hangchow lines had the almost immediate effect of stopping all shipments of smuggled goods by rail freight southwards from Tientsin. Certain quantities of sugar, artificial silk yarn, and cigarette paper were, however, transported to Tsinanfu as passengers' baggage by Korean *ronin*, who not only ejected members of the travelling public from passenger coaches in order to provide the necessary space for their goods but also caused considerable damage to the coaches themselves when loading at Tientsin and discharging at Tsinanfu. Attempts by Customs officers to interfere with these desperadoes resulted in a series of incidents in which many of the former suffered severe injuries, and it was not until late in July, when overwhelming forces of armed Chinese military and railway police boarded one of the trains at the Tientsin Central Station and ejected the Koreans by force and seized their goods, that the transport of illicit cargo as passengers' baggage finally ceased. With the closing of railway channels for the distribution of smuggled goods southwards and the consequent accumulation of stocks in Tientsin, the volume of smuggling in East Hopei diminished, and for a brief spell the situation showed marked signs of improvement. Towards the end of August, however, further attempts were made to break through the cordon created by the various preventive measures instituted, this time by road. Motor-trucks loaded with sugar, artificial silk yarn, etc., and escorted by Japanese and numerous Koreans armed with revolvers and less dangerous weapons, began to make their way from Tientsin southwards towards Shantung. Customs land barriers at points outside Tientsin were thereupon established with a view to check this new menace, but in the face of armed threats these barriers, lacking the necessary force and adequate protection, were unable to function effectively, with the result that smugglers availed themselves of this means of transportation more and more, and illicit goods continued to reach Shantung in increasing quantities.

"Approximate statistics of illicit goods arriving at Tientsin by rail from East Hopei during the year are as follows: artificial silk yarn, 3,994,200 kilogrammes; sugar, 897,070 quintals; cigarette paper, 378,600 kilogrammes; kerosene oil, 2,166,600 gallons; piece goods, 78,400 cases (particulars of contents unknown); sundries, 220,800 cases (contents unknown). The estimated duty evaded on the artificial silk yarn, sugar, cigarette paper, and kerosene oil is in the neighborhood of $30,500,000, and, although particulars of the other goods are unknown and the duty is therefore difficult to calculate, a figure of $20,000,000 is conservative, so that the total duty evaded during the year on goods brought in illicitly through East Hopei under conditions of *force majeure* reached the staggering figure of over $50,000,000. It is true, of course, that, had the Customs Preventive Service been permitted to execute their normal functions and the vast majority of goods been compelled to follow legitimate channels paying National Tariff duty rates, the demand for such goods would not have reached the proportions indicated by the above figures, and it does not follow, therefore, that normally the total amount of duty evaded on the illicit cargo brought in would have accrued to the national revenue. Be that as it may, the losses sustained were sufficiently serious to call forth a public statement from Sir Frederick Maze, the Inspector General of Customs, during the middle part of the year, to the effect that the orgy of organized smuggling in North China must necessarily affect the indemnity and loan services secured on the Customs, and, as Shanghai and the Northern Ports are responsible for 88 per cent of the total Customs revenue, the question was no longer a purely domestic one but an international issue. Representations were made in Tokyo by both the British and American Ambassadors, and General Chang Chun, Minister of Foreign Affairs, filed several protests with the Japanese Government against Japanese interference with the preventive powers of the Customs in Hopei and connivance at the smuggling activities of their nationals enjoying extraterritorial protection. Other than a decrease in the volume of goods entering the smuggling area, brought about by the palliative measures instituted by the Customs to check distribution and by an accumulation of stocks, however, the general smuggling situation in the North remained unchanged at the close of the year."

The watchword of Sino-Japanese "economic cooperation" in North China, which came to the front in the summer of 1936, expressed the positive side of Japan's economic penetration of the northern provinces. A comprehensive Japanese program designed to secure a monopoly of North China's economic resources, which will be considered later in another connection,[15] underlay this slogan. Immediate efforts were devoted to strengthening Japan's political influence over the Hopei-Chahar Political Council, as a prelude to the full execution of the economic program. In many respects these efforts appeared to be meeting with marked success. On the surface, at least, the measure of the Council's "autonomy" was steadily increasing. General Sung Che-yuan's appointees, one after another, took over the major revenue-producing offices, affecting such items as the consolidated taxes, salt, and the Peiping-Mukden Railway.[16] Appointments to the Council itself added more members of the Anfu clique, such as Tsao Ju-lin, Li Ssu-hao and Lu Chung-yu, or tools of the Japanese military, such as Generals Chi Hsieh-yuan and Shih Yu-san. Beginning from May 15, 1936, with the gradual arrival of at least 5,000 additional troops, the political leverage exerted by Japan in the Peiping-Tientsin area was still further increased. These reinforcements brought the North China Garrison up to brigade strength, or four times larger than the normal effectives maintained by any foreign power in this region for over twenty-five years. Kanichiro Tashiro, the new garrison commander, held the rank of Lieutenant-General instead of Major-General, as had been customary. The step was carried through in the face of a strong protest from the Chinese government. Its repercussions in China were nation-wide. In the north it brought the students once more into the streets in large and effective demonstrations, while in the Southwest it was taken as the signal for a virtual declaration of war on the Central Government.

The government's emergency law of February 20, de-

[15] See Chapter V.
[16] See *North China Star,* February 2, 1936.

creed in an effort to bring an end to student agitation, had given risen to a state of guerrilla warfare between the various local authorities and the students, especially in North China. Large-scale police raids on the Peiping university dormitories had resulted in the arrest of numerous students, some of whom had been detained for months at a time.[17] Despite a partial crippling of its leadership and activities, the movement had continued its struggle. In April a preparatory committee for the organization of an All-China Students' Union, comprising delegates representing approximately 200,000 students from schools and universities throughout the country, had met in Shanghai. During these months the movement had steadily broadened its scope, drawing people of all ranks and occupations—teachers, workers, women, journalists, and even business-men—into National Salvation Associations established in many different cities. This continuous organizational work culminated in two notable conferences at Shanghai. On May 29-30 student delegates from twenty-one districts, representing organizations from Peiping to Canton, formally inaugurated the Students' National Salvation Union. On May 31 sixty delegates, representing more than fifty national salvation groups, launched the All-China Federation of National Salvation Unions. The manifesto issued by this second conference asserted a belief in "the possibility of consolidating the country," even while deploring the continued "strife for political hegemony." To break the deadlock it made the following proposals: "(1) that all parties and groups immediately put an end to civil war; (2) that all parties and groups

[17] The student-police warfare in Peiping during the early months of 1936 forms a lengthy story in itself. For details, see the series of articles appearing under the title "On the Peiping Student Front" in *China Weekly Review*, March 7, p. 35-36; March 21, p. 107-108; April 11, p. 215-216; May 23, p. 440-441; June 13, p. 72-73.

immediately free the political prisoners in their custody; (3) that all parties and groups immediately send formal delegates, through the national salvation front of the people, to begin joint negotiations, so as to formulate the joint anti-enemy program and to build a united anti-enemy political power; (4) that the National Salvation Front of the People will guarantee with all the force at its disposal, the faithful fulfilment of the anti-enemy program by any and all parties and groups; (5) that the National Salvation Front of the People will with all the forces at its disposal, use sanctions against any party and group that violates the joint anti-enemy program, and acts to weaken the united strength against the enemy." [18]

Even while these meetings were being held, a new crisis had developed in the north. The Japanese troops added to the North China Garrison had moved steadily into Tientsin and Peiping during the last two weeks of May. A crop of incidents, including an explosion at a railway bridge outside Tientsin, had occurred. The stage was evidently being set for a new series of Japanese demands. On May 28 several thousand Tientsin students had paraded the streets, overcome police resistance, presented demands at the Mayor's office, distributed handbills, addressed crowds of people, and held a mass meeting, in protest against the increase of Japanese troops in North China, on the Nankai University campus. Spurred by strong Japanese representations, the local Chinese authorities had clamped down martial law and occupied school and university campuses. The Tientsin students then declared a five-day strike, which spread to Peiping. In this latter city, on June 2, the students had taken advantage of a Japanese demand for occupation of the Nanyuan barracks to send

[18] For complete text of the manifesto, see *The Voice of China*, Shanghai, June 15, 1936, p. 7-8, 21-22.

delegates to the 29th Army units stationed there. Staff officers sympathetically received a petition from the students, reminding the officers and men of the 29th Army of their heroic defense of Hsifengkou pass in 1933 and urging them to protect China to the last. In reply, the officers expressed their approval of the patriotic activities of the students, and pledged themselves not to disappoint the masses when the time came. At Shanghai, on May 30, the delegates who had inaugurated the All-China National Salvation Union proceeded directly to a vast mass meeting at which the new program was publicly announced. After the meeting, an orderly procession passed through the International Settlement into battle-scarred Chapei, where thousands of workers, as well as a number of policemen, joined the demonstration before the graves of the martyrs of May 30, 1925. This public demonstration was the first of its kind held legally on May 30 in Shanghai since 1927.

Early in June, striking into the midst of these events, came word that the Southwest was organizing an anti-Japanese expedition, under command of General Pai Chung-hsi, and demanding free passage into the north to fight against Japan. This move was supported by the powerful military leaders of Kwangtung and Kwangsi provinces. It had been preceded by a circular telegram from the Southwest Political Council, issued on May 28, urging the nation "to oppose to the death the increase of Japanese troops in North China." [19] Since the action proposed could not possibly receive the sanction of the National Government, unless the latter were prepared to declare war on Japan, its immediate effect was to produce a sharp political crisis involving the threat of serious civil strife. Announcing their adherence to the national salva-

[19] For text, see *The Voice of China*, June 15, 1936, p. 10.

tion front, the Southwestern authorities sponsored large anti-Japanese demonstrations, both at Canton and in the cities and towns of Kwangsi province; while the northern expeditionary force was given the title of Anti-Japanese National Salvation Army. The sudden emergence of this crisis faced the patriotic movement, organized under the auspices of the National Salvation Unions, with a difficult problem. It was realized from the first that political animosities and differences between the leaders at Nanking and in the Southwest played a part in the situation. On the other hand, the Southwest was apparently taking the lead in carrying out the program which the National Salvation Unions were strenuously advocating. The first reaction was one of enthusiastic acceptance of this new ally. In a mass demonstration at Peiping on June 13, for example, the students put forward a demand that the National Government accept the Southwest's anti-Japanese program.[20]

During the month which followed, there were times when a disastrous civil war seemed inescapable. General Chiang Kai-shek rapidly concentrated a large force of government troops in southern Hunan province, within striking distance both of Kwangsi and Kwangtung. Meantime the Kuomintang was summoned in plenary session at Nanking. At its second meeting, held on July 13, the plenum ordered abolition of the Southwest Political Council. It also ordered the dismissal of General Chen Chi-tang of Kwangtung, and appointed General Yu Hanmou in his place; but Generals Li Tsung-jen and Pai Chung-hsi were confirmed in their Kwangsi posts. The latter decisions were highly significant, arguing an effort

[20] For an account of this highly emotional demonstration, marked by extreme expressions of support from the public and also from members and officers of the police, see "On the Student Front in Peiping", *China Weekly Review*, June 27, 1936, p. 150-152.

to eliminate Chen Chi-tang from the political scene, while
retaining the services of Generals Li and Pai. This dis-
tinction was shrewdly calculated to gain popular support.
General Chen Chi-tang was an old-type militarist, mainly
bent on conserving his own interests and political power;
during the spring, he had vigorously attempted to crush
the student movement in Kwangtung province. On the
other hand, Generals Li Tsung-jen and Pai Chung-hsi
were generally recognized to be capable administrators
and military commanders. They had never enforced the
National Government's emergency law of February 20,
but had allowed the student and national salvation movements virtually free play in Kwangsi province.

At the Kuomintang plenum, twenty-eight members of
the Southwest Political Council had submitted a motion
calling for the immediate launching of an anti-Japanese
expedition. Speaking to this motion, which was rejected
by the plenum on July 13, General Chiang Kai-shek
further clarified the National Government's foreign
policy. Recalling the previous declaration on foreign
policy made at the Fifth Congress, he sought to define
the point at which the maintenance of peace became
hopeless and the necessity for sacrifice inevitable: "What
the Central Government considers to be the absolute
minimum in foreign relations is the maintenance of our
territorial sovereignty intact. If any nation should seek
to violate our territorial sovereignty, it would be absolutely impossible for us to endure. We shall definitely
refuse to sign any agreement that violates our territorial
sovereignty, and shall definitely refuse to endure any
actual violation thereof. To put it more plainly, if others
should seek to force us to sign an agreement violating our
territorial sovereignty such as that for recognition of the
puppet state, it would be impossible for us to endure any

longer, it would be time for us to make sacrifices. This is one point. Next, beginning with the National Congress in November last year, if our territorial sovereignty is found violated by others, in the event that all political and diplomatic means are exhausted and the violation is still not repelled, it will mean that the fundamental existence of our nation is threatened, it will mean that it is impossible for us to endure any longer. When that time comes, we shall not hesitate to make sacrifices. This is what we mean by the absolute minimum." [21]

This statement, no less than the vote on the motion proposed by the Southwestern members, clearly indicated that the National Government was still committed to the maintenance of peace with Japan. Yet its firmer tone suggested that the government did not remain unaffected by the strong nationalist feelings aroused in the Chinese public since December 1935. During the month of July the attitude of the national salvation movement also changed, and the weight of its attack shifted. With the Southwestern drive taking on the aspect of an anti-Nanking expedition, the National Salvation leaders condemned it as a disguised civil war. At the same time, they directed an equally heavy fire against any attempt by the Central Government to make the revolt a pretext for dispatching a punitive expedition against Kwangtung and Kwangsi provinces. Though the full aims and proposals of the national salvation movement as yet mustered only minority support in the country at large, its attitude on this question undoubtedly harmonized with general Chinese public opinion. This fact registered an important advance. From the period of the February emergency law, which had banned the student movement and ordered its forcible suppression, the progress of events had carried

[21] Quoted in Shuhsi Hsu, *The North China Problem*, cited, p. 90-91.

it to a position of neutrality in an issue vitally affecting the national government. In this position, moreover, particularly in the condemnation of resort to civil war, it stood side by side with the overwhelming majority of the public. The breach between government and people was closing.

The collapse of General Chen Chi-tang's power in Kwangtung province was foreshadowed before the meeting of the Kuomintang plenum at Nanking. General Yu Han-mou, appointed by the plenum to Chen Chi-tang's posts, had placed the First Kwangtung Army, of which he was commander, under control of the Central Government on July 9, when he suddenly arrived at Nanking by airplane from the Kwangtung border. His example was soon followed by other Kwangtung military commanders, while a number of the Cantonese aviators flew their planes to Nanking on July 10. Accepting the inevitable, Chen Chi-tang fled from Canton to Hongkong on July 18. The reestablishment of the National Government's authority in Kwangtung province, which had been lost since 1931, automatically followed. The event was a notable step toward political unity. Its effects were reinforced, on the material plane, by the newly completed Canton-Hankow Railway; and it enabled the application of the government's monetary reforms to Kwangtung province, thus strengthening China's economic foundations.

The problem of the Kwangsi armies, which still held the field, remained to be settled. In early September, after a prolonged crisis, the issues between the Kwangsi leaders and the Central Government were peaceably adjusted. By government mandate of September 5, Li Tsung-jen was appointed Pacification Commissioner for Kwangsi province, while Pai Chung-hsi was named a member of the standing committee of the Military Affairs Commission, of which Chiang Kai-shek was chairman. Reconstituted as the Fifth National Army, the Kwangsi forces were enrolled as national troops under nominal jurisdiction of the Central Government. The terms of this settlement, which brought the Kwangsi armies and commanders closer to Nanking than they had been since 1929, represented still another considerable advance toward national unity. The gains thus achieved, both in Kwangsi and Kwangtung, were noteworthy in one further respect: they had been won without resort to armed hostilities. This result could be largely attributed to the gathering strength of a nationalist public opinion, which henceforth forbade recourse to civil war in the settlement of internal political differences. The student movement, and the patriotic associations which were its outgrowth, had speedily leavened the thought of the Chinese people, had brought into being a real public opinion, and endowed this public opinion with a specific political leverage which had made it a vital force in national affairs.

The Kwangtung-Kwangsi crisis had lasted for three months, from June to September. Throughout this period there had been a marked relaxation of Japanese pressure, symptomatic of a deferred expectation of Chinese civil strife—which, however, never materialized. Shigeru Kawagoe, the Consul-General at Tientsin who had presented the demands of October 29, 1935 to the North China authorities, had meanwhile been appointed Japanese Ambassador to China. In elevating this junior official to such a responsible post, the Foreign Office had deferred to the insistence of the military at Tokyo, who wished the forthcoming negotiations to be placed in strong hands. After a brief visit to Nanking early in July, during which he called on General Chiang Kai-shek, the new Ambassador had gone to North China to deal with problems relating to Sino-Japanese "economic cooperation" in that area. In mid-September, following the Kwangsi settlement, he had begun discussions with General Chang Chun, Chinese Foreign Minister, taking as his point of departure two incidents in which Japanese nationals had lost their lives. The Chengtu incident of August 24 had been precipitated by Japan's insistence on opening a consulate at the Szechuan capital. This move was opposed both locally and at Nanking on the ground that Chengtu was not a treaty port; when the attempt was persisted in, two Japanese were killed during the riot which ensued. The second incident took place at Pakhoi, in southern Kwangtung, where on September 3 a Japanese was the victim in a murder case. Seizing upon these incidents, Mr. Kawagoe presented a set of demands at Nanking which, in effect, translated the three principles of Hirota into specific terms. The demands were carefully formulated by the Japanese Cabinet and were solemnly ratified by the Emperor.

Ambassador Kawagoe's discussions with General Chang Chun began on September 15 and continued until December 3, when the last of eight successive conferences was held. During the first two conferences Mr. Kawagoe seems to have held the floor, while "the Chinese Foreign Minister listened patiently." [22] The Ambassador's two major demands called for recognition of Japan's special position in North China, accompanied by appropriate measures to give it effect, and organization of a joint Sino-Japanese front against Communism. Five so-called minor demands involved establishment of a Shanghai-Fukuoka airline, reduction of China's tariffs, control of subversive activities of Koreans, employment of Japanese advisers, and suppression of anti-Japanese activities. Of these de-

[22] Shuhsi Hsu, cited, p. 93.

mands only the last had any direct relation to the Chengtu and Pakhoi incidents. At the third conference, held September 23, the Chinese Foreign Minister presented a set of counter-demands, including suppression of smuggling, abolition of the East Hopei régime, and control by Japan of its Korean nationals. Following this meeting, Mr. Kawagoe threatened to leave Nanking if the Chinese authorities "unnecessarily delayed" the readjustment of Sino-Japanese relations. On the same day unidentified assailants shot and killed a Japanese seaman at Shanghai. Japanese naval vessels thereupon moved to Nanking and Hankow, and fleet reinforcements were sent to Chinese waters. On September 28 Foreign Minister Arita declared to the foreign press at Tokyo that if the negotiations terminated without result "the lives and property of the large Japanese population in China could not be left exposed to any further danger. It will therefore be necessary to consider the steps to be taken in case of that eventuality. . . . China is now at the momentous crossroads, to decide whether or not to shake hands with Japan. I very earnestly hope that China will grasp our hand in friendly response, whatever difficulties she may have to surmount." [23] Despite these gestures of disapproval from Tokyo, the negotiations at Nanking were temporarily suspended. On October 8 Ambassador Kawagoe, in an evident effort to go over the head of the Foreign Minister, obtained an interview with General Chiang Kai-shek, but the latter referred him to Chang Chun for negotiations on concrete issues. Three more conferences between Mr. Kawagoe and the Chinese Foreign Minister followed on October 19, 21 and 26, but the deadlock remained unbroken.

During this period the National Government went to

[23] *New York Times*, September 28, 1936.

great lengths to curb untoward popular manifestations of anti-Japanese sentiment. At the first conferences in mid-September General Chang Chun, in response to Ambassador Kawagoe's expressed apprehension over possible anti-Japanese disturbances on September 18, anniversary of the fall of Mukden, replied that all provincial authorities had been ordered to take stringent precautions.[24] These orders were fulfilled to the letter, even to the extent of not allowing Chinese flags to be flown at half-mast. Rifle butts of the Chinese police broke up a demonstration at Shanghai; at least thirty persons were injured and several score arrested. In Peiping and Tientsin police guards, posted at schools and colleges both before and after the anniversary, prevented any large-scale demonstrations.

The government's stiffer tone toward Japan, however, clearly expressed the growing nationalist spirit of the people. On October 12 sixty-six leading Peiping intellectuals issued an outspoken manifesto, to which the Foreign Ministry replied that the principles advocated were in complete harmony with the fixed policy of the Central Government. The national salvation movement, especially at Shanghai, was enrolling figures of national prominence under its banner. In his speeches General Chiang Kai-shek, taking over the slogan of the movement, was now referring to his task of accomplishing national salvation. His prestige in the country at large was steadily increasing. At this time he was engaged in a series of conferences with national and provincial military commanders, apparently with an eye to threatening developments in the north, where the Japanese military were

[24] *North-China Daily News*, September 17, 1936. On August 29, following the Chengtu incident, the government had issued a second mandate prohibiting "hostile utterances and deeds" tending to stir up international ill-feeling.

growing restive under the continued stalemate in the negotiations at Nanking. Beginning with Hangchow, on October 16-18, successive military conferences were held at Sian and Loyang. The latter, held on October 31, was the scene of a celebration in honor of Chiang Kai-shek's fiftieth birthday. This occasion was also greeted with large meetings at many centers throughout the country, marked by the presentation to the government of gift airplanes purchased by funds popularly subscribed. Fifty-five planes were actually presented on this day; an estimated total of over one hundred planes was eventually realized by the fund-raising campaign. In the course of an address to the nation from Loyang, General Chiang Kai-shek declared: "So long as we have not recovered our lost sovereign rights and restored our territorial integrity, we will never be free as a people nor independent as a nation." [25]

The seventh Chang Chun-Kawagoe conversation took place on November 10. At its conclusion, the respective views were said to have come closer on several of the issues under discussion, although no full agreement had been reached. The negotiations at Nanking were already over-shadowed by a renewal of Japan's military pressure in North China. Several warning signals had been issued in the north since the middle of September. On September 18 an incident had occurred at Fengtai, strategic railway junction near Peiping. As reported, the details of this incident seemed trivial. A Chinese soldier, at the end of a column which had just passed a Japanese contingent in a narrow street, slapped the hindquarters of a Japanese officer's horse. The steps taken were important. Japan's forces surrounded the Chinese barracks, exacted an apology, and forced all Chinese units to evacuate Fengtai. Japanese troops then moved into the Chinese barracks;

[25] *China Weekly Review,* November 7, 1936, p. 336.

henceforth Japan retained military control of the Fengtai junction. Five weeks later a second premonitory sign appeared. Japanese troop maneuvers, which began on October 25, were of an unprecedented size, ending with a large-scale sham battle aimed at the capture of Peiping. The maneuvers concluded without incident but not before the Chinese Foreign Ministry, on October 30, had lodged a strong protest with the Japanese authorities. These events occurred in Hopei province; the scene of action now shifted to Suiyuan.

Following the occupation of North Chahar by Japanese-sponsored irregular forces in December 1935, methodical preparations had been made for a further advance into Suiyuan province. During this period several changes in the political line-up within the two Inner Mongolian provinces had occurred. By decree of January 25, 1936 the Nanking government had set up a new Mongolian Political Council, limited mainly to the Suiyuan banners. This move had thrown Te Wang, outstanding leader of the Mongolian nationalist movement, into the hands of Japan, and some of the Chahar Mongols had been organized as a military unit under Japanese direction. This force, together with pro-Manchoukuo irregulars under Li Shou-hsin, had made a tentative thrust into eastern Suiyuan in early August, but had been repulsed by General Fu Tso-yi's provincial troops. After this setback, additional Chahar forces had been mobilized and supplied with arms and equipment from Japanese sources. In mid-November they returned to the attack. Though aided by Japanese planes, the initial assaults in eastern Suiyuan were again thrown back. General Fu Tso-yi's troops then took the offensive; Pailingmiao, a base of operations for the invaders in north Suiyuan, was captured on November 24. Prior to this counter-attack, mutinies among the Mongolian-Manchurian irregulars near Pailingmiao had cost the lives of several Japanese officers. Although the military phases of this struggle in Suiyuan were relatively insignificant, the effects upon China were profound. The defense of Suiyuan became a rallying cry which stirred the patriotism of the whole country. In this issue China's newly developed nationalism found its first complete expression, and received a powerful additional stimulus. One further point was made clear: Japan's Mongolian and Manchurian allies, even though staffed by Japanese officers and equipped with Japanese supplies, were neither reliable nor strong enough to complete the conquest of Inner Mongolia. To accomplish this task, an invasion in force by Japanese troops would be required.

The Sino-Japanese negotiations were concluded on December 3, when a final conference took place at Nanking. At this meeting the Chinese Foreign Minister "first lodged a protest with Mr. Kawagoe against the landing of Japanese blue-jackets at Tsingtao and their subsequent raiding of the Kuomintang offices"—events that had followed disturbances in connection with a strike of the workers in Japanese-owned mills. General Chang Chun then "reported on the facts gathered by investigation of the Suiyuan situation" and requested that "the Japanese government should promptly suppress the participation of Japanese military and civilians in the Suiyuan affair." [26] The Japanese Ambassador, in an effort to commit Chang Chun on the issues under negotiation, next read a memorandum purporting to detail the points on which agreement had been reached. The latter, however, drew attention to certain inaccuracies in the memorandum;

[26] From official statement issued by the Chinese Foreign Ministry, quoted in Shuhsi Hsu, cited, p. 95-99.

when the document was later sent to the Chinese Foreign Office, it was formally rejected in a note addressed to the Japanese Embassy. At the end of December the Chengtu and Pakhoi incidents were settled by the normal methods of apology and reparation.

Further details as to the course of these momentous negotiations were supplied in a semi-official Chinese statement issued on December 8 by the *Central News Agency*.[27] Taking note of Japanese reports that agreement in principle had been reached on five questions under discussion, this statement claimed that the true attitude of the Chinese government on these issues was as follows:

"(1) The discussions of direct China-Japan air traffic were confined to the question of the linking of Shanghai and Fukuoka by a civil air line. This question was first brought up by Japan even before September 18, 1931. Last year, the ministries of Communications of Japan and China, after several discussions, reached a draft agreement, based on the principles of equality and reciprocity. Unfortunately, since last winter, Japanese airplanes have been freely flying over North China without going through the legitimate procedure of obtaining the consent of the Chinese Government. Such illegal flights are a violation of China's sovereignty. The Chinese Government maintains that before a stop is put to these illegal flights, it will be extremely difficult to proceed with further discussions to link Shanghai and Fukuoka by a civil air line. The Chinese Government has not modified this attitude.

(2) Revision of China's import tariff is China's domestic affair. The tariff may be readjusted at any time as required by national financial and commercial conditions.

[27] Shuhsi Hsu, cited, Appendix B, p. 110-112.

But when tariff readjustment is being studied the Chinese Government regards the suppression of smuggling and freedom of the Chinese Customs Preventive Service as questions to be first considered.

(3) In connection with the question of suppressing unlawful activities of Koreans, it is pointed out that the Chinese Government naturally does not like to see illegal acts committed on Chinese soil by nationals of whatever foreign country. But the Japanese Government should also suppress unlawful activities, committed under its protection by Koreans, Formosans and other subjects of Japan.

(4) On the question of employing Japanese advisers, it is pointed out that the employment of foreign advisers by the Chinese Government depends upon the requirement of the Government and the technical ability of those to be employed. The question of nationality does not enter. Should Sino-Japanese relations have taken a turn for the better, it would not be impossible for China, on her own initiative, to employ Japanese technicians as experts. But this is not a matter which can be made the subject of a demand by a foreign government.

(5) Referring to the question of suppressing so-called anti-Japanese activities in China, the Chinese Government has repeatedly issued orders to the people stressing the necessity of maintaining friendly relations with foreign nations. These orders have been strictly carried out by the local authorities. While the Chinese Government will continue to suppress illegal acts according to law, cognizance must also be taken of the fact that there must be a cause which excites the sentiments of the masses. If Japan can change her policy toward China and really cooperate with her with sincerity, then all the so-called anti-Japanese activities will completely disappear and a

sincere friendship will always exist between the two peoples."

This statement omits consideration of the two main demands relating to Japan's special position in North China and a joint front against Communism. Even in Japanese circles, it was generally admitted that General Chang Chun had turned down these demands. Mr. Kawagoe's pressure, however, seems to have strengthened the Central Government's determination to suppress anti-Japanese activities and the Chinese Communists by its own efforts. On November 23, for example, seven officers of the All-China National Salvation Association, all of whom were prominent national figures, were arrested at Shanghai under charges of violating the February 20 emergency law. Those arrested included Shen Chung-ju, dean of the Shanghai Law College; Chang Nai-chi, noted economist and former vice-president of the Chekiang Industrial Bank; Li Kung-po, a school president; Sa Chien-li, lawyer; Wang Tsao-shih, professor of political science in Kwang Hua University; Sze Liang, a woman lawyer; and Tsou Tao-fen, well-known writer and editor. This *cause célèbre* dragged on for many months, attracting both national and international attention and casting doubt on the sincerity of the National Government's patriotic and nationalist pronouncements. No less significant was a speech delivered by General Chiang Kai-shek at Loyang on November 1, 1936 in which he declared that all traitors should be eliminated, "especially the Communists." [28] This declaration presaged a determined attempt to renew the anti-Communist campaign. It was clear that, in the mind of the Generalissimo, the popular demand for an end to civil strife was not taken to include

[28] *China Weekly Review,* November 7, 1936, p. 336.

surcease to warfare with the Communists, on which Nanking had squandered enormous resources since 1930 without achieving final success. Chiang's adherence to this fixed idea was to usher in the most crucial phase of China's recent political evolution.

CHAPTER FIVE

CHINA ACHIEVES UNITY

THE drama enacted at Sian during the fortnight before Christmas 1936 seemed, for the moment, to shatter the prospects for national consolidation. Strands from ten years of China's political history were woven into the crisis precipitated by the arrest of Generalissimo Chiang Kai-shek on December 12, 1936.[1] It climaxed the five years of exile suffered by General Chang Hsueh-liang, the Young Marshal of Manchuria, and his Northeastern troops. The protracted struggle between the Nanking government and the Chinese Communists, which began with the split between the right and left wings of the Kuomintang in 1927, was central to the story. Finally, the popular demand for unity in the face of Japanese aggression, for an end to the civil strife between rival Chinese factions, brought the whole issue into direct relation with the burning problems of contemporary political development. Unpromising though the Sian coup appeared at the time, its eventual results placed the finishing touches on China's newly reared structure of political unity.

During the year which preceded the Sian events, the Chinese Communist forces had completed their "Long March" from Kiangsi province *via* Szechuan into the

[1] For a notable first-hand account of the events of the Sian coup and the issues at stake, see James M. Bertram, *First Act in China,* New York, The Viking Press, 1938; see also *Red Star Over China,* cited, Part Twelve, chapters 1-5.

northwest. In the autumn of 1936 the last of the main Red armies had entered Shensi. For the first time in their history, all of the outstanding Communist leaders had joined forces in one contiguous belt of territory. The remarkable fighting ability, tactics and generalship, which had accomplished the march through sections of eight provinces against bitter opposition from central and provincial troops, had again testified to the disciplined morale of the Communist armies and added new prestige to the almost legendary names of their commanders. These men had established a new Soviet area in the northwest, embracing northern Shensi and parts of Kansu and Ninghsia provinces. Though sparsely populated, it was far larger than the former central Kiangsi-Fukien base and even better adapted for defensive warfare. Much more important, in the minds of the Communist leaders, it was within striking distance of the advancing Japanese forces in North China. The center of gravity of their policy had shifted from immediate prosecution of social revolution to the achievement of a united national front against the invader. In its manifesto of August 31, 1935, the Chinese Communist Party laid chief stress on the organization of a united anti-Japanese army and a national defense government. As the general platform for such a government, it proposed the following points: (1) resistance to Japanese invasion and the recovery of lost territories; (2) confiscation of all properties of Japanese imperialists in China to finance the war against Japanese invasion; (3) confiscation of all properties, stored food and land owned by Chinese traitors and agents of Japan, to be used by the poor countrymen and anti-Japanese fighters; (4) abolition of onerous taxes and fees, reorganization of finance and currency, and development of industry, agriculture and commerce; (5) increase of salaries, wages and soldiers' pay, and improvement of the living conditions of workers, peasants, soldiers, students and teachers; (6) exercise of full democratic rights, and release of all political prisoners; (7) free education and provision of jobs for the unemployed youth; (8) equality for all nationalities in Chinese territory, and protection of the life, property and freedom of residence and business of Chinese emigrants; (9) union with all anti-imperialist elements—the toiling people of Japan, Korea, Formosa and other oppressed nations—as China's allies; union with all nations which are sympathetic to the liberation movement of the Chinese nation, and establishment of friendly relations with those nations which maintain good-will and a neutral attitude toward this movement.[2] Many features of this declaration, far removed though it was from a challenge to the conservatives, were by no means acceptable to the dominant groups at Nanking. Indeed, the Nanking government was not even mentioned as one of the constituent elements of the proposed national defense organ.

By the spring of 1936, however, Mao Tse-tung, chairman of the Communist party's Central Executive Committee, no longer excluded the possibility of an armistice with the Nanking authorities, provided only that they gave evidence of determination to struggle against Japanese aggression. At this time Mao declared: "The war still raging in the interior of China is what is called the 'war of extermination' against Communism conducted by Chiang Kai-shek with all the military forces at his disposal. The Red Army, at the command of our people, is the only resolute and courageous body of troops struggling against Japanese imperialism. It goes without saying that we shall never allow Chiang Kai-shek to lay a finger on

[2] For full text, see *China Today,* December 1935, p. 58-59.

it. . . . I solemnly declare here, in the name of the Chinese Soviet Government, that if Chiang Kai-shek's army or any other army ceases hostilities against the Red Army, then the Chinese Soviet Government will immediately order the Red Army to stop military action against them. . . . If Chiang Kai-shek really means to take up the struggle against Japan, then obviously the Soviet government will extend to him the hand of friendship on the field of battle against Japan." [3] In August 1936 this evolution was carried one step further by a manifesto of the Central Executive Committee of the Chinese Communist Party which offered to conclude a united front agreement with the Nanking government based on the premise of resistance to Japan. The offer was implemented by proposals to moderate the internal program of the Communist Party along lines which would call a halt to the seizure of the property of landlords and merchants and enable them, on giving evidence of allegiance to the anti-Japanese front, to play a full part in the economic and political life of the Soviet regions.

None of these proposals was accorded serious consideration by the Nanking authorities, who continued to adhere to the policy of "extermination of the Communist bandits" which had been rigorously pursued since 1927. Prosecution of the anti-Communist campaign rested at this time in the hands of General Chang Hsueh-liang, Commander-in-Chief of the Northwestern Bandit-Suppression Forces. The bulk of the *Tungpei* [3a] troops was concentrated under his command at Sian; another Manchurian force, the 51st Army under General Yu Hsueh-

---

[3] Interviews by Mao Tse-tung *et al., International Press Correspondence,* London, March 14, 1936.

[3a] *Tungpei,* i.e., Northeastern, from the Northeastern provinces or Manchuria, is the name by which Chang Hsueh-liang's troops are known all over China. The word is pronounced "doong-bay."

chung,[4] was stationed further west at Lanchow, capital of Kansu province. The Northeastern, or *Tungpei,* troops in the neighborhood of Sian and Lanchow numbered approximately 130,000 men; they were further assisted by some 40,000 local troops under command of General Yang Hu-cheng, Pacification Commissioner of Shensi province. These forces were located mainly in the central and southern areas of Shensi and Kansu provinces, with the Communist armies holding sections in the north.

General Chang Hsueh-liang had originally been transferred to his post at Sian in October 1935. Even before his transfer, he had begun to entertain doubts as to the wisdom of the Central Government's temporizing policy toward Japan. These doubts were much more sharply formulated by the rank and file of the *Tungpei* troops, who had grown weary of the round of internecine warfare, during which they had fought against the Communists in several provinces, and asked only to be led against the Japanese aggressors so that they could "fight back to their homeland" in Manchuria. Nevertheless, on arrival in Sian, General Chang had immediately initiated offensive operations against the Communist forces in northern Shensi. Two of his crack divisions, won over by nationalist and anti-Japanese propaganda, had deserted *en masse* to the Communists. The campaign continued, but with ever diminishing momentum. Gradually a truce was established. By the autumn of 1936 the *Tungpei* armies and the Communists were virtually cooperating on a common program, in which each recognized the other as a component element of an anti-Japanese front.

This result had come about so gradually and naturally that it was not recognized in the country at large, nor

---

[4] The same which had been driven from Hopei province under terms of the Ho-Umetsu agreement in June 1935. See Chapter II.

even fully appreciated at military headquarters in Nan-king. Contact with the Communist armies had convinced the Northeastern troops and leaders that they were deal-ing with a force as anti-Japanese as themselves. *Tungpei* officers and men, captured by the Communists, had been released and permitted to return to Sian, where they had given glowing accounts of the discipline, morale and anti-Japanese spirit animating the Soviet organization. A group of young Northeastern officers, revolving around a newly established Military Academy near Sian, had in-creasingly won the ear of General Chang Hsueh-liang. These *"Tungpei* radicals" were determined to call a halt to civil warfare, so that all Chinese guns, as the slogan ran, could be turned outward against the common enemy. Chang Hsueh-liang himself met and talked with Chou En-lai, one of the Communist leaders, in June 1936 at Sian.[5] Throughout this year he pleaded with Chiang Kai-shek for active resistance to Japan. To urge his case, he made two special trips to Nanking, where he canvassed the views of all groups, some of which were sympathetic to his proposals. The Generalissimo turned a deaf ear to these pleas, insisting that the time for action against Japan had not yet arrived and that meanwhile the Com-munists had to be exterminated.

One year after the Young Marshal's transfer, the na-tionalist forces that had been germinating at Sian came out into the open. On September 18, 1936, despite the ban placed on such actions by the central authorities, an enthusiastic demonstration followed by a mass meeting of some 12,000 people was held in the Shensi capital. In answer to a petition demanding immediate mobilization of the Northeastern troops against Japan, General Chang Hsueh-liang delivered a passionate speech to the assembly.

[5] See Bertram, *First Act in China,* cited, p. 106.

After that day the city was covered with slogans. Some of these, such as "only by resisting Japan can the real unification of China be manifested," ran directly counter to the Central Government's slogan of "unification before resistance." On October 4 a Northeastern Peoples' National Salvation Association was formally inaugurated at Sian. Its charter membership of two hundred included *Tungpei* officers and soldiers, as well as local officials, students and representatives of the professions.[6] Undergirding this organization was a coalition of students and the young officers. Part of the old Northeastern University at Mukden, which had been transferred to Peiping in 1931, was now moved to Sian. In addition, several hundred picked students from Peiping had formed a special political training school under command of Colonel Sun Mingchiu, one of the leading *"Tungpei* radicals." The sentiment of these groups, as well as of the *Tungpei* soldiers, was fanned to white heat by the invasion of Suiyuan. Six large patriotic demonstrations were held at Sian between September 18 and December 9, the period during which the show-down that led to the coup was maturing.

No effort was made to hide from the central authorities what was taking place in Sian. Long before these crucial months, General Chang Hsueh-liang had gone straight to Nanking with his proposals as to policy and program. Now, in late October, he despatched urgent telegrams to General Chiang Kai-shek and General Chen Cheng, a leading central commander, asking not only for military resistance to Japan but also for a united front to include the Red armies. General Chiang Kai-shek was already engaged in the series of military conferences summoned to deal with the emergency in Suiyuan. In the conferences at Sian and Loyang, held during the last days of October,

[6] For these details, see *China Weekly Review*, October 24, 1936, p. 272.

General Chiang delivered a categorical refusal to the requests of the Young Marshal. Chiang's public addresses at both cities still listed the Communists among the "traitors" that had to be exterminated. His attitude toward Chang Hsueh-liang was somewhat like that of a father toward a wayward son. The latter continued to obey the orders of the Generalissimo, despite Chiang Kai-shek's declaration before the Military Academy at Sian to the effect that the Communists, and not the Japanese, were the nearest and most dangerous enemy. This speech precipitated a near revolt of the young *Tungpei* officers, which Chang Hsueh-liang managed to control only with considerable difficulty.

General Chiang Kai-shek had sent no airplanes and few central troops to Suiyuan; the latter did not participate in the actual fighting. Instead, three divisions of the crack First Army under General Hu Tsung-nan, the Generalissimo's trusted subordinate, were moved into Kansu to initiate the anti-Communist campaign. This action represented a sharp rebuff to Chang Hsueh-liang, who, however, accepted it calmly and merely advised General Hu of the dangers attending an offensive against the Communist armies. The First Army advanced warily into Kansu for three weeks until November 18, covering some twenty-five miles without encountering the enemy. On this day, and again on November 21, the Red forces swept down on the Nanking troops. Two brigades of Hu's army, with all their equipment, were captured and disarmed; some of the captives, after receiving a lecture about fighting Chinese during a national emergency, were sent back to tell their fellow-soldiers what they had learned. The First Army had meanwhile beat a hasty retreat to its starting-point, this time covering the distance in three days.

The outcome of this affair offered Chang Hsueh-liang a new opportunity to press his views upon the central authorities. On November 27 he sent a letter to the Generalissimo at Loyang, which presented his case in these terms: "Nearly one month has elapsed since I last saw Your Excellency. Knowing that Your Excellency had personally gone to Shansi and Shantung to give instructions at these respective places, I was deeply moved by Your Excellency's undaunted spirit of devotion to the affairs of the country. The situation in Eastern Suiyuan becomes more and more critical. . . . For the period of nearly half a year, I have continuously laid before Your Excellency my principle and program of struggle against Japanese imperialism for national salvation. . . . Now the war against Japanese imperialism is beginning. . . . I have therefore waited patiently for Your Excellency's order of mobilization. To my greatest disappointment, I have so far received no such order at all. . . . Pressed by the zealous sentiments of my troops and urged on by my personal convictions, I ventured to present my recent appeal, but Your Excellency instructed me to wait for an opportunity. Since then I have ordered my troops to wait patiently, although their desire to fight against Japanese imperialism was already flaming. . . . In order to control our troops, we should keep our promise to them that whenever the chance comes they should be allowed to carry out their desire of fighting against the enemy. Otherwise, they will regard not only myself but also Your Excellency as impostors, and will no longer obey us. Now is exactly the right time. Please give us the order to mobilize at least a part, if not the whole, of the *Tungpei* Army to march immediately to Suiyuan as reinforcements to those who are fulfilling their sacred mission of fighting Japanese imperialism. If so, I as well as my troops numbering more than a hundred thousand will follow Your Excellency's leadership to the end." [7] In reply to this virtual ultimatum, General Chiang Kai-shek asked the Young Marshal to meet him at Loyang. At this conference the Generalissimo again waved aside Chang Hsueh-liang's proposals, but agreed to visit Sian to talk with the *Tungpei* commanders.

Affairs had now reached the breaking point. Within Shensi an open rift had developed between the military commanders and the officials representing the central authorities. Of these latter, the civil governor, Shao Li-tzu, was the most important, but for military support he could count only upon a small police force. The *Tungpei* troops of the 51st Army under General Yu Hsueh-chung in Kansu province were of one mind with those under Chang Hsueh-liang in Shensi. When General Yang Hu-cheng, commanding the 40,000 local Shensi troops, openly affiliated himself with the *Tungpei* program, the civil authorities were powerless. They possessed only one well-tried weapon—the special gendarmerie controlled by the Blue Shirts, a secret terrorist organization which had been active throughout China in suppressing movements deemed hostile to the Central Government. In the circumstances prevailing at Sian, the activities of this organ, while annoying, could not affect the balance of power and merely added fuel to the fire. Blue Shirt efforts to disrupt the national salvation movement in Shensi had led to a series of incidents. In one case, word was brought to Chang Hsueh-liang that three student delegates from North China had been kidnaped and were being held at the local Kuomintang headquarters in Sian. In answer to telephoned inquiries, the people at the headquarters replied that they knew nothing of such students. That

[7] From text released at Sian on January 2, after the revolt.

night General Chang posted troops around the building; when they were refused admittance, they broke through the doors—and found the students imprisoned inside. The Blue Shirts in the place were arrested and deported from Sian.

Following his conference with the Young Marshal at Loyang, General Chiang Kai-shek prepared to deal with the Shensi problem in his usual decisive fashion. For some time stores of supplies and military equipment had accumulated in great quantities along the Lunghai Railway in the neighborhood of Loyang. Ostensibly these supplies were for use on the Suiyuan front; in reality, they were ear-marked for a renewal of the anti-Communist campaign on a grand scale. On December 4 the Generalissimo and his staff arrived at Sian. With him came eighty bombing planes, presented to Nanking only a month before on the occasion of Chiang Kai-shek's birthday. None of these planes had been sent to Suiyuan, but their presence at the Sian airfield was symbolic. Obviously the Generalissimo had come to give orders to the *Tungpei* commanders, and not to listen to their proposals. Though prepared to meet with some difficulty, he had underestimated the explosive possibilities of the situation at Sian. He has himself written: "My opinion was that the foundation for national unity had already been laid; that the Northeastern troops under conditions created by our national crisis, might have [been] given occasion for the expression of unorthodox views, but that if they were given sound and earnest advice they would realize the importance of our national interests and all as one man would submit to authority." [8] With his bodyguard, some-

[8] *Sian: A Coup D'Etat*, by Mayling Soong Chiang; *A Fortnight in Sian: Extracts from a Diary*, by Chiang Kai-shek, Shanghai, The China Publishing Company, 1937, p. 54.

what enlarged but all told less than a hundred men, and a few of his close associates, Chiang Kai-shek was accommodated at temple quarters near Lintung, twelve miles from Sian. The greater part of his staff, accompanied by one or two other important military commanders, stayed within the city at the Sian Guest House, a newly constructed modern hotel.

The meetings which began after December 4 are thus described in Chiang Kai-shek's diary: "There I sent for the Commanders of the bandit suppression troops in Shensi and Kansu and received them one by one on a number of successive days. I inquired about the conditions at the front and gave them my orders. I told them that the bandit suppression campaign had been prosecuted to such a stage that it would require only the efforts of 'the last five minutes' to achieve the final success. I urged them to perform their duty with courage and determination." [9] What the *Tungpei* commanders themselves said the diary does not state. It is known, however, that they one and all protested that they wanted to fight back to Manchuria, that they could not go on killing their own people.[10] On this clear issue of policy, the Generalissimo found that the Young Marshal and Generals Yu Hsueh-chung and Yang Hu-cheng were as inflexible as any of the subordinate commanders. They wanted orders to fight Japan; General Chiang Kai-shek insisted that their duty was to suppress the Communists.

The feeling in Sian, which already ran high, was not improved by an incident that occurred on December 9, anniversary of the first big student demonstration in Peiping. Thousands of students, some from the university but many more from middle schools, paraded the streets

[9] *Sian: A Coup D'Etat*, etc., cited, p. 54-55.
[10] Bertram, *First Act in China*, cited, p. 114.

and demanded that reinforcements be sent to the Suiyuan
front. The civil governor, Shao Li-tzu, received them
with smooth words; meanwhile, he had given orders to
the police to suppress the students by force, if it proved
necessary. A demonstration at this moment, with the city
and environs filled with central government officers, was
as awkward to the Northeastern commanders as to Shao
Li-tzu. The students sought to have their petition received by the local military commandants, but Chang
Hsueh-liang and Yang Hu-cheng were both out. Chafing
at these failures, they decided to march out to see General
Chiang Kai-shek at Lintung. The police authorities became alarmed, and a police unit fired on the marching
line while it was still inside the city; two middle school
students, twelve and thirteen years of age, were seriously
wounded. Several thousand students, their determination
strengthened by this attack, broke through the gate and
started the march to Lintung. Only the personal intervention of Marshal Chang Hsueh-liang, who pledged satisfaction to their demands within a week, turned them
back.

The Generalissimo chose this moment to show his
hand. On December 10, for the first time, there was a
combined meeting of the leading military officers on both
sides. The old arguments were repeated, with no better
results than before. General Chiang Kai-shek thereupon
presented his ultimatum. He was determined to proceed
with the anti-Communist campaign. Since Chang Hsueh-
liang would not prosecute these operations, he would have
to be replaced by General Chiang Ting-wen, Pacification
Commissioner for Fukien. The latter officer had accompanied the Generalissimo's party to Sian; an official order
installing him in the post of Commander-in-Chief of the
Northwestern Bandit Suppression Forces had, in fact,

been already issued.[11] This order was now shown to General Chang Hsueh-liang. The *Tungpei* troops, he was told, were to be transferred to the south, even further away from the anti-Japanese front in Suiyuan; the Central Government, moreover, was issuing orders on December 12 for general resumption of the anti-Communist operations. At Nanking the Executive Yuan actually did issue orders to this effect on December 12 to twelve provincial governments.[12] Not until some hours later did the Nanking authorities learn that the Generalissimo was a prisoner at Sian.

Chiang's ultimatum, in effect, gave the Northeastern commanders and General Yang Hu-cheng two days to come to terms. Their decision was taken on December 11 at a night conference attended by the leading commanders and several of the younger *Tungpei* officers, thirteen in all.[13] The coup was carried into effect early on the following morning. Colonel Sun Ming-chiu, with part of a special regiment which included a number of the Peiping students, was entrusted with the task of capturing the Generalissimo alive. The bodyguard at the Lintung temple was taken by surprise and quickly overwhelmed. Chiang Hsiao-hsien, a nephew of Chiang Kai-shek and well-known Blue Shirt leader, was shot down out of hand when discovered. The Generalissimo could not at first be found, but was shortly discovered on the mountain-side behind the temple and brought back to Sian. In the city Yang Hu-cheng's men had occupied the Guest House and captured all of Chiang's retinue, as well as Shao Li-tzu, the Shensi governor. They had additionally taken over the police stations, the Blue Shirt head-

---

[11] See *Sian: A Coup D'Etat*, etc., cited, p. 117.
[12] *New York Times*, December 14, 1936.
[13] Bertram, *First Act in China*, cited, p. 115-116.

quarters and secret cells, and the bombing planes at the airport. In Kansu General Yu Hsueh-chung's troops similarly took control of Lanchow, disarming a brigade of Hu Tsung-nan's First Army in the process.

Responsibility for these acts rested squarely on the shoulders of the ranking commanders in the northwest. Their actions were motivated by an effort to effect a change in national policy which, they believed, was supported by majority opinion. Under the conditions in China, the difference of views that reached its climax in Sian on December 12 could be settled through no pacific democratic medium. After months of rebuff, capped by dismissal from their posts, Chang Hsueh-liang and his associates had, in their own phrase, offered the Generalissimo "advice by military force." Their objectives were expressed in the following eight points: (1) reorganization of the Nanking government in such a way that all parties might share the joint responsibility of saving the nation; (2) cessation of all civil war; (3) immediate release of the patriotic, i.e., National Salvation, leaders arrested at Shanghai; (4) release of all political prisoners throughout the country; (5) removal of all restrictions on the patriotic movement of the people; (6) safeguarding of the people's freedom to organize and call meetings; (7) effectual realization of Dr. Sun Yat-sen's last testament; (8) immediate convocation of a National Salvation Conference. This program was smothered by the Nanking press censorship, and never appeared before the country at large in complete form. The eight points, as generally reported, were vulgarized into demands for an immediate declaration of war on Japan and an alliance with the Communists. Even more unfairly, Chang Hsueh-liang was alternately painted as a villain seeking greater political power, huge monetary bribes, or better treatment for his troops. Against this background of misrepresentation, the practical difficulties facing accomplishment of the ends envisaged by the coup were greatly increased. The Generalissimo, not unnaturally, refused to treat with the rebels. At Nanking the military machine, in the hands of General Ho Ying-chin, insisted on a punitive expedition against the northwest irrespective of the possible danger to Chiang Kai-shek.[14] The message despatched to Wang Ching-wei inviting him to return at once from Europe to Nanking smacked suspiciously of an effort to reorganize the government on the basis of an anti-Chiang coalition. Throughout the two weeks of General Chiang's captivity, it seemed not unlikely that the conservatives at Nanking might precipitate a disastrous civil war—the very thing which the coup had aimed to prevent.

The position of the Communist leaders during this period was of crucial importance. They had taken no part in the planning or execution of the coup, which was solely the work of Chang Hsueh-liang and his associates. On the other hand, once the step had been taken, alluring possibilities opened up before the Red commanders. They had already established a basis of working cooperation with the forces in Shensi and Kansu under Generals Chang Hsueh-liang, Yu Hsueh-chung, and Yang Hu-cheng. Under conditions created by the coup, this co-operation might be cemented into a firm alliance which would muster 300,000 troops and dominate the northwest. Other forces, say in Kwangsi, could possibly be mobilized in support of the eight-point platform; with the Generalissimo held captive, the conservatives at Nanking might be isolated and the Central Government remodeled on the basis of the liberal program. Inviting though these

[14] See Madame Chiang Kai-shek's comments, *Sian: A Coup D'Etat*, etc., cited, p. 5-9.

vistas were, the Communist leadership firmly set itself against such action. Along that path the threat of large-scale civil war was too great.

The alternative involved a frank approach to Chiang Kai-shek. Taking the *Tungpei* platform on its professed basis of "advice" to the Generalissimo, the Communist leaders could reenforce the appeals of Chang Hsueh-liang for a change of policy. Further, by using their influence to secure Chiang Kai-shek's release, the Communists could demonstrate beyond peradventure of doubt the sincerity of their united front offers. Success of this policy would conserve the strength and prestige of the Generalissimo for establishment of a national united front behind which all forces in China, both conservative and radical, could rally. Its dangers were patent. No pledges could be exacted from General Chiang at Sian which he might not easily repudiate once he had returned to Nanking. Release of the Generalissimo would almost surely lead to the break-up of the local united front in the northwest. The younger *"Tungpei* radicals" would bitterly oppose such a step without sure guarantees; some of them were not averse to placing Chiang on trial at Sian for his "crimes" to the state. They would feel that their main surety had disappeared with Chiang's return to Nanking, and would naturally resent Communist pressure toward this end. The results of this line of policy were thus highly problematical; in the end, both the local and the national united fronts might well be lost. This alternative, nevertheless, seems to have been chosen with virtually no hesitation.[15]

The choice was not rendered any easier by the successes

[15] Actually, the policy was enforced by the ranking Communist leaders against fairly serious opposition from some of the secondary Red commanders.

attained almost without effort by the united front in
Shensi and Kansu at the end of December and early in
January. During these weeks a revolutionary base of mass
proportions appeared virtually overnight in the northwest. Sponsored by the authorities, instead of being
subjected to official repression, the national salvation
movement achieved its first completely untrammeled expression in China. Enthusiastic mass demonstrations on
a vast scale, addressed by Chang Hsueh-liang, Yang Hu-
cheng and other leaders, were successively held in Sian.
These activities, contrary to reports disseminated outside,
were carried through under disciplined control. Martial
law, imposed in Sian on December 12, was lifted on the
following day; only a few scattered incidents occurred
in the city during the course of the *coup d'état*. Organization work went on among the peasants in the villages,
who came by the thousands to participate in meetings
held throughout the country-side. Newspapers devoted to
the cause of the national salvation movement sprang up
in Sian and won a wide circulation in the northwestern
provinces. Political prisoners, including many Communist youths in the local jails, were released. Although no
Communist troops entered Sian, Red army men frater-
nized with the provincial troops in the north. A United
Northwestern Military Council was set up, with headquarters at Sian. The future of this movement, cherished
possibly more by the young *Tungpei* officers than the
Communists, was at stake in the negotiations which were
to decide the fate of Chiang Kai-shek.

From the first these negotiations were impeded by
refusal of the forces in control at Nanking to give a
hearing to the Young Marshal. Madame Chiang Kai-shek's
efforts to get in touch with General Chiang's captors had
to break through a wall of resistance at Nanking. The

proposals of the rebels reached the capital on the day after the revolt, but the eight-point platform was disregarded and its contents suppressed. On December 14 a telegram from Sian sent by Mr. Donald, the Generalissimo's adviser, informed the central authorities that Chiang Kai-shek was well and indicated that Chang Hsueh-liang wished Dr. H. H. Kung, acting head of the Executive Yuan, and Madame Chiang to go to Shensi. Doubts were cast on this telegram by the Nanking officials, who resolutely opposed Madame Chiang's efforts to leave for Sian and pressed ahead with preparations for a punitive expedition against the rebels. The state of affairs at the capital was soon realized by the Generalissimo, who could also hear the Nanking bombers droning over Sian. Initial hostilities, including the bombing of Weinan, northeast of Sian, occurred three days after Chiang's detention. The outbreak of large-scale warfare was prevented only when General Chiang Ting-wen, one of the Sian captives, was released and sent to Nanking with an autographed letter from the Generalissimo ordering the Minister of War to cease bombing and fighting for three days. Dr. T. V. Soong had meanwhile gone to Sian; on December 21, after conferring with Chang Hsueh-liang, both he and Mr. Donald returned to Nanking. Only then was Madame Chiang Kai-shek, in the face of continued objections from the authorities, able to return with these men to Sian during a prolongation of the truce arranged at Nanking with the greatest difficulty.

During these two weeks the leaders in the northwest were finding it impossible to shake the Generalissimo's determination to refuse political commitments. After some hesitancy, overcome partly by the state of affairs in Nanking, he entered for the first time into a serious discussion with Chang Hsueh-liang of the political issues at

CHINA'S COMMUNIST LEADERS: MAO TSE-TUNG, CHOU EN-LAI, PO KU, CHU TEH.

stake. Chou En-lai, one of the chief Communist leaders, participated in these conversations.[16] He made it clear to Chiang that the Communists were unwilling to exploit the situation on the narrow plane of partisan advantage; they desired the Generalissimo to return to Nanking, establish nation-wide political unity embracing the Red armies, and make preparations to resist Japan.[17] The efforts of Chou En-lai and other Communist representatives at Sian to prevent the hot-headed *Tungpei* officers from staging a mass trial of the Generalissimo, which would almost certainly have resulted in a death sentence, convincingly underlined the sincerity of these proposals.[18] Chang Hsueh-liang finally agreed to the release of Chiang Kai-shek; he succeeded, moreover, in winning the assent of his fellow-commanders. The young *Tungpei* officers, however, were apparently not thoroughly reconciled to this procedure—an element which lent a clandestine atmosphere to the flight from the Sian airport. General Chang Hsueh-liang accompanied his erstwhile captive to Nanking. The act was perfectly understandable. Only thus could he clear his name of the aspersions cast by the rebellion, and demonstrate the sincerity and patriotism of the motives which inspired the coup.

To the end Chiang Kai-shek seems to have refrained from committing himself to specific political pledges. In the later speeches of General Yang Hu-cheng and others,

[16] No mention of Chiang's talks with Chou appear in the former's published diary of his sojourn in Sian. The omission is natural, as such a revelation would have intensified the suspicions of the conservatives at Nanking and of Japan.

[17] Interview by the author at Yenan in north Shensi, June 1937.

[18] Note Madame Chiang's statement: "We heard nothing of menaces from the Reds during all this time. Quite contrary to outside beliefs, we were told, they were not interested in detaining the Generalissimo. Instead, they preferred his quick release." *Sian: A Coup D'Etat*, etc., cited, p. 39.

there are references to verbal assurances by Chiang Kai-shek that there would be no further civil war in China. If this evidence can be accepted, it marks the limit of the concessions made by the Generalissimo. Chou En-lai may possibly have watched the airplane that bore Chang Hsueh-liang and Chiang Kai-shek away toward Nanking, where the latter would again come under the influence and pressure of China's conservative elements. He could not be certain of the outcome. He and his Communist associates in northern Shensi had one assurance. Their analysis of conditions in China, and of the tempo of Japanese pressure, had convinced them that Chiang Kai-shek, whatever reservations he might have, would eventually be forced to assume the leadership of a national united front.

The immediate results were far from reassuring. In the northwest the spirit and enthusiasm of the mass movement persisted well into January; outwardly, few changes were noticeable in Sian after Chiang's departure on Christmas afternoon. As the weeks passed, however, ominous signs began to appear. The Nanking troops, which had at first been withdrawn from Shensi's eastern borders, reappeared and a strict blockade closed down against the northwest. Chang Hsueh-liang's sentence of ten years' imprisonment was commuted, after a plea for clemency from Chiang Kai-shek, but he was kept under surveillance and not permitted to return to Shensi. The Generalissimo had gone into self-imposed retirement at Fenghua, and affairs at Nanking were evidently dominated by the conservatives; once more the possibility of a punitive expedition against the northwest emerged. In Shensi and Kansu the political liaison between the various military units gradually weakened. Chang Hsueh-liang's guiding hand was sorely missed; neither the other *Tungpei* commanders or Yang Hu-cheng were able to take his place.

Collapse of the northwestern front was signalized by a second coup on February 2, carried out by the young "*Tungpei* radicals," in which General Wang I-che and two other officers were killed. This mutiny was directed against the settlement, accepted by the high *Tungpei* commanders, whereby the central authorities were to take over control in the northwest; in the end, it merely hastened the process. On February 9 General Ku Chu-tung, Director of the Generalissimo's Provisional Headquarters in Sian, entered the Shensi capital to assume control of military readjustments in Shensi and Kansu. The mass organizations that had centered in Sian were dissolved and their leaders went into hiding. Full reorganization of the troop dispositions in the two provinces was still to be effected, but the last stage of the revolt had ended. One favorable sign might be noted: General Ku Chu-tung's title was no longer that of "bandit-suppression" commander.

The Third Plenary Session of the Kuomintang, which met at Nanking on February 15-22, was devoted mainly to winding up the last phases of the Sian affair. For the third time Chiang Kai-shek's offer to resign his posts, in token of responsibility for the mutiny, was rejected. He presented a report on the Sian events which included, possibly as a result of prior agreement with Chang Hsueh-liang, the eight-point program of the northwestern rebels. The Kuomintang plenary session, in voting to accept this report, noted that since Chang Hsueh-liang's proposals had been "submitted through rebellious action" they could not be accorded consideration. On the other hand, the session restored the Young Marshal's civil rights, of which he had been deprived for five years. This action removed his last substantive penalties, although he was not allowed to resume his military command nor permitted to stray far from the capital.

A telegram from the Central Executive Committee of the Chinese Communist Party was brought before the plenary session. This message, after congratulating the nation on the peaceful settlement of the Sian affair and expressing hopes for political unification of the country, outlined five proposals which it hoped would be adopted as basic national policies. These were: (1) cessation of all civil wars and concentration of national strength to cope with external aggression; (2) freedom of speech and assembly, and release of all political prisoners; (3) summoning of a National Salvation Conference to be attended by delegates from all parties, factions, public bodies, and armies; (4) acceleration of preparations for positive armed resistance against Japan; (5) improvement of the people's living conditions. The Communist Party was prepared, in case these proposals were adopted, to demonstrate its desire for national unity by pledging to take the following steps: (1) suspend all armed activities throughout the country aiming at overthrow of the National Government; (2) change the title of "Soviet Government" to "The Special Area Government of the Republic of China" and re-name the "Red Army" as "The Chinese National Revolutionary Army"—this latter to be placed under direction of the Military Affairs Commission of the National Government; (3) realize democracy in the area under jurisdiction of the Special Area Government through introduction of popular suffrage; (4) suspend enforcement of the land confiscation policy, and resolutely carry out the national program of resistance to Japanese aggression.[19]

The Kuomintang session also received a lengthy peti-

[19] *China Weekly Review,* February 20, 1937, p. 408.

tion from the All-China National Salvation Association, which advocated the adoption of eight proposals similar in tenor to the *Tungpei* platform. Even more notable was a joint proposal submitted by fourteen of the liberal party and government members, including Feng Yu-hsiang, Sun Fo and Madame Sun Yat-sen, which openly advised a return to Dr. Sun Yat-sen's policies of coopera-tion with the Communists and alliance with the Soviet Union.[20] At its sixth general meeting, held on February 21, the plenary session adopted a resolution outlining its stand on the issue of rapprochement with the Commu-nists. The resolution listed four conditions on which rec-onciliation could be effected: (1) abolition of the Red Army and its incorporation into the nation's armed forces under unified command; (2) unification of political power in the hands of the Central Government and dis-solution of the so-called Chinese Soviet Government and other organizations detrimental to governmental unity; (3) absolute cessation of Communist propaganda, which is diametrically opposed to Dr. Sun Yat-sen's Three Peo-ples' Principles; (4) termination of class struggle, which splits society into antagonistic classes and invites mutual destruction.[21] The historical account which accompanied this resolution bitterly excoriated the Communists, while the session's concluding manifesto endorsed the govern-ment's pacific policy toward Japan and reiterated the necessity of exterminating the "Communist scourge" throughout China.

Adjournment of the Kuomintang plenary session ush-ered in a trying period of four months' apparent inde-cision on all vital political issues. The morale of the country at large was high. For this a combination of

[20] For text, see *China Weekly Review*, February 27, p. 445.
[21] *The Peiping Chronicle*, February 23, 1937; also *China Weekly Review*, February 27, 1937, p. 442-443.

factors was responsible: peaceful settlement of the Sian crisis; the successful defense of Suiyuan; Chang Chun's stand against Ambassador Kawagoe's demands; and the obvious relaxation of Japanese pressure. The prestige of General Chiang Kai-shek was undimmed, as witnessed by the popular expressions of relief and rejoicing on his return from Sian. If the leaders in the northwest had expected the Generalissimo to press immediately toward reorganization of the Nanking government and realization of the national salvation program, they must have experienced a keen sense of disappointment. At Nanking all seemed to go on as before. In this respect, the outcome of the February plenum was but one example. The trial of the seven National Salvation leaders, to whose number three more had been added, was scheduled to open at Soochow on April 28; despite all protests in behalf of the defendants, the case dragged on from one postponement to another through May, June and into early July.

During these months the national salvation movement seemed to mark time, devoting itself chiefly to strengthening mass organizations through activities which constituted no direct challenge to the National Government. Nanking agents succeeded in splitting the Peiping student movement, and on May 4, during a meeting commemorating the eighteenth anniversary of the 1919 student movement, an open wrangle occurred between rival student factions in the city. The National Government made no open efforts to retrieve the lost positions in North Chahar and East Hopei at a time which many thought to be opportune. In March it received the Kodama Economic Mission, sent by Japan to strengthen "economic cooperation" between the two countries, with fine formality, though the Chinese business-men suggested to their Japanese colleagues that revision of the status of

East Hopei was required to place Sino-Japanese relations on a sounder basis of cooperation. The relations between Nanking and the Communists seemed to have reached a stalemate. Rumors persisted that negotiations were proceeding, but there was no concrete evidence to this effect. The military authorities were still engaged in operations against Communist partisan bands in provinces outside the northwest; in Shensi and Kansu, however, there were no hostilities between the Communists and the local or central troops.

This pattern of events presented no clear picture as to the basic policies and attitude of the National Government. Against an indecisive political background, important advances toward military centralization were nevertheless being made. The *Tungpei* armies, which had at first remained in the northwest, were transferred to Honan, Anhwei and Kiangsu provinces during the month of April. The bulk of these troops was placed under the control of a Military Affairs Rehabilitation Committee, which included *Tungpei* commanders but was headed by General Liu Chih, Pacification Commissioner for Honan and Anhwei. General Yu Hsueh-chung, whose 51st Army had carried out the revolt in Kansu, was transferred with his troops to Kiangsu province, where he became Pacification Commissioner. General Yang Hu-cheng, last of the triumvirate who led the mutiny, resigned his command and left China for a trip abroad to study military affairs. These various steps marked the final liquidation of the Sian revolt, and brought the Northeastern troops under direct control of the National Government. By the end of June the five *Tungpei* armies had been reorganized as national units and formally incorporated into the regular forces under the Ministry of War, with maintenance provided by the central treasury.

Immediately following this settlement, a serious issue arose in Szechuan province over the Central Government's efforts to reorganize the motley array of more than 200,000 local troops. This attempt was the culmination of a process in the southwest which had begun at the end of 1934, when central troops had entered Kweichow and Yunnan provinces to cut off the Communist armies on their long trek. While the latter objective was not achieved, the central authorities had established firm control both in Kweichow and Yunnan, hitherto quasi-independent. In May 1937 a similar effort in Szechuan raised complications which, for a short time, threatened to result in civil war. The Central Government had by this time become virtually unassailable, the situation was handled tactfully, and the outcome was a success for Nanking. In July a Szechuan-Hsikang Military Affairs Readjustment Committee, with the War Minister as chairman and General Ku Chu-tung as vice-chairman, reached an agreement which provided for reorganization of the local military forces according to the central system by the middle of August. With this agreement, another major stride toward a consolidated national army had been taken.

These achievements during the late spring of 1937 left no further room for doubt that the country was being knit together, both politically and militarily, at a faster rate than at any time since the founding of the Republic. The one big question-mark was the extent to which the National Government would be willing to bring the Communists within the scope of the developing union. Early in June a group of four foreigners [22] set out from Peiping for Yenan, in north Shensi, to seek information from the Communist leaders as to the status of their relations with Nanking. Statements made at this capital of the Chinese

[22] Including the author.

Soviet Republic on June 21-24 by Mao Tse-tung, Chu Teh and Chou En-lai breathed a certainty that the split between the Kuomintang and the Communists, which had existed for ten years, was in the process of being healed. In reply to reservations expressed by the interviewers with respect to the contradictory features of Nanking's domestic and foreign policies, and the continued evidences of reactionary tendencies, Mao Tse-tung, chairman of the Central Executive Committee of the Communist Party, made the following statement:

"As to a Kuomintang military dictatorship, it is very clear that from September 18, 1931 to now Nanking has always been a military dictatorship. In the first period, up to July 1936, there was dictatorship plus a pro-Japanese policy. Now that it has changed its foreign policy, it must also change its internal policy. It is impossible for the Kuomintang at one and the same time to suppress the people and fight against Japan. It may be true that Nanking is not deeply and permanently committed to an anti-Japanese policy. There is not yet the anti-Japanese war, not yet democracy. This can only be a temporary situation. The present period bears a transitional character; it is passing from one stage to another. We are now in the midst of this transitional period. The same holds true in the world at large. So it is possible to observe many unhealthy phenomena. In China we see the arrest and trial of the National Salvation leaders, the suppression of the mass movement, the remnants of the old policy not yet fully given up. On the other side is the struggle of the healthy trend against evil remnants. It is not necessary to be overanxious, because we can see the other side. Look at the struggle that is going on objectively; this struggle is the specific character of this period. If some Kuomintang members maintain the old policy and don't want to change, they are free to adopt this attitude. But the new anti-Japanese, democratic forces are growing up, and will call a halt to the activities of these people. Even Justice Hughes must change a little, or be carried away."

From conversations with Chu Teh, Commander-in-Chief of the Red Army, it was learned that the main Communist forces in the Shensi-Kansu-Ninghsia areas, under direct centralized command through radio connection, numbered about 90,000 troops. These regulars were, on the whole, well armed; their equipment as to clothes, food and supplies was still inadequate, although steadily improving. Fairly large partisan forces, engaged mainly in police duties, provided reserves which, however, were not undergoing actual military training. Outside the central Shensi-Kansu-Ninghsia district, Red partisan areas existed in southern Shensi, the Fukien-Kiangsi border, the Honan-Hupeh-Anhwei border, northeastern Kiangsi, the Hunan-Hupeh-Kiangsi border, the Kwangtung-Hunan border, the Kiangsi-Hunan border, and the Shensi-Szechuan border. Each of these groups numbered from one to three thousand men, but it was impossible to give an exact estimate of their total figure. The central command maintained irregular and uncertain connections with only a few of these scattered partisan areas. In several cases, the Kuomintang forces were carrying on expeditions against such partisan groups; their ultimate disposition depended on the outcome of the negotiations being conducted with Nanking. After considerable difficulty, the Communists had succeeded in establishing friendly relations with certain Moslem communities in the west and Mongols to the north. The People's Anti-Japanese Military Academy at Yenan enrolled over two thousand students, who were obtaining instruction over a wide range of military, political, and cultural subjects.

Chou En-lai indicated that the negotiations toward a Kuomintang-Communist rapprochement were progressing favorably. After Sian, he had conferred with General Chiang Kai-shek both at Hangchow and Kuling; delegates from Nanking had also visited the Soviet region. The negotiations were proceeding within the frame-work of the respective proposals made public during the Kuomintang plenary session in February. For their part, the Communists were implementing the pledges contained in the telegram to the Kuomintang plenum. Confiscation of landlord property and attempts to overthrow the Kuomintang had already ceased; the Red Army was resting on its arms within the northwestern districts then occupied. In this region, educational and propaganda efforts had been under way for some months to prepare the people for the transition to a democratic form of government. Before the end of July it was expected that the existing Soviet organization would give way to a representative system of elections to local and higher offices, with all classes of the population enfranchised. During July, also, the Red Army would be coordinated with the central military command at Nanking. Its name would probably be changed to the "National Revolutionary Army," and its various divisions would be appropriately numbered in relation to other units of the national armed forces. No commanders would be sent in from Nanking. The army would be officered by its own leaders, who would operate under direction of the Military Affairs Commission, the chairman of which was General Chiang Kai-shek.

On the Kuomintang side, certain conditions stipulated by the Communists were also in process of fulfillment. Internal peace had been realized with the cessation of Nanking's anti-Red campaigns. Nationalization of the Communist military forces, when complete, would in-

volve maintenance and pay from the central treasury. This
condition had already been partially met by the lifting of
the economic blockade, and the shipment of food, trucks
and equipment to the Red armies. The general Communist demand for democratization of the Kuomintang
political system had been specifically applied to the issue
of the forthcoming Peoples' National Congress, scheduled
to inaugurate the new Constitution in November. The
Communist leaders, during the negotiations with Nanking,
insisted that this Congress should be democratically elected
on a basis that would include all parties and groups, so
that it might be transformed into a comprehensive representative organ capable of dealing with all problems
affecting salvation of the country. They also insisted that
the new Constitution, which had been formulated by the
Kuomintang, should be so modified that it might serve as
the organic law for a genuinely democratic republic. On
these questions, the Communist point of view had been
only partially accepted. The basis of representation of the
Congress had been somewhat broadened, and Communist
delegates were to be included, but on the whole it would
still be dominated by the Kuomintang. A third Communist proposal, to the effect that a National Defense
Conference representative of all military groups be summoned, was under consideration, but the appropriate time
for such a conference was thought to have not yet arrived.
The Communist leaders were also discussing with Nanking
concrete measures for preparation of the defensive war
against Japan, stimulation of the national defense economy, and improvement of the people's livelihood. Their
last condition, involving full guarantee of civil rights and
democratic liberties, stipulated that all political prisoners
should be released and the Communist Party given a legal
position. These points had not yet been conceded; in the

northwest all politicals had been freed, but in the rest of the country the Communists estimated that roughly ten thousand were still imprisoned, if the war prisoners were included.

In vivid metaphor, Chou En-lai summarized the progress that was taking place. "Peace is achieved," he said. "There is now no fighting between us. We have the opportunity to participate in the actual preparations for the defensive war against Japan. As to the problem of achieving democracy, this aim has only begun to be realized. This is more difficult than the development of the anti-Japanese movement, but it has begun to grow both among the masses and within the Nanking government, although the pace is still slow. One must consider the anti-Japanese war preparations and democracy like two wheels of a bicycle, one before the other, and not like the two wheels of a 'rickshaw, for example. That is to say, the preparation for the anti-Japanese war comes first, and following it the movement for democracy—which can push the former forward. Both wheels move together, but the anti-Japanese movement occupies the front position." These comments were suggestive of the determination manifest in Yenan to close the breach between the two parties, irrespective of the difficulties to be surmounted. On the other side, it was clear that Nanking, in view of the concessions already made, was equally convinced of the desirability and necessity of cooperation. Public announcement of the Kuomintang-Communist agreement was scheduled to take place on or about July 15. Such a declaration would have had an electric effect on China, galvanizing the centripetal forces at work in the country and hastening the advent of national unification. The announcement was forestalled by the hostilities at Lukouchiao.

Japan's military onslaught was timed no less carefully

than its previous retreat. The full results of the Sian
mutiny were not apparent in the early months of 1937.
During this period, with Mr. Naotake Sato in the Foreign
Ministry at Tokyo, Japanese military-political pressure
on China noticeably relaxed. The result was not as anticipated; centrifugal tendencies failed to reassert themselves
in Chinese political life. On the contrary, as the spring
wore on it became clear beyond the shadow of doubt that
China was rapidly pulling itself together. This process
could not be permitted to go past a certain point; above
all, it could not be allowed a period of years in which to
demonstrate its full potentialities. The blow fell in July
1937 for another equally valid reason. Japanese aggression
in China, which had progressed steadily since 1931, had
been brought to a halt all along the line. The Chang
Chun-Kawagoe negotiations at Nanking brought the diplomatic offensive to a full stop, while the Suiyuan hostilities
marked the limit to advances in the north which could be
achieved by reliance on the "irregular" allies. Uprisings in
Chahar in the spring of 1937, in fact, suggested that the
Japanese positions already won in North Chahar and East
Hopei were none too stable. There was still the program
of "economic cooperation" to fall back upon in this time
of need. In the hands of Foreign Minister Sato, with the
backing of strong groups of Japanese capitalists, the program was capable of extensive development under more
or less pacific auspices. The testing-ground for this policy,
however, was North China, and here military considerations impinged directly on the nature and objectives of
Japanese economic penetration.

The cleavage within Japan between the heavy industries, which supported the War Ministry's aggressive
policy, and the light industries, which hesitated to disrupt

trading relations with China,[23] found direct expression in North China at this period. Up to a certain point, the interests of these two groups in the economic invasion of China's northern provinces could be harmonized. The vast illicit trade, assisted by the Japanese military for reasons of their own, consisted mainly of the products of light industry, especially cotton and rayon textiles. In another respect, by contributing directly to the bankruptcy of the Chinese cotton mills in Tientsin, this trade played into the hands of Japan's liberal industrialists. After 1935 these mills were one after another forced to shut down, and then to sell out to Japanese textile firms. By the spring of 1937 the cotton textile industry in Tientsin had become predominantly Japanese. The Osaka firms were also directly interested in the efforts being made, through Japanese pressure on the Hopei-Chahar Political Council, to induce the Chinese authorities to improve and extend cotton cultivation in North China.

On the other hand, the Japanese army was seeking to force the Chinese officials to carry through a number of economic projects which were much more closely related to military objectives. Pressure toward this end reached its height during the closing months of 1936. In August Ambassador Kawagoe had participated in a series of conferences with the Japanese consular and military officials at Tientsin and Peiping, through which efforts were made to hammer out a concerted economic program. He also conferred with the Chinese authorities, and urged General Sung Che-yuan "to seek Japanese technical and financial assistance in the exploitation of North China's natural resources." [24] The subject was followed up by the army

[23] For more detailed treatment of this key factor in Japan's internal political struggle, see Chapter VII.

[24] North China Star, August 21, 1936.

chiefs. In late September and early October Lieutenant-General Tashiro, commander of the North China Garrison, assisted by his chief-of-staff, held several meetings with General Sung. The result was the so-called Sung-Tashiro agreement, by which General Sung was reported to have agreed in principle to Sino-Japanese "cooperation" on various economic projects in North China. These included construction of a railway from Shihchiachuang to Tsangchow, which, aside from its strategic potentialities, would afford a direct outlet for Shansi's coal through Tientsin; construction of a harbor at Taku; exploitation of the Lungyen iron mines; improvement of air communications in the north; development of radio and telegraph communications; expansion of cotton and wool production in North China; and preference to Japanese capital. The items of this program served the needs both of Japan's light and heavy industries, but were weighted strongly in favor of the latter and of military aims.

Impressive efforts were made to inaugurate this large-scale "exploitation of North China's economic resources." The Hsing Chung Corporation, a subsidiary of the South Manchuria Railway Company, was established with head offices at Tientsin to direct the program of Sino-Japanese economic cooperation. Months passed, however, and the results achieved hardly measured up to expectations. The scarcity of available Japanese investment capital represented a basic limitation on the scope of the Hsing Chung Corporation's activities. By the middle of 1937 the progress actually made could be summed up in a relatively modest list of achievements.[25] The growing Japanese monopoly of the textile industry in Tientsin undoubtedly

[25] For details, see "Sino-Japanese Economic Cooperation in North China", *Information Bulletin*, Council of International Affairs, Nanking, April 1, 1937.

constituted the most significant item. Through direct military pressure the salt output of the Changlu fields, situated in the East Hopei area, had been largely diverted to Japan at prices ruinous to the producers.[26] Chinese shipping interests, operating a line between Tientsin and Dairen, were forced into bankruptcy through Japanese competition and restrictions imposed by the Manchoukuo authorities; in September 1936 the company was reorganized under Japanese ownership and management. The Hui Tung Aviation Corporation, with airlines between Manchuria and North China cities, inaugurated traffic early in 1937. The Tientsin Electric Company, designed to supply light and power and operate the municipal tramways, was organized under Japanese control and ownership in the fall of 1936. Lesser enterprises, affecting the rayon, woollen, match, cement, glass and paper industries, had been projected but had only partially materialized.

It was noteworthy that this list included none of the more important projects which specially engaged the attention of the Japanese military. By the spring of 1937 the growing authority of the National Government was exerting a larger measure of influence over the attitude and policies of the North China officials. This influence was definitely slowing up the rate of progress of Sino-Japanese economic "cooperation" in the north. In March General Sung Che-yuan declared that such cooperation could only be carried out on the basis of reciprocity and equality. He admitted to having exchanged views with the Japanese authorities regarding exploitation of the Lungyen iron mines and construction of the Shihchiachuang Railway, but asserted that no specific plans had been worked out

[26] Export of this salt, which possessed qualities specially adapted to manufacture of explosives and chemical gases, had hitherto been prohibited by the Chinese government.

and positively denied that building of the railway would shortly be started. As to political issues, he stated that it was beyond his power to "discuss such problems, as they should be handled by the diplomatic authorities of the Central Government." [27] Some weeks later General Sung went into retirement at his native town in northern Shantung, from which he did not emerge until the middle of July—a week after the opening hostilities at Lukouchiao.

During the period of Sung's retirement, Japan's army circles were forced to take stock of the new situation which confronted them in China. The National Government was stronger than at any time since the Kwantung Army launched the Manchurian invasion in September 1931. Prospects of civil strife in China had definitely receded into the background. A period of peace would offer the chance to round out the structure of national unity on the foundations already laid. Political unity was undergirded by a strong national consciousness that was gradually permeating the whole Chinese people. The rapid centralization of command at Nanking indicated what these developments would mean to China's military strength. Industrial conditions, foreign trade, and central revenues were rapidly recovering from the low levels of 1934. An ambitious program of railway and highway construction, correlated with the extension of telephone, telegraph and radio communications, was strengthening the material basis of political unification; nowhere was this factor so visible as in China's large and growing network of commercial airlines. To the Japanese military, it was obvious that the growth of a strong and unified China, capable of a real defense of its legitimate interests, could not be allowed to continue. It was no less clear that Japan's policy of piecemeal encroachment in the north, pursued by

[27] China Weekly Review, March 20, 1937, p. 91.

threat and cajolery with a minimum use of military force since the middle of 1933, had reached the limit of its possibilities. They could stand on their existing positions, gained through six years of steady aggression, or they could advance toward a large-scale military operation aimed to annihilate China's central military forces. If a halt were called, the positions already won might soon become untenable and force a retreat. They chose to advance.

CHAPTER SIX

POLITICAL CRISIS IN JAPAN

THE dramatic military uprising at Tokyo on February 26, 1936, turned a corner in Japan's political evolution which has proved to be no less decisive than the changes occurring at that period in China. For up to that time a relatively small clique of army extremists had been the propelling force behind the military-fascist program; and although its members had exerted a determining influence on the course of Japan's foreign policy since September 18, 1931, they had remained on the fringes of control over the machinery of government and the direction of policy at home. The failure of the February coup resulted in the virtual elimination of the direct influence of this army clique and the relegation of its leaders to obscurity. Retirement of these army extremists, however, did not mean that their program of regimentation in the political and economic spheres was discarded. On the contrary, the drive toward an authoritarian régime was taken up by a more conservative army leadership working, not through the methods of assassination and *coup d'état,* but through the increased measure of control at the centers of government power thrown into its hand as a result of the February events. The new army leadership was placed in a far more advantageous position to realize its internal program. Its control over budgetary appropriations for the armed forces became much stronger and more direct—a factor which cemented an alliance with the large and growing industrial interests engaged in the production of war supplies. Its more cautious tactics enabled it to draw closer even to the conservative elements of Japanese business and finance, which had been repelled by the uncontrolled demagogy and direct action of the former clique of army extremists. When it appeared on the political scene, the new army group was faced with only one serious handicap: the Japanese people's disillusionment with the results of the expansionist program in China, its fear of war, and a general anti-militarist sentiment intensified by the February coup. The scenery had shifted, but the political struggle that had begun five years earlier in Japan went on unabated.

This struggle has been carried on within the framework of one of the most complicated governing systems of any modern nation. Perhaps the closest parallel to the Japanese state régime is the pre-war Tsarist autocracy. Japan's pseudo-democratic government apparatus is intertwined with a set of monarchical institutions which still flourish in full vigor. The backbone of the system is provided by the highly developed police organization and the extensive monarchist bureaucracy, which performs the day-to-day tasks of routine administration. This pattern is further complicated by the feudalistic survival of a semi-independent military and naval command.

At the apex of the state pyramid stands the Emperor—demi-god, and as such knitting the whole people together by the religious veneration he commands; constitutional ruler; and wealthy landlord and capitalist. Under normal conditions, the Emperor himself has the greatest stake in the preservation of the constitutional régime, which enables him to exert a considerable measure of direct political influence. There is little room for doubt that military-fascist control would curtail the Emperor's powers and relegate him to a position analogous to that under the Shogunate. For this reason, if for no other, he has tended to throw his support to the moderates during the crises of the internal political struggle in recent years. In evaluating the Emperor's political role, consideration must also be taken of the fact that he is the largest landowner and one of the wealthiest capitalists of Japan. The possessions of the Japanese royal family are even more extensive than those of the British crown. In 1927 the royal domain of Japan consisted of 1,397,656 *cho,* or about 3,800,000 acres of landed property, including tenements, agricultural lands, and forests, the whole being valued at 637,234,000 yen.[1] The Japanese throne also owned buildings, furniture, cattle, and farm implements to the value of nearly 83,000,000 yen in that year. In addition, the Imperial family holds a considerable block of shares of the Bank of Japan, the South Manchuria Railway, the Yokohama Specie Bank, the Formosan Bank, the Nippon Yusen Kaisha, and the Imperial Hotel in Tokyo, amounting to about 300,000,000 yen. Finally, the Emperor enjoys an annual civil list of 4,500,000 yen.[2]

The democratic front of the Japanese state apparatus consists of the Diet and the Cabinet, but equally effective centers of political power lie behind this facade. Many factors combine to reduce the lower house of the Diet to a subordinate position. Among these may be noted the equal powers exercised by the House of Peers, the ordinance power of the Cabinet, and regulations which even affect its control over the budget. In the Cabinet, the authority of the Prime Minister is impaired by the embry-

[1] Since 1927 over 200,000 *cho* of the Imperial estates have been sold or transferred to public or private ownership.

[2] For these figures, see Kenneth W. Colegrove, "The Japanese Emperor", *American Political Science Review,* October 1932, p. 837-838.

onic development of the parliamentary commons and challenged by the virtually independent position of the military and naval branches. The Army and Navy Ministers, by imperial ordinance, cannot be civilians but must be ranking military or naval officers. On occasion, the refusal of army officers to serve in a cabinet has led to its downfall or prevented its formation. The latent threat of such action always exerts a certain degree of pressure on the composition and policies of a cabinet, the strength of this influence depending on political circumstances. The War and Navy Ministers, furthermore, have the right of direct access to the Emperor, without reference to the Prime Minister. This right is also shared by the military and naval chiefs of staff and by members of the Supreme War Council, a body which is in no way subordinate to the War and Navy Ministers. Finally, since the general staffs exercise supreme command over the armed forces, they can initiate or conclude military action without authorization of the government, although such action is normally the result of imperial sanction given to a decision of the cabinet.[3] In addition to the military-naval organs, the position of which conduces to "dual government" and "dual diplomacy", the threads of actual political power in Japan lead to a number of other institutions. Prince Saionji, last of the *Genro* or Elder Statesmen, has wielded virtually dictatorial power over the choice for Prime Minister when a government is overthrown. The Privy Council, a collection of aged conservatives, must be consulted on legislative measures and on the ratification

[3] For a detailed analysis, see Harold S. Quigley, *Japanese Government and Politics*, New York, Century Co., 1932, Chapters 6-11; also Colegrove, "Powers and Functions of the Japanese Diet", *American Political Science Review*, December 1933 and February 1934; "The Japanese Cabinet", *ibid.*, October 1936; "The Japanese Privy Council", *ibid.*, August and November 1931.

of treaties—powers which amount to extensive restrictions on the authority of Cabinet and Diet. Less visible, but no less important, is the influence exerted by the officials of the Imperial Household Ministry through their control over access to the Emperor. In times of crisis, the latter himself has a determining voice.

The intense political struggle that has developed in Japan since 1930 has mainly involved four groups: the capitalists, the landowners, the monarchist-bureaucratic elements, and the military cliques. Of these, the first and last have been the central protagonists. The conflict between these two leading members of Japan's ruling bloc does not at all represent war *à l'outrance*. The basic necessity of preserving their ruling position, particularly against the threat of social revolution, constitutes a strong bond of union. Before the military-fascist movement had acquired momentum, the bourgeois moderates had already proceeded to stamp out revolutionary groups and drive Communism underground. The capitalists, no less than the military, are interested in external aggression and have not been slow to take advantage of its results in China; at the same time they tend to be more cautious than the military, and are unwilling to plunge into a big war for which adequate diplomatic and financial preparation has not been made. On the internal front, they have struggled bitterly against the army's demand for a monopoly of political power and the scrapping of the parliamentary régime. With the emergence of a decisive crisis, however, as of war or revolutionary upheaval, all the ruling groups— including the capitalists—tend to close ranks around the military-fascist program.

Following the world war, which enriched and strengthened the Japanese capitalists, they increasingly pressed their way into the traditional ruling corporation of the clan bureaucrats, who had dominated the state since the Constitution of 1889 from their entrenched positions in the Army and Navy, Cabinet, Privy Council, House of Peers, *Genro,* and the Imperial Household Ministry. Japan's industrial and financial barons had established close connections with the political parties even in the pre-war years. After 1925 the extension of the electorate, which forced Diet members to spend vast electioneering sums, firmly cemented the capitalists' control over the Minseito and Seiyukai parties. The close relation between the Mitsubishi interests and the Minseito is commonly acknowledged; while the Seiyukai, though it continues to represent the landowners, is closely allied with the house of Mitsui. By this time, moreover, the bourgeois interests had penetrated into the House of Peers, the Privy Council, and the Imperial Household Ministry. Above all, the passing of Prince Yamagata, long the dominant *Genro* who worked in the interest of the army, and Prince Matsukata had left Prince Saionji—himself connected with the Sumitomo banking house—the sole surviving Elder Statesman. Through his influence, in the period from 1925 to 1931, six consecutive Cabinets were formed by party Premiers who headed either a Minseito or Seiyukai majority in the lower house of the Diet. It was noteworthy that General Tanaka, who headed a strong militarist Cabinet from 1927 to 1929, achieved the Premiership by virtue of his presidency of the Seiyukai party. The Tanaka interregnum was significant in another sense: it indicated the persistence of the military bid for control of government even during an adverse period. This nearest approach to democracy in Japan at the end of the 'twenties was reached in a time of relative stability, and corresponded to the actual position which the capitalists had achieved in Japanese society.

Various factors combined to narrow the term during which even an approximation of orthodox parliamentary democracy could successfully function in Japan. The concentration of financial, industrial and commercial control in the hands of the leading Japanese capitalists had already reached an advanced stage. Although the landowners still maintained an important position,[4] with an independent role as collectors of tribute from the countryside, the capital squeezed from the peasantry in the form of rent was largely invested in industry and the banks. Japanese industry and trade had not only grown in relative size and importance but had increasingly fused with monopolies of finance capital. A half-dozen of Japan's huge family combines had come to constitute one of the most powerful financial oligarchies of the world. Five years ago the banking houses of Mitsui, Mitsubishi and Sumitomo—comprising the Big Three—already held one-fourth of Japanese finance capital, while the Big Eight held one-half.[5] In the decade of the twenties, Japan's national economy reached the stage of an advanced monopoly capitalism, which, however, was rendered peculiarly unstable by a set of unique drawbacks. The economic structure was top-heavy, and prevented from attaining all-round development by the relative importance of an agriculture with a low level of technique and a chronically impoverished peasantry.[6] Restrictions thus imposed on the size of the domestic market also obstructed the complete growth of a modern large-scale industry. Over wide areas, except for textiles and a few other notable

[4] In 1925 over 50 per cent of the population still depended on agriculture for a livelihood. See John E. Orchard, *Japan's Economic Position*, New York, McGraw Hill, 1930, p. 182.

[5] See "The Control of Industry in Japan", *Problems of the Pacific, 1933*, University of Chicago Press, 1934, p. 255.

[6] For detailed analysis, see Freda Utley, *Japan's Feet of Clay*, London, Faber and Faber, 1936, Chapters IV and V.

exceptions, Japanese industry was characterized by insufficient concentration and inadequate technical modernization.[7]

With the onset of the world depression in 1929, Japan's national economy suffered the same catastrophic reverses that were experienced by all of the highly developed capitalist nations. In the two years 1929-1931 Japan's total foreign trade declined by nearly one-half, while the income from rice and silk—the agricultural staples—declined in the same proportion between 1929 and 1933. The condition of the farming population, already serious in the period before the crisis, deteriorated until a virtual state of famine prevailed in certain districts. Industrial unemployment, which the rural areas could no longer absorb, rose to nearly three millions. Small-scale industrial establishments were squeezed by the large monopolies, as well as by the gradual closing of the smaller banks, and the middle-class intelligentsia either suffered wage cuts or joined the ranks of the unemployed. Widespread social unrest developed among the lower and middle classes. Tenant-farmer and industrial-labor conflicts multiplied, while the middle classes inveighed against monopoly and demanded lower taxes, cheaper credit, and employment. Under conditions such as these, the basic defects and weaknesses of Japan's national economy stood out in bold relief. The domestic market, half of which was constituted by a poverty-stricken peasantry, afforded no possibility of recovery, unless the possessing classes became willing to undertake drastic social reforms that would trench on their own privileged position. Neither the landowners nor the great banking houses could be expected to engage in such a task. They would not take, in point of fact, even the

[7] Orchard, *Japan's Economic Position*, cited, Chapter 11; also Utley, cited, Chapters III, VII.

mildest of steps toward a new deal. At the same time, something had to be done to retrieve the economic situation from disaster and divert the existing discontent into safe channels. The solution—fascism at home and aggression abroad—was hit upon by the military. Its advantages were soon realized by the capitalists, despite certain reservations as to the nature of the internal program and who was to control it.

The growing crisis had found the Minseito government wedded to an economic platform that was quite out of line with the needs of the moment. A return to the gold standard, retrenchment, and deflation—conservative measures adopted at the height of the boom in 1929—enormously aggravated the difficulties of the depression period in 1931. They had been carried through by a government which, more clearly than any that had gone before, expressed the newly won political hegemony of the capitalists. A single-party cabinet, with a large majority in the Diet, was guided by distinguished leaders: Shidehara, Hamaguchi, Inouye, Wakatsuki. Baron Shidehara's policy of Sino-Japanese cooperation, which had reversed the "positive" policy enforced by the previous Seiyukai government under General Tanaka, stood squarely in the path of the military-fascist program. It was grounded on a different premise: that friendly relations with China provided the soundest basis for an expansion of Japan's trade and the solution of its economic difficulties. Even more anathema to the military was the Minseito government's policy of disarmament and reduction of defence expenditures. The effort to achieve the latter by small cuts in the budget led to a minor skirmish with the military-naval leaders; while issues involved in the former, revolving around the London Naval Treaty of 1930, gave rise to a first-class struggle of major proportions. In protest against the signature of this treaty, Admiral Kato, Chief of the Naval Staff, memorialized the Emperor on April 2 and ultimately resigned on June 11. Public opinion and the press, however, were practically unanimous in support of the government's position, and the Privy Council, which had delayed action on the treaty for several months, eventually yielded to this pressure by recommending unconditional ratification on October 1, 1930.

More than the question of cruiser ratios was involved in this struggle. It brought to the fore the basic issue of the Emperor's constitutional prerogatives with regard to the seat of control over the naval and military establishments.[8] Did this reside in the Cabinet, by reason of the Emperor's prerogative over affairs of state, or did it rest with the military-naval leaders, by virtue of the Emperor's prerogative over the supreme command? The issue concerned a fine point of constitutional interpretation. Liberal jurists such as Professor Minobe lined up in favor of the Cabinet, and their opinions were supported on the editorial pages of such progressive newspapers as the Tokyo *Asahi*. If this view were to prevail and become established constitutional practice, the Cabinet's supremacy over the military-naval organs would be unchallenged and "dual government" abolished. The progress being made toward full parliamentary government would have reached its triumphant conclusion. Obviously, the significance of the Minseito government's success in achieving ratification of the London Naval Treaty of 1930 could hardly be overestimated. As it turned out, this victory was the swan song of parliamentary government in Japan. In November Premier Hamaguchi was shot by an assassin; eight months later he died from the wounds. His death was a portent.

[8] See Kenneth W. Colegrove, "Militarism in Japan," New York, World Peace Foundation, 1936, p. 16-27.

Economic conditions and social unrest provided an advantageous field of action for the military; defeat on the naval treaty issue supplied the incentive. Leadership for a military-fascist movement was already at hand. The decade of the twenties, when capitalist elements were establishing themselves more firmly in the organs of government, had witnessed profound changes in the army. With the declining influence of the Choshu clan, formerly dominant in the supreme military command, the social composition of the officer ranks had undergone a marked change. From 1920 to 1927, thirty per cent of the new officers came from families of small landowners, rich farmers, and lower middle classes in urban areas; in later years, this percentage steadily increased.[9] These young officers had observed the crushing effects of monopoly capitalism on the rural and urban middle classes, and had developed a bitter hatred of the parliamentary régime and its capitalist supporters. Their personal interests led them to challenge the positions held in the army by the older conservative clan generals, aside from the fact that many of these had long since made their peace with the capitalists. The older clan generals, however, were already being pushed out by middle-rank officers coming from the poorer and less influential clans, whose social-economic background was not very different from that of the discontented young officers. By 1930 this middle group of officers, including Generals Muto, Araki and Mazaki, began to take over control of the Supreme War Council. The authority and influence of these incoming generals was reinforced by the prestige they bore in the eyes of the young officers, whom they were enabled to utilize as a revolutionary threat to the established order. The "young colonels" Itagaki, Doihara,

[9] See Tanin and Yohan, *Militarism and Fascism in Japan*, New York, International Publishers, 1934, p. 180.

Okamura, Nagata and Ishihara,[10] who all exercised great sway over the young officers, were the underpinning of the Muto-Araki-Mazaki triumvirate. On the surface, at least, these generals had not been compromised by connections with the big concerns, the bureaucrats or the party leaders. Assuming the position of the disinterested soldier, they were enabled to come forward as a force uniting the nation, and so to take the lead in a "national-socialist" reformation. By deflecting the suppressed grievances of the young officers and the general discontent of the lower middle classes into this movement, they sought to strengthen the position of all of Japan's ruling groups, including the capitalists.

To this end, they developed an extensive chauvinist, anti-capitalist and national socialist demagogy.[11] In the political sphere, they excoriated the alliance between the capitalists and the parties, which was corrupting Japan's institutions of government, and called for abolition of the parliamentary system. They demanded that the army should be given political leadership, since it was the sole disinterested force that could be trusted to uphold the dynasty and subordinate conflicting interests to the welfare of the nation as a whole. In the realm of foreign affairs, they asserted that the "weak-kneed" policy of Foreign Minister Shidehara was threatening Japan with disaster; that his conciliatory policy toward China, by encouraging Chinese aggression, was destructive of Japanese prestige in the Far East; and that the ratification of the London Naval Treaty had dangerously weakened Japan's national defense. To correct this situation, national policy required the creation of a powerful colonial empire on the Asiatic mainland, the crushing of the Soviet Union,

[10] These have since advanced to the rank of Lieutenant-General.

[11] Tanin and Yohan, cited, p. 184-203; also for the economic program, *New York Herald Tribune*, April 28, 1932.

and thus the spread of the "kingly way"—*Kodo* or *Wang Tao*—to other countries. On the economic side, they declared that capitalism had to be replaced by state socialism; that is, the government—the army leaders under the Emperor—should assume control of industry and finance, and end the agricultural crisis. Finally, they demanded the merciless eradication of the "Red menace."

For the dissemination of this propaganda, the army extremists possessed at the outset or soon controlled an extraordinary set of facilities.[12] The Ex-Servicemen's Association, with a membership of three million, came under the control of the Muto-Araki-Mazaki triumvirate in 1932. This association, with its allied patriotic societies, had tens of thousands of local posts and branches scattered throughout the country, embracing an active membership estimated at half a million. Through this agency tons of literature were distributed; in recent years, some of the army pamphlets have gone into editions of several hundred thousand copies. In addition, there existed a host of reactionary societies of all shades, with possibly a quarter million of active members, which were all connected in one way or another with the army chiefs. These societies varied greatly in social composition; they also performed many different functions. Some specialized in espionage work abroad under the War Ministry, some were devoted to breaking up strikes or combatting Socialism and Communism, while others were out-and-out terrorist groups. Several of the more conservative and dignified patriotic societies enrolled members from the highest ranks of Japanese society. Only one, the Great Japan Production Party, ever held out the possibility of bridging the gap between

[12] For detailed analysis of the various societies, see Colegrove, *Militarism in Japan*, cited, p. 27-39.

the people and the upper classes, and establishing a Fascist party of mass proportions along more or less orthodox lines. The great numbers of these societies, their heterogeneous composition and aims, and the jealous efforts of the military to preserve a monopoly of political control militated against the rise of a single united mass movement. As an unrivalled propaganda vehicle, and as participants in terrorist outbreaks, the societies exercised their most important role. The position of the Ex-Servicemen's Association as a channel for propaganda was buttressed by the Japanese Youth Association with over two million members, and the Young Women's Association with more than a million members. The Imperial League of Young Officers was significant for its part in directing the attention of the younger officers to a study of the social and economic conditions of the country and to an attack on parliamentary government. Finally the *Kokuhonsha,* or Society of the Foundations of the State, with nearly one hundred thousand members, was the most notable representative of the conservative type of Fascist society. Its membership was drawn from the highest social strata, including landed proprietors, capitalists, government officials, bourgeois intelligentsia, and military and naval officers.[13] During the 1932-1935 period the *Kokuhonsha* groomed its leader Baron Hiranuma, then vice-president of the Privy Council, for a Fascist Premier. In 1930-1931 the society conducted a vigorous agitation against the London Naval Treaty, and became closely associated with the Muto-Araki-Mazaki group. This con-

[13] On its directorate were such men as Seihin Ikeda, manager of the Mitsui interests; Fumio Goto and Keinosuke Ushio, one-time finance and home ministers respectively; Dr. Kisaburo Suzuki, president of the Seiyukai party from 1932 to 1937; Generals Araki and Ugaki; and Admirals Mineo Osumi and Kanji Kato.

nection, given the social composition of the *Kokuhonsha*, was indicative of the real aims of the army extremists despite their anti-capitalist demagogy.

In the summer of 1931 the campaign of the army leaders definitely entered the sphere of political action. Seizing on provocative developments in Manchuria, not unconnected with the activities of the army itself,[14] the general staff openly pressed the Foreign Office to take "positive" action. At this period General Minami, Minister of War, headed an aggressive military clique which was competing with the ultra-aggressive Muto-Araki-Mazaki group for the leading role in the army. The loss of public confidence in the political parties, hastened by the economic depression and army propaganda, was meanwhile sapping the foundations of the Minseito government. Allegiance to the cabinet wavered among influential sections of the capitalists, some of whom began to advocate a reversal of the Minseito's deflationary policy, while others felt the need of a stronger hand to control the developing crisis. These conditions enabled General Minami, acting more or less secretly within the Minseito Cabinet, to prepare for a military coup in Manchuria. Plans were carefully laid, and on September 18, 1931 the military took independent action at Mukden, Changchun and other points in Manchuria. Never was there a clearer example of "dual government" and "dual diplomacy" in Japan. The efforts of Baron Shidehara to limit the scope of military operations proved unavailing, and the Foreign Office was forced into the position of apologist to the world for events in Manchuria which it had not initiated and was powerless to control.

Under cover of the excitement engendered by war con-

[14] For details, see "Japan and Manchoukuo," *Foreign Policy Reports*, June 22, 1932, p. 89-90.

ditions, the military chiefs were able to press forward all along the line with their political program. Extreme Fascist propaganda, fostered by direct and indirect censorship and the rigorous suppression of pacifist views, took the center of the stage. Broad sections of the lower middle classes, the peasantry and the workers, who, only a year previous, had supported the Minseito's fight to ratify the London Naval Treaty, succumbed to the nationalizing process. With popular support rallied behind them, the army cliques intensified their assault on the correspondingly weakened Minseito government. Military conspiracies directly aimed at the seizure of political power occurred in rapid succession. A *coup d'état,* planned by the group surrounding General Minami, was prematurely revealed on October 17, 1931, and failed to materialize; although Colonels Hashimoto and Shigeto were directly implicated, neither suffered more than minor penalty, and the whole affair was hushed up. An even more ambitious effort, in which General Araki's clique took a direct part, was planned for November 3. It involved the *Kokuhonsha,* the Ex-Servicemen's Association, the Imperial League of Young Officers, and Ryohei Uchida's reactionary societies, as well as the Fascist section of the Social Democratic Party led by Katsumaru Akamatsu. The police again discovered the plot; gendarmes were detailed to guard the residences of Premier Wakatsuki, Foreign Minister Shidehara and Count Makino, Lord Keeper of the Privy Seal; and the conspiracy was forestalled. Financial groups, now strongly committed to abandonment of the gold standard, powerfully seconded the attacks of the military. Britain's suspension of gold payments on September 20, by accentuating the difficulties facing Japanese trade and shipping, and intensifying a specie drain that was already severe, had dealt the Minseito government's eco-

nomic program a crippling blow. A clamor for reimposition of the gold ban arose.

The Seiyukai, the opposition party, was in a strong position to capitalize these Minseito difficulties. Not only was
it the more nationalistic of the two parties and, to this
extent at least, more acceptable to the military. It was also
traditionally inflationist, and had criticized the Minseito's
deflationary policy since its inception. The unsavory circumstances attending the resignation of the Minseito government on December 11, and the formation of a Seiyukai
Ministry on December 13, played into the hands of the
military by arousing renewed public antipathy to party
politics. The immediate cause of the Minseito's resignation was an intrigue led by its reactionary Home Minister,
Kenzo Adachi, ostensibly directed at setting up a coalition
ministry composed of the nationalistic wings of the
Seiyukai and Minseito parties. It was widely believed,
however, that Adachi had received a liberal fortune to
accomplish the downfall of the Minseito and thus facilitate a departure from the gold standard.[15] In any case,
the chief benefit derived from the precipitate reimposition
of the gold embargo by the Inukai Ministry, announced
immediately after its appointment, was reaped by Japanese financial interests which had been faced with heavy
losses on dollar-buying speculations so long as Finance
Minister Inouye maintained gold payments. It was charged
that departure from the gold standard netted the Mitsui,
Mitsubishi and Sumitomo interests sums ranging from
thirty to sixty million dollars.[16] Popular condemnation

[15] *New York Herald Tribune*, May 22, 1932; *The Trans-Pacific*, August
4, 1932, p. 14.
[16] It was estimated that some 200 million dollars was held speculatively,
the principal holders being the Mitsui house with 50 millions, Sumitomo
with 20 millions, and Mitsubishi with 10 millions. In these dollar-buying
operations, Mitsui was recouping losses suffered by depreciation of some
50 million yen of sterling holdings in London. *New York Times*, December 14, 1931.

was intensified when it was revealed that the private financiers' gain was the government's loss, since the hurried restoration of the gold ban left the Yokohama Specie Bank with foreign obligations amounting to some 170 million gold yen, which had to be covered by a much larger sum of depreciated yen.[17]

In the War Ministry of the Seiyukai Cabinet, formed by Tsuyoshi Inukai, was placed General Sadao Araki, outstanding leader of the army extremists. Unhampered by any save minor Cabinet restrictions, the military-naval leaders completed the conquest of Manchuria, organized the Manchoukuo government, and carried through 'the attack on Shanghai. Despite these gains, the army extremists were still far from satisfied. Prince Saionji had followed parliamentary procedure in advising the choice of Inukai, who was president of the opposition party, for the post of Prime Minister. In the general election of February 20 the Seiyukai won a sweeping victory. Having just overthrown the Minseito government, the military were again confronted with a single-party cabinet, drawing its chief strength from an unchallenged majority in the lower house of the Diet. The political struggle therefore continued with unabated intensity. Junnosuke Inouye, the ex-Finance Minister, was assassinated on February 9 and Baron Takuma Dan, head of the Mitsui interests, was shot on March 5. These assassinations were carried out by the Blood Brotherhood League, dedicated to the use of terrorism against the "corrupt political parties, slaves of the capitalists." [18]

Late in March the Japanese police discovered that the

[17] *Japan Weekly Chronicle*, December 31, 1931, p. 840; *New York Times*, December 21, 1931.

[18] Colegrove, *Militarism in Japan*, cited, p. 38. The *Ketsumeidan* had been founded in 1930 by Lieutenant-Commander Hitoshi Fujii and one Nissho Inouye, a Buddhist priest of the Nichiren sect who had had a varied career as spy for the South Manchuria Railway and agent of Chinese generals.

Blood Brotherhood League had planned the assassination of a score of prominent political leaders, financiers and industrialists. Even this plot was dwarfed by the affair of May 15, 1932, in which Premier Inukai was assassinated, bombs were hurled at the residence of Count Makino, at the Tokyo police headquarters, the Mitsubishi bank and the offices of the Seiyukai party, and an attempt was made to blow up the metropolitan power stations. These acts were carried out by several terrorist societies, composed mainly of young naval officers, military cadets and peasant youths, including the Blood Brotherhood League, the *Jimmukai*,[19] and the *Aikyojuku*.[20] They were part of a wider conspiracy, involving high army commanders, which aimed to take control of the capital by a military *coup d'état*.[21] Partially forewarned, the government had mobilized the police and placed the defense of the capital and

[19] The *Jimmukai*, or Society of Emperor Jimmu, was a secret terrorist organization of young military and naval officers, founded by Shumei Okawa in 1931. Prominent army figures were connected with it, including Lieutenant-General Kikuchi, a leader of the *Kokuhonsha*. Lieutenant-Colonel Hashimoto acted as head of the *Jimmukai's* military department. See Tanin and Yohan, *Militarism and Fascism in Japan*, cited, p. 225.

[20] The *Aikyojuku*, or School of Love for the Native Soil, was founded in 1930 by Nissho Inouye of the Blood Brotherhood League and Kozaburo Tachibana, head of an agricultural settlement at Mito. Peasant youths studying in Tachibana's school were imbued with the belief that the rural crisis resulted from the actions of the politicians and plutocrats, and that by killing these men they could "reestablish in its original purity the power of the Emperor who would depend upon only the army and people." This society was connected with the higher commanders through Lieutenant-General Kikuchi of the *Kokuhonsha*. Tanin and Yohan, cited, p. 220-222; see also Colegrove, *Militarism in Japan*, cited, p. 36-38.

[21] The police report of the trial stated that the officers were trying "to create a condition for the proclamation of martial law, to open a way for other forces to make a move for the acceleration of a national reform." *The Trans-Pacific*, November 16, 1933. Colegrove brings out the fact that funds used in this affair by the *Jimmukai* and *Aikyojuku*, which passed through Shumei Okawa's hands, came from the South Manchuria Railway directorate. See also Tanin and Yohan, cited, p. 28.

the Emperor's residence in the hands of the chief of police instead of the garrison commander. The May 15th affair, as it came to be known, sounded the death-knell of party government.

Before advising on the choice of a new Premier, Prince Saionji devoted a full week to thorough canvass of the views of the Army, Navy, Diet, Privy Council and Imperial Household officials. The army chiefs refused to support a party Cabinet and demanded the establishment of a "national" government headed by Baron Hiranuma, leader of the *Kokuhonsha*. Dr. Kisaburo Suzuki, who was hurriedly chosen president of the Seiyukai on May 16, was the logical choice for the head of a party government. Prince Saionji elected neither of these alternatives, but secured agreement of the army and parties to the appointment of a compromise candidate—Admiral Saito, former Governor-General of Korea. A super-party coalition Cabinet emerged, with three posts allocated to the Seiyukai, two to the Minseito, two to the military, and six to nonparty men. The outstanding figures were General Sadao Araki, who kept the War Ministry, and the new Finance Minister, Korekiyo Takahashi. In the general compromise the political parties suffered the most decisive loss. The theory of government responsibility to the Diet, which had been reinforced by six successive party administrations, experienced a grave set-back. On the other hand, although the basic demand of the militarists that the government must stand above party allegiance was satisfied, the army extremists failed to set up a Cabinet exclusively dominated by the military. To this extent the compromise represented a victory for the capitalist elements, despite the loss of authority by the parties, especially since the key post of Finance Minister was placed in the capable hands of Takahashi.

The passing of this crisis ushered in a three-year period of comparatively peaceful political evolution. Trials of the various persons implicated in the terrorist affairs attracted much attention, and stirred political passions.[22] The comparatively light sentences meted out to the defendants encouraged further plots, of which the most serious was that by the *Shimpeitai,* or Soldiers of God, in July 1933; this and others, however, were successfully forestalled by the police. Toward the end of this year General Araki's prestige gradually waned; although his views prevailed in connection with the advance into North China, he had relatively little success in affecting the course of domestic policy. The Manchoukuo régime, at first headed by General Muto, Araki's close collaborator, and after the former's death by men sympathetic with extremist aims, carried the state socialist ideology to its clearest practical expression, and wrung capital from Japan for an economic program devoted to military-strategic aims. Thorough-going supporters of the military-fascist program were to be found only among a small minority of the big concerns. In January 1934 Araki resigned from the War Ministry, and was replaced by General Senjuro Hayashi.

Six months later the Saito Cabinet was forced out of office by the Teikoku Rayon scandal, in which its Minister of Communications was involved. The succeeding Cabinet, under Admiral Okada, was formed on the basis of a super-party coalition similar to that of its predecessor. Its stability testified to the gradual reassertion of authority by a new group of moderate statesmen—a phenomenon which had become clearly marked by the end of 1935. At no point were the army extremists enabled to break through the wall that was again rising up before

[22] For course of the trials, see *Foreign Policy Reports,* February 13, 1935, p. 323-324.

them. Despite all efforts by the military, the inner group of Imperial advisers continued to be dominated by the moderates. Of these, Prince Saionji was still the most influential; in the Imperial Household Ministry, also, Count Makino, as Lord Privy Seal, and Admiral Suzuki, the Lord Chamberlain, were both moderates. A difficult situation had arisen when the presidency of the Privy Council fell vacant in the summer of 1934. The vice-president, who, according to precedent, should have been appointed to the post, was Baron Hiranuma, head of the *Kokuhonsha*. Hiranuma was passed over, and the post was given to Baron Kitokuro Ikki, a moderate. Despite the furore over the "Minobe affair",[23] which was an oblique attack on Baron Ikki, who held the same liberal views as to the Emperor's constitutional status, the latter had maintained his position as president of the Privy Council throughout 1935. Count Makino finally resigned as Lord Privy Seal, but his successor—Viscount Saito, the former Premier— was hardly less objectionable to the extremists. Despite the steady attacks to which Admiral Suzuki was subjected, he too retained his office as Lord Chamberlain. Every post in the circle of inner advisers surrounding the Emperor was sealed tight against encroachment from the military.

The same struggle went on in the Cabinet, with not dissimilar results. Budgetary expenditures on Japan's armed forces mounted rapidly during these years. From 442.8

[23] Professor Minobe has already been noted as a champion of the liberal interpretation of the Emperor's prerogative in connection with the struggle over ratification of the London Naval Treaty in 1930. He was one of the foremost constitutional jurists of Japan, his text-books were required study material in the great universities, and he had been appointed to the House of Peers. In 1933-1935 the extremists bitterly attacked the basic theory underlying his writings—that the Emperor was an organ of the state, and not the state itself. Attempts were made on his life; his textbooks were eventually withdrawn; and Premier Okada was forced to issue a statement clarifying Japan's "national polity" in the sense required by the extremists.

million yen, or 28 per cent of the total, in the fiscal year 1930-1931, appropriations for the military and naval establishments advanced to 937.3 millions, or 43.7 per cent of the total, in the 1934-1935 year. Each autumn, however, Finance Minister Takahashi pared down the lavish army-navy estimates; the increases actually allotted were sufficient to cover the necessities arising out of the conquest of Manchuria, which Japanese capitalists unreservedly supported, but not sufficient to unduly hasten preparations for a large-scale conflict, say, with the U.S.S.R. Foreign Minister Hirota finally succeeded in arranging an agreement on March 23, 1935 for purchase of the Chinese Eastern Railway from the Soviet Union, although at one time the military seemed bent on taking it over by force. General Araki's demands for greater arms expenditures conflicted with his demagogic pleas for vast subsidies to relieve the farmers. In this matter, as well as the issue of higher taxes on the big concerns, Finance Minister Takahashi had listened to Araki's extravagant proposals but quietly shelved their practical application. In the summer of 1935 General Hayashi, after more than a year in the War Ministry, undertook a general transfer of extremist army officers from key posts. The purge started at the top with General Mazaki, Inspector-General of Military Education and, since General Muto's death, the closest associate of Araki. The assassination on August 12, 1935 of Lieutenant-General Nagata, the official directly charged with the task of carrying out shifts in army personnel, constituted a vigorous return thrust by the army extremists. General Hayashi resigned from the War Office; he was replaced by General Kawashima, who put a stop to the purge. The struggle was then transferred to North China where Major-General Doihara, one of the original "young colonels" of the extremist movement, staged the five-province autonomy movement in November-December 1935. Foreign Minister Hirota, during the preliminary conferences with the War and Navy Offices,[24] had been forced into grudging assent to the scheme. He had adroitly managed to bring it to a halt, as soon as the moderates became worried by the growing opposition from China and the Western powers.

While the capitalist interests had kept their grip on the advisory posts to the Emperor and had largely reasserted their dominance in the Cabinet, one difficulty still remained. The Seiyukai, the more extremist of the two major parties, controlled a majority in the lower house of the Diet. When the Okada Cabinet was formed on July 7, 1934, the first steps toward a change in this state of affairs had been taken. As in the previous Saito Cabinet, three ministries were allotted to the Seiyukai and two to the Minseito. From the Seiyukai, however, Admiral Okada had chosen Mr. Takejiro Tokonami and two of his followers, all of whom were members of a clique opposed to Dr. Suzuki, president of the party. This action tended to discredit Dr. Suzuki, who was one of the founders of the *Kokuhonsha* and supposedly had pro-army leanings. It also contributed to the disruption of the Seiyukai, which proceeded to expel all members who supported Mr. Tokonami. Finally, since Home Minister Fumio Goto, one of the bureaucrats appointed to the Cabinet, had Minseito leanings, the Okada government was obviously establishing its parliamentary support on a Minseito basis, plus the followers of Mr. Tokonami. If necessary, it was apparently prepared to go through with an election in order to wipe out the Seiyukai majority. This became even clearer when Mr. Tokonami and his adherents organized a new third party, called the Showakai. Since the Seiyukai had proved

[24] See Chapters II and III.

tractable, the Okada government had permitted the Diet, which had been elected in February 1932, to live out its full four-year term. An election, therefore, fell due in February 1936, in accordance with statutory requirement.

Following reassembly on January 21, after the usual winter recess, the Diet was dissolved as soon as the Premier and Finance Minister had finished reading their declarations on administrative policy. The step was forced by the Seiyukai, which sought a vote of non-confidence in order to use the Diet as a sounding-board for announcement of its campaign stand. An interesting reflection of the actual political status, prior to the election, is supplied by editorial comment of a leading bourgeois journal to the effect that "Japan today is in a peculiar condition with respect of business and industry being immune from any high degree of political unsettlement. This is entirely due to the general assumption that, no matter who is entrusted with the steering of the ship of state, he will have to follow the policy of Finance Minister Korekiyo Takahashi, insofar as that concerns economic and financial affairs." [25] In the election which followed the Seiyukai was roundly defeated, as shown in the table.

Results of the General Election, February 20, 1936

Parties	At Dissolution	Elected	Change
Minseito	127	205	+78
Showakai	25	20	— 5
Seiyukai	242	174	—68
Kokumin Domei	20	15	— 5
Shakai Taishuto	3	18	+15
Local Proletarians	0	3	+ 3
Independents	10	31	+21
Vacancies	39	0	—39
Total	466	466	0

[25] *The Oriental Economist*, Tokyo, February 1936, p. 70.

Virtually every feature of these returns witnessed to the running of a strong anti-Fascist tide in the electorate. The seats lost by the Seiyukai affected several of its party leaders, including Dr. Suzuki, who failed of reelection. The *Kokumin Domei,* or Nationalist League, a right-wing party organized by the Kenzo Adachi who had wrecked the last Minseito government, lost five seats. An unusually large number of right-wing candidates stood for election; most of them suffered disastrous defeats. On the other hand, aside from the Minseito successes, the *Shakai Taishuto,* or Social Mass Party, gained fifteen new seats, while three additional proletarian candidates were elected in Tokyo. Labor representatives polled nearly 700,000 votes, as against 268,000 in February 1932. Most of the independents were liberals rather than reactionaries, including the veteran liberal Yukio Ozaki; while in the great majority of cases the heaviest votes cast were polled by the Shakai Taishuto, the Tokyo proletarians, and the independents. The Minseito, combined with the Showakai, the labor members, and the liberal independents, commanded an absolute majority in the lower house of the new Diet. The policies of the Okada Cabinet were thus vindicated; if a new Cabinet were to be formed, it would probably witness an increase of party influence. To their strongholds at court and their growing control in the Cabinet, the moderates had now added the Diet, thus closing the last parliamentary door to the army extremists. Unless the military were willing to admit defeat, they were forced to take direct steps either through independent action in the field or a frontal attack at home. The latter course was chosen. Its results are detailed in the following official version of the February 26th incident, issued on March 4 by the martial law headquarters:

"Early on the morning of February 26, officers and men

of the 3rd Infantry Regiment of the Imperial Guards Division and the 1st and 3rd Infantry Regiments and the 7th Field Artillery Regiment, numbering about 1,400, left their barracks without authorization and in violation of military discipline. In the insurrection that followed they attacked the official residence of Premier Keisuke Okada; the private residence of Viscount Makoto Saito, Lord Keeper of the Privy Seal; the private residence of General Jotaro Watanabe, Inspector-General of Military Education; the quarters of Count Nobuaki Makino, the Itoya at Yugiwara; the official residence of General Kantaro Suzuki, Chief Aide-de-Camp to His Majesty; and the private residence of Finance Minister Korekiyo Takahashi. They killed Viscount Saito and General Watanabe and seriously wounded Chief Aid-de-Camp Suzuki and Finance Minister Takahashi. They then took up positions in the neighborhood of Nagata-cho, Kojimachi Ward, Tokyo, and cut off all traffic, within and without. Their aim, according to their declaration, was to exterminate at this moment of great crisis at home and abroad the arch-traitors who were destroying the national polity, such as the Genro, statesmen close to the Throne, financial magnates, military cliques, bureaucrats, and members of political parties.

"Upon the outbreak of the incident, the garrison commander directed the units in the city to maintain order. At 3 o'clock in the afternoon, wartime garrisoning under the jurisdiction of the 1st Division was ordered. Units from Kofu, Sakura, Mito, Takasaki and Utsonomiya were meanwhile called to Tokyo, and on their arrival the same night they placed themselves under the direction of the garrison commander. The next day, on February 27, it was decided to apply part of the martial law ordinance to the City of Tokyo. Martial law headquarters were set up. Lieutenant-General Kohei Kashii, commander of the Tokyo Garrison, was appointed commandant of the martial law area and ordered to have his forces restore peace and order in the capital. It was feared that the taking of forcible measures to suppress the insurgents would result in bloodshed. Had an unfortunate situation arisen in which an exchange of shots would have been unavoidable, unfathomable damage would have been caused and evil effects produced on the public mind, for the locality involved was in the neighborhood of the Imperial Palace, the mansions of Imperial Princes, various Government offices, foreign diplomatic establishments and many private residences. To avoid this, the insurgents were surrounded and placed under heavy guard.

"For three days, their superior officers and colleagues endeavored to the best of their ability to persuade the insurgents to return to their barracks quietly, but they refused to listen. At last, on February 28, in view of their disobedience to the Imperial commands, the martial law headquarters were compelled to decide on forcible means to liquidate the situation. That night, re-enforcements were summoned from Utsunomiya, Matsumoto, Mito, Sendai and Wakamatsu. Upon arrival in Tokyo, they were placed under the direction of the martial law commandant. On the morning of February 29, residents in the neighborhood of Nagatacho, Kojimachi Ward, were ordered to refuge. All traffic in the city was suspended, and other preparations were made for forcible settlement of the issue. At the same time, airplanes and tanks were sent out to distribute handbills among the insurgents in order to give them a last chance to surrender. As a result, non-commissioned officers and men gradually laid down their arms in groups, and by afternoon almost all had given themselves up. They were disarmed and sent back to their

barracks for confinement. Of the ringleaders of the insurrection, Shiro Nonaka disposed of himself, and the majority of the others were confined in military prisons.
Thus, without any exchange of fire, the insurgents were
quelled." [26]

What in this statement is described as the aim of the
insurgents constituted, in reality, their method. Their
objective was nothing short of a full-fledged military dictatorship, which they hoped to establish after physical
extermination of the moderate leaders of the government
and court. During the first day or two of the rebellion,
it seemed not unlikely that the ruling groups would be
constrained to accept this result. Many high officers of
the army, including War Minister Kawashima, tacitly
supported the revolt; army extremists, such as Generals
Araki and Mazaki, openly came forward as mediators
between the rebels and the court. Prince Chichibu, hurriedly summoned to Tokyo from his division at Hirosaki
in the north, was thought to be *persona grata* with the
extremists. The moderate leaders were either dead, scattered or in hiding. On the other hand, the rebellion failed
to awaken a popular response, hardly surprising in view
of the clear expression of public opinion in the election
of six days before. The army extremists, moreover, hesitated to take the dangerous step of calling out other
military units to assist the rebels; in the face of this hesitation, many officers who sympathized with the aims of
the uprising were impelled to protest against its methods.
Thus the army was disunited, while the navy was definitely hostile. After a period of confusion and perplexity,
the court circles realized these facts; they then mobilized
the navy, called in safe detachments of the army, and
forced the rebels to surrender.

[26] *The Oriental Economist,* March 1936, p. 136.

The initiative now passed momentarily to the moderates. Their losses had been severe, particularly in respect of Takahashi, who succumbed to his wounds on February 26, and of Viscount Saito. For a time Premier Okada was also thought to have been killed; not until February 29 was it disclosed that his brother-in-law, Colonel Denzo Matsuo, who resembled him, had been mistakenly killed in his stead. Following Admiral Okada's reappearance, Prince Saionji and Count Makino were called into consultation by the Emperor. The opportunity to form a new Cabinet was offered on March 4 to Prince Konoye, who declined on the plea of ill-health and lack of ability to cope with the crisis. Koki Hirota, former Foreign Minister, then assumed the task. His first choices, announced on March 6, included a set of liberal Ministers, who, if they had been confirmed, would have constituted a Cabinet not dissimilar to that under Admiral Okada. This result was immediately forestalled by army pressure.

After their initial set-back, the army leaders had quickly reorganized their lines and rallied for a counter-attack. On March 7 the seven ranking generals on the Supreme War Council resigned *en bloc*. Four of these generals, comprising Araki, Mazaki, Hayashi and Abe, withdrew from active service. The remaining three were appointed to executive posts: Terauchi to the War Ministry, Uyeda to the proconsulship in Manchoukuo, and Nishi to the Inspectorate-General of Military Education. Having carried through this voluntary purge, the army command held a vantage point from which it could exert renewed pressure on the moderates. General Terauchi's refusal to assume the War Ministry wrecked the Cabinet line-up first proposed by Hirota. In particular, the army opposed appointment of Shigeru Yoshida, son-in-law of Count Makino, as Foreign Minister; of Naoshi Ohara, who in the previous Cabinet had insisted on prosecuting the assassins of Premier Inukai, as Minister of Justice; and of Dr. Hiroshi Shimomura, editor of the then liberal Tokyo *Asahi,* as Overseas Minister. After three days of negotiation with the army leaders, Hirota dropped all three of these appointees. General Terauchi also refused to allow Mr. Kawasaki, a Minseito party man, to occupy the Home Ministry, which was finally awarded to Keinosuke Ushio, a non-party bureaucrat and member of the *Kokuhonsha.* Instead of five party members as before, the new Cabinet contained only four—two from each party, and these in minor posts. Important changes also occurred among the inner circle of the Emperor's advisers. Baron Ikki resigned as president of the Privy Council; he was succeeded by Baron Hiranuma, founder of the *Kokuhonsha*—a decided advance by the extremists. In the Imperial Household Ministry, however, the moderates retained control through the appointment of Kurahei Yuasa as Lord Privy Seal, in place of the murdered Viscount Saito, and of Tsuneo Matsudaira as Minister of the Imperial Household.

This counter-offensive by the military was carried out in the midst of a number of contradictory political crosscurrents. The revolt led to a temporary eclipse of the movement that had been led by the army extremists, as typified by Generals Araki and Mazaki. The latter was kept under unofficial detention for more than a year after the February events; not until October 1937 was Mazaki officially cleared of complicity in the rebellion. The minor officers who openly led the revolting soldiers, however, were executed—a sharp contrast to the leniency displayed toward offenders in the earlier terrorist outbreaks. Popular reaction was no less pronounced. Whereas, in previous cases, there was general sympathy for the "patriotic" motives of the terrorists, in this case public condemnation was virtually unanimous. An outgrowth of this sentiment was the marked alienation between the army and the people which soon developed. On the other hand, the revamping of the Hirota Cabinet was passively accepted, both by the public and the ruling elements. The leaders of the political parties, forgetting their election pledges, played for peace at any price and offered no resistance to General Terauchi's demands. Even the Social Mass Party avoided an appeal to the people; instead, through its general secretary, Hisashi Aso, it declared that it abstained from "hasty commentary." The court circles and the capitalists, content with suppression of the rebellion, sought to defend their own narrow interests and shunned a head-on collision with the army, chief pillar of the régime.

Under these circumstances, and despite popular antipathy, the part played by the military in the Cabinet became far more influential than at any time in the previous five years. Under the cautious and conservative leadership of General Terauchi, with far greater unified support from the army as a whole, the military-fascist movement now proceeded to work for its objectives from the top. Terrorism was eschewed and its exponents curbed, except as a latent threat held over the heads of the moderates to force acceptance of demands presented in the Cabinet. Aside from revising the ministerial personnel, General Terauchi had exacted a number of pledges from Hirota in the course of the negotiations leading to formation of the new government. These pledges were along four major lines: vastly larger appropriations for the military-naval establishments, to be financed by heavier taxation; definite steps toward a controlled economy, beginning with nationalization of certain selected enterprises; a revision of the parliamentary structure; and a "positive" foreign policy. The full outlines of this program did not become apparent until toward the close of Hirota's term of office. Nevertheless, its implications were immediately grasped by the capitalists, as indicated by the mingled note of hope and dread in the following editorial comment: "While it is true that Mr. Hirota made a certain revision of his Cabinet program on the advice of General Terauchi, to brand the General's action as military meddling shows lack of a correct conception of the circumstances. It would be rash to conclude that this conceded fact presages the Hirota government's taking orders from the Army so as to become its puppet and adopt fascistic economic measures. To be sure, some among the army officers entertain varied ideas, and it would not be surprising if a few are sympathetic with views akin to the fascist ideal. But this is not true of the larger section of the Army. Even those who advocate fascist principles have no concrete plans prepared in such a form to suit the practical needs of this country, for ready application. Viewed from the angle of Japan's social structure, entirely dissimilar from Italy's, whether better or worse, conditions are lacking to make a similar evolution possible. Even granted that the Army lorded it over the Cabinet, it is entirely unthinkable that social and economic changes of any magnitude might occur. Moreover, neither is the Army equal to such a task, nor has it the intention to undertake it." [27]

The reaction in Japanese business circles to the statement issued on March 9, the day the government assumed office, by the new Finance Minister, Eiichi Baba, belied these optimistic views. The first sentence of this statement read as follows: "Our Government finances are in such a state that not only are curtailments probably impossible,

[27] *The Oriental Economist*, April 1936, p. 213.

but one must be prepared for increased expenditure, as the country stands in need of pushing its Manchurian policy, amplifying the national defense, effecting the economic regeneration of agrarian and fishing communities, and enforcing other important State policies so as to build up national strength and reserve resources." From this starting-point, the Finance Minister went on to advocate the need for continued heavy borrowings, fundamental reforms in the system of taxation so as to increase revenues and distribute burdens more fairly, and cheap money to facilitate industrial prosperity and bond financing.[28] Here, at last, was a Finance Minister who understood the army's requirements.

Its effect on business proved unsettling. The journal quoted above observed that "the Baba announcement was received as though it were a bombshell in the financial community. After an extended closure, from February 26 to March 9, stock exchanges reopened throughout the country on March 10, the day after the formation of the new Cabinet, and a stampede developed. The Baba statement was held directly responsible. There were some rallies during the next two days, but on the 13th shares again slumped violently, conditions for a time verging on panic. This unsettlement lasted only a short while, and towards the end of the month a seeming composure returned to the market, although below the surface there still lurked some feeling of nervousness and uncertainty, stock prices being held down at low levels. . . . Share vulnerability, however, was not by any means solely due to the Finance Minister's statement. The market was stirred and agitated also by a rumor that the new government had made up its mind to exert control of a fascist

[28] For full text of the statement, see *The Oriental Economist*, April 1936, p. 212.

type over many industries. In particular, rumor said, electric power, coal mining, sugar and fertilizer industries might be nationalized. . . . One prominent feature of the Baba statement which proved a particularly discouraging financial factor was the reference to the forthcoming boosting of taxation. And what aggravated the situation was the circulation of the rumor that the Finance Department had up its sleeve a program of drastic tax increase, so as to make good its chief's announcement." [29] These, however, were merely the first difficulties which the financial community was to have with the Cabinet's new outlook; the later issues came to a head with the Baba budget and the proposal to nationalize the electric power industry.

During the early months of the Hirota government, General Terauchi made extraordinary efforts to counteract the hostile popular sentiment toward the army. In his speech to the prefectural governors at Tokyo on March 26, he had specifically deplored the loss of "social support" suffered by the army as an aftermath of the February uprising. Serious steps were taken to rectify this situation. The young officers involved in the revolt were court-martialled and shot. Four ranking generals on the Supreme War Council were retired, and three shifted to new posts. These personnel shifts, ordered immediately after suppression of the uprising, were the first of many that took place throughout the spring. Generals Minami, Kawashima, and Honjo were also retired, as well as four Lieutenant-Generals and five Major-Generals, bringing the total retirements in the top ranks to sixteen. In March wholesale shifts and a number of retirements were enforced among the lower-rank officers. Terauchi utilized this purge to concentrate control in his own hands, as

[20] *The Oriental Economist*, April 1936, p. 212-213.

well as to strengthen army unity. He removed not only those who supported the rebels, but officers who had connections with the court circle. He also succeeded in revoking the ordinance which had permitted generals on the reserve list to become Minister of War, and this at a time when the number of generals in active service had become very limited. The army was thus regrouped and to a certain extent consolidated.

These measures somewhat relieved the apprehension of the bourgeois moderates but they awoke no popular response, despite the wide publicity which attended the purge and the "restoration of discipline" in the army. Mainly for this reason, martial law was prolonged for nearly six months until the middle of July. Under its provisions, the press was rigidly controlled and opposition voices silenced. Government authorities, both local and national, strenuously attempted to change the humor of the masses. Labor demonstrations on May 1 were banned. These efforts were aided in some cases by leaders of the political parties. Further steps in this direction were taken during the extraordinary Diet session which convened on May 4, 1936. Departing from his customary formally prescribed speech, the Emperor included in the opening address the following words: "We regret the outbreak of the recent incident in Tokyo. It is expected of Our faithful subjects that they will unite as one, government and people, civilians and military, to promote the development of national prosperity." This unprecedented Imperial intervention was a rebuke to the army, but it served at the same time to soften the popular resentment against the military. General Terauchi reinforced this effect by roundly declaring that soldiers should place limits on their interest in politics.

Nevertheless, several reactionary bills were introduced under army pressure in this session of the Diet. A law was passed for the protection and surveillance of persons charged with "dangerous thoughts" after their release from prison; this measure strengthened the notorious Peace Preservation Law of 1925, which had made it a crime to organize associations designed to alter Japan's national polity or repudiate "the system of private ownership of property." The army then sought to pass a Mobilization Secrets Bill and a Seditious Literature Bill, both of which could have been utilized to stifle freedom of speech and the press. These bills met with intense opposition. The first was eventually abandoned while the second was passed, with amendments which weakened its force and made it apply solely to emergency situations, only after the Diet session had been prolonged for two days. The opposition to these bills, both within the Diet and from the general public, reflected a dissatisfaction with the Hirota government which steadily increased. It also witnessed to General Terauchi's failure to moderate popular suspicion of the army's motives and activities.

Although the government came under severe fire at this session, notably in a fiery speech by Mr. Takao Saito, a Minseito member of the Diet, excoriating army activities and defending parliamentarism,[30] it did not give way its hand. The session had been summoned mainly to pass a working budget, but since the government limited itself to minor revisions of the last budget framed by Mr. Takahashi, the new principles of Finance Minister Baba were not yet applied. On the other major issues of parliamentary "reform" and foreign policy, the Cabinet restricted

[30] For summary of this speech, see *The Trans-Pacific*, May 14, 1936, p. 10-11.

itself to safe generalities. All these questions assumed great prominence during the autumn months.

Premier Hirota's speeches had from the beginning stressed the need for "renovations" and "reforms" in the administrative structure. These euphemisms were understood on all sides to stand for modifications of parliamentary government in the direction of suppression of party influence and increase of army control. At the special May session of the Diet, attacks were already made on certain rumored proposals of this nature. The army, it was said, would push for the establishment of a Minister without Portfolio, in whose hands would be concentrated problems of state reorganization and wartime economics. Then it was declared that the army would demand the fusion of certain Ministries, especially those under party control, with a view to reducing the total number to five or six.[31] It was also believed that a new Ministry of Aviation would be established. All these proposals, however, remained in the field of conjecture and rumor until the autumn. Meanwhile two policy commissions, aside from a previously organized Parliamentary System Investigation Commission which contained Diet members, had been set up within the Cabinet. Toward the end of October the press reported a set of reform proposals which was said to be receiving strong backing from the army authorities. This scheme, as reported, provided for the organization of an inner Cabinet to be composed of only a few Ministers; separation of the legislative and executive powers in such a way as to deny a political party the right to organize a government; annulment of the Diet's right to impeach a government by vote of non-confidence; abolition of universal suffrage by enfranchising only the head of a family or a person

[31] *The Japan Advertiser*, September 30, 1936.

who had served in the army; and functional instead of territorial representation.[32]

Publication of these proposals raised a storm of protest. General Terauchi, on November 6, and Premier Hirota, on November 16, both made statements tending to allay suspicion, but only succeeded in intensifying the unrest. The Parliamentary System Investigation Commission finally demanded an explanation from the War Minister. General Terauchi at first rejected the demand but eventually, following Premier Hirota's intervention, agreed to attend an informal meeting of the Commission. At this meeting, on December 2, General Terauchi denied the authenticity of the news reports and indicated that an individual in the military affairs bureau of the War Department, from whom the reports had emanated, had been properly punished for his imprudent conduct. He then stated: ". . . some are engaged in spreading the rumor that the Army is bent upon a revision of the Constitution or the abolition of the Diet, which is, of course, absolutely without foundation. The Army is opposed to the operation of the parliamentary institution along democratic ideas of the Western type. It is hoped that the Diet and the Election Laws will be so amended that fair popular opinion and national intellectual faculties shall be given full opportunity for their demonstration. It is keenly desired that a constitutional government based on a Constitution which is all our own be allowed to develop." [33] The Hirota Cabinet's efforts to secure parliamentary reform ended at this point, with an aroused public opposition in full cry and the War Minister covering his retreat.

[32] *The Japan Advertiser*, October 30, 1936; also *The Oriental Economist*, December 1936, p. 750.

[33] For full text, see *The Oriental Economist*, December 1936, p. 751; also *The Trans-Pacific*, December 3, 1936, p. 25-26.

Premier Hirota's "positive" foreign policy had also reached an *impasse* by the middle of December. The prolonged Sino-Japanese negotiations, initiated at Nanking by Ambassador Kawagoe three months earlier, had produced no tangible results.[34] Failure of the China negotiations coincided with equally serious diplomatic complications which had arisen over the German-Japanese anti-Communist pact, concluded on November 25, 1936. Abroad, especially in Great Britain and the United States, the pact met with an exceedingly unfavorable reaction. Apprehension over its possible effects was also felt by the Japanese public. These feelings became even more pronounced when the U.S.S.R. refused to ratify the Soviet-Japanese fisheries agreement, which had just been brought to final form after lengthy negotiations. The "clumsiness" of the Foreign Minister's diplomacy was brought under review by the Privy Council on December 10, when Mr. Arita was quizzed by members of this body. As to China, he told the Privy Councillors that the negotiations had reached a deadlock but had not actually broken down; by mentioning the Suiyuan invasion, he indirectly suggested that the army was responsible for the lack of diplomatic results at Nanking. He admitted that efforts to explain Japan's position on the anti-Communist pact to Great Britain were "being made under unfavorable conditions." In the matter of the Soviet Union, he promised to consult further with the Privy Council if it proved impossible to sign the fisheries agreement before the year was out.[35] The results finally attained by Mr. Arita on these questions were meager enough. On December 29 the Soviet Union agreed to extend the old

<hr>

[34] See Chapters III and IV.

[35] For a summary of this examination of the Foreign Minister, see *The Trans-Pacific*, December 17, 1936, p. 14.

fisheries agreement, which was much less favorable than the new instrument, for one year; while at Nanking the best that could be secured was the settlement, effected on December 30, of the Chengtu and Pakhoi incidents, with no political concessions attached.

The practical application of Finance Minister Baba's new program had meanwhile created equally burning issues in the economic sphere. In July Premier Hirota had decided that budgetary considerations should rank second to the formulation of important national policies,

Takahashi vs. Baba Budgets
(in millions of yen)

	Takahashi		May 1936	Baba		
	1935-36	1936-37	1936-37	1937-38	Gains	Per Cent
Ordinary revenue	1,443	1,598	1,608	2,234	626	38.9
Loans	772	680	704	806	102	14.5
Total revenue	2,215	2,278	2,312	3,041	729	31.5
Administrative expenses	1,155	1,218	1,252	1,632	380	30.4
Army	493	508	508	728	220	43.3
Navy	530	552	552	681	130	23.6
(Army and Navy	1,023	1,060	1,060	1,409	349	32.9)
Total expenses	2,215	2,278	2,312	3,041	729	31.5

which should be threshed out in the Cabinet. The various Ministries immediately drew up a long list of expensive projects, all of which were professed to be supremely advantageous to the national welfare. Of these, the army-navy replenishment programs and the proposal to nationalize the electric power industry attracted the most attention. The latter scheme, which had been drafted under army influence, was vigorously attacked by the private interests affected and after months of acrimonious controversy was temporarily shelved. Hostilities on the economic front became more general when the full terms of the Baba budget, approved by the Cabinet on November 27, were announced. The accompanying table shows the comparative figures of the last two Takahashi budgets, the working budget adopted in May 1936 which slightly increased Takahashi's estimates for 1936-1937, and the Baba budget.

The last budget prepared by Mr. Takahashi, that for 1936-37, levied no additional taxes. Allowing merely for the natural increase in revenue, it covered a 63 million yen net increase in expenditures by a 154 million net increase of revenues, thus permitting a reduction of 91 millions in borrowings. The increases in the army and navy expenditures were held down to 15 million and 22 million yen respectively, or a total of only 37 millions. This conservative policy contrasted sharply with the Baba budget, which was unprecedented both in total and in respect to the army-navy estimates. The fact that army-navy expenditures swallowed most of the total increase is masked by the apparent large increase in general administrative expenditure. This sum, however, was swelled by a 220 million yen subsidy which the national treasury, as an element in Baba's tax reform plan, was to extend to the local and prefectural governments in order to permit of a corresponding reduction in their tax burden. Omitting this amount, the actual increase in general administrative expenditure was only 160 million yen, or 12.8 per cent, while the increase in national defense expenditure was 349 millions, or 32.9 per cent.

Along with this budget went a fundamental revision of the Japanese taxation system, the details of which were made public on September 22.[36] The main object of the change was to effect a large total increase in the annual revenue derived from taxation, thus reversing one of Takahashi's cardinal policies. Other purposes were also

[36] For details, see *The Oriental Economist,* November 1936, p. 690-692.

served, of which one—long advocated by the army—was to relieve the agrarian community. To this end the land taxes were not increased, while prefectural and local taxes were to be reduced by some 220 million yen the first year and 289 millions thereafter. The resulting deficit in local government finances was to be made good by Treasury disbursements. This amount, as well as the higher army-navy expenditure, had therefore to be met by a wholesale boosting of nearly all tax rates. These increases bore directly on the industrial and financial communities in a number of ways. The rates on corporation and individual income, on inheritance, on stock and produce exchanges, and on business profits were raised; while new levies were imposed on movable property, on the transfer of stocks and bonds, on gasoline, and on corporation capital and reserves. In view of the prosperity for the monopoly concerns which attended the current munitions and trade boom, as well as the large profits derived from underwriting the government loans, these measures did not appear objectionable. On the other hand, the heavy additional burdens, both direct and indirect, imposed by the Baba tax reforms on the mass of the people hardly bore out the Hirota Cabinet's professed policy of the "stabilization of the national livelihood." The already low exemption limit of 1,200 yen for income tax was reduced to 1,000 yen. In addition, a national sales tax was introduced, while the excise duties on sugar, wheat-gluten, textiles, silk and woollen hosiery, felt manufactures and liquor were increased, tobacco sales prices were marked up by the government monopoly, and postal stamps and charges were raised.

This large advance in the direct and indirect levies on mass consumption was additionally increased by an extensive tariff readjustment, in which 964 out of a total of 1,610 items were affected. Rates were raised on 692 items; 62 duty-free items were placed on the dutiable list; and 210 were revised downward.[37] In view of the fact that the benefits of the much-touted reduction of 220 million yen in local taxes were mainly derived by the middle and upper agrarian strata, it would seem that the masses of the Japanese people were paying far more than their proportionate share of the increased army-navy expenditure. Especially was this true since the economic position of workers and farmers, unlike that of the merchant-industrial-banking monopolies, had deteriorated during the years of territorial expansion in China.[38] Finally, it should be noted that the Baba budget, despite the tax increases, had still to be balanced by loans considerably in excess of those called for by Takahashi's last budget.

Taken as a whole, the Baba budget met with no insuperable objections from the capitalist groups, which concentrated their attention on the elimination of certain of the new tax proposals distasteful to them. In the country at large, however, this "war budget" was viewed with disfavor, and added to the unpopularity of the Hirota Cabinet created by its essays in parliamentary reform and foreign policy. When a serious financial-economic crisis developed at the turn of the year, the position of the Hirota Cabinet, as it appeared before the Diet in January 1937, had become exceedingly vulnerable.

[37] *The Oriental Economist*, January 1937, p. 6.

[38] The agrarian crisis was but slightly mitigated in 1935 and 1936; as for the workers, unemployment had declined but so had wage rates, while the cost of living mounted slowly but steadily from 1931 to 1936. See the wage-rate and cost-of-living tables in *The Oriental Economist*, 1931-1936, *passim*.

CHAPTER SEVEN

JAPAN'S DRIVE TOWARD FASCISM

JAPANESE politics, for the first six months of 1937, was dominated by a parliamentary and extra-parliamentary struggle of serious proportions, which turned almost solely on Fascist issues. The lines of battle, which were gradually forming during the Hirota administration, became clear-cut under the Hayashi Cabinet. Behind the Fascist drive, giving it "propelling force", was thrown the determined political weight of the military. The army leadership, both in personnel and methods, had accomplished its divorce from the strong-armed gangsterism of the previous epoch. Generals Terauchi, Sugiyama, and others of their group had "disciplined" the army extremists. In the process, the latter's aims had come to dominate the greater part of the army command, including the former moderate and conservative generals. This leadership had adjusted its policies not only to changed conditions in Japan but to new problems raised by the gradual metamorphosis in world politics since 1931. In the early years of the Manchurian invasion, Japan had virtually a clear field in the Far East. The economic depression, and the low level of European and American armaments, prevented effective interference from that quarter; the U.S.S.R. was militarily and economically weak and unprepared; China was disorganized and helpless. Five years later the outlines of this picture had changed in important respects. The army leaders were conscious of a gradual shift against Japan in the Far Eastern balance of power, resulting mainly from the arms programs of the Soviet Union, the United States, and Great Britain. They felt that this shift was strengthening Chinese resistance and undermining their drive toward hegemony in China. Retreat or a settlement negotiated on the basis of the status quo could not be tolerated. They chose, instead, to enter on the task of bringing Japan's armaments up to a level that would restore the pre-1936 balance of power in East Asia.

The goal set by the army necessarily demanded serious innovations in Japan's national economy; above all, it required an immense expansion of Japanese heavy industry. To accomplish this task, the mobilization of Japan's entire financial resources had to be effected. Five years earlier, the resistance of the financial community would have negatived any such attempt at the outset. In the interim, the business prosperity attendant on the trade boom had enlarged the scope of possible internal financing. The moderate inflationary policy of Finance Minister Takahashi, combined with the refusal to increase taxes, had apparently provided resources which could now be tapped to expand heavy industry. Even more important, the enlarged armaments budgets since 1932 had given the army a strong ally in the group of industrialists whose products supplied the ever-growing requirements of the War and Navy Ministries. The munitions manufacturers, ship-building firms and various heavy industries, including mining, chemicals and metallurgy, were all directly concerned in war preparations. Old industrial combines, such as Furukawa, Fujiwara and Okura, tended more and more to acquiesce in the army's program. New and vigorous industrialists, speculating on the possibilities of the inflation and armaments boom, had arisen to challenge the positions of the bigger houses, such as Mitsui and Mitsubishi. Of these the Aikawa interests were outstanding. Nippon Sangyo Kabushiki Kaisha (Japan Industrial Company, Ltd.), the Aikawa holding company, was capitalized at 225 million yen. Its associated enterprises included Nippon Mining Company, with 160 million yen capital; Hitachi Works, manufacturing tools and machinery, at 118 million yen; and Nissan Chemical Industrial Company, at 62 millions. Through the Nippon Marine Products Company, capitalized at 91 million yen, Aikawa had bought up the Mitsui and Mitsubishi fishery interests and established virtually a complete monopoly over the fishing industry, including manufacture, refrigeration and catch.[1] In his business methods, Aikawa had brought a new technical efficiency into industrial management, and a vigor and dash which contrasted with the safer and more conservative policies of the older houses. Somewhat similar, though on a smaller scale, were the activities of the Noguchi interests, specializing in mining and heavy industry, and the Mori interests, with large investments in the chemical industry.

Even these aggressive industrial promoters, it should be noted, had hesitated to link themselves too closely to the army extremists headed by General Araki. The new army leadership, however, with its solid program of arms and industrial expansion, found in them ardent supporters. This evolution was not confined to industrial upstarts; it had also affected the older financial-industrial combines. The heavy industries of Mitsui and Mitsubishi, to a much greater extent than their parent financial cen-

[1] For complete figures on the Aikawa enterprises, see *The Japan Times*, December 15, 1937.

ters, gravitated toward support of the army program. In some cases their representatives moved into controlling positions in the older houses, as when Mr. Chichi, former manager of the Mitsui Mining Company, was appointed managing director of the Mitsui Bank. Younger men, who rapidly pushed out the older leaders after 1932, were coming to the fore in the traditional strongholds of orthodox finance. Their aggressiveness and ambitious designs increasingly outweighed the counsels of caution advanced by the conservatives. A new factor of basic significance was thus introduced into Japan's political struggle. The solid wall of capitalist opposition to the army's internal program, which had existed during Takahashi's reign over the Finance Ministry, was crumbling. By 1937 important sectors of the business community were prepared to join hands with the more conservative leaders who had established their control over the army. This reactionary grouping, in order to defend and enlarge the gains won by six years of aggression in the Far East, was prepared to discount the strain that would be imposed on Japan by an arms race with the first-class Powers. Gathering up the reins of political power, it moved steadily toward a series of fixed objectives. These included vastly larger armament expenditures, the expansion of heavy industry to meet the enlarged military-naval requirements, establishment of a semi-wartime controlled economy, large tax increases and bigger deficit loans, elimination of parliamentary influence in government, and the complete suppression of all opposition voices.

The forces of the right were a compact and closely knit minority. Linked firmly to the reactionary magnates of finance and heavy industry, the army possessed the advantages of initiative, position and driving political power. The constituents of the liberal opposition were three-fold: the moderate business and financial groups, the parties, and public opinion. At first glance it might seem that such a combination was amply sufficient to throw back the Fascist attack. In reality this opposition, save for certain adherents in the inner circle of the Emperor's advisers, lacked any clearly articulated channels through which its influence could be effectively brought to bear on government policy. Political trends, both at home and abroad, were undermining the strength which the business conservatives had mustered during the earlier onslaught of the army extremists. Their platform, no less than that of the reactionary industrialists, was rooted in economic necessity. The industrial and trading interests of the Osaka area, specializing primarily in the products of light industry, constituted the stable, cautious elements of Japanese monopoly capital. Enriched by the export boom and dependent on an uninterrupted flow of international trade, they looked askance at any influence that threatened to upset the status quo. Like the conservative centers of finance with which they were merged, they battened on the accomplished fact of territorial aggression but fought shy of too risky or too costly military adventures. Budgetary disequilibrium, an abnormal commodity price rise, runaway inflation, weakness of the yen—such dangers could be curbed when it was a matter of local military operations restricted to China, especially in the latter's previously weak and disorganized state. But these difficulties attained formidable proportions when it became a question of inaugurating a vastly enlarged armaments program, particularly one that attempted to keep pace with the expanding preparations of the first-class Powers, which now included Great Britain and the United States as well as the U.S.S.R. At the end of such a race, aside from its immediate strain on Japanese economy, the conservative business circles foresaw the likelihood of war with one or more of these Powers, or a large-scale clash with China, and had no confidence in the ultimate result.

These apprehensions were generally shared by the Japanese public, which clearly sensed the dangers inherent in the army platform. If conservative capitalists struggled against a government-sponsored controlled economy, the people were opposed to rising prices, increased taxes, and the offensive against their few remaining democratic rights. If conservative business distrusted military adventurism and swollen budgets and scented financial crisis, the people reacted against military conscription, service in Manchuria, and the danger of war. But this coalition, strong in numbers and outwardly powerful, was politically ineffective because the main levers of control rested in the hands of its opponents. The natural political instrument to effect its policies was the parties, more especially when the moderate business elements began to lose their grip on the Finance Ministry. Since the middle of 1932, however, the parties had been relegated to a few of the minor Ministries and excluded from any real influence on policy. The promise of a new lease on life held out to the parties by the election of February 20, 1936 had been withdrawn by the military uprising less than a week later. In any case, the Minseito and Seiyukai were far from homogeneous political entities; both contained elements that properly belonged in the reactionary camp, and the same was true of the Social Mass Party. These parties, even in combination, were an unstable defense against the Fascist drive; only the strong anti-Fascist public opinion current at this period served to force them to hew to the line of a fairly vigorous opposition. Despite its inherent weaknesses and strategic handicaps, the liberal opposition managed to obstruct the progress of the military-fascist program at least partially until June 1937.

When the Diet members reassembled in January 1937, after the customary holiday recess, they were provided with a full store of ammunition for an attack on the Hirota Cabinet. The lack of results attending the China negotiations, the unpopularity of the German-Japanese pact, and the difficulties over the Soviet-Japanese fisheries agreement laid the government's foreign policy open to wholesale condemnation. General Terauchi's efforts to emasculate parliamentary government by way of Diet reform were generally resented by the public. Finally, the prospect of the Baba budget, with its tax increases and increased deficit financing, and the indications of a sizeable excess in the year's imports had led to an incipient financial panic over the year-end. A sharp rise in prices had set in. The Bank of Japan's index of wholesale commodity prices for January 1937, taking October 1899 as 100, stood at 233.3, the highest on record. This figure represented an advance of 8.6 per cent over December 1936 and 21.6 per cent over January 1936.[2] In December 1936 the Bank of Japan's retail price index was 2.26 per cent higher than the previous month. When the yen showed signs of weakness in December, a flight of capital accompanied by speculative imports developed. The demand for imports was intensified by efforts to place orders for shipment before the new tariffs went into effect. To cope with this situation, the Finance Ministry subjected import exchange on January 8 to a rigid licensing system. The resulting difficulty in obtaining import exchange placed a premium on import commodities, especially textiles and textile materials, and exaggerated the rise in

[2] *The Japan Times*, February 6, 1937.

commodity prices. Underlying these untoward manifestations was the fear of a serious inflation, indicated by difficulties in marketing government bonds and a decline in bond quotations.

The vigorous attack launched on the Cabinet by party members when the Diet reconvened in January immediately created a governmental crisis. None of the ranking party leaders had sought this result, which was mainly the work of young progressive members in the two major parties. In November the younger Minseito deputies had twice met in conference to devise means of overcoming the party leaders' hesitancy in taking up General Terauchi's challenge on the Diet reform issue. Representatives of this group, including Seiyukai deputies, had been the chief interlocutors of Terauchi before the Parliamentary System Investigation Commission. On the eve of the Diet session fifteen Minseito and Seiyukai deputies held a conference at which they decided to take a strong stand against the government.[3] The interpellation of one of these deputies, Kunimatsu Hamada of the Seiyukai, was the outstanding feature of the turbulent session in the lower house of the Diet on January 21. In the course of this speech, Mr. Hamada declared: "Of late the army has taken upon itself the role of 'the propelling force of the nation,' and in all the recent major incidents it has made this force felt. It is true of the May 15 incident, the February 26 incident, the dictatorial views broadcast by some sections of the army from time to time, the political views expressed by the War Minister at the meeting of the Diet System Inquiry Commission. . . . Thus dictatorial political ideology is at all times the undercurrent of thought within the army, and there is danger of this current destroying the dam that is set between the civil and military

[3] *Japan Weekly Chronicle,* January 21, 1937, p. 66.

in accordance with the Imperial will. The people realize this and are afraid. If the Hirota Cabinet is really to enforce renovation of general administration, it must first of all undertake the disciplining of the army, and at the same time it must lift the heavy pressure brought to bear on the people by the army. The present Cabinet, however, through its weakness and indecision, is seeking its propelling force in a section of the army. Under a vague totalitarian banner, the Cabinet is feverishly trying to establish administrative Fascism. . . . In disregard of the capacity of the people to bear the burden, it has compiled an enormous and abnormal budget and planned heavy tax increases that are exceptionally crude and lacking in balance. Thus a general economic panic is threatening. By rash economic control measures, it is brewing industrial confusion. The general impasse in international relations characterized by armed diplomacy is also a product of the Fascist ideology." [4] When General Terauchi stated that words in this talk seemed "like an insult to some military men," Mr. Hamada made a vigorous rebuttal and then challenged examination of the stenographic record. If the War Minister's charge were borne out, he was ready to apologize by committing *harakiri;* if not, the former should assume full responsibility. After the session, the Cabinet obtained Imperial sanction to prorogue the Diet for two days, January 22 and 23.

Active political maneuvering featured the period of prorogation. The ranking leaders of the Minseito and Seiyukai denounced the step as unconstitutional. Within the Cabinet, a sharp struggle was caused by the War Minister's demand that the Diet be dissolved. Approached by reporters immediately after the Diet session, General Terauchi refused all comment except to say that he had

[4] *The Japan Advertiser,* January 22, 1937.

taken "a firm resolve." On January 22, after conferring
with other army officers, he privately submitted his resignation, apparently in an effort to force the Premier to
dissolve the Diet. Navy leaders sought to arrange a compromise, and this attempt was seconded by the Emperor's
advisers. The Cabinet was divided, and at first it seemed
that the War Minister might have his way. Eventually, on
January 23, the Cabinet submitted its resignation. In this
first round the victory belonged to the parties, which had
avoided dissolution by the army and thrown out the government. Despite his inglorious downfall, Hirota had won
and held new positions for the military-fascist drive: the
sedition and surveillance laws, import exchange control, and the German-Japanese pact. More important, he
passed on the Baba budget to his successors. The Cabinet
had outlived its usefulness, even to the reactionaries. Its
support of the Fascist program had compromised it in
the eyes of the public, and the army let it fall.

General Kazushige Ugaki received the Imperial command to form the next Cabinet at one o'clock on the
morning of January 25. His choice came as a severe
shock to the army leadership. General Ugaki had recently
concluded a five-year term as Governor-General of Korea;
earlier, he had been War Minister in three Minseito cabinets. In 1925 he had forced through a reduction of the
standing army by two divisions. An emergency conference
of the army leaders, meeting as soon as Ugaki's nomina-
tion became known, decided to oppose his efforts to form
a Cabinet. The reasons given for this stand were that
Ugaki's views on the situation confronting the nation
fundamentally differed from those of the army, and that
under his leadership they could not succeed in strengthening military discipline. These two points were made explicit in later statements. For the first, he had "too many

ties with the status quo camp, composed of the parties, financial interests, et cetera"; as to the second, he was under suspicion of "having plotted a dictatorship." [5] This latter charge was understood to refer to Ugaki's implication in one of the abortive military coups during the autumn of 1931.

From the determination first taken, the army chiefs never wavered through five days of intense political crisis. The success with which this opposition was maintained showed conclusively the extent to which General Terauchi's judicious personnel changes had riveted a stranglehold of his own on the army. Japan's military affairs have traditionally been controlled by the occupants of the "Big Three" positions—Chief of the General Staff, Minister of War, and Inspector-General of Military Education. [6] At this time these offices were respectively held by Prince Kanin, General Terauchi, and General Gen Sugiyama. Prince Kanin had been a fixture at the Staff Office since 1932; by virtue of his rank, he was immune to political changes. The latter two generals, since the eclipse of Araki and Mazaki, had come to dominate the "upper strata" of the army. They had been purging or disciplining the "middle strata", i.e., chiefly the former "young colonels" of the extremist wing who had moved up to the rank of major-general. The changes had been carried out in such a way as to place adherents of the Terauchi-Sugiyama clique in key posts, until its influence had become paramount. In this process Terauchi's following had become increasingly affected by extremist views; their methods of a gradual advance toward Fascism through government reform, though eschewing violenc:, equally

[5] *The Japan Advertiser*, January 23, 1937.
[6] In the heyday of the extremists' power, General Araki was at the War Office and General Mazaki in the Inspectorate-General of Military Education.

involved them in efforts to gain control of the Cabinet. All their actions were rationalized by the claim that they contributed to renovation of the army.

Terauchi now held his stand despite the recognized ability of Ugaki, and in face of the latter's overwhelming support by the press, public, the parties and the business world, as well as the Emperor's advisers. The full force of the liberal opposition was mobilized against the military-fascists, and was calmly waved aside. The army's "Big Three" suggested the names of three men for War Minister; each of them declined the post. No others dared come forward. Never before in Japan's constitutional history had the inability to appoint a civilian to the War Ministry testified so clearly to the army's power to wreck the formation of a Cabinet.[7] At times it was thought that General Ugaki would resort to Imperial intervention on his behalf, but this critical step was not taken. On January 29, after announcing his determination to resign his rank of full general on the retired list in protest against conditions in the army,[8] he finally abandoned his efforts to form a Cabinet.

A statement by Ugaki, in the form of a note transmitted on the previous day to one of his old army associates, was made public in the morning editions of the papers but was immediately banned. Its essential portions

[7] Between 1912 and 1936 it was constitutionally possible to appoint a general or a lieutenant-general on the retired list to the War Ministry. Through General Terauchi's pressure, the ordinance which made this possible had been repealed by the Hirota Cabinet—a factor which strengthened his position in this political crisis.

[8] In submitting his resignation, he stated: "A general in the army, whether on the first or second reserve list, must as long as he retains his rank go to the front and command an army in the event of war. By observing the attitude of the army since I received the Imperial command to form a Cabinet, I have realized that I could not possibly discharge my duty as a commander in the field. Thus I think I should hand in my resignation." *The Japan Advertiser*, January 30, 1937.

read: "The present conditions in the army and public opinion are as you see. What I see is that only a few men in authoritative positions in the army have formed a group and are forcing their views on the authorities, propagandizing as if their action represents the general will of the army. The army belongs to the Emperor. Whether their action during the last few days represents the general will of the army of the Emperor or not is not too clear. The selection of a War Minister by the Big Three of the army was too formal and lacked sincerity. Some of the officers in active service are willing to come forward and cope with the present difficult situation but their way is blocked. What I can do in these circumstances is to resort to an abnormal measure. I have not thought of requesting an Imperial message. I am very anxious regarding the future of Japan and the future of the army should I decline the Imperial command. I believe that Japan stands today at the crossroads between Fascism and parliamentary politics. I am partly responsible for the present condition in the army, which has become a political organization. I feel sorry for the Emperor because of this state of affairs. Moreover, I greatly regret that the army which I have loved so long has been brought to such a pass. . . ." [9]

Throughout this period the party leaders showed themselves to be mainly interested in smoothing over the difficulties with the army, instead of continuing the outright struggle which they had begun on the floor of the Diet. On January 27 Yukio Ozaki, the veteran liberal deputy, proposed that the parties should assemble the Diet, which was still formally in session, to pass a resolution expressing "the will of the people". This offer was summarily rejected by the Minseito and Seiyukai leaders,

[9] *New York Herald Tribune*, January 29, 1937.

who preferred to watch developments passively. Mr. Ozaki then proposed that the lower house should adopt a resolution inquiring after the health of the Emperor. With considerable qualms, the party leaders finally agreed to allow the Speaker of the House to perform the errand in his own capacity, but refrained from meeting in plenary session to pass a resolution to this effect. On January 27 the Social Mass Party issued an innocuous statement calling on both Premier-designate Ugaki and the army to clarify their intentions with regard to national policy. After the crisis was over, the Minseito put forth a declaration expressing sympathy with General Ugaki over his difficulties and asking the army to clarify the reasons for its opposition. In conclusion, the declaration stated that "the Minseito, together with the people, is keenly observing the situation." Surprised by the vigor of General Terauchi's counter-attack, the parties had never resumed the offensive after January 21. The next moves turned strongly against them.

The new choice for Premier was announced late on the night of January 29. Prince Saionji's first nominee was Baron Hiranuma, president of the Privy Council. The latter's army connections had been with the former extremist clique; knowing that he would be unacceptable to the Terauchi group, he declined the offer. In evident expectation of this refusal, Prince Saionji had suggested an alternate choice. Shortly before midnight, General Senjuro Hayashi was vested with the command to form a Cabinet. The suggestions made by Saionji were indicative of the new political current. Though Hayashi was not one of the officers close to General Terauchi, he was far more extreme in his views than Ugaki and to that extent more acceptable. Nevertheless, difficulties at once arose over his attempt to secure Lieutenant-General Seishiro Itagaki,

chief of staff of the Kwantung Army, and Admiral Suetsugu as War and Navy Ministers. The "Big Three" of the
army and the naval authorities strongly objected to these
men, who were both extremists of the first water, and
eventually induced Hayashi to accept Lieutenant-General
Kotaro Nakamura and Vice-Admiral Mitsumasa Yonai.

Considerable surprise was occasioned by the extremist
nominees at first advanced by the Premier-designate for
the War and Navy portfolios. The explanation offered
was that Shinji Sogo, chief of Hayashi's cabinet organization headquarters, had been planted in this strategic
position by the extremists in order to put over a vigorous
reform Cabinet. When the Premier-designate finally accepted the nominees of the Terauchi-Sugiyama clique,
Sogo withdrew from his post at Hayashi's headquarters.
This incident, however, shed further light on the new
Premier's political views, hitherto none too clearly
marked. Equally revealing was his ready acceptance of
the army's demand that the Cabinet should include no
party members. Three political leaders were approached
with an offer of Ministerial portfolios, but only on condition that they severed connections with their parties.
These men were Mr. Chikuhei Nakajima, a director of
the Seiyukai; Mr. Ryutaro Nagai, chief secretary of the
Minseito; and Mr. Tatsunosuke Yamazaki of the Showakai, a small third-party group. Of these, the latter accepted
office as Minister of Agriculture and Forestry, and resigned from his party; the other two refused the proffered
Ministries.

In this time of trial the parties received little support
from the capitalists. The latter centered attention on
reaching an agreement with the army over a Finance Minister who would be able to remove some of the "iniqui-
tous" features of the Baba budget. Mr. Toyotaro Yuki,

the compromise choice finally selected, summed up in his person the basic political evolution that was taking place in Japan's ruling circles. He was at the time president of the Industrial Bank of Japan, and concurrently president of the Japan Chamber of Commerce and Industry; in earlier years, his connections were with such moderate financial leaders as Inouye and Takahashi. His past ties and undoubted practical abilities reassured the conservative business-men, who trusted him to bridge over the immediate difficulties and revise the budget to their satisfaction. On the other hand Mr. Yuki had in recent years drawn close to the army, and was known to favor arms and industrial expansion—factors which won him the allegiance of heavy industry. He was thus uniquely fitted to harmonize all capitalist interests and marshal them behind an economic program adapted to army requirements. Ten days later he appointed Mr. Seihin Ikeda, former Mitsui managing director, as Governor of the Bank of Japan, a move equally symptomatic of the inroads of the reactionary platform in financial circles. Ikeda himself had become an outspoken expansionist, and vigorously set about his task of channeling large credits into the development of heavy industry.

On February 15 Yuki was already advancing proposals for a revision of the Bank of Japan Act to enable the bank to lend money directly to industrial enterprises and to receive debentures and stock shares, in addition to government bonds and notes, as security for such loans.[10] Pending this revision, Ikeda had begun open market operations, featuring the purchase of government bonds by the Bank of Japan, in order to augment funds at the disposal of private banks for investment in industrial enterprises. Still another figure in the new Cabinet was worthy of

[10] *The Japan Advertiser*, February 17, 1937.

note. Vice-Admiral Takuo Godo, president of the Showa Steel Works in Manchoukuo, was appointed Minister of Commerce and Industry, with the object of pushing forward the campaign to make Japan self-sufficient in the heavy metals.[11] These appointments were made with one object in view: to bring the nation's industrial production up to a level that would match the large additions to the armaments budget. Having won this major point, the army was content to make certain concessions to the big concerns on the new tax scheme, and to lessen immediate pressure toward a controlled economy.

After two additional prorogations, made necessary by Finance Minister Yuki's revision of the Baba budget, the Diet reassembled on February 15. Lieutenant-General Nakamura had meanwhile resigned from the War Ministry due to serious illness, and General Gen Sugiyama had replaced him. When General Terauchi assumed the Inspectorate-General of Military Education, vacated by Sugiyama, these key men had merely exchanged places in two of the "Big Three" posts and thus retained dominance in the army. Their success in ousting party men from the Cabinet constituted a bold advance toward exclusion of the parties from governmental authority, and left the latter no option except to continue the struggle.

Many factors combined to weaken the parties' position at the outset of this new period of conflict. The Hayashi Cabinet, as was customary, had issued a colorless declaration of policies, which offered small grounds for direct attack. Taken aback by the army offensive, the leaders of the major parties were inclined to hesitancy and compromise. This tendency was reinforced by the feeling that

[11] Godo's first essay in unifying sales of Manchurian and home-produced pig-iron, however, seemed to have been drawn mainly with an eye to the interests of the home producers and had to be dropppd after objections from the Kwantung Army.

Yuki's revision of the budget would conduce to the interests of their capitalist supporters; the generally passive attitude of the Minseito and Seiyukai leaders was not materially affected by pressure from the younger progressive deputies and from the left-wing parties. Throughout the Diet session, the army continued to hold the threat of dissolution over the heads of the party leaders. Its force was strengthened by efforts to disrupt the two major parties and organize a new Fascist party out of dissident elements. The Seiyukai was in the throes of a serious internal crisis, with a strong "reformist" faction under army influence disputing for leadership. When Dr. Kisaburo Suzuki resigned as president, the guidance of the party had to be placed in the hands of a committee representing the several factions. Under these conditions, the opposition during the Diet session was confined mainly to occasional courageous criticism from individual deputies.

Finance Minister Yuki's handling of the budget inherited from Baba was admirably adapted toward restoring business confidence, while at the same time maintaining untouched the enlarged armaments program. The revised budget figures laid before the Diet for the 1937-1938 fiscal year aggregated 2,814 million yen, a reduction of 224 millions over the Baba total. Army-navy expenditure stood unchanged at 1,409 million yen, although 46 millions of this total was to be postponed to the next fiscal year. The reduction of 224 million yen was accomplished entirely on the civilian side of the budget, comprising 150 millions lopped off the projected grants to local governments and 74 millions cut from the budgets of the civilian Ministries. This latter sum, the sole actual reduction of expenditure in the new budget, chiefly affected certain social welfare measures which had been projected in the Baba budget. The proportion of the budget taken by the defense services had thus increased to slightly over half of the total. Bond emissions for general account aggregated 771 million yen, a reduction of 35 millions.

The Yuki budget was still slightly more than 500 million yen in excess of that for the preceding fiscal year, so that ordinary revenue had to be increased by 441 millions. In accomplishing this end, important changes were made in the taxation scheme which Baba had fostered. The two new levies on property and on combined income instead of on income at the source, which financial quarters had particularly opposed, were eliminated. Propertied interests, however, were still affected by increases in income tax, emergency earnings tax, and the newly imposed corporation tax. The people at large were forced to assume additional burdens with respect to advanced tobacco prices, tariff increases, higher postal stamp charges, the new gasoline tax, and increases in the liquor tax and sugar excise.

With Minseito and Seiyukai support, and some slight opposition mainly from the Social Mass Party, the amended budget was adopted by the lower house on March 8. Confidence inspired by Yuki, rather than the nominal budgetary revision, exerted a marked psychological effect which speedily overcame the unsettlement which had gripped Japan's business and financial circles in December and January. The basic economic outlook remained none too favorable. Commodity prices continued to soar and the increased excess of imports, already notable in 1936, achieved much larger proportions during the early months of 1937. On February 18 the Finance Minister announced that recourse to shipments of gold to balance Japan's international accounts, which had virtually ceased for five years, might have to be resumed.

Soon afterward the government forwarded 50 million yen in gold to the United States, the first of successive shipments during later months as the import excess steadily mounted. At the same time, business promotion in Japan assumed proportions that had not been experienced in many years. The Bank of Japan placed the volume of new capitalizations for March at 489 million yen, an increase of 327 millions over the preceding month and 442 millions over March 1936. Munitions industries led the advance, with 89 millions for mining, 72 millions for chemicals, and 39 millions for metals.[12] Speaking before a committee of the lower house on March 26, Finance Minister Yuki stressed the importance of extending industrial productive capacity; clearly, this policy was already being effected. On the other hand, no important economic control measures were passed. The Hirota Cabinet's plan to nationalize the electric power industry was allowed to lapse. As envisaged by Yuki, the "repletion of national defense" was to be obtained by private rather than governmental enterprise. The latter might be called upon where costs loomed larger than profits. A bill to set up an Imperial Fuel Industry Promotion Corporation, to conduct enterprises for the manufacture of artificial petroleum, was introduced in the Diet; although passed by the lower house, it had not yet been approved by the House of Peers when the session ended.

Several projects for administrative reform, which the army was still intent on achieving, continued to attract attention during this period. A number of Ministerial portfolios in the Hayashi Cabinet were held concurrently for longer or shorter periods, and it was thought that this fact signified an intention to reduce the number of Ministries. In particular, it was feared that the Overseas

[12] *The Oriental Economist*, April 1937, p. 201.

Ministry would be abolished, while the merging of Agriculture and Forestry with Commerce and Industry, and Railways with Communications, was also rumored. The army was further seeking to establish a General Affairs Board within the Cabinet, professedly to coordinate Ministerial policies and functions. This idea was borrowed from Manchoukuo, where the General Affairs Board was utilized by the Kwantung Army to dominate the government from behind the scenes. Finally, the long delay in appointment of the Parliamentary Vice-Ministers or Counsellors, one of which is usually attached to each Ministry, was also viewed with suspicion by the parties. These Counsellors were chosen from the Diet to help maintain liaison between the executive and legislative branches; they are to be distinguished from the Vice-Ministers, who are administrative officials. In the end, none of these various threats materialized, but they served to maintain an undercurrent of hostility between the deputies and the army throughout the Diet session.

A highlight of this guerrilla warfare was the publication on March 1 of a ten-point questionnaire, addressed by Yukio Ozaki to the Cabinet, which flayed the army's interference in politics. The ten questions, each of which was accompanied by lengthy commentary, were as follows: (1) Why are the true facts that caused the Hirota Cabinet's resignation being kept a secret? (2) What were the reasons that reputedly prompted the former War Minister to demand the Diet's dissolution? (3) What were the facts that prevented General Kazushige Ugaki from forming a cabinet? (4) Why has the Cabinet failed to curb political opinion among the army? (5) Is it true that fulfilment of the Imperial wish by General Ugaki was prevented entirely by the army? (6) Why has the nation not known the authors of political opinion within the army? (7) What are the actual circumstances which enabled General Hayashi to form the present Cabinet? (8) Does the Cabinet intend to recommend to the Throne an amendment of the system of appointing a Premier? (9) Is the Cabinet in favor of direct exercise of the Imperial prerogative for selection of a Premier? (10) Is the Cabinet willing to consider a change in the procedure of Imperial recommendation as a substitution for the Genro system? [13]

A more indirect, but hardly less forceful, attack on the army was the resolution adopted by the Diet on March 14, the seventieth anniversary of Emperor Meiji's Charter Oath, which explicitly sanctioned democratic government. This resolution, which was submitted to the Throne, was worded as follows: "Emperor Meiji, on March 14 of the fourth year of the Keio Era, promulgated the Charter Oath containing five articles and inaugurating the national principle that all affairs of the State be referred to public opinion before final decision. Subsequently the Imperial Constitution was granted to the nation, leading to the development of the national will and to the prosperity of the country's destiny. This day is the 70th anniversary of the promulgation of the Oath. On this auspicious occasion, it is proper and desirable that the members of the House look back upon the past and fully recall to mind the Imperial wishes underlying the Oath, so that in the future they may even more appropriately express their faith in the Constitution, and exert all efforts in harmony and cooperation, and, by their conduct and achievements, help to illustrate the beauty of the Constitution throughout generations." [14] Article I of the Char-

[13] For full text of this questionnaire, including the commentary, see *The Japan Advertiser*, March 1, 1937.
[14] *The Oriental Economist*, March 1937, p. 135.

ter Oath, to which the resolution particularly referred, reads: "An assembly widely convoked shall be established and all affairs of the State shall be referred to public opinion before final decision."

These diversions could not serve to conceal the position to which the parties and parliamentary politics had been reduced under the Hayashi Cabinet. The basic trend was indicated by the smooth functioning of the Yuki-Ikeda combination, which was intent on forcing Japan's industrial development into the straight and narrow path of preparation for war. It was indicated by the huge army-navy appropriations, to which the business interests had easily accommodated themselves. The parties had logically followed suit, swallowing the insult of exclusion from Cabinet posts in their approval of the budget. Their defense was conceived solely in terms of an effort to maintain their parliamentary rights, and not of an attack on the fundamental aims of the military-fascist program.

In one field the more moderate financial groups may be said to have had a representative of their opinions in the Hayashi Cabinet. The new Foreign Minister, Mr. Naotake Sato, introduced a marked change of emphasis into the truculent policies of Hirota and Arita, especially in reference to China. In response to interpellations in the lower house on March 11, the Foreign Minister declared that Japan could avert war at any time if it so chose, that he would negotiate with China on a basis of equality, and that formation of economic blocs, such as that between Japan and Manchoukuo, was premature. These remarks were highly indiscreet, and were bitterly resented in army circles. The first, in particular, could hardly be reconciled with Premier Hayashi's interpretation of the international situation in terms of "explosion at a touch." On the following morning the Premier and the defense Ministers conferred with Mr. Sato, who considerably modified his statements that afternoon in an explanation before the budget committee of the House of Peers.[15] His concept of "economic diplomacy" awoke distinct echoes of Baron Shidehara, who also sought peace and an uninterrupted flow of international trade in the interests of Japan's export industries. In pursuit of this policy, Foreign Minister Sato despatched the Kodama Economic Mission to China and sent a similar mission to the United States and England.

At the moment even the military circles could see no real harm in this shadow-play. So far as China was concerned, there was every advantage in waiting to see the ultimate outcome of the Sian crisis. With an internal struggle of major proportions on its hands, a truce to foreign adventures by the army was nothing more than an elementary precaution. Foreign Minister Sato's policy meanwhile provided an admirable stop-gap which tended to mitigate the international suspicion aroused by the Suiyuan hostilities, Ambassador Kawagoe's demands at Nanking, and the German-Japanese pact. The groundwork for a liberal foreign policy of any permanence was cut away by the actualities of the military-fascist program being carried through at home.

Premier Hayashi's sudden dissolution of the Diet on March 31 came as a general surprise. Despite a steady drum-fire of criticism, the parties had given the Cabinet little real difficulty. On one relatively minor point, the addition of 30 million yen to the grant for local governments, the party leaders had wrung a concession from the Cabinet. Yuki had reduced the original Baba grant of 220 million yen to local governments to 70 millions; the additional amount raised the total grant to 100 millions. A

[15] *The Japan Advertiser*, March 12-13, 1937.

supplementary budget of 58 million yen, including the
added 30 millions, was passed by the Diet during the
session. On another point of considerable interest to the
parties, the government had remained obdurate. The six
parties in the lower house had agreed on the text of an
election reform bill, designed to forestall possible essays
in this direction by the army, and late in the session submitted it to the Cabinet. When the latter's approval was
withheld, proceedings in the lower house appreciably
slowed down. On March 25 an Imperial edict extending
the Diet for six days, from March 26 to 31, was issued.
At the end of this period a number of bills still awaited
consideration, and some were deadlocked. The Premier
seemed to have been waiting for some such opportunity.
On March 31 he obtained Imperial sanction for dissolution of the lower house, charging that it had unduly
obstructed the passage of legislation. A general election
was set for April 30.

The arbitrary nature of Hayashi's action betrayed the
army's impatience with parliamentary politics and its
determination to crush the opposition in the Diet. In
choosing the tactic of dissolution and general election,
however, the Premier committed a first-class political
blunder. The party leaders, who had been engaged in
damping down the fires of political struggle, were obliged
to assume an intransigeant opposition. The hands of the
progressive forces within the two big parties, as well as
of all left-wing elements, were immensely strengthened.
A head-on clash between the army and public opinion, on
a much more serious scale than during the election of
February 1936, was precipitated. In 1936 the public was
generally opposed to reactionary tendencies, but not specifically anti-army. Since then the February coup, the
policies of the Hirota Cabinet, General Terauchi's role

in opposing Ugaki, the exclusion of party men from the Hayashi Cabinet, and the latter's abrupt dissolution of the Diet had opened the eyes of the people to the source of danger. They now saw, much more clearly than before, that the army leaders were the bearers of war and Fascism. The general election of April 30 was fought on this clean-cut issue, and mobilized much stronger forces of popular opposition to the army.

At the outset of the election campaign, Premier Hayashi was confronted with the basic difficulty that his government had no organized party to represent it at the polls. The threat that a new party, essentially dominated by the army, would be organized by the government persisted until nearly the end of the campaign. In his statement when the Diet was dissolved, the Premier declared: "I think, however, that there would be nothing wrong should the Government decide to cooperate with a new party that might come into existence that would support it. The Government has not yet considered whether it should take positive action in the direction of forming a new party. It would be good if a party ready to support the Government came into being of its own accord. There is no intention on my part to take the initiative in forming such a party. I am afraid I have yet to make up my mind regarding the matter." [16]

The rather lame conclusion to this statement was suggestive of the difficulties facing such a project. In the existing state of public opinion, the reformist elements in the major parties were compelled to think twice before openly allying themselves with the military-fascist program. The possible leaders for a new party, as suggested in the press, were nevertheless highly significant. Outstanding was the name of Prince Konoye, president of the

[16] *The Japan Advertiser,* April 1, 1937.

House of Peers, whose leadership was considered essential for any degree of success. Of the other suggestions, one was Chikuhei Nakajima, a Seiyukai leader, and the other was Ryutaro Nagai, chief secretary of the Minseito. None of these men considered the time opportune for announcing their adherence to the army platform. On April 2 Mr. Nagai had already given favorable reception to a proposal by Mr. Seijun Ando, chief secretary of the Seiyukai, that the two parties should cooperate in the election. This proposal was later implemented in a number of constituencies, where the weaker candidates of the two parties withdrew in favor of the stronger.

The Hayashi Cabinet encountered almost as much difficulty in formulating a set of policies as in finding a party. On April 10 it published an eight-point platform consisting mainly of vague generalities. Kinship with the Hirota program was evident in such items as perfection of armaments, reform of the Diet, control of the electric power industry, and establishment of a Cabinet Planning Board. Statements by individual members of the Cabinet, and by its associates, left no doubt as to its real purposes. On April 8 the War Minister, General Sugiyama, defined the objective in a classic sentence: "The myriad affairs of the State must be made to harmonize with the keynote of full armament." [17] Seihin Ikeda, Governor of the Bank of Japan, in an interview given on April 17, called for "perfection of national defense" by operating "Japan's financial and monetary policies on a semi-wartime system." [18] Finance Minister Yuki, after addressing a round-

[17] Commenting on this speech, the *Domei* news agency noted that its statements were regarded "as a manifestation by the army that its highest aim is construction of a national-defense State and that its determination is to be the pilot in leading the nation toward that goal." *The Japan Advertiser*, April 9, 1937.

[18] *Shanghai Evening Post and Mercury*, April 20, 1937.

table conference of Osaka industrialists on April 6, was sharply criticized. The business-men pointed out that "production capacity may expand in the munitions industries alone as a result of the arms program, and warned the Minister that the Government should be ready to turn munitions plants to more productive purposes when the military program is completed." [19] The actual issues of the campaign were also revealed by the Cabinet's orders to prefectural chiefs of police to prohibit "utterances liable to alienate the people from the army" during the election. These were defined as utterances "charging the military with trying to provoke a war, alleging that the fighting services mean to reject the parliamentary system, arousing suspicion about obedience to orders in the services, or affecting the attitude of the people toward the conscription system." [20]

During the months preceding the election campaign, there had been a general leftward swing among the people, based on the rise in the cost of living and the fear of Fascism and war. Economic struggles of the factory workers had increased throughout the country. Actual labor shortage in some lines of business had greatly strengthened the workers' bargaining power. For the first quarter of 1937 labor disputes totalled 609, as compared with 353 in the first quarter of 1936, while the number of workers involved in strikes had risen from 13.8 per thousand to 38.4 per thousand in this period.[21] These strikes revolved almost solely around demands for wage increases, and nearly all resulted in successful settlements for the workers. In many cases the employers voluntarily offered wage increases, in order to avoid labor difficulties.

[19] *The Japan Advertiser*, April 8, 1937.
[20] *The Japan Advertiser*, April 8, 1937.
[21] *The Oriental Economist*, May 1937, p. 263.

This situation contrasted notably with the 1931-1936 period, when wage rates steadily declined in spite of increased employment.

It was partly affected by a movement for unity and consolidation of the trade unions, begun by the Osaka metal workers in 1935. Their demand for fusion of the two labor federations was at first resisted by the leaders of these organizations, but pressure from below led to a formal decision for unity in January 1936, which was partially effected at the center and in some prefectures. Where unity was achieved, trade union membership rapidly increased. In the case of the Osaka arsenal workers, for example, the membership soon rose from 5,000 to 7,000. At this point the military authorities stepped in and forced the arsenal workers to dissolve their union, on the ground that they were "working members" of the army and "in an entirely different category from the workmen of civilian factories and companies, which operate on a profit basis, in respect of their social standing, responsibility and their mission."

The majority of the trade unions were associated with the Social Mass Party, including 270,000 members of the united labor federation, 70,000 members of two farmers' unions, and some 5,000 members of lower middle class organizations. In addition to these "supporting organizations", the Social Mass Party recruited an individual membership, much on the order of the British Labor Party. Taken together, these trade unions included only a small fraction, considerably less than ten per cent, of the Japanese working class; the organizational base among the farmers was even less important. The cohesion of the Social Mass Party depended mainly on the prestige of the aged social-democratic leader, Dr. Abe; within its Diet representation, social democrats—some of whom were outspoken anti-Fascists—were forced to rub elbows with potentially Fascist elements. This factor accounted for the continued inability to establish unity with the "legal leftists", headed by Kanju Kato, who controlled a more militant minority following of some 40,000 trade unionists. The overtures of the "legal leftists" for a formal united front were turned down by the Social Mass Party, although the trade union and peasant organizations of Kato's group had forged certain links with the latter's trade union following. In 1936, after the setting up of formal trade union and political party organs by the "legal leftists", the split between the two groups deepened. This picture of disunity was further accentuated by the existence of a considerable fraction of "patriotic", or Fascist, unions. During the election campaign of April 1937, however, the voting strength of the left wing was materially increased by the general leftward movement of public opinion. The leaders of the Social Mass Party, much more than those of the Minseito and Seiyukai, were able to take up a fairly vigorous anti-Fascist position and count upon popular support.

Threats from both sides enlivened the final days of the campaign. Minseito and Seiyukai leaders, it was said, were prepared to introduce a vote of non-confidence at the special session of the Diet to be called after the election. The Cabinet countered by letting it be known that it was ready to dissolve the Diet a second time, if the results of the poll did not prove satisfactory. In this case press reports suggested that Premier Hayashi would seek through Imperial ordinance to reduce the number of Diet members by half or more, with the expectation that the enlarged constituencies would enable a new party to crush the influence of the old-line parties. In spite of all efforts, the Hayashi Cabinet found itself unable to

organize a new party by April 30 that would stand any
chance of success in the election. It was thus forced to
rely on the election of reactionaries under the banners
of the two major parties or of the Showakai and Kokumin
Domei, which favored the government. Early in the campaign the *Nichi Nichi* had noted: "The outstanding
aspect of the 20th general election is that it is not a
struggle for political power between opposed parties but
a struggle for supremacy between the status quo and reno-

Results of the General Election, April 30, 1937

Parties	At Dissolution	Elected	Change	Votes (in 000's)
Minseito	205	179	—26	3,668
Seiyukai	172	175	+ 3	3,584
Social Mass Party ..	18	36	+18	947
Showakai	24	18	— 6	398
Kokumin Domei ...	11	11	....	282
Tohokai	9	11	+ 2	221
Other groups	7	7	....	335
Independents	18	29	+11	769
Vacancies	2	0	— 2	....
Total	466	466	0	10,204

vation forces to be found side by side within all the
parties. What will be important is not how many seats
the Minseito or Seiyukai will win, but how many seats
the reformist elements in all the parties gain in comparison with the status quo elements. If the election results
in a majority of reformist members of the lower house
who will coalesce in a new party, the Government will
consider itself fortunate." [22] The votes cast on April 30
decisively crushed any such hope.

Although the Seiyukai gained appreciably in relative
standing as against the Minseito, the two major parties

[22] Quoted in *The Japan Advertiser*, April 3, 1937.

still represented a combined opposition controlling 354 seats, or well over an absolute majority. The Showakai, main government supporter, lost six seats, while the Kokumin Domei barely retained its 11 seats. Among the newly elected deputies of all parties, the Cabinet could muster hardly fifty adherents. The outstanding result of the election was the doubling of its representation by the Social Mass Party, which polled nearly one million votes and took rank as the third largest group in the lower house.

Under normal constitutional procedure, the election result would seem to have called for immediate resignation of the Cabinet. Nothing of the sort occurred. Despite the emphatic popular repudiation of his reformist platform, Premier Hayashi elected to remain in office. His statement issued on May 3 had the effrontery to instruct the new Diet members to fulfill their duties in "the spirit of self-abnegation and service to the country, hold high the ideals on which the nation was founded in accordance with the cardinal principles of our national polity, promote the development of a constitutional government which is entirely our own, and have a correct perspective of the existing situation." [23]

Although the Cabinet made preparations to face a special session of the Diet, it postponed the date for this session until August, or five months after dissolution—the final limit permitted by law. During May the Cabinet inaugurated three new policy-making commissions or boards. One of these was a Price Policy Commission, charged with the task of devising remedies for the untoward rise of commodity prices, while another was the Education and Culture Commission, formed to "inquire

[23] *The Oriental Economist,* May 1937, p. 259; also *The Japan Advertiser,* May 4, 1937.

and study all important matters relating to thorough per-
meation of the concept of the national polity and promotion of the national spirit." [24] A Cabinet Planning Board,
headed by Finance Minister Yuki, was formally inaugurated on May 14. Established by Imperial ordinance, this
board was a continuing organ of government with significant potentialities as the economic general staff of an
army dictatorship. Its immediate tasks, aside from preparing bills for submission to the special Diet session,
were to solve the iron and fuel supply questions, to
consider a five-year industrial program being studied by
the Ministry of Commerce and Industry, revise the Election Law, and deal with the problem of creating an
aviation department. [25] This board later framed the National Mobilization Bill passed in March 1938.

The most serious problem of the Cabinet was how to
cope with the parties, as a spate of statements issued by
the Premier testified. Organization of a new party out of
the material thrown up by the election was patently impossible, and had to be abandoned. For a few days the
Premier toyed with the hope of seducing the party leaders
by the offer of some of the three Ministerial portfolios—
Overseas, Railways, and Education—which were still held
concurrently. With the parties becoming daily more intransigeant, any such step was soon out of the question.
On May 19 a meeting of Minseito and Seiyukai representatives decided to establish a joint headquarters "for
the overthrow of the Hayashi Cabinet." This movement,
which centered its efforts on achieving "a real national
union Cabinet," was carried further by a joint rally of
the two parties in Tokyo on May 28. The conservative
party leaders, however, were careful to see that they did

[24] *The Japan Advertiser,* May 11, 25, 1937.
[25] *The Japan Advertiser,* May 14-15, 1937.

not arouse a genuine mass movement against the military-fascist program. In this connection, the comments of *Kokumin* were instructive: . . . "the parties are really expected to proceed carefully to keep the military from thinking that the anti-Cabinet combination is taking on the nature of a popular-front movement against Fascism. To guard against such consequences, the parties, at every available opportunity, will seek the understanding of the military and the upper strata in political circles on their contentions." [26] Sentiment in the House of Peers, expressed in meetings of several of its groups, turned against the Cabinet. The Showakai, considered the Ministry's only organized support in the Lower House, voluntarily dissolved on May 21 as an example to the other parties. Later its president was said to have suggested to Premier Hayashi that he should resign in the interests of national unity. The position of the Hayashi Cabinet had become hopeless; on May 31 it suddenly resigned.

During its short term in office, the Hayashi Ministry had carried forward under the onus of difficulties bequeathed by its predecessor. It had passed the 1937-1938 budget and won acceptance of the arms expansion program by business circles, after modifications of the tax reforms. Three new consultative agencies, of which the Planning Board was outstanding, had been established. A truce to military aggression was enforced in foreign policy, marked especially in May by a serious effort to reach agreement with Great Britain on China questions. The Premier's efforts at complete suppression of the remnants of parliamentarism had led to an outright clash with the parties, in which the former had been worsted. Before his resignation, Hayashi's tactic in this respect was accepted on all sides as a serious blunder. It had widened

[26] Quoted in *The Japan Advertiser*, May 16, 1937.

the gap between the army and the people, and strengthened the left wing in each of the parties, reflecting the
anti-Fascist, anti-government, and anti-war sentiment of
the country at large. This result was not at all to the
army's liking, and had seriously compromised its domestic standing. The two major parties were not alone in
demanding a government of "national union." Views of
the army leaders, canvassed at an emergency meeting after
Hayashi's resignation, were reported as follows: "The
feeling prevailing in the army is that the new Premier
should be capable of embracing the fighting services, the
bureaucracy and the parties in order to form a strong
Cabinet with unanimous national support. He must be
able to put through renovation policies in spite of obstacles. The new Cabinet must not, therefore, be partial
to any party or faction. Instead, it should embrace the
army, navy, bureaucrats, people, parties and financiers,
with its personnel strongly coordinated. As long as they
cooperate, the parties will not necessarily be ostracized." [27]

This program was faithfully carried out in the formation of the next Cabinet. At its head was placed Prince
Konoye, favored no less by the army than by the parties
and business quarters. There were valid grounds for be-
lieving that Prince Konoye's liberal front masked basically
reactionary views. The comment of a bourgeois journal
on this complex individual, who seemed to be all things
to all men, is noteworthy: "A keen student of politics,
Prince Konoye is much a reformist in his views but never
an extremist, people say." [28] Obviously he was an ideal
choice to reestablish a semblance of cooperation between
all of Japan's ruling groups, including the two big parties,
in realizing the military-fascist aims. For the main posts

[27] *The Japan Advertiser*, June 1, 1937.
[28] *The Oriental Economist*, June 1937, p. 326.

in the new Cabinet, Prince Konoye chose the leading reactionary figures of the two previous governments. General Sugiyama and Admiral Yonai were carried over as War and Navy Ministers, affording the clearest evidence that no real change in policy was contemplated. The Justice Minister, Suehiko Shiono—a close intimate of the Fascist-minded Baron Hiranuma, president of the Privy Council—was also taken over from the previous Ministry. The bureaucrats were represented by Okinobu Kaya, as Finance Minister, and Shinji Yoshino, Minister of Commerce and Industry. These men were advanced from the posts of Vice-Minister; they were typical of the "new bureaucrats", who had decisively swung over to support of the army since the February coup and had been instrumental in framing many of the economic control measures put forward by the Hirota and Hayashi Cabinets. Equally notable were the appointments of Koki Hirota, as Foreign Minister, and Eiichi Baba as Home Minister. The former had launched the army's excursion into Fascist reforms at home, and seen to the signing of the German-Japanese pact; the latter had drafted the 1937-1938 budget, which included the army's proposals as to military-naval appropriations and tax reforms.

The roll of these Ministers—Sugiyama, Yonai, Shiono, Kaya, Yoshino, Hirota, and Baba—showed a compact reactionary team, holding all of the important portfolios. To party members were delegated two of the lesser portfolios: the Communications Ministry, given to Ryutaro Nagai, and the Railways Ministry, assumed by Chikuhei Nakajima. These choices were the most reactionary figures of the two major parties; both had been prominently mentioned as possible leaders of a new party. Mr. Nagai had been chief secretary of the Minseito; Mr. Nakajima, an airplane manufacturer, had been a leader and large financial supporter of the Seiyukai. Their willingness to enter a Cabinet of the complexion outlined also reflected the eagerness of the two parties to come to terms with the army. Thus the result of their struggle with the Hayashi Cabinet had left the parties with two minor portfolios under Konoye, as against four under Hirota and five under Okada. Before entering the Konoye Cabinet, moreover, both Nagai and Nakajima agreed that, though they would not resign from their parties, they were not representing their parties in the new Ministry. However this jesuitical compromise might be interpreted, there was no question that it constituted at least a technical concession to the army viewpoint that party members should be excluded from the government.

The Agriculture and Forestry, and the Overseas, Ministries were both taken by members of the House of Peers; Konoye, Hirota and Baba were also members of the Upper House. Two of the auxiliary Cabinet posts were given to deputies in the Lower House. Mr. Akira Kazami, a member of the Kokumin Domei, was made Chief Secretary of the Cabinet; and Mr. Masao Taki, an independent deputy personally connected with the Premier, was appointed Councillor of the Bureau of Legislation. Including these two men, the Cabinet contained nine members of the Diet. The following comment on this phenomenon is significant: "In spite of this sprinkling of Diet members the Konoye Cabinet is by no means a party government. While Communications Minister Nagai and Railways Minister Nakajima are leaders respectively of the Minseito and Seiyukai, they are not representing their parties in the present Cabinet. In this respect the administration is even less closely linked to the House of Representatives than the two cabinets preceding General Hayashi's, namely those under General Keisuke Okada and Mr.

Koki Hirota." [29] The army, in other words, had not given up its hope of securing control of the lower house, although it had reversed the tactic of frontal assault. Nagai and Nakajima, it was hoped, would turn the parties toward collaboration with the military or possibly even facilitate the emergence of a new party through which the army could establish a firm parliamentary support for its policies.

The effects of the sharp internal strife which had existed under the Hayashi Ministry could not be eliminated merely by a change of government. Echoes of that conflict would not die out at once, and popular suspicion of the army would continue to exist. At all costs the army's rear, or public confidence and support at home, had to be consolidated. With a strong national Cabinet such as Konoye's in office, there was little danger to be apprehended from a renewal of military aggression in China. Such military operations, in view of the greater unity and new nationalism of China, might have to be conducted on an extensive scale. The risk was worth taking, especially since the international auspices were favorable, thus reducing the possibility of outside intervention to a minimum. Under cover of a serious external emergency, nationalist sentiments at home could be re-kindled, opposition voices silenced, the prestige of the army re-established in the public mind, and the military-fascist program for a "controlled economy" pushed ahead at an accelerated rate. The Konoye Cabinet was inducted into office on June 3; less than five weeks later, the first shot of a war with China had been fired at Lukouchiao. Within this brief period, the army had retrieved victory from apparent disaster. The downfall of the Hayashi Cabinet had been in the nature of a rout. Under the

[29] *The Oriental Economist*, June 1937, p. 326.

Konoye Cabinet, the army had skillfully re-formed its lines. With the beginning of war in China, the liberal opposition, composed mainly of elements which never dared to repudiate the military entirely, was swept away and its cause was lost.

CHAPTER EIGHT

THE DEFENSE OF SHANGHAI

THE preliminary fighting in North China during the month of July,[1] though comparatively restricted, had already carried the Japanese troops well beyond the territorial limits of the hostilities in 1933. At that time Japan's armed forces had stopped short of the northern metropolitan district; by the end of July 1937, they had effectively occupied the Peiping-Tientsin area. After withdrawal of the 29th Route Army from Peiping, the full extent of the next phase of hostilities was not apparent for some weeks. The steady stream of Japanese reinforcements flowing into North China, as well as the large amounts of munitions and supplies being concentrated there, indicated that Japan was preparing for an extensive campaign in the northern provinces. Factors on both sides militated against the possibility of a swift local campaign and a compromise settlement in the north at this time. The central authorities at Nanking could no longer hope to compromise with Japanese aggression and retain political power. For a year General Chiang Kai-shek had been declaring that the government was determined not to permit further encroachments on China's territorial sovereignty. Neither the nation's armed forces nor the general public, which were equally aroused, would admit of retreat without resistance. On the other hand, Japan's

[1] See Chapter I.

ruling groups, notably the military and the dominant elements of big business, had become convinced that war was necessary both to consolidate their home front and break China's growing unity and strength. A campaign restricted to the north might have been prolonged indefinitely without seriously affecting the military strength or

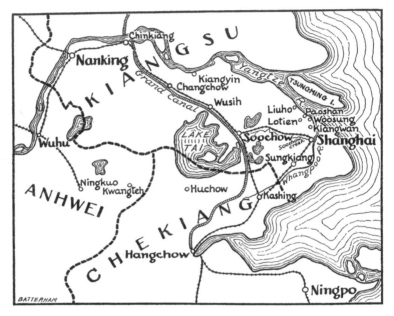

THE SHANGHAI-NANKING REGION.

economic resources of the Chinese government. To attack the latter at its vital point, operations in the Shanghai area would have to be undertaken.

Before the end of July a typical incident in Hongkew, reminiscent of earlier affairs, had plunged a large part of Shanghai's northern district into a fever of excitement. On the evening of July 24 a Japanese civilian reported that three Japanese bluejackets had been involved in a fight with a group of Chinese. At the end of the fracas, the informant claimed, the Chinese party had bundled a first-class seaman, Sadao Miyazaki, into a car and carried him off. This civilian informant gave a false name and address; despite thorough search, he could never be located for further questioning. His information had been relayed to the Naval Landing Headquarters, which immediately went into action. Japanese marines in full war kit, with steel helmets and with rifles at fixed bayonet, were speedily stationed along the roads where the incident had occurred. Trucks crammed with fully equipped Landing Party contingents tore through the streets, depositing men at various points in Hongkew. Patrols were sent through the area, cars were stopped, people were interrogated and searched. As the seaman was indisputably missing, these precautions continued for several days. The Chinese population, fearing that hostilities were about to begin, was greatly alarmed and a general exodus of Chinese citizens from the adjoining Chapei areas began.

Local Japanese officials called on the Chinese authorities in connection with the affair. Mr. O. K. Yui, Mayor of Greater Shanghai, pointed out to the Japanese Consul-General that the Naval Landing Party had despatched fully-equipped patrols to the territory outside the Settlement before investigating the facts regarding the incident. The alleged kidnaping was brought up on the floor of the Diet at Tokyo, contributing to stir nationalist passions in Japan. On July 29 the true facts of the incident came to light. There had been no fight between Chinese and Japanese, nor had Miyazaki been abducted. He had deserted, changed into Chinese clothes, hidden for two nights on the Bund, and then stowed away on a Chinese river steamer. At Chinkiang he had been taken into custody by Chinese police, who sent him to the Nanking

Foreign Office for questioning on July 28, under suspicion
of being a spy. There his identity was established, following which the Chinese authorities turned him over to the
Japanese Embassy.[2] In its details, this affair was reminiscent of the missing Japanese consular officer two years
previously, who, after Japan had mobilized war vessels at
Nanking and threatened dire action, was found un-
harmed, although he had run away and attempted suicide
in despondency over failure to be promoted. The handling of the Miyazaki incident by the Naval Landing
Party was a fair sample of its high-handed methods at
Shanghai, where for several years the Chinese and foreign
populace had been continually alarmed by Japanese maneuvers carried out at all hours of the night in the heart
of the Settlement. Aside from provocative use of the
Japanese marines, the higher officers showed no intention
of expanding the Miyazaki case into cause for war. It
served nonetheless to increase the apprehension at Shanghai, where feeling was already running high over events
in the north.

In the two weeks' grace which followed, China's political unification was carried several steps further. Under
threat of imminent war, the leaders both at Nanking and
in the provinces seemed impelled to overcome the last
remnants of separatism. On July 31 the National Salvation leaders were released from their prison at Soochow,
where they had been detained for eight months. They
proceeded to Shanghai and thence to Nanking, where one
of their number interviewed General Chiang Kai-shek
and assured him of their determination to assist in re-
pelling Japanese aggression. The ban on songs of the
national salvation movement, which had been imposed
in deference to Japanese susceptibilities, was lifted; and

[2] *North-China Daily News*, Shanghai, July 25, 29, 1937.

these stirring tunes, created out of the nationalist revival, were allowed to be broadcast. General Han Fu-chu arrived at Nanking on the morning of August 1, consulted with Generals Feng Yu-hsiang and Chiang Kai-shek, and left by return train to Shantung the same afternoon. Before large mass meetings on August 2 at Canton and Kweilin, the ranking military leaders of Kwangtung and Kwangsi pledged their support of the National Government. On August 4 General Pai Chung-hsi, one of the two Kwangsi leaders, landed at the capital in a plane despatched by the Generalissimo. The subsequent meeting of these two men, who had been bitter enemies since March 1929, was the first in eight years. One after another, during the early days of August, the leading provincial commanders appeared at Nanking to consult with the central authorities. General Yen Hsi-shan of Shansi reached Nanking on August 2, while Generals Ho Chien of Hunan and Yu Han-mou of Kwangtung arrived on the following day. General Liu Hsiang of Szechuan, arriving on August 7, announced that the troop readjustments in his province were being rapidly completed, after which Szechuan would be able to contribute its man-power to the state. On August 9 General Lung Yun, chairman of Yunnan, appeared at Nanking for the first time in his career, and declared that his province was ready to offer its full support to the Central Government. One of the last schisms was healed when General Tsai Ting-kai, leader of the 19th Route Army during the Shanghai hostilities of 1932, visited the capital and offered his services to the Generalissimo; he was later followed to Nanking by associate commanders of the same army, including Generals Li Chi-shen, Chen Ming-shu and Chiang Kwangnai, all of whom had participated in the Fukien rebellion of 1933-1934. This period also witnessed the successful completion of the Kuomintang-Communist negotiations. The Communist forces were reorganized as the Eighth Route Army, commanded by General Chu Teh; the vice-commander was General Peng Te-huai. These appointments were formally gazetted on August 22 by General Chiang Kai-shek, in his capacity as chairman of the Military Affairs Commission. By the end of August, every military leader in China was directly responsible to the central command of the National Government at Nanking.

This new-won military unity was at once put to the supreme test. A steady evacuation of Japan's nationals from the Yangtze valley was capped on August 6 by official orders for all remaining Japanese to leave Hankow. The subsequent concentration of Japanese vessels from the upper Yangtze in and around Shanghai fostered Chinese apprehension that a renewed invasion of the city was being planned. On August 9, as the result of a shooting affray near the Hungjao Airdrome, two members of the Japanese Naval Landing Party and a Chinese member of the Air Force Auxiliary were killed. The Japanese authorities claimed that a sub-lieutenant, with a seaman as chauffeur, had been driving along an outside road, when Chinese with rifles and machine-guns surrounded the car and suddenly opened fire. According to the Chinese version, the Japanese marines had attempted to drive into the military airdrome; challenged by a Chinese sentry, they shot him down with a revolver. Attracted by the firing, Chinese members of the Peace Preservation Corps rushed to the scene, exchanged shots with the Japanese bluejackets, and killed them. Mr. O. K. Yui, the Shanghai Mayor, called attention to the fact that previous disputes had occurred in that vicinity, and that repeated protests had been lodged with the Japanese authorities over attempts of their marines to enter the Hungjao Airdrome.[3]

The efforts of a joint Sino-Japanese investigation committee to fix responsibility for the incident were nullified by the rapid progress of events. On August 11 a Japanese Naval Squadron of four cruisers and seven destroyers arrived in Shanghai with marine reinforcements. A stream of arms, ammunition and supplies poured from the Japanese cruisers and destroyers onto the Yangtzepoo Wharf of the Osaka Shosen Kaisha, where they were loaded into lorries and taken to the barracks of the Naval Landing Party's headquarters on Kiangwan Road. A large detachment of bluejackets, in full marching kit, was landed; it was reported that the Landing Party's force of about 5,000 men was to be increased to 9,000. At the same time the Japanese authorities requested the Shanghai Mayor and General Yang Hu, the local Chinese garrison commander, to withdraw the Peace Preservation Corps and dismantle all Chinese military defense works in and around the Shanghai area. The same demands were presented to the Chinese Foreign Office at Nanking on the following day.

August 12 marked the eve of the outbreak at Shanghai. Five additional Japanese naval vessels, and a transport carrying 1,000 reinforcements for the Landing Party, reached the city. It was estimated that 28 Japanese war vessels of all types were concentrated in the Whangpoo River. Late that afternoon the Chinese authorities threw a boom across the Whangpoo River from the Nantao Bund to Pootung, with the object of protecting the Kiangwan arsenal and naval dockyards, which were located some distance above the barricade. Vanguards of the 88th division, part of Nanking's crack Fifth Army,

3 *North-China Daily News*, August 10, 1937.

entered Chapei, where sand-bag barricades were erected. The Chinese population of Hongkew and Chapei was thrown into panic, and evacuation reached a peak never equalled even in 1932. The Shanghai Volunteer Corps was mobilized to protect the foreign-controlled areas of the Settlement, exclusive of Hongkew. At a special meeting of the Joint Commission, a representative body of the major Powers organized to supervise execution of the Shanghai Armistice of May 5, 1932, the Japanese and Chinese delegates mutually accused the other of violating the truce agreement. This was the last diplomatic gesture; hostilities began on the following morning.

The first stage of the warfare in Shanghai, up to August 23, was confined mainly to Chapei and Hongkew, where the Japanese naval landing forces were compelled to stand on the defensive against incessant Chinese attacks. At times during this period, the Chinese troops pushed well into the Japanese lines, but were unable to consolidate their advances owing to the heavy shelling from the Japanese naval vessels. The Chinese air force continuously sought to sink the *Idzumo,* flagship of the Japanese fleet in the Whangpoo, but never succeeded. On August 14, during the course of one of these raids, Chinese planes dropped bombs in two thickly settled quarters of the Settlement, resulting in 3,609 casualties, of whom 1,741 were killed.[4] Official sources at Nanking claimed that shell fire had wounded the airmen and damaged the bombracks, releasing the bombs accidentally. On August 20 a shell struck the *Augusta,* flagship of the United States naval forces at Shanghai, resulting in the death of one seaman and the wounding of eighteen members of the

[4] Official figures published October 26 by the Fire Brigade. On August 23 a large projectile, from an unidentified source, also took a heavy toll of 773 casualties, with 215 deaths, in the Settlement.

crew; investigation failed to establish the source of the projectile. Japanese air-raids on cities in widely separated areas of the Yangtze valley carried the war well into the interior of China. In dog-fights over these cities, especially Nanking, the Chinese aviators proved their mettle by downing some two score Japanese planes.

During the week beginning August 23, Japanese army contingents, aided by heavy naval concentrations, effected costly landings at several points on the lower Whangpoo and Yangtze rivers. A severe struggle for possession of the key points of Paoshan, Lotien and Liuho was thus inaugurated, with additional Japanese troops gradually concentrating in this region. For some weeks the warfare continued indecisively at two separated areas, the one immediately around Shanghai and the other on the banks of the Yangtze River near Woosung. On August 26 two Japanese planes machine-gunned and bombed motor-cars containing a party of British officials traveling from Nanking to Shanghai. The British Ambassador to China, Sir Hughe Knatchbull-Hugessen, was seriously wounded. A lengthy diplomatic controversy ensued, at the conclusion of which Britain's demands for satisfaction, including immunity for non-combatants, were only partially met by the Japanese government. Japanese disregard for the safety of non-combatants was strikingly illustrated on September 8, when the bombing of a crowded refugee train standing at the Sungkiang station, on the Shanghai-Hangchow Railway, resulted in the deaths of at least 300 Chinese civilians. A blockade of the Chinese coast from Shanghai to Swatow, proclaimed by the Japanese naval authorities on August 25, was extended to the whole of the coast from Chinwangtao to Pakhoi on September 5. This blockade was applied only to Chinese shipping, although the Japanese authorities reserved the right to hail foreign merchantmen to ascertain their identity. After three weeks of dogged defense, the Chinese troops were forced to withdraw from their advanced coastline positions along the lower Yangtze. Lotien was surrendered on September 15, following the loss of Paoshan. In the Shanghai area a slight withdrawal had been effected on September 13. A new line, running from the North Station through Tachang and Liuhong to Liuho, was firmly consolidated.

The fighting in the lower Yangtze region was of the highest strategic importance, since a sufficient advance in this sector would enable the Japanese army to turn the flank of the Chapei-Kiangwan front and force a Chinese retreat from Shanghai. During the next six weeks, Japanese assaults in this area were bitterly contested and advances won only at heavy cost. Chafing at the stubborn opposition, the Japanese military authorities decided to extend and intensify their bombardments of Chinese cities behind the lines. On September 20 Vice-Admiral Hasegawa, in communications to the foreign consuls at Shanghai, served notice that Nanking would be severely bombed after noon on September 21 and warned all foreign nationals to evacuate the city. To this demand the local foreign authorities made strong protests, which were echoed in capitals abroad. On September 22 some thirty or forty Japanese planes subjected Nanking to a drastic bombardment. The bombs landed on more than thirty places, including a refugee camp where approximately 100 civilian refugees were killed. A series of Japanese raids on Canton, also carried out at this time, had even more disastrous effects, resulting in an estimated total of roughly 2,000 casualties. Widespread destruction was also caused on September 24 by a raid on Hankow, with approximately 700 casualties, of which the major proportion consisted of refugees and children. In the face of mounting sentiment in Europe and the United States against these exhibitions of Japanese "frightfulness", and the adoption by the League Assembly on September 28 of a resolution condemning the bombing of open towns, the Japanese naval authorities saw fit partially to curtail the air-raids and restrict them to more specifically military objectives. Large Japanese reinforcements were thrown into the fighting in the Liuho-Tachang sector during October. Sanguinary engagements, featured by continuous Chinese counter-attacks to regain ground temporarily lost, continued until nearly the end of the month. The capture of Tachang, key position of the Chinese center, was finally effected on October 26. Japanese forces at once pressed into the rear of the Chapei-Kiangwan front, from which the Chinese troops withdrew in good order across Soochow Creek on October 27.

The new Chinese line, running from Soochow Creek to Liuho, promised to afford an equally stern defense against a frontal attack. Initial Japanese efforts to break the Soochow Creek front were turned back. Additional troops were brought in from Japan, and early in November landings were effected as several points on Hangchow Bay, some fifty miles southwest of Shanghai. This flank movement was pushed rapidly north toward the Shanghai front; within a week the Japanese forces involved had covered more than half the distance. The Chinese troops in Pootung withdrew on November 7 through the narrowing gap left by the Japanese advance from the south. On the following day the bulk of the Chinese forces evacuated the Soochow Creek area, with rearguards covering the retreat. A force of several thousand Chinese troops was cut off in Nantao; after severe Japanese shelling, it was compelled to hand over its arms on November 12.

The occupation of the Shanghai area had taken exactly three months, during which Japan's military forces had suffered their heaviest losses since the Russo-Japanese War.

During the last three weeks of November, the Japanese armies rapidly cleared the triangle formed by Shanghai, Hangchow Bay and the Tai Lake, and began an advance on Nanking in several parallel columns. From the southern and inner sides of the Tai Lake, one column pushed inland toward Wuhu, in an effort to flank the capital's defenders, while another moved overland toward Nanking. The more vital offensive was made from north of the Tai Lake, where Japanese forces pressed up the Shanghai-Nanking Railway and along the banks of the Yangtze River. In this sector the Kiangyin-Wusih defense line was the immediate objective of the Japanese drive. Wusih fell first, followed by reduction of the Kiangyin forts at the beginning of December. The last major obstacle to a direct assault on the capital was thus removed. By December 7 the outer defenses of Nanking were under attack; one week later, the Japanese military forces had won complete control of the city.

Japanese bombing planes, with what seemed to be deliberate intent, had meanwhile engaged in several attacks on British and American ships in the Yangtze River. On December 5 several Japanese planes bombed the steamers *Tuckwo* and *Tatung,* as well as the British gunboat *Ladybird,* at Wuhu. All three vessels plainly displayed the British colors. Both steamers were filled with Chinese civilian refugees; one of them burned, while the other was beached. Scores were killed, while the American Mission Hospital at Wuhu treated more than a hundred burned and mangled Chinese. Japan's apologies for the attack on the steamers were delivered on December 8.

Four days later the American gunboat *Panay* and three

oil tankers, anchored 28 miles up-river from Nanking, were bombed by Japanese planes. The gunboat was sunk, and the tankers were either destroyed or beached. Although the *Panay* was clearly marked with American flags and other insignia, and was resting in an open stretch of the river, it was subjected to four successive bombing attacks. Parties of the gunboat's survivors, making their way toward shore in small boats, were machine-gunned by the planes. A Japanese military launch machine-gunned, boarded and searched the *Panay* before it sank. Three Americans and one Italian were killed, or subsequently died of their wounds, and nearly two score were wounded. Stern protests from the United States, including a request that they be brought to the attention of the Emperor, eventually elicited replies from the Japanese authorities which were accepted as satisfactory by Washington.

For several days after Japan's victorious entrance into Nanking, no word as to what was transpiring at the capital, or as to the fate of the foreigners who had remained to supervise a safety zone for Chinese civilians, could be obtained. When the news finally leaked out, it became apparent that a complete breakdown of discipline had occurred among the Japanese troops. Wholesale looting, terrorism, and violation of women's security had taken place in all quarters of the city. The feeling of relief at first experienced by many of Nanking's residents, who expected an end to minor disturbances and looting by evacuating Chinese troops, was engulfed in a much greater horror. These excesses at Nanking, which duplicated scenes in Paotingfu and other captured cities and towns in North China, were clearly connived at by the Japanese officers, some of whom were seen directing the looting of street shops. The rounding up of former Chinese soldiers, who were tied together by ropes and executed in batches of forty or fifty, was also directed by Japanese officers. Looting of American residences both at Nanking and Hangchow, the latter of which fell to Japanese forces on December 24, formed the subject of protests later presented at Tokyo by the United States government.

Dispatches from Tokyo, prior to the fall of Nanking, indicated that the Japanese Cabinet expected to be able to conclude a peace treaty immediately after the fall of the capital. The stubbornness of the Chinese resistance at Shanghai had confounded Japan's military leaders. With the relatively easy and rapid advance on Nanking, a considerable degree of confidence had been restored. On December 8 Hugh Byas wirelessed from Tokyo: "Chinese leaders are conferring, and it is known a peace party exists, so the Japanese hope a new government, sufficiently representative to be recognized by the world and disposed to conclude a peace treaty, will replace Chiang Kai-shek's administration. . . . The prospect of a victorious termination of what has been a short, easy, inexpensive war arouses great exuberance here." [5] At the time Japan was already sending peace feelers to the Chinese authorities. For a while Tokyo was apparently led to believe that Wang Ching-wei, chairman of the Kuomintang Central Political Council, and General Chang Chun, former Chinese Foreign Minister, would take over the government and seek to obtain the best peace terms possible. The Chinese armies had been defeated; obviously, they would now have to sue for peace.

The danger of a split among China's leaders, some of whom undoubtedly voted for compromise, was probably very real during the first two weeks of December. Japan's brutal excesses at Nanking did not help to uphold the

[5] *New York Times,* December 8, 1937.

hands of the compromisers. The crucial period passed with no overt signs of capitulation. The peace was not concluded. An answer to Japan's overtures may be read in General Chiang Kai-shek's statement of December 17, broadcast to the nation from his military headquarters: "To capitulate is to court sure national disaster. No matter how the international situation turns, we must do our utmost and not depend on others. The time must come when Japan's military strength will be exhausted, thus giving China the ultimate victory. Appraising the probable outcome of hostilities, we are convinced that the present situation is favorable to China. The basis of China's future success in prolonged resistance is not found in Nanking or big cities but in villages all over China and in the fixed determination of the people. Since the beginning of hostilities Chinese army casualties on all fronts have exceeded 300,000. The loss of civilian life and property is beyond computation. Such huge sacrifices in resisting foreign aggression are unprecedented in the history of China. My position and responsibility do not admit of evasion of duty. As long as I live I shall pursue to the utmost of my ability China's determination to resist the aggressors and secure the ultimate victory for China." [6] The political unity forged in China during the early months of 1937, Japan was to learn, had substance to it. Various departments of the Chinese government had withdrawn from Nanking some weeks previously. The active Ministries, such as Foreign Affairs and Finance, were established in Hankow, while other offices were removed to Chungking, on the upper Yangtze. New armed forces were recruited and placed in training, and measures to continue resistance to the Japanese armies of invasion were vigorously pushed.

[6] *New York Herald Tribune*, December 17, 1937.

CHAPTER NINE

THE STRUGGLE IN THE NORTH

IN North China, at the end of July 1937, the Chinese military forces in the Peiping-Tientsin area had retreated along three railway lines: the Tientsin-Pukow, the Peiping-Hankow, and the Peiping-Suiyuan. The Japanese command had two alternatives. It could continue its efforts to clear Hopei province by pushing along the two trunk railways which ran south from Tientsin and Peiping, or it could advance north and west through the Nankow Pass into the Inner Mongolian provinces of Chahar and Suiyuan. Obvious strategic considerations dictated the latter course, since the mountains west and northwest of Peiping flanked the Hopei plain and exposed it to the threat of raiding attacks. Relatively small forces were therefore detailed to keep the Chinese units south of Tientsin and Peiping at bay, while the bulk of the available Japanese troops sought to force the Nankow Pass. Strong Chinese resistance in this quarter held up the Japanese drive until nearly the end of August. One Japanese contingent made the frontal attack; another flanking detachment pushed up parallel with and some ten miles south of the pass. Nearly a month elapsed before this latter force had debouched on the high plain behind the pass; on August 27 it entered Huailai, a town on the Peiping-Suiyuan line between Nankow and Kalgan. On the same day units of the Kwantung Army, which had

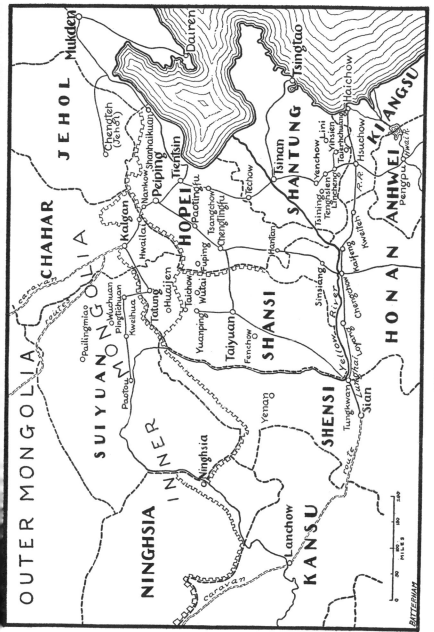

THE NORTH CHINA PROVINCES.

marched across Chahar from Manchuria, occupied Kalgan. Faced with this threat to their rear, the Chinese forces defending the pass had already effected a retreat toward the southwest. Before withdrawing they had blown up several locomotives in one of the Nankow tunnels, but failed to destroy the tunnels themselves; within ten days, the Japanese military had cleared the railway and established communication between Peiping and Kalgan. The Japanese expeditionary forces had continued along the railway to Tatung; here they divided, with one group pushing westward into Suiyuan and another southward into Shansi.

During the course of these operations, the Japanese command had made extensive preparations for a drive in Hopei province. Early in September, Japanese munitions and food trains were still being unloaded at intermediate stations between Tientsin and Peiping, and their stocks added to the mountainous piles of crates, boxes, bags and baskets of all kinds stacked along the platforms. Pontoon bridges were brought in for river crossings. A force of Japanese troops estimated at 300,000 was disposed in readiness for the offensive. On September 10 a concerted attack was launched along a seventy-mile front stretching between the railways leading south from Peiping and Tientsin. The Japanese forces had an overwhelming superiority of armament. They were equipped with about 30 tanks, more than 100 airplanes, and all types of modern artillery, ranging from one-pounders to five-inch howitzers and heavier guns. Against the weight of such an offensive, backed by methodical preparation for every eventuality, even the best Chinese force would have been at a hopeless disadvantage. As it was, the Chinese commanders on this front made no effort to overcome their mechanical inferiority by resort to mobile warfare or

attacks on the Japanese lines of communication. The in-
trenched armies, lacking adequate artillery and without
anti-aircraft guns or a single war plane, waited almost
fatalistically for the attack. When it came, the center of
the Chinese front collapsed and both wings were rolled
up. Blasted from their first-line positions and mercilessly
bombed and machine-gunned from the air during their
retreat, the withdrawing troops were never able to consolidate their secondary defense lines. The Japanese forces
rapidly pushed their way down both railways. Paotingfu,
capital of Hopei province, was occupied September 24;
on the same day Tsangchow, a large town on the Tientsin-
Pukow Railway, also fell to the advancing Japanese
armies.

The actions of the Japanese troops in Paotingfu beg-
gared description. For more than a week some 30,000 soldiers indulged in an unrestrained orgy of looting and
massacre. Virtually every shop and home in this city of
70,000 people, most of whom had already fled, was systematically broken into, looted, and wrecked. Chinese
refugees were shot and bayoneted on the streets. A foreign
correspondent, who reached Paotingfu several days after
its fall, watched the work of destruction. On his way back
to Peiping he was placed under arrest by the Japanese
military authorities and detained for seventeen days before
he was allowed to return. One of the foreigners in the city
had his watch lifted by a Japanese officer. Sporadic firing
went on day and night, although the battle front was
miles south of the city. No Chinese woman was safe, either
in the city or in the surrounding villages. Cases of Chinese
civilians, all with tales of one tenor, filled the hospitals.
A young farmer was shot in the leg; his wife and sister
had been killed by Japanese soldiers. A middle-aged barber
was stabbed in the abdomen by a bayonet; two other Chi-

nese were killed outright in his shop. Usually there was not the vestige of an excuse for this wanton killing. Chinese refugees quartered at different places in the city were hounded by Japanese soldiers, threatened with drawn bayonets, and stripped of their few remaining belongings. Other phases of Japanese action at Paotingfu betrayed more systematic design. For days the city was lighted with bonfires, fed by tens of thousands of text-books from schools where 15,000 students had formerly pursued their education. The destruction did not stop with text-books. Laboratory equipment and part of the library of the Hopei Medical College were fed to the flames; so also were the crop-statistics of the Agricultural Institute, which represented the results of a decade of careful study and investigation designed to help the Chinese farmer.

The Japanese military advance had meanwhile continued steadily down the two railway lines. On October 3 Techow, in northern Shantung, was occupied, while Chengtingfu, junction of a railway line running west into Shansi province, was taken on October 13. The occupation of this strategic junction-point proved of inestimable value to the hard-pressed Japanese divisions in northern Shansi. A large force, estimated by correspondents at well over 100,000 troops, was detached from the main armies operating in Hopei province; this army immediately started an advance along the branch railway from Chengtingfu to Taiyuan, capital of Shansi province. The end of its march belongs to the story of the Shansi campaign, and will be told in that connection. Events at Chengtingfu were a repetition on a smaller scale of those in Paotingfu. News of the deaths of eight Catholic missionaries and one other foreigner, who were bayoneted and cremated in a group at Chengtingfu, was withheld by the Japanese au-

thorities for nearly six weeks; investigations conducted by
foreigners at the end of November tended to incriminate
Japanese troops, despite strenuous denials of responsibility
by garrison headquarters officials at Tientsin. With the
capture of Chengtingfu, the spectacular phase of the campaign in Hopei was concluded. During October and
November the Japanese troops left in this province gradually fought their way down the Peiping-Hankow Railway
into northern Honan; to the east, along the Tientsin-
Pukow line, they worked their way to the north bank of
the Yellow River in Shantung, where the large bridge near
Tsinan was blown up by retreating Chinese troops. On
both railway lines the 29th Route Army, which had been
driven from Peiping in July, doggedly held its ground
against the more powerful Japanese forces in a series of
sustained, courageous actions; months later, this army was
still fighting off the Japanese attacks in southern Shantung
and north of the Yellow River near Chengchow in Honan
province. At the end of November the Japanese command
postponed general operations south of the Yellow River
in Shantung, either through a desire to protect Japan's
investments or in the hope that General Han Fu-chu,
local Chinese governor, would yield the province without
a struggle.

In Shansi province the scheduled plan of Japanese
operations had meanwhile been rudely upset by the desperate resistance of the Eighth Route Army, assisted by
the Shansi provincial troops. The details of this campaign,
which was covered by none of the foreign correspondents,
were virtually unreported during the month of October,
when some of the severest engagements were fought along
the passes through the mountain barrier. Not until December did the correspondents in Peiping begin to piece

together, from reports of missionaries and information gathered by the foreign military attachés, the full story of these operations.

The preliminary stages of the Shansi invasion, including the capture of Tatung, were successfully handled. By the middle of September, the Japanese divisions—mainly from the Kwantung Army—had left the railway and taken Huaijen, some fifty miles south of Tatung. The mountain passes along the Great Wall in northern Shansi were before them. Here the Japanese troops were split into three or four columns which attempted to force their way southward through the passes, of which Pinghsiangkuan, Juyuehkou, and Yenmenkuan were the most important. Sections of the Eighth Route Army, commanded by General Chu Teh, had taken up positions along the mountain barrier. In late September the Communist forces isolated a full division of Japanese troops in a narrow defile at Pinghsiangkuan, the easternmost pass, and cut them to pieces. General Chu Teh later stated that 2,000 Japanese troops were killed in this single engagement. At about the same time, however, another invading column broke through at Juyuehkou, and debouched into more open country at Fanchih and Taichow. Large Japanese reinforcements also increased the pressure at Pinghsiangkuan and finally forced the pass, whereupon a considerable portion of the Eighth Army fell back to Wutai and the Hsinkou range, covering the approaches to Taiyuan.

During these operations the Eighth Army leaders refused to be drawn into a positional battle in which they might have been destroyed by the bombing planes and superior artillery of the Japanese. Marching often at night, and guided by information supplied by the local population, they swiftly attacked carefully chosen objectives and then withdrew. The Japanese forces which first broke

GENERAL CHU TEH, COMMANDER OF THE EIGHTH (COMMUNIST)
ARMY, DONS A KUOMINTANG UNIFORM.

through at Juyuehkou, as well as the neighboring pass of Hsiaoshihkou, totaled about 50,000 troops. They were soon surrounded south of Taichow by overwhelming Chinese armies, including provincial troops and units of the Eighth Army, and for a time were in desperate straits. Even with supporting reinforcements, which brought the combined Japanese force to more than 100,000 troops, it proved impossible to break the Chinese resistance which developed along the Hsinkou range. From the middle of October to the end of the first week in November, the Japanese divisions which had penetrated the northern passes were held up north of Taiyuan. Sections of the Eighth Route Army, still operating in the passes, completely disrupted the supply lines of the invaders. Pinghsiangkuan and Yenmenkuan were twice recaptured and held for a time by Eighth Army detachments, and a continuous series of engagements occurred in the rear of the Japanese columns. These swift attacks, often in considerable force, made it impossible for all except large and heavily mechanized Japanese contingents to move south from Tatung to the aid of their fellow armies south of the passes. The Kwantung Army commanders' whole offensive bogged down. They were bailed out by the army which had started into Shansi from the east, at Chengtingfu, three weeks earlier.

This force was also operating in difficult country. The Chengtai Railway, which runs from Chengtingfu to Taiyuan, climbs steadily from the Hopei plain toward the high plateau on which Taiyuan, the capital of Shansi, is situated. It passes through a series of mountain ranges, cut by deep river valleys. The Niangtsekuan passes, along this route, are virtually as impregnable as the Great Wall barrier in northern Shansi. As it happened, the few Chinese troops defending this quarter were unequal to their task; the bulk of the local troops and the Eighth Army were all in the north. The Japanese army from the east smashed its way steadily through the Niangtsekuan passes; by the end of the first week of November, it had reached the outskirts of Taiyuan. Its appearance was decisive, in so far as the defense of the capital was concerned. Taken from the rear, the Chinese defense along the Hsinkou range was compelled to give way, and the Japanese advance guards entered Taiyuan on November 9.

Weighing the results of the Shansi campaign, the Japanese army command could find little cause for self-congratulation. The task of conquering north Shansi, at first entrusted to several relatively small Japanese columns, had eventually required an army of between 200,000 and 300,000 men. After the fall of Taiyuan a good portion of this force was needed to hold the ground already won. Until late February the city of Fenchow, distant only about eighty miles from Taiyuan on a good motor highway, was still held by Chinese troops. The Eighth Route Army ranged across the Japanese line of communications from Tatung to Taiyuan, rendering it useless as a source of military supplies.

On the basis of these first clashes with Japan's war machine, General Chu Teh had formed certain preliminary judgments which reveal his coolly calculating temper. The Japanese, he remarked in an interview with a newspaper correspondent,[1] had superior arms and used them well; they could act according to their plans and keep their plans secret; they did not surrender their guns but fought until killed, mainly because they feared death if taken captive; they could retreat and bring in reinforce-

---

[1] *China Weekly Review*, November 13, 1937, p. 239; for other details, see also *Domei* dispatch, *Peking & Tientsin Times*, September 29, 1937; and editorial, September 30, 1937.

ments more quickly than the Chinese. On the other hand, the war spirit among the rank and file was low; the Japanese soldiers did not like to build defense works; their intelligence service worked slowly; and—this he thought a fundamental weakness—they feared hand-to-hand battles. He pointed out that most of the Japanese killed had fallen in hand-to-hand combat; hand grenades accounted for the second largest number. Not a man of the Eighth Army had been captured; without exception, the Japanese had put to death every soldier captured from other Chinese forces in Shansi. At Yenmenkuan on October 18 units of the Eighth Route Army had attacked the Japanese airfield; using hand grenades it had destroyed twenty-one Japanese planes, leaving only three on the field before it retreated. In engagements following that at Ping-hsiangkuan, Chu Teh stated, the Eighth Army had killed between three and four thousand Japanese troops, suffered less than one thousand killed, and had virtually re-equipped its troops with captured Japanese arms and munitions.

The severe losses inflicted on the Japanese army during this campaign, its protracted character and inconclusive results, and the number of troops required for the capture of Taiyuan demonstrated the efficacy of the mobile warfare employed with such skill by the Chinese Communist leaders. Formal conclusion of the campaign left the Japanese command with a military problem scarcely less serious than the one it faced at the outset of its operations. Its chief opponent in Shansi, the Eighth Route Army, by avoiding positional battles, had emerged virtually intact to continue the struggle. The Eighth Army's war base in the mountains of northern Shansi is the most strategic area in the whole of North China. As long as the Chinese forces led by Chu Teh and his associates can operate in this region, the consolidation and pacification of Japan's conquests in the northern provinces will be a long-drawn-out and inconclusive affair, engaging the efforts of large and expensive armies of occupation. From north Shansi, during the early months of 1938, the Eighth Route Army sent raiding detachments into Suiyuan, Chahar and Hopei which harried all the main Japanese lines of communication in these provinces.

Of basic importance is the fact that the population of this whole area has been opened to the organizational efforts of the Eighth Army, which for the past ten years has been demonstrating the extraordinary military potentialities of the Chinese masses when properly led. Paradoxically, the Japanese invasion, which claims to be saving China from bolshevism, has enabled the Communist leaders to exercise their talents for making effective soldiers of workers and peasants in a larger area than they had ever dreamed of. It was the pressure of Japanese aggression, in the first place, which forced the Nanking authorities into a position where they became willing to bury the hatchet with their erstwhile foes. Many observers felt that the Kuomintang-Communist agreement of last spring, which restricted the Red forces to the comparatively poor Shensi-Kansu-Ninghsia districts, would eventually bring about the decline and disintegration of the Chinese Communist movement. Japan's invasion of North China has completely altered this perspective. The Eighth Army has now a large and important sector of the national defense front to hold against the invaders, in which it can apply the lessons of its rich guerrilla campaigning experience of a decade.

The Communist leaders are already devoting a major portion of their energies to the speedy organization of partisan forces, which can immediately take the field to harry the enemy outposts and supply lines. Japanese excesses in the North China countryside, reported in Peiping by a succession of eye-witnesses, may be counted on to induce the peasants to lend a willing ear to the appeal for enlistment in military service. Thousands of the peasants, as well as the townspeople, have been torn from their surroundings or embittered by wanton murders of their closest relatives. A correspondent who traveled through rural districts swept over during the Hopei campaign found that an almost unparalleled reign of terror existed. Forced requisitions, reckless killings, and worse had been the universal experience of the villagers. Some had been shot down while they ran in terror, others had suffered the same fate because they had not obeyed a command barked at them in the Japanese language. Many villages had lost as many as two score killed in this way, others had lost ten or a dozen. In many cases, the survivors were herded together by bayonet and forced to carry out tasks imposed by the Japanese military.[2] Chinese peasants, shot or bayoneted in the villages around Paotingfu, were coming into the hospitals two months after the fall of the city. In Mentoukou, a small town not far from Peiping, shops and homes were stripped bare by the Japanese forces of occupation: villages in the region around Mentoukou had lost every young Chinese woman. A first-hand observer reported similar conditions at Tatung, in north Shansi. Such circumstances tended to produce sympathy and support when the Eighth Army organizers entered a village or town and began the task of winning the people to active resistance against the invader.

The extent to which these efforts have been rewarded is indicated by the testimony of missionaries and other

[2] The author witnessed an example of this in Kalgan, in the middle of September 1937.

observers from the interior of Hopei province. North Shansi, by virtue of its geographical position, dominates the greater part of the Hopei plain from the Peiping environs south. The mountain ranges extending from Shansi into western Hopei offer excellent cover for military forces entering this region, especially if they possess the confidence of the Chinese peasants. During the fall months of 1937, a small and locally recruited guerrilla force maintained its position in the mountains a few miles west of Peiping. At the outset of the war the Eighth Army leaders sent upward of 10,000 regulars into western Hopei. This force later split up into numerous smaller bands which, accompanied by experienced political organizers, scattered across the interior areas and began to establish friendly contacts with the villagers. These units have been reorganizing remnants of defeated Chinese troops, collecting all available arms and ammunition, and organizing new worker and peasant guerrilla forces. Similar activities were being carried on in much of Shansi province, and in areas of Suiyuan and Chahar. It is safe to say that tens of thousands of new guerrilla forces have been put into the field in North China as the result of these efforts. At first these detachments may be poorly armed, but past experience suggests that the Eighth Army leaders may rapidly overcome this deficiency with captured enemy equipment. Chu Teh declared that in many of the new partisan units only fifteen or twenty out of a hundred men possessed rifles, the rest being armed with hand grenades. With the support of this type of campaigning by the central military authorities, which is now assured, supplies of small arms and ammunition can be procured from the government arsenals. Early in February nearly 100,000 silver dollars, raised by public subscription in Hankow, was expended for uniforms and other supplies to equip newly organized Shansi guerrilla forces.[3] Dr. H. H. Kung, the chairman of the Executive Yuan and himself a native of Shansi, contributed 10,000 dollars to this fund. On the leadership and morale of guerrilla troops depends much of their effectiveness. In its simplest terms, the strategy applied by the Eighth Army consists in keeping out of the way of superior forces and attacking when the enemy is weak or unprepared. Hundreds of leaders trained in this strategy in the People's Anti-Japanese Military Academy at Yenan are available for the present emergency, and can be placed in command of newly formed partisan units.

Eighth Army detachments in Hopei province were fighting as well as organizing. In Peiping during the last two weeks of November the correspondents had reports of from sixteen to twenty attacks on Japanese detachments along the Peiping-Hankow Railway. A Japanese airfield at Hantan, near the southern border of Hopei province, had been attacked with hand grenades and a number of airplanes destroyed; the Japanese aviators had returned by rail through Peiping. Only heavily armed Japanese detachments, usually escorted by airplanes, dared venture into the interior of Hopei. Actual Japanese military control embraced but a narrow strip of approximately five miles on either side of the railway, with somewhat larger areas around the more important cities, such as Paotingfu. East of the Peiping-Hankow Railway the countryside was still controlled by remnants of the Chinese divisions which had been swept aside in the big September push. In this area at the beginning of December the Japanese command was still unable to utilize the motor highway from Tientsin to Paotingfu as a regular supply line. In Suiyuan and Chahar units of the Eighth Army were also operating. The

[3] *New York Times*, February 5, 1938.

continuous reports of raids, captured towns, and torn-up railway tracks during the early months of 1938 suggested that the guerrilla campaign was acquiring increased momentum in North China.

In addition to the operations in Hopei and Shansi, the Japanese armies had fought a third major campaign in Inner Mongolia during the autumn of 1937. Following the capture of Kalgan and Tatung, the fighting was immediately carried into Suiyuan during mid-September. Here the provincial troops under General Fu Tso-yi proved no match for the crushing thrusts of the Kwantung Army divisions, assisted by Mongol forces. Three parallel columns participated in the early phases of the invasion. Pingtichuan, main strategic defense of the province, fell to the combined onslaught of the two southerly columns before the end of September. The Mongol force operating in the north took Pailingmiao during the first week of October and then pressed on to Wuchuan, twenty miles north of the capital. Kweihua, capital of the province, was occupied on October 14; three days later Paotou, western terminus of the Peiping-Suiyuan Railway, fell to a Japanese force. Japanese domination of the Inner Mongolian provinces, save for the western reaches of Ninghsia, had finally been achieved. Years of scheming by the Kwantung Army had gone into the accomplishment.

On October 29 a so-called National Assembly of the Mongol princes, meeting under Kwantung Army auspices at Kweihua, formally established the Federated Autonomous Government of Mongolia. Prince Yun was chosen Chairman, and Te Wang Vice-Chairman of the new government. The territories embraced by the new régime consisted mainly of the Chahar and Suiyuan banners; the Mongolian province of Hsingan in Manchoukuo was not included. Future expansion of this Mongolian kingdom was envisaged by the wording of Article 2 of the organic law, which stated that the government "shall rule over the territory originally possessed by Mongolia, but for the time being it will function" over the Chahar-Suiyuan banners. Echoes of the Manchoukuo state builders rang through many portions of this document. The new régime, according to Article 3, was "founded on the policy of anti-Communism and racial unity." [4]

The Kwantung Army's state-building activities did not stop with the Mongols; there were still the southern areas of Chahar and Suiyuan, populated mainly by Chinese, to be considered. For these regions an Autonomous Government of Chahar was set up at Kalgan, while at Kweihua an Autonomous Government of Suiyuan was formed. A committee to coordinate the work of the three new Inner Mongolian régimes was organized at Kalgan toward the end of November. The Kwantung Army's future relationship with the province of Shansi has not yet been made clear. The problem involves a certain amount of rivalry with the Japanese armies in North China under the command of General Terauchi. Both groups participated in the invasion of Shansi, but the title of the Kwantung Army, whose divisions entered the province from the north, does not seem entirely clear. Its entrance into Taiyuan was made possible only by the assistance rendered by the Japanese forces from Hopei, without which it might have pounded vainly at the Hsinkou range for some time longer. There can be no doubt that the Kwantung Army will surrender its tutelage of the three new Inner Mongolian régimes, or allow them to be merged with the provisional government established at Peiping, only with the greatest reluctance. Inner Mongolia is considered as

[4] For text of the organic act, see *The Peiping Chronicle*, October 30, 1937.

a natural extension of the Kwantung Army's exclusive sphere of jurisdiction in Manchoukuo.

At Peiping, in the autumn of 1937, conditions seemed outwardly normal, and the general routine of life went on much as usual. External signs of Japanese occupation, though quite apparent, were limited to a few sights which soon became customary and accepted. Columns of marching Japanese troops or long lines of supply carts might be encountered at any point in the city, instead of the Legation Quarter or its environs. Khaki-colored motor trucks, carrying Japanese troops or military supplies, drove recklessly through the streets, causing many accidents and not a few casualties among Chinese pedestrians, 'rickshaw pullers and their passengers, bicyclers and cartmen. To supply the large influx of Japanese residents, new Japanese shops were being continually opened on Hatamen Street, subtly changing its appearance and giving it a pronounced flavor of Japan. Most spectacular were the balloon streamers floating over Peiping—a wholly new sight, and typically Japanese. In late September and October, the lines of Chinese characters on these streamers usually reported the new cities captured by the Japanese armies. Later, possibly in deference to the susceptibilities of the local Chinese population, the sentiments expressed by the streamers changed to more general themes. Of these, the most favored read: "The Japanese Army preserves the peace of East Asia." Some Japanese doctor had evidently examined the water supply, and probably been horrified at the number of bacilli; the result was an overdose of chlorine, which confounded the digestion and rendered even tea undrinkable.

Economic life, as the result of many factors, had dropped to a low ebb, and a serious business depression prevailed.

The virtual closing of the port cities of Tientsin and Tangku to all but military supplies had throttled the foreign trade of North China. Collapse of the former Chinese government, and the withdrawal of the 29th Route Army, registered severe economic effects. An investigation covering but part of the city disclosed that 20,000 white-collar workers, including clerks, lower government officials, staff employees in factories and hotels, and those connected with the Chinese military, had been thrown out of employment. Among the lower classes the conditions were even more serious; more than 200,000 destitute were being fed at twenty-three local gruel kitchens, mostly conducted by charitable organizations under Chinese or foreign auspices. Normal agricultural life in the surrounding countryside was disrupted. In November there were still more than forty refugee centers at Peiping, housing upwards of 10,000 refugees from neighboring towns and villages. Retail business was seriously affected by the fear of looting; in many Chinese shops, all valuable articles had been taken off display and hidden for safe-keeping. Large losses were suffered from Japanese soldiers who would put down a tithe of the price for an object, offer a small sum in Japanese currency, or else walk out without paying anything. Early in September this situation became so serious, and was attracting so much comment, that the Japanese military authorities were forced to take cognizance of it and issue special regulations to hold it in check.[5] The tourist traffic of the summer and fall, an important item in the economic income of Peiping, had been frightened off in large part by the hostilities. This untoward situation is to be set right in 1938. Japanese tourist and other government agencies

[5] *The Peiping Chronicle,* September 5, 1937.

have prepared an extensive advertising campaign, which will feature the attractions of Peiping for European and American tourists.

Behind these surface phenomena, much more fundamental changes were occurring in Peiping's political life and social organization. During this period the city was nominally governed by a so-called Peace Maintenance Commission, which had been set up early in August. For months, despite strenuous efforts, the Japanese had been unable to secure the services of any Chinese puppets who would command the respect of the people. Chiang Chao-tsung, head of the Peace Maintenance Commission, was a conservative Confucian scholar who had held office in former Peking governments. Pan Yu-kwei, chief of police in this nondescript régime, had spent a term in jail for nefarious practices some years earlier. Marshal Wu Pei-fu, aged leader of the former Chihli Party, although resident in Peiping, had steadily refused Japanese overtures and spurned Japanese threats designed to make him become titular head of North China. As in Manchoukuo, this Peiping régime was controlled by a set of Japanese advisers which directed every phase of the administration. These advisers enforced the application of a series of measures which were rapidly molding North China into the likeness of Manchoukuo.

Within a few months the Chinese population was deriving its information of events in the rest of China and the outside world from sources controlled or directed by the Japanese civilian or military authorities. Any possible misuse of the forest of radio antennae over Peiping, which had at first caused the Japanese some concern, was speedily set right. Agents disseminating propaganda material were placed in the local broadcasting stations. The programs soon failed to supply any news, even from Japanese

THE STRUGGLE IN THE NORTH

agencies. A shriek, set up on the wave-length of Nanking's powerful station, effectively prevented successful reception from that quarter. Possession of short-wave radio sets was prohibited. The few short-wave radios owned by foreigners were heavily patronized.

A number of startling transformations occurred in the newspaper and news agency field. Following the Japanese occupation, the many Chinese newspapers that had appeared in Peiping and Tientsin were forced to suspend publication. In Peiping the Chinese staff of the *Central News,* a government agency, was imprisoned and kept under detention for several weeks. The important newspapers, each with its set of Chinese figure-heads, were reorganized and placed under Japanese direction. Filled with news items and dispatches of *Domei* and *Kokutsu,* these newspapers were hardly distinguishable from those published in Japan or Manchoukuo. The editors were held strictly responsible for what appeared in their papers. They were instructed to emphasize the number of Chinese casualties and the number of Chinese planes shot down or destroyed. They were forbidden to use the term "Chinese National Government", forced to vilify Chiang Kai-shek and the central authorities, and compelled to play up and praise Japan's "holy war" to deliver China from the clutches of its corrupt rulers. In Peiping such papers were forced on the Chinese shopkeepers by visitations from the police.

The evolution of the two English-language newspapers in Peiping took a characteristic course. At the end of July the editors of *The Peiping News,* a paper owned and managed by Chinese interests, were arrested; the editor-in-chief, Dr. Wilson S. Wei, was held in jail for months. After a temporary suspension, the paper reappeared on August 14 with a new set of Chinese editors;

thereafter its editorials and news items were thoroughly colored with a Japanese viewpoint. Pressure from the authorities forced *The Peiping Chronicle,* which was foreign owned and edited, to suspend publication on August 22. After considerable negotiation, the paper was allowed to resume on August 31, but difficulties still continued. Its delivery boys were shanghaied, and two of its Chinese sub-editors were attacked by thugs. At the beginning of November new interests, with Chinese names to the fore, bought up the *Chronicle.* In accordance with the change in the city's name decreed by the authorities, the title of the paper was altered to *The Peking Chronicle.* On December 1 the *News* suspended publication, leaving the *Chronicle* as the only English-language paper in Peiping. The latter's nominal editors are Chinese, but it is understood that the actual editorial work is carried on by a Mr. Gorman, who has long worked with the Japanese. The character of the paper is indicated by a scare head-line, published on November 20, which read as follows: "Mutiny and Coup D'Etat Led by Feng at Nanking has Communism as Centre." This was based on a *Domei* dispatch, itself taken from the *Asahi,* which "indicated" that "mutiny has reportedly occurred at Nanking"; a second *Asahi* message quoted by *Domei* said that General Feng Yu-hsiang was "reportedly planning to stage a coup d'état." Under these conditions, exaggerated reports of Chinese victories spread among the Chinese population, which is compelled to choose between such rumors or distorted materials from Japanese sources.

Peiping has always been the foremost educational center of China; in this sphere, wholesale changes were wrought by the Japanese occupation. The normal enrolment of approximately 80,000 elementary and middle school students, who came from all parts of North China, was cut nearly in half. With the loss of a substantial educational subsidy from the Nanking government, public school finances were seriously crippled. During the first two months of the school term, the teachers received only 30 per cent of their regular salaries. A Japanese-language teacher was attached to each of the 190 primary and middle schools, and the study of Japanese made compulsory. Text-books in history and civics were revised. All reference to the three principles of Sun Yat-sen or other ideas involving Chinese nationalism was eliminated, and the history of Sino-Japanese relations recast to illustrate Japan's benevolent intentions toward China. Use of the documents of the League of Nations was banned. Study of the Confucian classics, with particular reference to their encomiums on humility and obedience to authority, was emphasized. Abstruse tomes such as the *Yi Ching*, which no scholar pretends to understand, were offered as intellectual fare for pupils in the lower schools. Ultimately the whole set of Chinese text-books used in the primary and middle schools is to be revised. At one meeting of the local school principals, a Chinese teacher had the temerity to suggest that it would hardly be necessary to change all text-books, especially those in the natural sciences. He argued that the expense of purchasing a complete set of new text-books would impose a heavy burden on poor Chinese families. A Japanese sitting in at the meeting immediately stated that, considering the large expenditure which Japan was incurring for the benefit of China, it was unfortunate if the Chinese people should not be willing to contribute their small share. Early in September the authorities had attempted to organize a Student Union in Peiping. At the inaugural meeting, not more than half a dozen students appeared. A second meeting fared no better and the effort was given up, although the organization continued to exist on paper. The teachers, who were dependent on their positions for a livelihood, did not escape so easily; they were formed into clubs to promote Sino-Japanese friendship.

When Paotingfu and Taiyuan fell to the Japanese armies, brightly colored *pailou* symbolic of the victories were erected across the main streets of Peiping, and celebrations were organized. Each shop was compelled to send at least one representative to the street parades and demonstrations, or else contribute one dollar in local currency to help cover expenses. The primary and middle school principals were called together in advance, and notified that their pupils must take part in the street parades. Each school had to prepare flags and banners, inscribed with slogans furnished by the Japanese authorities. Thousands of students, many of whom had participated in the earlier anti-Japanese demonstrations in Peiping, paraded the streets on these occasions. They marched with lowered heads, in almost complete silence. No slogans were shouted; in many cases the flags were not even unfurled. Missionary schools, including Truth Hall and Bridgman Academy, were forced to send their pupils to these demonstrations.

On the occasion of the fall of Paotingfu, the turn-out of the students was not complete. The school principals, on the eve of the capture of Taiyuan, were therefore called on the carpet and told that they must see that every student appeared or there would be reprisal. This time the students were all out; again they were herded through the streets by Chinese police and an occasional Japanese soldier. At one point two thousand students were lined up before a military headquarters; officers inspected them from behind sand-bag barricades, and Japanese sentries pointed bayonets at them. They were ordered to cheer for the Japanese army. After the first feeble response the command was barked out more gruffly, and the cheers were louder. Nevertheless, when the demonstration was over, many of the students threw their flags into the moat around Central Park, where they were later seen floating on the water. The effects of these parades, which embitter the local population, would hardly seem to be worth the effort expended on them. A possible explanation is offered by the fact that many photographs of the demonstrations are taken; these are apparently sent home to illustrate the enthusiastic support which the Chinese people are giving to their deliverers from mis-rule and oppression.

University students were not compelled to join the demonstrations, mainly because the former flourishing college life of Peiping has been almost entirely swept away. Of some 13,000 former Chinese university students, only 1,700 were left in Peiping during the autumn of 1937. Where formerly there had been 2,200 professors and college teachers, there were less than five hundred. Sixteen of the twenty-six colleges and universities were shut down. Of those left, only three could be termed *bona fide* universities; the others included Peking Union Medical College, the College of Chinese Studies, and a business school. All of these were either under foreign auspices or had a considerable number of foreigners on their faculty staffs. Peking National University, the Oxford of China, had become a barracks for Japanese troops. The same was true of three other Chinese national universities at Peiping, including Tsinghua, the institution founded by American Boxer Indemnity funds. Part of the National Normal University was used as a stable for Japanese cavalry horses. The three real universities still functioning comprised Yenching, with American Protestant backing; Fu Jen, the Catholic University; and the Sino-French

University. Their enrolments were considerably reduced, but on giving pledges that no political activities would be permitted by the student body they were enabled to continue under watchful supervision.

From late November Japanese representatives made desperate efforts to enlist the political services of a more imposing set of Chinese figure-heads in the north. The patch-work régime formed by amalgamating the Peace Maintenance Commissions of Peiping and Tientsin had outlived its usefulness. Despite the approaching fall of Nanking, none of China's national leaders had swung over to cooperation with Japan. The real capital of China was already at Hankow, and the Japanese could substitute no rival authority at Nanking that would not be dwarfed by the galaxy of Chinese leaders up the river. Something had to be done toward setting up a more respectable alternative in the north. On December 14 a "provisional government of all China" was proclaimed in Peiping. No leader of sufficient stature to become president or chief executive of this provisional régime could be found. Wang Keh-min, twice Finance Minister in the old Peking governments dominated by the pro-Japanese Anfu clique, headed the executive council. Tang Erh-ho, veteran North China politician educated at Tokyo Imperial University, was made Minister of Education in the abbreviated cabinet. Another of the council members was Wang Yi-tang, also educated in Japan; once an adviser of Yuan Shih-kai, he had helped to organize the Anfu clique, which had contracted the notorious "Nishihara" loans in 1918. General Chi Hsieh-yuan, an old-style warlord who had fled to Japan after defeat in the civil wars of 1924, headed the Ministry of Public Safety. Every man on this list had long before been thoroughly discredited in the eyes of progressive Chinese public opinion. Premier Konoye welcomed the régime as heralding "the birth of a new China", but he did not see fit to extend Japan's immediate recognition. The provisional government's title to authority rested on Japanese bayonets. Its figure-heads were fairly safe on the main railways; off the trunk lines they might encounter responsible Chinese citizens. The first visit of Wang Keh-min, Tang Erh-ho, Wang Yi-tang *et al.* was to Tientsin, where they were herded in to pay their respects to General Terauchi, commander-in-chief of the Japanese military forces in North China. This was symbolic. For their continuance in office depends on Japan's ability to win the war. Against this a question-mark was being set by the rising tide of guerrilla opposition in the northern provinces. The new government was hardly ensconced in office when raiding activities were carried to the outskirts of Peiping and Tientsin. This, too, was an omen.

While the facts with regard to Chinese guerrilla campaigning in the north are of primary significance, they should not be exaggerated. They do not suggest that the Japanese military position in North China is untenable, or that new areas may not be overrun by heavily mechanized armies. They do mean that the Japanese command is faced with a military problem of large dimensions, which will continue to require a costly army of occupation for many years to come. The "pacification" of North China, certainly of any considerable section of the interior, will not be accomplished unless the Eighth Route Army is completely annihilated.[6] Failing this, from fifteen to twenty divisions of Japanese troops will be required to maintain control of the lines of railway communication in the northern provinces. And the problem may become steadily more serious if the Eighth Army is able to com-

[6] This was the reported objective of a Japanese drive across Shansi and into Shensi in late February of 1938, which had petered out by April.

plete its mobilization of the peasants in areas off the railway lines. In March 1938 a Chinese administration, embracing an estimated total of seven million people, was functioning in the interior of Hopei province.

Guerrilla operations in the north were being carried on at an increasing tempo during the winter months of 1937-1938, when the grain had been cut and cover was meager—a season when the armed Manchurian volunteers are normally driven into the most inaccessible areas of the Northeastern provinces. The campaign, in other words, had got off to an early and auspicious start. Consisting of an initial force of 100,000 troops seasoned by a decade of mobile warfare under the most difficult circumstances, and led by experienced commanders, the Eighth Army will carry on a wasting conflict that will try Japanese nerves to the utmost and place an increasing strain on Japan's economy and finances. The Communist leaders are convinced that China, because of its semi-colonial status and backward technique, cannot defeat Japan by engaging solely in positional warfare. Chu Teh made this point, during an interview last June,[7] in these succinct sentences: "China must depend on its peasant and worker strength if it is to fight Japan victoriously. For China this war must be a totalitarian war. Even all of our four hundred millions are not quite enough."

[7] Interview by author at Yenan in north Shensi, June 23, 1937.

CHAPTER TEN

JAPAN'S HOME FRONT

AUTHORITARIAN trends in Japan's political and economic life, which had rapidly become predominant after the February uprising in 1936, received new impetus with the outbreak of hostilities in China. The three weeks' delay between the Lukouchiao incident of July 7 and the launching of the Japanese attack in the Peiping-Tientsin area was utilized to cement public opinion behind the Konoye Cabinet and overcome the damaging effects of the political strife that had divided Japan under the Hayashi Ministry. For this purpose, nothing could have served so well as the long series of sporadic clashes in the neighborhood of Peiping from July 7 to 28. The relatively small Japanese forces on the ground in North China were depicted as under danger of imminent attack from overwhelming Chinese armies. During these three weeks the *Domei* news agency carried almost daily reports of the vast numbers of Chinese central troops that were being mobilized in southern Hopei for an advance on Peiping. All the newspapers in Japan, including such formerly progressive papers as the *Asahi,* joined in denunciations of China's "provocative" actions. The responsibility for the continued local clashes near Lukouchiao was unhesitatingly assigned to the Chinese troops.

Although the regimented press did yeoman work, the Japanese people refused to be swept off their feet. The public displayed marked suspicion of the army's motives, according to well-informed observers, throughout the month of July. Not until after the Japanese troops began to move on July 28, when the barrage of propaganda was intensified, did the war shibboleths win any measure of general acceptance. By dint of sheer repetition, the claims that Japan was "preserving peace in East Asia", "saving China from Communism", and "serving the welfare of the Chinese masses" gradually affected Japanese public opinion. Official circles were not wholly satisfied. As insurance against any flagging of patriotic sentiment, the government organized a national "spiritual mobilization" campaign. The movement was inaugurated at Tokyo on September 11 by a patriotic rally addressed by the Premier and other Cabinet Ministers, and broadcast by radio throughout the country. Despite all official efforts, the spontaneous popular enthusiasm generated during the earlier phases of the invasion of Manchuria was not apparent. The mobilization of approximately one million troops affected all sections of the country—a marked contrast to the Manchurian campaign and later advances, which had been handled by the regular army. This conflict with China was taken much more in the spirit of grim necessity.

The Cabinet organized by Premier Konoye, with its "national union" basis, was well fitted to take advantage of the change effected in public opinion. In the political parties, progressive tendencies were submerged by the flood of nationalist propaganda. The political leaders vied with each other in demonstrating their firm support of the Cabinet in its prosecution of the war. At the conclusion of the extraordinary session of the Diet on September 8, the lower house adopted the following resolution: "Let it be resolved that the House of Representatives shall, in accordance with the wish expressed in the gracious mes-

GENERAL SUGIYAMA, JAPANESE WAR MINISTER, ADDRESSES HOUSE OF PEERS BEFORE VOTE ON WAR APPROPRIATIONS IN SEPTEMBER 1937.

sage granted to it by the Emperor and with the principles of justice and equity, seek to realize national unanimity, cope with the situation with perseverance and tenacity, urge the lawless Republic of China to reflect on its attitude and establish peace in the Far East." [1] Many of the party leaders went abroad as unofficial ambassadors to explain the aims and purposes of Japan in relation to the China hostilities. Among others, these included Bunji Suzuki, of the Social Mass Party, who visited the United States in an effort to influence the American labor movement against taking hostile action toward Japan. The Social Mass Party openly supported the war. Fascist elements within the party, headed by such leaders as Hisashi Aso, Kanichiro Kamei and Manabu Hirano, were enabled to come to the fore under stress of the national emergency. One of the planks in the party platform adopted at its annual meeting, held in Tokyo on November 15, reads as follows: "To strive for the progress and development of Japan in accordance with the fundamental principles of national policy for the advancement of mankind's civilization and culture." [2]

Although the apparent political unanimity should have served to strengthen the Cabinet's position, Premier Konoye saw fit to add to it in October an advisory council of ten impressive personages. Meeting regularly once a week, this set of virtual unofficial Ministers was empowered to advise jointly or severally with members of the Cabinet. The personnel of the Board of Cabinet Councillors included General Kazushige Ugaki, General Sadao Araki, Admiral Nobumasa Suetsugu, Admiral Kiyotane Abo, all retired from active service; Mr. Chuji Machida, president of the Minseito; Mr. Yonezo Maeda, representing the

---

[1] *The Japan Advertiser*, September 9, 1937.
[2] *The Japan Advertiser*, November 16, 1937.

Seiyukai; Mr. Kiyoshi Akita, former speaker of the lower house; Baron Seinosuke Goh, of the business community; Mr. Seihin Ikeda, former governor of the Bank of Japan; and Mr. Yosuke Matsuoka, president of the South Manchuria Railway Company. This group was organized as a temporary organ "in order to participate in the Cabinet's discussion and planning of important State affairs concerning the China Incident." The Councillors were "to be accorded the Court treatment due to State Ministers in view of their Cabinet duties," but they were "not to become regular members of the Cabinet Council." [3] The Privy Council, in examining the draft ordinance establishing the Board, was somewhat concerned lest the Councillors might represent a set of Ministers without portfolio, but was assured that they constituted merely an advisory group whose recommendations need not be accepted.[4] One unexpressed function of the Board was to smooth over any rifts that might develop in Japan's ruling circles over the handling of the war. Its personnel was representative of the army, navy, the business community, and the political parties. The military and naval members of the Board, in particular, were obviously chosen with an eye to reconciling opposing points of view. General Araki and Admiral Suetsugu, two outstanding extremists, were balanced by the more moderate views of General Ugaki and Admiral Abo. In this connection, the editor-in-chief of the *Asahi* writes: "The Sino-Japanese conflict having been aggravated to an unexpectedly serious extent, failure to settle the situation properly may possibly involve internal strife in this country. The new system of Cabinet Counsellors

[3] Taketora Ogata, "Behind Japan's Greater Cabinet," *Contemporary Japan*, Tokyo, December 1937, p. 380.
[4] *The Japan Advertiser*, October 12, 1937.

represents a precaution taken by the Government to guard against this grave possibility." [5]

For the first six months of the war, the additional expenditures appropriated by the Japanese government reached the impressive total of nearly 2,600 million yen. The aggregate cost of the Russo-Japanese war to Japan was approximately 1,700 million yen; of this sum more than half, or roughly 900 millions, was borrowed abroad. Expenditures for the China war began with a sum allotted early in July from the reserves of the 1937-1938 fiscal term. At the first special Diet session, which convened for three weeks on July 25, two supplementary budgets were passed; a third supplementary budget was passed by the special session in September. These appropriations and their destination are shown in the following tables.

Authorized Expenditures		*Destination*	
	Yen		*Yen*
From 1937-1938 reserve	10,198,223	Army 1,736,019,270	
Passed by 71st Diet:		Navy 454,058,381	
First estimate	96,809,496	Debt service 10,220,499	
Second estimate	419,635,200	Reserve 350,000,000	
Passed by 72nd Diet:		Other ministries 41,623,175	
Emergency military.	2,022,671,158		
General account ...	42,607,248		
Total	2,591,921,325	Total 2,591,921,325	

These appropriations all came within the 1937-1938 fiscal year, ending March 31, 1938. They were in addition to the regular budget of 2,814 million yen, plus the first supplementary budget of 58 millions voted by the Diet in March, bringing the total estimated expenditures for the 1937-1938 fiscal term to 5,464 million yen. The 71st Diet approved a set of China war taxes in July which, with special reserve transfers, were estimated to produce an additional revenue of 106 million yen. Total bond emissions

[5] Taketora Ogata, "Behind Japan's Greater Cabinet," cited, p. 379.

to cover the anticipated deficit for the 1937-1938 fiscal year were estimated at over 3 billion yen. The leading Japanese economic journal comments editorially on the fiscal problem thus created as follows: "As it is out of the question that bonds in such vast amounts can be successfully placed in the market for assimilation within a few months, the Government appears to have decided on the policy of first selling the bonds in several blocks to the Bank of Japan, receiving in exchange a line of credit with which to meet fiscal expenditure. When the money market begins to show increasing signs of slackness as a result, the central bank is expected to sell bonds out of the above holdings and thereby contract the expanded credit supply. It is hardly necessary to say that this method involves the danger of provoking inflation. Much the same method has been used since 1932 whenever the Government issued bonds, and as this system served the purpose of the reflation policy for which there was a widespread demand in the Japanese financial community, no evil result was experienced. The present situation, however, is entirely different. The industrial mechanism is now being given almost full employment and a large number of able-bodied men have been called to the colors. To adopt such a fiscal policy at such a juncture is essentially to tread the path which the European belligerent nations followed during the world war. The probable duration of the fighting should dictate what sort of fiscal method is to be followed. We are, however, of the contention that the most sensible policy that can be adopted by this country is a taxation increase to be effected without delay, and we are convinced that both the Government and people will presently recognize the soundness of this contention."[6]

Japan's inability to borrow in foreign capital markets

[6] *The Oriental Economist,* September 1937, p. 501.

during recent years has enhanced the difficulty of its fiscal problem. All loans since the Manchurian invasion of 1931 have been floated in the home market. By the end of the current fiscal year Japan's national debt will amount to nearly 13 billion yen. Though relatively small in comparison with other major powers, this sum is equal to Japan's entire national income for 1936. In the near future it will continue to increase at a rapid rate. The fiscal problem is rendered even more acute by the large adverse balance of Japan's merchandise trade. For the first eleven months of 1937, the excess of imports for the Empire amounted to 647 million yen, as compared with 130 million yen in the full year of 1936 and 15 million yen for 1935. The increase may be partially accounted for by excess stocks of raw materials accumulated by light industry, but more largely by the rise in world prices and the demand for war supplies. These latter factors will doubtless continue to operate in 1938. The invisible items of Japan's balance of payments were also adversely affected by the decline in shipping income, attributable mainly to the requisitioning of ships for transport service.

To balance Japan's international accounts and maintain stability of the yen, the Japanese government has been forced to resort to large shipments of gold for the first time since 1931. During the five months from March to July 1937, the total shipments of gold reached the sum of 380 million yen.[7] Japan's gold reserves, however, are extremely limited. Specie reserves of the central banks and the new exchange equalization fund aggregated possibly two billion yen in August 1937. The production of gold in Japan and Korea, which has greatly increased in recent years, was still only slightly in excess of 100 million yen in

[7] *Contemporary Opinions*, Tokyo Information Bureau, November 11, 1937, p. 1.

1936.[8] Finally, Japan's nationals owned foreign securities and held deposits and loans in foreign currency at the end of April 1937 valued at approximately two billion yen. Japan's war chest was thus one of the smallest possessed by any first-class power. Combined gold reserves and foreign assets were worth about four billion yen; calculated at the present exchange rate, this sum was equivalent to hardly one and one-quarter billion dollars. To this may be added the annual gold production of the Empire, which should reach 200 million yen in 1938, and the amount which could be obtained by collecting the ornaments and gold hoarded by private individuals.

The difficulties consequent on war financing have sharply accelerated the trend toward controlled economy in Japan. On January 8, 1937 the Finance Ministry had already decreed that foreign exchange contracts for financing imports valued at 30,000 yen or over, later reduced to 1,000 yen, would be subjected to license.[9] Government permission also became mandatory for export shipments made without negotiation of an exchange draft, unless payment had been received in Japan. Even export shipments used to cover imports, if made without negotiation of a draft, were subjected to license. Japanese nationals were further required to secure government permission to dispose or hypothecate foreign assets held abroad in payment for imports. Bank to bank payments under telegraphic instructions from abroad required a permit, as well as similar payments of 10,000 yen or more under

[8] In August 1937 the 71st Diet passed a Gold Production Law, which aimed to concentrate the country's gold supplies and augment the gold output. Plans were then laid down to increase the gold production of the Empire to 450 million yen by 1942; Manchoukuo, which produced gold worth 10 million yen in 1936, is scheduled to produce 200 million yen in 1942. It may be doubted whether these ambitious plans can be successfully fulfilled.

[9] For details, see *The Oriental Economist,* October 1937, p. 574-576.

mail instructions. Thus the movement of funds between the headquarters of a bank or corporation in Japan and its branch establishment abroad was placed under strict government supervision. The Finance Ministry stated that permits for foreign exchange contracts involving purchase of pig iron, steel products, petroleum, machinery and metals, all relating to the needs of war industries, would be unreservedly granted. As to other imports, licenses would be given within limits calculated on the past volume of shipments. The effort was directed, in other words, toward speeding up the import of materials for war purposes by giving them the right of way.

With the outbreak of war, which placed even greater pressure on the yen, three additional measures were speedily adopted. The 71st Diet, meeting from July 23 to August 8, enacted the Gold Fund Special Account Law, which authorized revaluation of gold on the basis of 290 milligrams per yen, or about ten per cent below the world price. The former statutory rate, unchanged since the gold ban was reimposed in December 1931, had been 750 milligrams, equivalent to the old par value of the yen. Gold reserves of the central banks of Japan, Formosa and Korea were revalued on the new basis and the resulting book profit was credited to the government. With these funds, the gold reserve of the Bank of Japan was increased to about 800 million yen, outstanding government debts to the Bank of 248 million yen were cleared, and a Gold Fund Special Account totalling 747 million yen was inaugurated. With these funds, the Special Account was to buy about 200 million yen of government bonds from the Bank of Japan, take up 250 million yen of Industrial Bank debentures, and use the remainder to adjust the balance of international payments.

This foreign exchange stabilization fund is not called

upon to control migratory short term transactions, which are virtually unknown in Japan. Even when restricted to adjustment of exchange fluctuations due to seasonal trade movements, its resources were exceedingly small. Another step was therefore taken in preparation for future emergencies. The Foreign Exchange Control Law was revised to enable the government to acquire control over and dispose of all foreign assets held abroad by Japanese nationals. Through data already supplied by applications under this act, it had been ascertained that Japanese nationals held abroad at the end of April 1937 assets valued at 1,476 million yen.[10] These included 761 millions in Japanese government and corporate securities, actually foreign currency obligations of Japan; 390 millions in foreign securities; 166 millions in foreign currency deposits; and 159 millions in foreign currency loans. Of these only the last three, amounting to 715 million yen, could be mobilized to support the Japanese currency. This sum was expressed in terms of the former gold parity; on the revalued basis, it placed approximately two billion yen at the government's disposal in case of need.

A third measure, designed to regularize the buying and selling rates for the yen, was also adopted at this time. Although foreign exchange transactions had been conducted on the basis of 1s 2d on London, uncertainty had existed as to whether this represented the buying or selling rate, leading to competition among the various banks in Japan. On August 20, through the offices of the Finance Ministry and the Bank of Japan, the various Japanese banks came to the following agreement: "Telegraphic transfers on London to be sold at or above 1s 2d. Buying rates on London 3 months credit bills to be 1s 2$\frac{1}{16}$d or above. Forward contracts to be no further forward than

[10] *Contemporary Opinions*, cited, November 11, 1937, p. 4.

three months, quotations to be flat for all months. Inter-
bank change-over transactions for providing funds, however, will be regarded as exceptions to this rule and can
be dealt in at differences to suit the occasion." [11] This
bankers' agreement clarified the basis of yen quotations
and established the government's intention to maintain
the 1s 2d rate. Foreign banks in Japan subscribed to the
agreement, which went into effect on August 23.

In September 1937 the 72nd Diet had enacted two further important economic control measures: the Foreign
Trade Control Law and the Capital Control Law. The
first of these empowered the government, whenever necessary, to restrict or prohibit the import or export of any
article or articles, or to place their manufacture, distribution and consumption under control. This act, which
reinforced the foreign exchange control law, was also designed to cut down the import balance to a minimum on
all commodities not directly required for war purposes or
the export trade. Three classes of commodities were made
subject to the law. Restrictions applied to the first two
classes, for which import permits had to be secured from
the Ministry of Commerce and Industry, sought to reduce
the value of imports by nearly 200 million yen annually.[12]
Under Class A was placed certain major import items,
comprising raw cotton, wool and lumber. The estimated
saving of 157 million yen on these commodities was calculated on the basis of a reduction of 1936 imports by 10
per cent for raw cotton, 30 per cent for wool, and 20 per
cent for lumber. Purchases of American cotton on this
basis would be reduced by 37 million yen. Under Class
B was grouped some 260 import items, but as most of
these were unimportant, a saving of only 39 million yen

[11] *The Oriental Economist,* October 1937, p. 576.
[12] *The Oriental Economist,* October 1937, p. 577-580.

was anticipated. The total estimated saving in these two classes came to 196 million yen, or only seven per cent of the import value for 1936. Class C included a list of commodities, such as naphthalene, nitric acid, cotton waste, rabbit furs, antimony and sulphate of antimony, mainly required for war purposes, which could not be exported without permit from the Ministry of Commerce and Industry.

This general measure received specific application to the cotton trade by a regulatory program introduced on October 23, 1937, by the Ministry of Commerce and Industry.[13] Raw cotton imports were restricted to 1,050,000 piculs a month, while the production of cotton yarns was limited to about 300,000 bales a month, as against the past average of from 340,000 to 350,000 bales. To maintain yarn and piece-goods exports at their existing level, domestic consumption was to be curtailed to the above extent. The ramifications of a control program of this sort were illustrated by the additional set of measures deemed necessary. It was feared that restricted imports of raw cotton might boost domestic yarn prices above world levels, and so hinder the export trade. To counteract this result, maximum prices were fixed for yarns and raw cotton to check appreciation, and a control duty of 10 per cent ad valorem was imposed on raw cotton to check its consumption. Since this latter impost would increase the production cost of cotton goods and hinder their export, refunds from the raw cotton control duty were granted to the cotton manufacturers. The home consumers were obviously expected to buy less cotton goods at higher prices in order to enable the cotton manufacturers to hold their export markets. Official maximum prices for cotton yarns and raw cotton, based on quotations of the New

[13] *The Oriental Economist*, November 1937, p. 643.

York Cotton Exchange, are set by the Ministry of Commerce and Industry once a week. The first official maximum price for cotton yarns was set on October 23 at 230 yen per bale, allowing an estimated profit of 30 yen to the Japanese manufacturer and a differential advantage of 66 yen over the British manufacturer.

The Capital Control Law, also enacted by the 72nd Diet, subjected all enterprises with a minimum limit of capital, as well as new financing of fixed capital, to government license. Regulations which became effective on September 27 gave absolute priority in capital increases or calls on shareholder capital to a list of "urgent" industries having relation to military necessities. The law also sought to make additional funds available for such wartime financing. It empowered the Japan Industrial Bank to issue government guaranteed debentures to a maximum limit of 500 million yen, intended to supply the capital needs of industries supplying emergency requirements. It also authorized the Japan Hypothec Bank to issue its premium savings certificates to the limit of 200 million yen, in order to absorb the savings of Japan's laboring classes. The Capital Control Law permitted capital increases to urgent concerns even before their authorized capital had been fully paid up, a procedure normally prohibited by the commercial code. Expansion of capital equipment in Japanese industry went on at a rapid rate throughout 1937.[14] Total capital increase during the first six months of the year amounted to 846 million yen, as compared with 828 million yen in the full year of 1936 and 577 million yen in 1935. For the third quarter of 1937, the Bank of Japan estimated that capital investment for new incorporations, capital increases and debenture

[14] *The Oriental Economist,* August 1937, p. 454-455; also October 1937, p. 564-565.

sales would total 984 million yen. In absolute amounts and in rate of expansion, such industries as machinery and shipbuilding, mining, metals, and chemicals stood in the forefront of this expansion. Japan's "national defense" state was being speedily rushed to completion. In the process, the bloc of the Japanese heavy industrialists and the military was consolidating its control over all phases of the national life.

While the details of establishing a wartime economy were thus being arranged, the army and navy authorities were entrenching their position as sole arbiter of the conduct of war operations through the establishment of an Imperial Headquarters. Sanction for this step was obtained by the War and Navy Ministers on November 11, 1937, and the ordinance authorizing the new organ was promulgated on the following day. The Imperial Headquarters was formally organized on November 20. This institution is peculiar to Japan. It clearly establishes the sole responsibility of the Supreme Command to the Emperor in directing military operations, side-tracking the Cabinet, and so emphasizing the "dual government" of Japan. Article 1 of the new Imperial Headquarters Ordinance states in part: "The highest body of the Supreme Command, to be called the Imperial Headquarters, shall be established under the supervision of the Emperor"; while Article 2 states: "The Chief of the Army General Staff and the Chief of the Naval General Staff shall as heads of their respective staffs assist the Emperor in the exercise of His Majesty's Supreme Command, formulating strategic plans for achievement of the final objective and coordinating the operations of the army and navy." [15] Under this system, even the War and Navy Ministers occupy a subordinate position, becoming in

[15] *The Japan Advertiser,* November 18, 1937.

effect liaison officers between the Cabinet and the Imperial Headquarters. At the first joint conference between the Cabinet and the Imperial Headquarters, held on November 24, the Premier and the chief secretary of the Cabinet were the only civilian representatives. The statement issued by the army and navy press sections of the Headquarters on November 20 declared that the Imperial Headquarters was "purely an agency of the Supreme Command based on the Supreme Command prerogatives of the Emperor in order to unify the command systems of the army and navy. Its establishment in no way signifies that the boundary between the functions and responsibilities of high command and those of the Government has been affected in the slightest, and any rumor that the Imperial Headquarters is intended to combine the Supreme Command and the Government is entirely without foundation. That is not in the least the purpose of the headquarters." [16] Despite this disclaimer, it was obvious that by the establishment of the Imperial Headquarters the army and navy had firmly taken in hand complete control of the military operations in China, which was the paramount political concern of the country. In respect of this enterprise, the Cabinet was relegated to a subsidiary role.

Political trends in Japan under the stress of war conditions were also marked by the re-emergence of the army extremists, whose influence had gone into partial eclipse after the February 1936 assassinations in Tokyo. The mobilization of an army of one million soldiers had forced the recall to active service of many extremist officers who had been placed on the retired list in 1936. Among the high commanders of the three main centers of military operations in China, the extremist wing of the army was

[16] *The Japan Advertiser,* November 21, 1937.

prominently represented. General Terauchi, in control of the North China front, had brought the influence of the new and ambitious, but somewhat more conservative, army clique to bear on developments in this region. In the Inner Mongolian provinces, however, the Kwantung Army pursued its own special political objectives, as indicated by the puppet régimes established under its exclusive jurisdiction in Chahar, Suiyuan and north Shansi. On the Shanghai front, General Iwane Matsui represented the viewpoint of the extremists; his successor, General Shunroku Hata, and the latter's chief-of-staff, Major-General Torashiro Kawabe, were of the same persuasion. No less significant was the return of the extremists to high government posts at home. General Sadao Araki, as previously noted, emerged from retirement in October to become a member of the Board of Cabinet Councillors. His closest exemplar in the navy, Admiral Nobumasa Suetsugu, was also appointed to this Board. Two months later, on December 14, Admiral Suetsugu succeeded Eiichi Baba in the Home Ministry. This appointment was an omen for the future. It was widely believed that Admiral Suetsugu was being groomed to succeed Konoye as Premier.

The new Home Minister's first act was to order a general round-up of all persons suspected of harboring "dangerous thoughts", that is, those with liberal or radical leanings. The arrests took place during the last two weeks of December. All mention of these arrests by the press was stringently prohibited. This press ban was faithfully observed until nearly the end of January, when the police released news of the scope and details of the raids. The official statement issued at the time declared that not only Communist ideas, but liberal and democratic thoughts which might become "hotbeds for Communist ideas" had to be "drastically suppressed." In the course of the police raids, which took place simultaneously throughout the country, 371 persons were arrested. In Tokyo alone 108 were detained. Kanju Kato, left-wing labor leader who visited the United States in 1936, was the most prominent figure taken in the police drag-net. The Japan Proletarian Party and the All-Japan Council of Labor and Farmer Unions, the most radical of legal political and labor organizations in Japan, both headed by Kanju Kato, were summarily dissolved. Mr. Kato was a member of the lower house of the Diet, having twice been elected from a working-class constituency in Tokyo with the largest majorities polled by any candidate. Four former university professors, two from Waseda, one from Tokyo Imperial and one from Kyushu Imperial University, were taken into custody. Baroness Ishimoto, prominent feminist known for her liberal-minded autobiography "Facing Two Ways", was also arrested. These persons, under Japan's legal system, may be detained indefinitely for examination without being brought to trial. Although the arrests were labeled "precautionary", they would seem to indicate that the authorities are not wholly at ease. The increased privations imposed on the Japanese people by the war demand a more rigid and drastic suppression of even potentially oppositionist elements.

Apprehension of the authorities is not without foundation. The existence of opposition to the war is testified by additional facts which occasionally come to light. Students of Tokyo Imperial University are known to have absented themselves from war ceremonies at the Imperial shrines. Liberal educational leaders are being weeded out of the universities. Dr. Hachiro Yuasa, president of Doshisha, one of the oldest mission colleges in Japan, was recently compelled to retire. Professor Tadao Yanaihara, economist and expert on Japanese colonial administration, has also been forced to resign his chair at Tokyo Imperial University. In September the Metropolitan Police Bureau of Tokyo, during a series of raids, seized large quantities of anti-war publications. Popular sentiment is further illustrated by the reaction to the Social Mass Party's adoption of a pro-war platform and relegation of its former socialist aims to the background. In the Tokyo municipal elections, held at the end of November 1937, the party elected only ten of its forty-two candidates; in 1936, it had elected two-thirds of its candidates. As the war drags on, and its effects on the living standards of the people become more pronounced, an even more thorough-going campaign of repression will be required to dam up the forces of opposition and unrest.

CHAPTER ELEVEN

THE TEST OF STRENGTH

THE initial phases of the war, despite the unexpectedly stubborn resistance encountered at Shanghai and in the north, had resulted in the occupation of considerable areas of China, important both politically and economically, by Japanese armies. With the conclusion of these operations, there were many signs that the Japanese Cabinet was prepared to make peace. The objectives set for Japan's military forces at the outset of hostilities had been triumphantly attained. Nanking, the enemy capital, had been captured; the North China provinces had been overrun. All that remained was to dictate the terms of peace. These terms, imposed by the victor on the vanquished, would more than repay the costs of the campaign. At this point, when success was within Japan's grasp, the scheduled program met with a disconcerting set back. Japan's military and political circles had confidently expected that the first powerful blows of their war machine would shatter the morale of the Chinese leaders. The influence of the compromisers in the Nanking régime, it was thought, would suffice to clear the road to an acceptance of the *fait accompli*. Failing this, the more conservative elements in the Chinese government would at least split away from the determined resisters, and offer themselves as tools in a puppet establishment dominated by Japan. Neither of these anticipated results occurred. China's newly won political unity stood the test of severe military reverses, and the Chinese authorities continued to maintain a solid opposition front to the invaders.

Japan's official leaders were loath to accept the evidences of this fact. Their first peace overtures, made just prior to the fall of Nanking, were rejected. Still they persisted. At the end of the year, a more detailed outline of Japan's peace terms was submitted to General Chiang Kai-shek at Hankow through Dr. Oskar P. Trautmann, German Ambassador to China. The reported terms included Japanese participation in the development of China's resources, aviation, transport and communications; increased Japanese control over the Maritime Customs; China's adherence to the anti-Comintern pact; establishment of permanent Japanese garrisons in China; specification of certain demilitarized zones by Japan; recognition of an independent government for Inner Mongolia; and payment of war indemnities by China. Early in January it became clear that these terms had also been rejected. The gravity of Japan's failure to obtain a peace settlement was recognized by the summoning of an Imperial Council, an action which had been taken only once before during this century. On January 11, in the presence of Emperor Hirohito, the Imperial Council formally considered the steps which it deemed necessary to pursue. The decisions of this meeting were not revealed for several days. In the end, the only new step adopted, aside from a determination to prosecute the war vigorously, was the withdrawal of recognition from the Chinese government. This action, in view of the wide publicity attracted by the Imperial Council's session, came as something of an anti-climax.

A general Japanese advance into Shantung province was already well under way. If the previous hesitation to

Times Wide World

IMPERIAL COUNCIL MEETS IN JANUARY 1938 TO DECIDE
JAPAN'S POLICY ON WAR WITH CHINA.

take this step had been due to anxiety over the fate of Japan's extensive investments in Shantung, there was nothing gained by the delay. Soon after the middle of December, Chinese troops had dynamited and fired the valuable Japanese cotton mills in Tsingtao, and had wrecked the Japanese-owned coal mines along the Tsingtao-Tsinan Railway. On December 23 several Japanese columns crossed the Yellow River and quickly invested Tsinan, capital of the province. Tsingtao was occupied without fighting on January 11, when a dozen vessels unloaded a Japanese force which took over the undefended city. The provincial troops under General Han Fu-chu had meanwhile offered little resistance in the interior of Shantung, and the Japanese troops had driven rapidly down the Tientsin-Pukow Railway. By the middle of January this offensive was seriously threatening Hsuchow, strategic junction point of the east-west Lunghai Railway and the Tientsin-Pukow line. On January 14 General Chiang Kai-shek took personal command of the operations on this front. His first act was to order the arrest of General Han Fu-chu, the Shantung governor, who was later executed for failing to resist the invaders. New Chinese forces were thrown into the struggle at Tsining, in southern Shantung, and the Japanese drive in this sector was brought to a full stop.

With the rapid massing of some 300,000 Chinese troops along the Lunghai Railway, the struggle for this strategic line soon developed large proportions. Halted in their drive through Shantung, the Japanese commanders began a new offensive against Hsuchow from the south. By early February, this force had covered approximately half the distance between Nanking and Hsuchow in its northward advance along the Tientsin-Pukow Railway. At Pengpu and Hwaiyuan, in the valley of the Hwai River, the

Chinese defense stiffened and little further advances were
made during February. An even more serious Japanese
thrust down the Peiping-Hankow Railway toward Chengchow had meanwhile developed. This drive, which was
aimed to cut the center of the Lunghai Railway in Honan
province, threatened to pinch off the Chinese forces defending Hsuchow in southern Shantung. Late in February a strong Japanese thrust into central and south Shansi
began. The extended lines of Japanese communication
were increasingly harassed by guerrilla forces. In Hopei
province, units of the Eighth Route Army occupied several towns near Paotingfu in mid-February and tore up
the tracks of the Peiping-Hankow Railway, the line of
communication of the Japanese forces advancing on
Chengchow. Serious fighting was also taking place at
Wuhu, where the Japanese troops were hard pressed, and
at other centers in the Shanghai-Hangchow-Nanking area.

In March 1938 the Japanese command threw additional
forces into the offensive against the Lunghai Railway.
Separate Japanese columns pushed southward in Shantung, Honan and Shansi provinces. In each province, as
the invading forces approached the Lunghai Railway, the
Chinese defense stiffened and held. Chinese operations in
these areas displayed unsuspected potentialities of effective
organization and staff work. New forces, speedily trained
and reorganized by Generalissimo Chiang Kai-shek after
the retreat from Nanking, were sent to the Lunghai fronts.
Under General Li Tsung-jen, the Chinese armies delivered strong flank attacks against the Japanese line of communications in central Shantung. Early in April a Chinese
counter-offensive at Taierhchuang routed the front-line
Japanese divisions in southern Shantung and temporarily
relieved pressure in this sector. As the war proceeded, the
Chinese forces were demonstrating the possibility of meet-

ing the Japanese invaders successfully in the open field
and holding their own in a combined warfare of position
and maneuver. The stubborn defense of the Lunghai
Railway front opened up new perspectives. As the Chinese
soldiers and officers gained experience, it seemed possible
that they might steadily reduce Japan's original margin of
technical superiority in orthodox positional fighting. Even
a partial lessening of Japan's ability to strike through to
specified objectives with heavy concentrations of mechanized troops would redouble the effectiveness of the growing numbers of Chinese guerrilla troops. These latter, instead of assuming a dominant military role, would then
take their proper place as an adjunct of an increasingly
effective army of Chinese regulars.

In any case, Japan's difficulties in covering such large
distances, as well as the problem of achieving conclusive
results, were becoming more apparent. There was no indication that the loss of the Lunghai Railway, serious
though this might be, would bring Chinese military resistance to an end or establish Japan's effective domination of China. Under the conditions imposed by a long
and wearing contest, there was no assurance that Japan's
superior military technique would eventually prevail.
The test of strength lay in the home fronts of the two
belligerents, and in the relative ability to procure the
sinews of war necessary to meet the vastly different requirements of the invader and the defender in the course
of a prolonged struggle.

During the early months of 1938, Japan's governing
authorities were compelled to deal with the fiscal problems consequent upon the continuance and enlargement
of the military operations in China. The general account
budget for the 1938-1939 term authorized expenditures
of 2,868 million yen, or 54 millions in excess of the record

budget for the previous year. Added to this were the "China incident" expenses, aggregating 4,850 million yen. Total appropriations for the 1938-1939 fiscal year thus amounted to 7,718 million yen. Of this sum, 694 million yen from the general account budget, 166 millions from the special accounts, and the bulk of the 4,850 millions of direct war expenditure had to be derived from bond flotations. Bond issues in this amount would swiftly bring on a catastrophic inflation.

Analysis of government bond issues during the 1937-1938 fiscal year, however, shows that the situation is not so serious as these figures might be thought to indicate. The budgets of the 1937-1938 term called for bond issues of 965 million yen for both general and special accounts, and of 2,428 millions for the "China incident" expenditures. Total bond flotations up to the end of 1937 amounted to 1,300 million yen, i.e., 900 millions of "China incident" obligations and 400 millions for the regular budgets.[1] Additional bonds were floated before the end of the fiscal term on March 31, 1938; even so, it was clear that actual expenditures were running well under total appropriations. Most of the bond flotations were taken up by the Bank of Japan. Some difficulty was apparently experienced in passing on these bonds, since at the end of the year the central bank's holdings had increased by 539 million yen. The net increase in the bank's note issue was 301 million yen, indicating some degree of inflation though hardly of serious proportions.

As expressed in prices, even if not in currency emission, there was rather more evidence of inflation. The level of wholesale and retail prices, as well as the cost of living index, has risen steadily since 1931 and notably during the past year. Tokyo's wholesale price index, based

[1] *The Oriental Economist*, January 1938, p. 3.

on 1913 as 100, rose from 116.0 in November 1931 to 209.8 in December 1936; in December 1937 the index stood at 232. This index includes certain imported materials, and possibly shows a disproportionate increase. Nevertheless, the same trend is evident in retail prices and the cost of living. The retail price index, based on 1914 as 100, which stood at 135 in November 1931, had risen to 163 in December 1936; in December 1937 it had reached 182. The rise in the cost of living index, based on 1914 as 100, has been almost equally pronounced. From 159 in November 1931, it rose to 186 in December 1936; in December 1937 it stood at 198.[2] The war was being brought home to the Japanese population in increased living costs.

There are several other aspects of Japan's internal financing which cannot be lightly dismissed. A bond emission of 1,300 million yen, even though it happens to be well under total appropriations, constitutes almost exactly 10 per cent of Japan's national debt. Bond flotations during 1938, moreover, will certainly exceed 1,300 million yen by a wide margin. The burden of servicing this debt is growing steadily heavier. In this connection, there is the matter of taxation to be considered. During the spring of 1937 the Hayashi Ministry obtained the Diet's approval for tax increases designed to raise 361 million yen over a full year. The Konoye Cabinet increased taxes by another 100 million yen, and this enactment has now been revised so as to yield about 300 million yen. Over the course of a single year, taxes have thus been boosted by some 631 million yen. Calculated on the basis of the tax revenue for the 1936-1937 fiscal year, which was 965 millions, the Japanese taxpayer has been forced to shoul-

[2] For these figures, see *The Oriental Economist*, January 1936, p. 37; January 1938, p. 44.

der an increase of 68 per cent over his burden of a year ago. These tax increases weigh heavily on the mass of the people, and their effects are not so easily shuffled off as an increase in the Bank of Japan's bond portfolio.

The Achilles heel of Japan's fiscal situation, however, resides not so much in internal financing as in the problem of the import surplus, yen stability, and the gold reserve. Complete trade figures for 1937 show an excess of imports of 608 million yen for Japan proper and 636 millions for the Empire, including Korea, Formosa and the South Seas.[3] An import surplus of this staggering amount has been registered only once before in Japan's history—in 1924. As already noted,[4] this deficit in merchandise trade forced resort to large gold shipments for the first time since 1931. During the first seven months of 1937, actually from March through July, gold shipments aggregated 380 million yen.[5] After July 1937, the Department of Finance at Tokyo ceased to publish figures on gold exports. As these shipments have been made exclusively to the United States, it is possible to gauge fairly accurately the amounts reaching this country since last July. By the middle of December total shipments to the United States since March 8 aggregated $245,300,000, according to figures issued by the Federal Reserve Bank of New York.[6] Up to July, calculated on the basis of $0.29 to the yen, Japan had shipped gold worth $110,200,000 to the United States. Shipments since then have therefore totaled $135,100,000, or well above the original amount. During 1937, on this basis, Japan had shipped gold valued at nearly 850 million yen to the United States. Since July

[3] *Monthly Return of the Foreign Trade of Japan*, Tokyo, The Department of Finance, December 1937, p. 3.

[4] See Chapter X.

[5] *The Oriental Economist*, January 1938, p. 44.

[6] *New York Times*, December 18, 1937.

it had dug into its gold reserves to the extent of 465 million yen. Nearly one-eighth of its total reserves in gold and foreign securities, estimated previously at four billion yen in July,[7] had been consumed in less than five months of war. Specie reserves had been virtually exhausted.

It is not surprising that the Japanese authorities had made drastic efforts to curtail imports during this period. These attempts were continued and intensified in the new year. On January 13, for example, the Ministry of Commerce and Industry decreed that cotton yarn used in the manufacture of textiles for domestic consumption had to be mixed with 30 per cent staple fiber, a synthetic material made from wood pulp with which Japanese industrialists had been experimenting for some years. The trend toward rigid economic control was made even more explicit in the provisions of the National Mobilization Bill, drafted by the government Planning Board in collaboration with the army, which the Konoye Cabinet fought to push through the Diet in February. This bill, by method of ordinance, would vest additional sweeping powers in the hands of the authorities to complete the establishment of a totalitarian state.[8] The provisions of the bill are so detailed as to encompass all phases of economic life. State officials would be vested with virtually unrestricted powers of industrial control, affecting such matters as contracts, prices, insurance, and transportation charges. They could order industrialists to install machinery, and producers and merchants to hold in stock fixed quantities of goods. They would control capital investment, issuing orders with respect to company promotion and amalgamation and increases of capital share and debenture issues. Trade control would be placed in official

[7] See Chapter X.
[8] *New York Times*, February 16, 1938.

hands, permitting tariffs to be altered and imports and exports regulated by decree. The labor provisions of the bill are no less typical of Fascist regimentation. State officials might regulate wages, prohibit strikes, and enforce compulsory labor service. The provision whereby people might be examined and registered according to vocation suggests that compulsory allocation of workers to various types of labor service is contemplated. Free speech, press and assembly, already drastically limited in Japan, are explicitly voided by this bill, which empowers the authorities to exert complete control over public meetings, the press, and organizations.

These latter provisions, no less than the economic control features, once again brought the parties into opposition to the Cabinet. This opposition was intensified by efforts of the Home Minister, Admiral Suetsugu, to curb the parties through police action. Following police raids on both the Seiyukai and Minseito headquarters in February, the parties carried the issue to the floor of the Diet, where they demanded guarantees from the Home Minister against recurrence of such incidents.[9] This controversy underlined the change that had come over Japan since the days when control of the Home Ministry was an accepted prerogative of the parties. Behind the parties in this struggle stood the group of industrialists whose interests are being seriously injured by the government's pressure to give the right of way to "necessary" industries. The textile manufacturers have particularly suffered from the application of the new program. All export industries, whose future is contingent on their competitive ability to sell abroad, are necessarily concerned over the prospects of unlimited state regimentation and control. Their experience has already indicated that such measures as

[9] *New York Times*, February 22, 1938.

official allocation of capital investment and control of imports are all applied in favor of the heavy industries supplying war requirements.

The point of view of the opposition is expressed in the following statement: "At the same time, it is essential that the Government shall exercise the utmost care to restrict its interference with national economic life to the absolute minimum. The Government's course just now, however, is diametrically opposed to this desirable policy. Not only are imports of such important raw materials as cotton, wool, etc., placed under restriction, but the foreign exchange license system is being enforced with growing rigidity, and under the two forms of control industrialists and traders are required to go through complicated formalities at the hands of Government officials who are complete novices in commercial affairs. The result has been to undermine alarmingly the competitive powers in the world markets of Japan's harassed business men, and the effect of the faulty wartime policy on the commodity price movement has already become apparent. . . . As measured by *The Oriental Economist's* index for which May 1936 is the base period, wholesale prices in Japan last December moved up to 129.8 as contrasted to 110.6 in Great Britain and 96.1 in the United States of America. . . . It is a noteworthy fact that imported articles alone were as high as 141.8 in December, while home trade factory manufactures remained at 117.7, farm products at 108.9 and exported articles at 117.2. It is obvious that the recent commodity upswing has chiefly been due to the obstruction of imports of articles of trade." [10] This quotation clearly illustrates Japan's economic dilemma. Even at the risk of losing vital foreign markets, it is compelled to place restrictions on export industries in order

[10] Editorial in *The Oriental Economist,* January 1938, p. 5-6.

to secure the necessary sinews of war. While the opposition may delay full application of industrial control for a time, it is fighting a cause which has already been virtually lost. The *mésalliance* of the war industries and the military is marching toward an unrestricted domination of the state. Before the Seventy-third Diet adjourned on March 26, it had passed the National Mobilization Bill and the long postponed measure for nationalization of the electric power industry.

Recent economic developments in Manchoukuo, notably the incursion of the Aikawa interests into the field of Manchurian industrial development, have special reference to the problem of Japan's current economic and political evolution. The position occupied by Yoshisuke Aikawa, president of Japan Industrial Company, Ltd., in the Japanese scene has already been briefly considered.[11] It must now be taken up in more detail. In January 1938 it was revealed that the Aikawa interests had approached Thomas J. Watson, president of the International Business Machines Corporation and also of the International Chamber of Commerce, for a loan of fifty million dollars. The credit was to be applied to the development of Manchurian heavy industries through the purchase of American machinery. Recognizing the difficulties likely to be encountered, the Japanese interests formulated their offer in the most attractive terms. They not only secured an undertaking from the Japanese government that payments on the loan would be exempt from operation of the Exchange Control Act, but apparently suggested that American experts might be retained to install the equipment and operate it during the period required for training the necessary staff and workers.[12]

[11] See Chapter VII.
[12] *New York Times*, January 16, 1938.

On the face of it, the execution of such a contract by an American business man at this time, when China is being ruthlessly overrun by Japan's war machine, would seem to merit condemnation. It places the executor in the category of those American operators who are now making profits by selling scrap iron to Japan. A credit of this amount for Manchuria's industrial development, moreover, would seem to be a gratuitous slap at the American government's official policy of refusing to extend recognition to the Japanese conquest of Manchuria. While normal American economic relations with Manchoukuo have not been suspended as a consequence of the non-recognition policy, a financial transaction of the size contemplated in this arrangement would have the effect of reducing the policy to an absurdity. It is therefore not surprising that official circles in Washington frowned on the carrying through of such a deal, when the details were made public.[13] In view of Mr. Watson's disclaimer of any formal approaches from the Aikawa concern, it may be hoped that the project is dead.

These reflections are incidental. Much more interesting details are concealed in the ramifications of the Japanese background. As the commentary in the *New York Times* brings out, the offer was made to sound more palatable by an effort to show that private industrial enterprise in Japan was staging a revolt against pressure of the military for a controlled economy, and particularly against the brand of state socialism enforced by the Kwantung Army in Manchoukuo. The obvious implication is that an American credit, given at this time for Manchurian industrial development, would tend to work against militarist domination in Japan and Manchoukuo. This interesting implication, which involves the crucial issue of

[13] *New York Times*, January 18, 1938.

the direction of Japan's internal development, demands closer examination.

The facts already considered hardly justify the conclusion that *laissez-faire* is on the up-grade in Japan. If the Japanese military can enforce their control over the opposing vested interests at home, they might reasonably be expected to do so even more effectively in Manchoukuo, which is the creature of the Kwantung Army. Nevertheless, it is asserted that the army advocates of state socialism in this colonial protectorate have admitted the error of their ways, and have appealed to the home capitalists for aid.[14] The evidence, so it is said, can be seen in the formation of the Manchurian Heavy Industrial Development Company, Ltd., organized in December 1937 to take over the exploitation of iron, gold and silver mines, to produce pig iron and steel, to manufacture automobiles and aircraft, and to refine Manchuria's light metals. The president of this company is Yoshisuke Aikawa. His new Manchurian enterprise shunts aside the South Manchuria Railway Company, which had previously carried on many of these enterprises in close cooperation with the Kwantung Army. The total capitalization of the Manchurian heavy industry holding corporation will be 450 million yen. Of this amount, however, only half is supplied by the Aikawa interests; the Manchoukuo government will provide the other half. The new company is thus not very different from the long string of Manchoukuo government monopolies, affecting coal, oil, telegraph, telephone and radio, electric light and power, munitions, and others, most of which were formed by absorbing a home Japanese interest. In this case, it is argued, the situation is different; under Mr. Aikawa the private interests will dominate. This

[14] *New York Times,* January 16, 1938.

argument, in view of the personality and undoubted managerial ability of Mr. Aikawa, has a certain amount of weight. The real issue thus becomes clear. What sort of man is this Aikawa? What are his connections, past and present? What tendency in Japan's business circles does he represent? Is he an acceptable champion of *laissez-faire*, or possibly of liberalism?

The details of his past history furnished by the *New York Times* are not entirely reassuring. It is said that "Yoshisuke Aikawa sprang into prominence as the chief aide of Fusanosuke Kuhara, his brother-in-law. Mr. Kuhara's fortunes were closely entwined in his early days with those of the late General Baron Giichi Tanaka. . . . When Mr. Kuhara became Minister of Communications in the Tanaka Cabinet [1927-1929], Mr. Aikawa became chief executive of their joint enterprises." [15] This is quite illuminating. Aikawa is the brother-in-law of Kuhara, who was closely connected with General Tanaka—militarist, expansionist, exponent of a "positive" policy in China, famed for the Tanaka Memorial, the man who ordered the Shantung intervention of 1927-1929, and whose Cabinet fell mainly because of the unexplained circumstances attending the implication of certain Japanese officers in the murder of Chang Tso-lin at the railway trestle outside Mukden in June 1928. But what of Kuhara's more recent history? About this nothing is said. Nevertheless, it is germane to the subject, and should be introduced at this point. Kuhara was a Seiyukai member of the Diet in 1935, when he covered himself with ignominy in a transparent effort to drag the Emperor into the political arena against the Okada Cabinet. Needless to say, he was working hand in glove with the military. This was not the climax of his career. After the assassi-

[15] *New York Times*, January 16, 1938.

nations of February 26, 1936, Kuhara was detained on charges of being an accomplice to General Mazaki, chief instigator of the attempted *coup d'état*. Both Kuhara and Mazaki were later officially cleared of complicity in the affair, chiefly because of their influence and high position. The evidence produced during the investigation tended to show that funds expended in behalf of the military uprising had passed through Mr. Kuhara's hands, if, indeed, they were not furnished by him.

Clearly, this brother-in-law of Mr. Aikawa is a very interesting person. But to continue with the narrative: "Taking advantage of the inflation boom which followed Japan's departure from the gold standard at the end of 1931, Mr. Aikawa started a career of rapid company promotion. On the foundation of the old Kuhara-Aikawa interests he erected the edifice of the Nippon Sangyo Kabushiki Kaisha (Japan Industrial Company, Ltd.) and commenced the formation of subsidiaries and the acquisition of control in going companies. The Nippon Sangyo 'empire', in which the paid capitalizations aggregate more than 500,000,000 yen and the 'going concern value' is probably triple that, includes such diversified interests as iron manufacturing, machinery manufacturing, glycerine, whaling, accident insurance, nitrogen fertilizers, gold mining, coal mining, shipping, industrial chemicals, fishing and automobile manufacturing. Through the Kyodo Fishery Company, which now operates off the coasts of Mexico and Australia as well as in the North Pacific, Mr. Aikawa now dominates the marketing of the Japanese catch of crab and salmon. All in all, the Nippon Sangyo interests make it second only to Mitsui in the Japanese industrial scheme." [16]

These facts are also of extreme value in gauging the

[16] *New York Times*. January 16. 1938.

position occupied by Mr. Aikawa. He is, first and foremost, a promoter of heavy industries—mining, iron manufacturing, industrial chemicals, machinery, and automobiles. His meteoric rise is said to rest on the inflation boom after 1931. It rests equally on the stimulus to heavy industry given by the expanding military budgets. He is *par excellence* the representative of the group of heavy industrialists which profit from the army program and which are the staunchest supporters of continental expansion, including the war in China. He is in the opposite camp from those light industrialists whose interests are really opposed to a controlled economy, twisted and warped to the purpose of building a war machine. One other fact, of considerable interest, might be added to this man's biography. In October 1936 Aikawa visited Manchoukuo on an inspection trip—made at the invitation and under the auspices of the Kwantung Army. This is the man, then, whose advent on the scene of Manchurian heavy industrial development is to be taken as the signal for a revival of *laissez-faire* in Manchoukuo, the precursor of the "open door" for private Japanese— and mayhap American—interests who may wish to invest in Manchuria. With a few more "enemies" like Aikawa, the leaders of the Kwantung Army would have nothing left to fear. Any classification of Mr. Aikawa as an exponent of laissez faire, liberalism, or anti-militarism must be decisively rejected. He is a compound of the opposites of all these terms.

Sound reasons led the Kwantung Army leaders to go out of their way to interest Mr. Aikawa in the development of Manchurian heavy industries. They needed capital, it is true, but they wanted this capital to come from an industrialist who stood shoulder to shoulder with them in their program of aggressive continental expansion. In

consummating this *entente cordiale*, they were cementing
the bloc with Japanese heavy industry and undermining
the position of the liberal business groups in Japan which
distrusted and opposed the army program. Since Nippon
Sangyo was already engaged in most of the lines of enterprise allocated to the new Manchurian holding company,
it was obviously in a most advantageous position to coordinate the development of the resources of Manchoukuo. In the second place, they needed the technical and
managerial equipment of Japan Industry, Ltd. Under
Mr. Aikawa's direction, this firm has become one of the
premier exhibits of advanced technical efficiency in Japanese industry. It disposes of a staff of hundreds of engi-
neering and economic experts, who thoroughly explore
every project and close every avenue of possible failure
before actual work is undertaken. When the signal to
go ahead is given, nothing is allowed to stand in the
way of results. The ruthless aggressiveness of Nippon
Sangyo is well illustrated by its purse-seine salmon operations off the Alaskan coast, which have been prosecuted
in complete disregard of the protests of American salmon
operators, who point out that the methods pursued by
the Aikawa fishery concern will destroy the salmon fields
in a few years' time.

One further reason was the most compelling of all.
Staggering under the financial burdens of the war, Japan
desperately needs the assistance of foreign capital to develop its new conquests. What a coup it would be, both
from the economic and political angles, if American
capital could be induced to invest in Manchoukuo. The
difficulties in the way of securing American cooperation
in such a project were obvious. Special preparation and
inducements would be necessary to assure success in the
delicate task of approaching American interests. The

introduction of Mr. Aikawa into the Manchurian scene seemed to be the proper answer. His reputation and the technical standing of Nippon Sangyo would be reassuring to any foreign investor. And lest the fear of government control might result in hesitation to rise to the bait, why not present Mr. Aikawa in the guise of a crusader for the revival of private enterprise in Manchoukuo? This was the crowning, the most subtle touch of the whole scheme.

If this reconstruction seems too Machiavellian, it is only necessary to refer to an editorial in *The Oriental Economist,* the most authoritative economic journal of Japan. As this editorial appeared in the November 1937 issue of the magazine, it must have been composed at some time toward the end of October. Its concluding paragraph reads as follows: "An interesting fact about the Manchoukuo holding concern is its reputed aim of obtaining as much foreign capital as possible, more especially American capital, for the operation of its variegated activities. As referred to elsewhere in this issue, while Manchoukuo has access to, by the present arrangement, personnel of executive and technical ability of an unusually high order which Japan Industry, Ltd. has taken several decades to build up, it has been recognized that assistance of foreign capital was needed to develop the vast resources of the country. Plans considered for the introduction of foreign capital include obtaining a line of credit on the security of heavy industrial assets in Manchoukuo for the purchase in the country where such credit is established of machinery and other producers' goods. It is also suggested that American capitalists be induced to take up the shares of various industrial concerns." [17] Presumably these will be shares in the new concerns which will spring

---

[17] *The Oriental Economist,* November 1937, p. 636.

up as soon as Mr. Aikawa has accomplished the revival of private industrial enterprise in Manchoukuo.

As the strain imposed by the war on Japan's financial position becomes greater, the search for foreign loans will be pursued with redoubled intensity. The weakest link in Japan's armor is the large merchandise trade deficit, which demands unprecedented amounts of foreign exchange. There is a definite limit to the restrictions which the Japanese authorities can apply to imports. Those already applied have begun to hamper export trade; they can be carried further only at the risk of adding to the trade deficit by reducing the volume of exports. The boycott of Japanese products by consumers in the outside world, which is growing in extent and intensity, strikes directly at this most vulnerable point. Even a relatively small decline in Japan's total export trade, occurring under present circumstances, would add greatly to its difficulty of securing adequate quantities of foreign exchange. The purchases abroad must be continued. Japan's import requirements for war purposes, owing to its paucity of natural resources and deficiencies in certain machine techniques, are greater than those of any other first-class power. It must purchase abroad the bulk of its raw cotton, rubber, antimony, nickel, mercury, lead, petroleum, scrap iron, manganese, tungsten, molybdenite, chrome and iron ore. It produces less than half of its needs with respect to aluminum, tin, zinc, cadmium, phosphorus and asbestos. It must import machinery, aircraft and military trucks in large amounts, as well as such raw materials as wool, timber and hides. This excessive dependence on the outside world for the sinews of war means that for Japan the problem of foreign exchange is crucial. To wage a successful war, it must sooner or later seek external financial assistance. Germany and Italy, its partners in the anti-Comintern pact, have no surpluses of foreign exchange to place at the disposal of their Eastern ally. Their deficiencies in this respect are as serious as Japan's. The best they can do is to establish barter arrangements, as in the triangular German-Japan-Manchoukuo trade agreement, by which Japan exchanges Manchuria's soya bean products for German machinery and munitions. Only in the United States or Great Britain, which possess large capital reserves, can Japan hope to obtain sufficient loans or credits to ease the strain on its finances. Mr. Aikawa's essay in this direction is likely to prove but the precursor of similar attempts in future months.

In the test of strength between China and Japan, the latter has the advantages of a superior professional army, better and more adequate munitions, and a higher industrial technique. These are of great importance. They explain the relative ease with which Japan's armies have been enabled to smash their way to military objectives set by the high command. Under the conditions of a protracted war, however, it may prove that China's economic front is the stronger, possessing certain advantages which Japan lacks. The more advanced financial-economic structure of Japan is also more delicately geared, and its equilibrium can be more easily upset. Dislocation or stress at any point immediately transfers its effects to the structure as a whole. There is a much more general dependence on the outside world, with more serious results if any of the connections are impaired or broken. Within Japan itself there is an imperfect fusion of a developed monopoly capitalism, which reigns over some but by no means all phases of industry, and a backward agriculture, characterized by the strip system, share-cropping, and predominance of hand labor.[18] In certain respects Japanese agriculture is closely linked up with the world market, and seriously dependent on these connections. This is true notably of silk; a sharp decline in the prices paid for raw silk by the United States, or in the amounts taken, has immediate repercussions on the whole Japanese countryside.

These considerations do not apply in nearly the same degree to China. While the loss of Shanghai is a serious blow, it does not have the crippling effects which the destruction of Osaka or New York would produce on the economies of Japan or the United States. As one careful student of Chinese economic conditions has noted: "In China, the loss or destruction of a city like Shanghai would not seriously affect the economy in the interior. There would be a dearth of imported articles and glut of commodities destined for export, but neither of these categories constitutes a significant proportion of the total products of the nation. Not only will the destruction of major port cities and stoppage of foreign trade not be of decisive importance, but the economy of China is so localized and the various localities are so self-sufficient that even a disruption of internal trade through the loss of certain regions in the process of the war will not be fatal to China's power of resistance." [19] A blockade will impose hardships on the interior population, especially as regards clothing and certain other necessities, but it cannot lead to a general economic collapse. The predominantly agricultural life of China's inland provinces will

[18] See Chapter VI.
[19] Ch'ao-ting Chi, "China's Economic Strength and the Sino-Japanese War", *amerasia*, October 1937, p. 345.

continue, with various necessary readjustments to compensate for the scarcities of imported articles.

As regards finance the Chinese government faces rather more serious handicaps, but even in this sphere there is no certainty that the difficulties cannot be surmounted. The loss of Shanghai, Tientsin and Tsingtao has already cut off the bulk of China's customs receipts, which supplied over 40 per cent of government revenue in 1935 and 1936. A considerable proportion of China's banking, industrial, and commercial interests have either suffered grave losses or been placed beyond the effective jurisdiction of the Chinese authorities. The financial contributions of this group to China's war chest must henceforth become much more of a voluntary offering than a taxable lien. To an increasing extent, China's government revenues must be derived from a narrowing section of the interior. These disadvantages are partially offset by the patriotic enthusiasm of the Chinese people, which, for example, facilitates the sale of government bonds. The war loan of 500 million silver dollars, sold in issues as low as one dollar, met with a surprising response and has been largely, if not entirely, subscribed. Other sources of revenue have also been made available by the existence of a war situation. In view of Japan's savagery, it would not seem unreasonable for the Chinese authorities to confiscate the considerable Japanese properties in the interior and convert them to war use. The same action might be legitimately applied to properties of Chinese found to be assisting the invader. Measures such as land tax reform, involving larger assessments on the landlords, and a graduated property tax are already under consideration for the inland provinces.

On the expenditure side, the Chinese government will find it possible to effect large savings. A moratorium on the loan and indemnity services, which averaged 300 million dollars in 1935 and 1936 or nearly one-third of total expenditure, is contemplated. Important reductions of administrative expenditure, including official salaries, have already been made. These savings will release considerable sums for direct military expenses, which must necessarily increase. China's problem in this regard, however, has certain differences from that of Japan which must be taken into account. The Chinese armies are fighting on their own soil, in the midst of a sympathetic and friendly population. Japan must transport huge armies, now aggregating possibly 800 thousand men, to the war fronts and supply them with food and other supplies, which must largely be sent from home by means of an expensive commissariat system. Its expenditure of munitions, notably with regard to bombs and shells, is on a prodigal scale compared with China. A burst of machine-gun fire from Pootung, for example, has been answered by a two-hour bombardment from Japanese war vessels in the Whangpoo River. The relative extent of military expenditure is vastly different in the two cases.

These are some of the underlying factors which have to be taken into account with respect to China's financial ability to continue the military struggle. Extensive year-end surveys by American and European financial experts have contributed specific information on certain elements of this problem.[20] Chinese foreign loan and indemnity bonds, as well as internal issues, have been regularly serviced throughout 1937; it is expected that during the year 1938 amortization payments on foreign obligations will probably cease, but interest payments will be met in full. A moratorium will be declared at the same

[20] *New York Times*, February 20, 1938.

time on Chinese domestic bonds; interest payments will continue, though at 3 or 4 per cent instead of the prevailing 6 per cent. To maintain service on its foreign and domestic loan obligations, the Chinese government paid out nearly 100 million U.S. dollars during 1937. Somewhat over 100 million U.S. dollars had been expended for munitions between July and January; on January 1, 1938 an additional 25 million dollars' worth of munitions and other war supplies had been ordered but not yet delivered. On the same date, cash reserves of the Chinese government held abroad, principally in New York and London, were estimated at roughly 300 million dollars. The reported summary of the experts' observations then stated: "Were it not for the necessity of keeping intact a large slice of this fund to act as a reserve back of Chinese national currency, China's financial position would indeed be bright, despite nearly six months of devastating war on her own soil."

For the immediate future, at least, the Chinese government apparently has sufficient funds with which to cover its minimum requirements for munitions. Another aspect of this problem involves the maintenance of lines of access to China through which such supplies can continue to reach the interior. The great bulk of China's military supplies have thus far entered the country through Canton, from which they have been carried north to Hankow by rail. This supply line was still functioning in the early months of the new year. At the beginning of 1938, it was obvious that a considerable additional supply of airplanes had been acquired by the Chinese military authorities and put into action at the front. Japan might adopt either of two methods to block this line of entrance. By a declaration of war, Japan would be enabled to attempt to block shipments *via* Hongkong. The risk of complications with foreign powers has thus far prevented such action. The alternative would be a direct military attack on Canton. Such a campaign would entail large-scale military-naval operations, involving very considerable forces; the exigencies of the war in the north have not permitted such a diversion.

It is not unlikely, however, that one or the other of these steps may ultimately be taken, thus eliminating Canton as a source of entrance for military supplies. Under such circumstances, it is also probable that the line of access through French Indo-China might be closed through blockade or threat of reprisal. Even so, there would still be several interior routes through which supplies might reach China. Access from the Soviet Union, either through Outer Mongolia or Sinkiang, could be blocked only by a general Japanese occupation of China's northwestern provinces. Under these conditions, there would still be access to Szechuan province *via* the southerly routes through Sinkiang, or Chinese Turkestan. Finally, an overland highway from Burma into Yunnan was being rushed to completion and was expected to be ready for use in the spring of 1938. All these overland routes would be subject to inconvenience and considerable delays, but would at least offer means of entrance for a certain amount of military supplies. Airplanes, in particular, can be flown into China from a number of different points on the borders of the peripheral provinces.

There is still another factor, which may well prove to be decisive, in China's ability to wage a successful war of defense. The positional warfare carried on in the Shanghai-Nanking area, and later on both sides of the Lunghai Railway, is of great military and strategic value. China's stand at Shanghai dealt a considerable blow to the prestige of the Japanese army. For nearly three months,

Chinese armies with inferior military equipment withstood the shock of Japan's heaviest blows and inflicted serious losses on the invaders. During the operations early in the year in Shantung and Anhwei provinces, both north and south of the Lunghai Railway, the Japanese offensives were held up for many weeks by a determined Chinese defense. Such campaigns exact a heavy toll from the Japanese side, in military supplies, in casualties, and in funds. At the same time, they involve a serious drain on the more scanty munitions stocks at China's disposal. As the Japanese armies penetrate further into the interior, positional warfare combined with the broad application of guerrilla tactics becomes both more feasible and more damaging to the morale and fighting ability of the invading forces. The effectiveness of the mobile warfare carried on by units of the Eighth Route Army in several of the northern provinces has already been noted.[21] These tactics have also been successfully applied in the Shanghai-Nanking area by former Communist partisan forces from the southern provinces, which have been reorganized and placed under the Chinese central command.

Statements made on February 21 by General Chen Chien, commander of the Peiping-Hankow Railway defenses, indicate that preparations have been made to inaugurate guerrilla fighting on a large scale. The Chinese forces operating north of the Yellow River, he declared, were under orders to adopt mobile tactics in that area, and establish liaison with the Eighth Route Army. Within Honan province, Chen Chien was recruiting soldiers for the regular armed forces; in addition, at least two million men of military age in 85 districts of the province were undergoing two hours of daily training. A mass mobilization of this sort, if thoroughly organized, can place

[21] See Chapter IX.

hundreds of thousands of additional guerrilla forces in the field. Large numbers of regular troops can also be diverted to mobile operations. The problem of supplying such units with munitions is relatively simple. Rifles, machine-guns, and small arms ammunition are the main requirements. Even in the interior provinces, China possesses a number of arsenals capable of producing these types of military equipment. The output of such centers can be expanded at slight expense.

Military resistance of this character, it is true, will not be able to win smashing victories. Its effects, in the long run, may be nonetheless devastating. By their control of wide areas of the interior, the guerrilla units can force Japan to maintain large armies of occupation in China indefinitely. These occupationary forces will be constantly harassed by swift attacks at various points of their extended lines. The support of the local population will not only afford the mobile detachments a continuous source of food supplies and other necessities; the people will also constitute an incomparable intelligence service, warning the guerrilla fighters of the approach of large Japanese forces and supplying information as to the numbers and disposition of isolated Japanese units. Such a guerrilla army will attest the truth of the statement of Generalissimo Chiang Kai-shek that "the basis of China's future success in prolonged resistance is not found in Nanking or big cities but in villages all over China and in the fixed determination of the people." The successes of the Manchurian volunteers, under even more difficult circumstances, is a pledge of what can be accomplished in the wider regions of China's inland provinces. At best the Japanese armies will be restricted to a defense of the main lines of railway and highway communication. The effective garrisoning of interior areas presents a problem of such vast proportions that it can be ruled out as a practical procedure. With the countryside in arms against the invader, there can be no question of economic revival or of a generally successful exploitation under Japanese auspices of the occupied provinces. The essential economic fact will be the staggering burden of expenditure for the Japanese armies of occupation, only a small portion of which could be recouped by taxes or forced requisitions.

The most serious danger for China has resided in a possible collapse of morale, particularly among certain elements in the ruling government circles. The critical period in this respect, however, seems to have passed with the fall of Nanking and the withdrawal of the government to the interior. There is every indication at present that the political unity established last spring has stood the test, and that a firm struggle in defense of China's national existence will be maintained. It is recognized on all sides that China's sole hope lies in prolonged resistance over a period of years, which may be ultimately counted upon to bring about Japan's financial and military collapse. Plans have been laid, and are being put into execution, to transfer the vital elements of China's national life to the provinces of the Southwest. Universities formerly located in the occupied areas have transferred students and faculties to Szechuan and the neighboring provinces. A reconstruction program for these regions, especially affecting improvement of communication facilities, is being planned and put into effect in the midst of war. These developments do not mean that the rest of China is being abandoned to Japanese rule. Even if the core of the central armies was eventually forced back into the Southwest, the real struggle would still be carried on by guerrilla forces behind the

Japanese lines in occupied territories, as the example of Hopei province clearly indicates. Off the main lines of communication, in any section of the country, the Japanese will be able to operate only in overwhelming force.

Democratization of China's political system, which is making steady progress, may be expected to contribute still further to the unity and strength of Chinese resistance. Measures adopted by the Kuomintang plenary session, held March 29 to April 2, 1938 in Hankow, witnessed to the most notable democratic trend in Chinese political life during the past decade. The session's outstanding achievement was the creation of a People's Political Council. As the representative of all party groups, and not merely the Kuomintang, this organ constitutes an embryonic legislature. This step toward democratic government was supported by the decree granting full freedom of press, speech and association. Since the beginning of 1938 newspapers of many political shades, including the Communist *Hsin Hua Jih Pao* or New China Daily, had been published in Hankow. The possibility of achieving these democratic reforms was originally considered during the negotiations which established the Kuomintang-Communist entente. Under a more liberal political régime, the Chinese people as a whole will play a fuller and more responsible part in China's broad anti-Japanese front.

The test of strength, as between China and Japan, pits two qualitatively different techniques and objectives against each other. For Japan the supreme objective must continue to be a smashing victory, and collapse of the opponent's morale and will to resist. Only a swift triumph, thorough enough to permit the withdrawal of excessively large forces of occupation, will leave an economic margin sufficient to balance its books. Every additional month of large-scale warfare diminishes the prospects of a successful outcome to the military adventure. The gambler's hands already betray their nervousness as the wheel spins, but shows no sign of settling on the lucky number. For China there is the necessity of maintaining a stubborn refusal to admit defeat in the face of overwhelming devastation and apparent disaster. The sources of such a spirit are reinforced by the objectives of the struggle. The Chinese soldier, long the plaything of internal struggle for wealth and power, now at last takes his legitimate place as the defender of an independent national existence. He is fighting in self-defense against a ruthless aggressor, and with a united country behind him. Among both the leaders and the rank and file, genuine patriotism rules more supreme than at any time in this century. In the opposing trenches, the motivating force is the zeal for conquest, domination, even for loot. The advantage in this regard clearly rests with China. It may well turn the scales. History shows other examples of a colonial country defeating a better equipped ruling power, whose troops had no stomach for the business. It was true of the American war for independence.

CHAPTER TWELVE

MANCHOUKUO—A PROTOTYPE FOR CHINA?

THE sixth anniversary of the founding of the Man-choukuo régime was marked by appropriate ceremonies in March 1938. This occasion, coming at a time when Japanese armies were operating in half the provinces of China south of the Great Wall, affords a not unfitting opportunity to review the record of Japan's administration in the Manchurian provinces. Attention might be legitimately directed, in particular, toward an examination of the effects of Japanese rule on the life of the thirty million Chinese in Manchuria. At the moment Japan is engaged in the task of establishing new puppet régimes which, if successfully consolidated, will control the destinies of scores of millions of the Chinese people south of the Wall. These new governments, it is claimed, will sweep away old abuses and confer the benefits of an honest and enlightened administration on the people which they are to govern. Fortunately, there exists the prototype of such an administration in Manchoukuo. The experiences and results of the past six years in Manchuria supply a mass of material which may be used to check the validity of the claims now advanced. For the methods and policies already enforced in Manchoukuo will be applied to the additional territories and populations which the Japanese are attempting to bring under their sway, as is clear from the evidence of developments in Peiping.[1]

[1] See Chapter IX.

What have been the distinguishing features of the methods and policies applied by Japan to the government of the Northeastern provinces? How have they affected the livelihood, physical well-being, and mental outlook of the Chinese in this region? What degree of initiative and self-determination is exercised by the Chinese in this state, the creation of which was claimed to represent the spontaneous will of its inhabitants?

The highest government offices of Manchoukuo, notably the various Ministries under the State Council, are held almost exclusively by Chinese and Mongols. Actual administrative control, however, is vested in the powerful General Affairs Board, which functions within the State Council and is dominated by Japanese officials. Foreign visitors to Hsinking, capital of the new state, at once find themselves in the hands of Japanese officials, who will accompany and assist them if they wish to interview the *de jure* Ministers or the Emperor. No less revealing is the data on the composition of Manchoukuo's Civil Service, as supplied by the Official Register. In 1933 there were 2,048 "Manchurian" [2] and 1,259 Japanese civil servants; by the middle of May 1936 the proportion was 5,514 "Manchurians" and 5,811 Japanese. The change was particularly striking in the lowest of the four grades of the Civil Service. In this category of civil servants, known as *wei-jen,* the figures show 1,547 "Manchurians" and 740 Japanese in 1933, while in May 1936 there were 4,540 "Manchurians" and 4,473 Japanese. Thus, even on the lowest level, the work of day-to-day administration was being carried on increasingly by Japanese under-officials.

Six months later, significantly enough, the Official

[2] Japanese officials make every effort to stress the "Manchu" character of the new state. In reality, the population is overwhelmingly Chinese; such few Manchus as remain have been almost entirely assimilated in customs and language.

Register for November 30, 1936 failed to include statistics for this lowest grade of civil servants. Nearly 500 "Manchurian" officials had meanwhile been added to the Department of Justice, bringing the figures for the three upper grades in this department to 527 "Manchurians" and 122 Japanese. Since most of the cases handled by the courts involve Chinese litigants exclusively, the change thus introduced was not of material importance. More noteworthy was the racial composition of the civil servants in the State Council, where the three upper grades comprised 43 "Manchurians" and 189 Japanese. In the Department of Industry the corresponding figures were 38 to 124, and in the Department of Communications 33 to 68. Taking the administrative branches of the government as a whole, including the provincial offices, the tendency was to approximate a ratio of 40 per cent "Manchurians" to 60 per cent Japanese in the three upper grades of the Civil Service. These figures show that the Manchoukuo régime is not only directed at the top by Japanese officials ensconced in the General Affairs Board, but that routine administration is predominantly carried on by Japanese civil servants. Whatever else may be true of this new state, it is not governed by the Chinese who constitute the overwhelming majority of its population.

Recognizing the inherent difficulties of this situation, the Japanese authorities have devoted special attention to the problem of controlling the intellectual life of the Chinese people in Manchuria. Every avenue of indoctrination—education, press and radio—is employed in the task of reconciling the local population to its inferior status. The more positive aspects of this effort are reflected in the activities of the Manchoukuo Concordia Society, which has the special function of inculcating a peculiar brand of Manchurian patriotism, and in the emphases of the school curriculum. At the same time, Japanese policy seeks to de-nationalize the Manchurian Chinese by deliberately circumscribing their educational opportunities and by carefully filtering all information that enters Manchoukuo from the outside world. This negative side of Japanese policy is probably more subtly effective and in the long run more damaging than the rather obvious propaganda for the "harmony of the five races." Both aspects, however, are correlated to achieve the supreme aim of destroying the national consciousness of thirty million people.

Even the most cursory survey of Japan's educational program in Manchuria brings to light a series of startling facts. It is not surprising that Japanese apologists for the achievements of Manchoukuo carefully sidestep any mention of what is taking place in the sphere of education. The budgetary appropriations for the Department of Education are not only unusually small, amounting to roughly one-half of that expended for educational purposes by the former Chinese governments of the four Northeastern provinces in 1929. They have declined, during the past four years, both in absolute amount and in relation to total government expenditure. The figures are as follows: 6,114,268 Manchoukuo *yuan*[3] in 1934-1935; 3,055,814 *yuan* in the last half year of 1935, when the term of the fiscal year was changed; and 5,090,043 *yuan* in the calendar year 1936.[4] In percentages of the total budget, these sums work out respectively at 3.24 per cent, 3 per cent, and 2.3 per cent. The estimate for educational expenditure in 1937 was 5,697,925 *yuan*, or 2.2 per cent of total budgetary appropriations.

[3] A Manchoukuo *yuan* is equal to the Japanese *yen,* or rather less than thirty cents in United States currency.

[4] *Fifth Report on Progress in Manchuria to 1936,* Dairen, The South Manchuria Railway Company, July 1936, p. 153.

The logical conclusion from these figures would seem to be that educational enterprise in Manchoukuo is declining, or at least is making no advance. Attempts to check such an assumption by reference to the educational statistics of the Manchoukuo government are unavailing, since the data issued are contradictory and incomplete. One source, for example, places the number of elementary schools in Manchoukuo at 12,896, with 830,960 pupils, at the end of 1934.[5] Another gives corresponding figures for 1935 as 13,451 schools, with 825,468 pupils.[6] Statistics recently issued,[7] showing 13,100 schools with 960,600 pupils, presumably refer to 1936, i.e., a sudden jump during a period when the appropriations had declined by about one million *yuan*, or one-sixth of the total. Yet these discrepancies are as nothing to figures by the Department of Education for the three-year period 1933-1935, which show the number of elementary schools fluctuating by well over 2,000 but give the constant figure of 596,688 pupils for each of the three years. These misleading data are possibly intended to conceal the actual status of Manchoukuo education. A conservative estimate would be that no more pupils are in school than under the pre-1931 Chinese régime; the highest figures cited above exceed but slightly those for 1929 during Chang Hsueh-liang's era. It is more likely that considerably fewer children are in school—a conclusion which is borne out by the testimony of foreign residents in Manchoukuo.

It will be noted that so far mention has been made only of elementary schools. The Japanese freely admit that they are not interested in providing secondary or advanced education. Statistics with respect to secondary

[5] *Fifth Report on Progress in Manchuria to 1936,* cited, p. 170.
[6] Department of Civil Affairs Bulletin, September 15, 1935.
[7] *General Survey of Conditions in Manchoukuo,* Department of Foreign Affairs, Hsinking, November 1936, p. 13.

education also exhibit puzzling discrepancies. One source gives 202 middle schools with 28,866 pupils for the end of 1934,[8] while another shows 178 middle schools with 32,900 students for 1936.[9] Both sets of figures appear to be well padded. The use of former middle school textbooks is prohibited, and new ones have been provided in but few subjects. There is not one *bona fide* university in the whole of Manchoukuo.[10] The half-dozen colleges and universities which flourished in Chang Hsueh-liang's day have been closed. The famous Northeastern *(Tungpei)* University at Mukden has suffered the same fate recently meted out to Peking National University; it is used as a barracks for Japanese troops. Indifferent training, not much above secondary grade, is provided in a few special normal and vocational schools, the latter specializing in business, agriculture, and mechanics. Vocational education is highly prized, evidently because it is less likely to provoke "dangerous thoughts" or stir up political unrest. Students who return to Manchoukuo from advanced schools in China or Western countries undergo police inquiries and supervision; while they are abroad, their parents are visited and questioned by the police. A few students are given the opportunity to pursue a university education in Japan. This favored handful of "Manchurians" is carefully selected. They must have a permit issued by the Manchoukuo Embassy in Tokyo, which supervises their activities and may send them back to Manchuria if they prove "unsatisfactory." The expectation seems to be that, after such a period of training in Japan, these students will be smoothly assimilated into the ruling caste of Manchoukuo. Private schools are not

[8] *Fifth Report on Progress in Manchuria to 1936*, cited, p. 170.
[9] *General Survey of Conditions in Manchoukuo*, cited, p. 13.
[10] Two medical colleges, one under missionary auspices and the other under the South Manchuria Railway Company, are located in Mukden.

encouraged; those under missionary auspices, in particular, are viewed with suspicion and subjected to strict regulation.

Since the Manchoukuo authorities direct their educational efforts primarily toward the elementary schools, it is instructive to examine the content of this education. Here the Japanese feel that they have their best opportunity to influence the minds of Manchurian youth who have not been previously affected by the virus of Chinese nationalism. The curriculum of these lower schools has several obvious emphases. Study of the Japanese language is compulsory. Manual training for boys and domestic science for girls are characteristic features. Most prominent of all are the courses in ethics, the central theme of which is Manchoukuo's guiding principle of "Wang Tao." This concept of the "Kingly Way" has been consciously borrowed from the Confucian classics. It represents the Confucian ideal of the upright sage, who rules not by force but by the persuasive effect of his gracious benevolence on all within his realm. It is the "Way of Right" as contrasted with "Pa Tao", the "Way of Might." There is a certain grim irony in the connotations of such a symbol for the state of Manchoukuo. Yet the emphasis on Confucian ideology, perfected through the centuries to buttress the ruling position of a privileged bureaucracy, has a deliberate and not inappropriate application. The pupil is taught to revere Kang Te, the Emperor of Manchoukuo, as the virtuous ruler who governs in accordance with the "will of Heaven." His mind is impressed with the Confucian ethical concepts of *te, i, li* and *jen,* or virtue, right conduct, propriety and benevolence—all of which tend toward submission and minimize self-assertion. There is no mention of that other strain in Confucian philosophy, represented notably by Mencius, which stressed the right and duty of the people to revolt against an unjust and tyrannous ruler.

Within this Confucian setting, attention is devoted toward creating and popularizing a set of patriotic shibboleths, especially in the history text-books. Manchuria is pictured as distinct from the China south of the Wall. It is a separate geographical entity, with an historically unique culture. It possesses the treasured precedent of the Manchu conquests. More recently Manchuria has been delivered from the corrupt Chinese warlords, mainly by the spontaneous will of its thirty million people, though benevolently aided by Japan. The pupil also learns that Manchoukuo derives great benefit from its intimate connections with Japan, that China is ground down by the militarists, and that his duty is to reverence the Emperor and act his part in achieving the "harmony of the five races." This latter concept seems to be a purely Manchoukuo creation. It has already undergone a degree of evolution. During the first year or two, the classification was Han (Chinese), Manchu, Japanese, Korean and Mongol, but it has since been revised to read Manchu, Japanese, Korean, Mongol and Russian. The Chinese have all become "Manchurians." These various school precepts, which seek to fashion a patriotic undergirding of the new state, are given free rein in demonstrations on the national holidays of Manchoukuo and Japan, when the pupils must parade, wave flags, cheer and listen to speeches.

The strands woven into Manchoukuo's educational policy form one consistent pattern. There is the decline in government expenditure and probably in the number of children who receive schooling, the absence of higher education, the prominence of elementary and vocational schools, the emphasis on Confucianism and unquestioning obedience to authority, and the importance attached to the inculcation of patriotism. What effect this sort of education may have on those of the younger generation who are subjected to it is somewhat problematic. Most of the children are affected by home influences which must act as a healthy counter irritant to the indoctrination they receive in school. Very soon they doubtless come to realize that patriotism for the "Manchurians" means the acceptance of an alien rule. They probably recognize that the burden of maintaining the "harmony of the five races" rests chiefly upon them. For the objective of Manchoukuo's educational system is clear. It aims to prepare the great bulk of the Chinese population for a well defined position of subservience in their new national life, with the ruling places reserved to the Japanese and those few Chinese who emerge acceptably from a university education in Japan.

This educational policy is supplemented by rigid provisions affecting control of the press and distribution of news in Manchoukuo. The press system now in vogue contrasts sharply with conditions in Manchuria prior to the Japanese occupation. Under the former Chinese administration censorship was exercised only during stress of emergency, and newspapers and periodicals were freely brought in from the outside. As in China south of the Wall, the literate population was growing and the number of newspapers increasing. By 1931 there were thirteen Chinese dailies in Manchuria, of which six were published in Mukden and three in Harbin. Following the occupation, these Chinese-owned papers were reorganized under Japanese control, with military censors directing their news and editorial policies. This *ad hoc* policy was regularized by an order of the Department of Education in October 1932, later enacted into law.[11] Under the provisions of this law, the publication of a wide range of material was prohibited. The limitations set up were so vaguely defined as to confer virtually unrestricted discretion on the censor. They covered news materials disturbing to peace and order, seeking unlawful alteration of the form of the state, affecting foreign relations, liable to cause public or financial panic, and revealing closed court proceedings or other subjects forbidden by the police. In addition, the Foreign, War and Finance Departments were empowered to forbid discussion of matters deemed to jeopardize peace and order or to interfere with their spheres of administration. Censorship of local and imported publications, enforced by the power of total suppression, was sanctioned by this law. Imprisonment up to one year could be visited upon violators of the law's provisions.

Some two weeks later, on December 1, 1932, the Manchoukuo News Agency, or "Kokutsu", took over the telegraphic and news facilities of existing Japanese agencies in Manchuria. By official action, this agency was soon given a monopoly of news distribution in Manchoukuo, including all despatches entering and leaving the country. Kokutsu obtains its Chinese news from its own branches in China, while its Japanese and foreign news is secured through "Domei", Japan's official agency. All news sent out or brought into Manchuria thus originates with and is approved by official Japanese organs. The Hsinking authorities were still not wholly satisfied. Regulations issued on August 17, 1935 by the Japanese Ambassador to Manchoukuo forbade the import of publications into the

[11] Department of Education, Order No. 130, October 13, 1932; Imperial Ordinance No. 11, March 1934.

Kwantung Leased Territory and the South Manchuria
Railway zone except by permission granted after copies
submitted for examination had been approved by the
appropriate censorship organs of these jurisdictions. Similar arrangements were already effective with respect to
Manchoukuo, under the provisions of its publications
law, so that foreign newspapers and periodicals must run
a double gauntlet before they can enter Manchuria. A
further step toward effective press control was taken on
April 9, 1936, when an ordinance was issued establishing the Manchuria News Publishing Association, Ltd.[12]
Ostensibly formed to develop the local press along "sound
lines", this organ was actually intended to coordinate the
press censorship. Offices established by the association,
which was composed of Japanese officials and publishers,
took over the onerous burdens of censorship, introducing
greater efficiency and uniformity and relieving police and
judicial authorities.

The older vernacular newspapers had long since become nothing more than a reflection of Japanese editorial
opinion of the most orthodox stamp. Staffs of the former
Chinese-owned papers had gradually been changed, usually with Japanese editors and business managers added
by the Kwantung Army. So colorless were these papers
that the Chinese reading public tended to shift allegiance
to Chinese-language dailies published and edited by Japanese interests in the Kwantung Leased Territory, which
were slightly less circumscribed in their treatment of the
news. At best, the Chinese population of Manchoukuo
is restricted to a reading fare totally alien to its viewpoint
and interests. In their press, no less than in their education, the Chinese in Manchuria are intellectually isolated
from the rest of China, and taught to look through

[12] Imperial Ordinance No. 51.

Japanese eyes at the world around them and the world outside.

In ways not so formal, though equally pervasive and compelling, the mental outlook of the Chinese people in Manchuria is affected by the activities of the Manchoukuo Concordia Society. Here the Kwantung Army, central and directing force behind the whole Manchurian adventure, is revealed in true perspective as the semi-secret yet dominant power in the new state. In the words of its official handbook,[13] the Manchoukuo Concordia Society's origins and early activities are described as follows: "The predecessor of the Concordia Society was the Bureau for Directing Self-Government, which for some years prior to the Incident was an organization of groups of Japanese and Manchurian volunteers united to solve Manchurian and Far Eastern questions. Under the influence of the Kwantung Army, this Bureau before the Incident worked strenuously to hasten the day of Manchurian independence. At the time of the Incident, when Manchoukuo was being established, this organization, in concert with the Army's military measures, took upon itself the burden of political measures. . . . After the nation was established, it split into two parts, one composing the Manchoukuo Government and the other forming the Concordia Society, a people's organization. From the historical viewpoint, therefore, while the Society has changed its form, its nature is the same as before; it was born and has developed as a nation creator."

These are notable admissions. Before the Mukden incident of September 18, 1931, the Kwantung Army was sponsoring a movement to detach the Manchurian provinces from China. After the success of "the Army's

[13] "Concerning the Manchoukuo Concordia Society", Central Affairs Office, Manchoukuo Concordia Society, May 9, 1935.

military measures", the members of this movement were responsible for the political steps which led to the formation of Manchoukuo. Some of them entered the government thus established, while the rest became members of the Concordia Society. The role which this Society was henceforth to play is clarified by another statement: "The government is the direct and the Society the oblique organization of Manchoukuo. In a primitive society a direct organization may be sufficient, but in a complex society such as that of Manchoukuo . . . if one does not bind the social mass by an oblique as well as a direct organization, the state will not develop unity and strength to resist external conflict and internal dissension. As for functions, the government administers the operation of the Wang Tao principle, while Concordia preaches this principle. . . . Thus the rule of Wang Tao is perfected by two coordinated but separate organs, the government taking the higher will to the people, the Society taking the people's will to the higher. . . . If we compare Manchoukuo to a kimono, the government is the outer cloth and the Society the lining, two pieces but nevertheless one garment." More specifically, the Society "will give substance to the spirit of national construction founded upon Wang Tao principles", and "bind officials with people and inferiors with superiors." It will "ease the execution of the government's plans by smoothing relations among the several races." It "works among and close to the people" and "must complete the structure of the nation and mould the minds of the people."

The Concordia Society is evidently an unofficial arm of the government, striving to reconcile the Chinese population to the new dispensation in Manchuria. Though not a statutory organ, its relations to the government are of the closest. Not only are the Emperor and Prime Minister its *ex officio* Governor and President respectively, but its revenue is mainly supplied by annual grants in aid from the government. These have been steadily increasing. In 1934-1935, the grant was 800,000 *yuan;* in 1935 (last half) 500,000 *yuan;* in 1936 (calendar year) 1,500,000 *yuan;* while in 1937 it was 1,800,000 *yuan.* Obviously, the task of developing patriotism, a feeling of nationality, and a harmonious relationship to the new régime among the Chinese in Manchuria is considered of the highest importance by the Manchoukuo government.

On the surface, the Concordia Society appears to be a democratic, self-governing organization. At its base are the local chapters, which may be formed by two or more members, organized by occupation or locality. The various chapters annually elect local congresses, which in turn elect the national congress. The national congress elects a Board of Directors, which chooses the Chief Director. The latter appoints the Central Affairs Office Committee, which is the actual executive organ of the Society. Despite this democratic facade, the Society is in fact a firmly controlled tool of Japanese policy intimately linked with the Kwantung Army. The various Commanders-in-Chief of the Kwantung Army have successively acted as its honorary advisers. A pamphlet issued by the Central Affairs Office on May 7, 1936 states: "These strides have been made by the Society *pari passu* with the progress of Manchoukuo, but the spur to them has been the Kwantung Army, which is the Society's inner supreme guiding force." [14]

In 1936 the Board of Directors was composed of 23 honorary directors (11 Japanese and 12 Chinese), including the highest officials of Manchoukuo, the Kwantung

[14] "Concordia's New Leadership Plans", Central Affairs Office, Manchoukuo Concordia Society.

Army, and the South Manchuria Railway Company. It also consisted of 85 acting directors (69 Chinese and Mongols and 16 Japanese), including the state Ministers and chief administrative officials. This Board, however, met only twice a year, while the majority of its 108 directors were high Chinese officials who were preoccupied with other business. Actual executive authority was concentrated in the hands of the nineteen commissioners (11 Japanese and 8 Chinese) of the Central Affairs Office. This body consisted of one chairman, four full-time commissioners, and 14 part-time commissioners. The chairman was the Minister of Civil Affairs, a Chinese and a figure-head. The vice-chairman and the other three full-time commissioners were Japanese. Of the remaining part-time commissioners, seven were Chinese with other positions and seven were Japanese. Control of the Society's affairs thus rested in the hands of the four full-time Japanese commissioners, and the Commander-in-Chief of the Kwantung Army normally participated in their business meetings.

Although the Concordia Society was organized as early as July 25, 1932, by an informal edict of Chief Executive Pu Yi, and was clearly backed by the highest sources of political power in Manchoukuo, it seems to have met with little success in recruiting members or promoting its various aims. Early in 1936 the vice-chairman of the Central Affairs Office Committee, i.e., the real director, publicly deplored the fact that after nearly four years membership consisted almost solely of employees of the Society, Manchoukuo officials, and Japanese "volunteers". He urged the necessity of greater efforts and activity, in order to expand and popularize the Society. Following this public airing, a special board of twenty Japanese members, functioning under a larger advisory commission, actively set to work to revitalize the Society's program. The grant in aid from the government was raised to 1,500,000 *yuan*. Additional regional field offices were set up, bringing their total to 10; while local field offices were increased to 76. A membership drive was energetically fostered. The Concordia Society absorbed the entire 43,000 members of another Japanese-sponsored organization, the "Manchuria Justice Party." New chapters were formed, until in June 1936 their total number was 1,377, with a membership said to aggregate 300,000. Eighteen months later the claimed membership was 700,000.[15]

During the past two years the Society has vigorously pushed its campaign to develop synthetic Manchoukuo patriotism and national unity. All channels of publicity are at its disposal. A half-hour Concordia program is broadcast from Hsinking every evening; a Chinese language daily is published for its members; pamphlets, handbills and posters are widely distributed. Movie films prepared by the Central Affairs Office or Japanese agencies are continuously shown in local towns and villages by a special corps of screen operators with several dozen screen projectors. Junior members are enrolled in the Concordia Young Men's Association. The Society sponsors contests in oratory and calligraphy among primary and secondary school pupils, and offers prizes for essays on Wang Tao and other Manchoukuo themes. In June 1936 it conducted a nation-wide competition, with monetary prizes as an inducement, for the best slogans in Chinese, Japanese, Korean or Russian to enliven the "national foundation spirit" and encourage the "fight against Communism." The Society organizes patriotic celebrations on national holidays and on the newly pre-

[15] William Henry Chamberlin, *Christian Science Monitor*, January 19, 1938.

scribed festival days. Airplanes scattering leaflets and handbills constitute a feature of these celebrations. The independent status of Manchoukuo, emphasized in this patriotic propaganda, is not allowed to stand in the way of efforts, similar to those in Korea, to Japanize the population. Concordia has established schools giving free instruction in the Japanese language; it arranges free trips to Japan to promising individuals, and gives constant lectures on Japan and its relation to Manchoukuo. Society officials find it necessary to make special efforts to enroll Japanese, who seem to manifest little enthusiasm over becoming "Manchurians". Mongols and White Russians exhibit the same apathy. Concordia's chief aim, of course, is to reach the Chinese. The Society has even sought to amalgamate the Japanese and Chinese Chambers of Commerce in the larger cities—a bold attempt to break down an age-long stronghold of Chinese exclusiveness. Members of Concordia are encouraged to wear the society's olive-drab uniform, which is now generally affected by Japanese employees of Manchoukuo.

This quasi-Fascist society presents certain novel features. Its original founders, who constituted little more than a conspiratorial sect, obviously could not build up a mass movement among the Chinese to overthrow their own government. The Kwantung Army captured political power by dint of military conquest, imposing its will by force on those whom it now seeks to woo into the Concordia Society. It has since continued to dominate the state which it created. After the conquest, however, the leaders of the Kwantung Army felt the need of winning the support of the conquered population. The Concordia Society was organized to meet this need. It is a vehicle of high-pressure propaganda, designed to conciliate the Chinese people, create a distinctive national consciousness among them, and present Japan's role in an attractive light. The work of Concordia is clearly synchronized with the objectives of Japanese policy in relation to education and the press in Manchoukuo. In each sphere, the aim is to break the ties between the Chinese in Manchuria and their kindred south of the Wall, choke off any spirit of genuine nationalism among them, and mold them to a passive acceptance of their lot as Japan's colonial wards.

The phases of life in Manchoukuo thus far considered all relate to the intellectual environment of the Chinese population. It is not extreme to say that the facts point toward a deliberate effort to stupefy the mental processes of the Chinese living in Manchuria. On the physical plane, these Chinese are also being drugged as a consequence of the growing sale of opium and its derivatives. In this case, too, the facts are too obvious to admit of dispute. In 1936 the Opium Monopoly Bureau of Manchoukuo specified that 133,333 acres might be sown to opium; in 1937 this legally permitted sown area was increased to 156,061 acres. The Manchoukuo budget for 1937 anticipated a gross revenue of 47,850,000 *yuan* from opium sales, as compared with 37,318,925 *yuan* in 1936. These figures, moreover, do not show the whole picture. Considerable areas of Manchuria are sown to opium by illegal cultivators, and there is a widespread sale of opium and its derivatives by illicit retailers, mostly Japanese and Koreans. In addition, a vast opium enterprise has existed in the Kwantung Leased Territory and the South Manchuria Railway zone, where the extraterritorial privileges of the Japanese producers and dealers placed them beyond reach of the regulations of Manchoukuo's Opium Monopoly Bureau. It remains to be seen whether, with the abolition of extraterritoriality, the Manchoukuo authorities will limit the traffic in the railway zone and the leased territory.

In theory, the laws of Manchoukuo and the regulations of its Opium Monopoly Bureau are designed to control and limit the production and sale of dangerous drugs. Only a specified total area can be sown to opium, retailers are licensed, and opium smokers must obtain permits. These restrictions are more honored in the breach than in the observance. In recent years the Kwantung Army, by tacit consent if not actively, has encouraged an extensive and lucrative opium traffic across the Great Wall. A flood of opium and opium derivatives swept into the former "demilitarized zone" of northern Hopei province, and thence throughout North China.[16] The opium grown in Manchuria had to cover this large external demand. Even more, the fierce three-cornered competition between the Manchoukuo Opium Bureau, the illegal Manchurian dealers, and the Japanese producers and retailers in the extraterritorial zones broke down any pretenses at limitation. In the effort to popularize legal consumption, the Monopoly Bureau was forced to relax its official restrictions all along the line. The area legally sown to poppies was increased; the number of licensed shops in the larger cities was nearly doubled; and the retailer's guarantee money was reduced by four-fifths in the smaller towns and villages. Permit requirements became virtually a dead letter. The fee for a smoking permit was first reduced from 1 *yuan* to 0.20 *yuan,* and then disregarded almost entirely. Hardly three per cent of the opium smokers in Mukden, it is estimated, have permits. The hard-pressed

---

[16] This opium traffic in North China has latterly been supplied to an increasing extent by the output of huge manufacturing establishments which have been set up in the Japanese Concession at Tientsin.

licensed retailers, in addition to winking at the permit requirements, have been forced to duplicate their competitors' practices in such matters as purchase of illegal opium, secret employment of female attendants, adulteration of opium with ash in preparation of the paste, and manipulation of standard weights and measures.

An increasing proportion of sales consists of the more dangerous opium derivatives, such as heroin and morphia. These derivatives, produced mainly in the leased territory and the railway zone, are distributed from Dairen and Mukden along the railway lines. Sold in many forms, designed to satisfy varying tastes or to suit differing incomes, they include heroin or morphia for injection, materials for a pinch of snuff, cigarettes, and certain types which may be eaten. A dose sells for 0.10 *yuan*, as contrasted with 0.20 *yuan* for an opium pellet in a licensed shop. Heroin cigarettes are the cheapest of all, and are therefore most popular among the poorer classes.

The weight of evidence indicates that consumption of both opium and its derivatives, mainly heroin, is rapidly increasing in Manchoukuo. A conservative estimate would be that at least one-fourth of the adult population smokes opium more or less regularly. Confirmed addicts must total at least half a million, and their number is steadily growing. A question put to a Chinese as to the number of opium smokers in Mukden elicited the reply *"shih fen yu pa"*, that is, eight out of ten, or 80 per cent.[17] There can be no doubt that every year thousands of Chinese throughout Manchuria die from the effects of narcotic drugs. Bodies of narcotic addicts may be discovered almost daily on ash heaps and other such places in the larger cities. On a morning in March 1937, although it was quite late and the bodies are usually removed

[17] Evidence by author while in Mukden.

quickly by the Red Swastika Society, the corpses of two such addicts were seen on an ash heap near the Mukden wall.[18] The immediate area was surrounded by filthy opium dens, housing the lowest type of prostitutes who openly dispense narcotic drugs. Whether the policy is deliberate or not, the existence of this situation, and the fact that it is growing worse instead of better, constitutes a black mark against Manchoukuo. The record in this respect adds little justification to Japan's efforts to extend its rule over the Chinese provinces south of the Wall.

The disabilities suffered by the Chinese in Manchoukuo, at least in the fields already touched upon, will hardly be disputed. In some quarters, however, the claim is put forth that the industrialization and economic progress achieved by Manchoukuo tend to counter-balance these negative aspects of the new régime. What do the facts indicate on this point? Has the livelihood of the mass of the Chinese people in Manchuria been improved under the ægis of Japan?

On this issue, the foreign trade figures of Manchoukuo offer some valuable suggestions. Prior to the Japanese occupation, Manchuria enjoyed a steadily favorable balance of trade, ranging from well over 100 million silver dollars to nearly 400 million—this latter in 1931. Beginning with 1933, the balance has been continuously adverse, reaching nearly 200 million Manchoukuo *yuan* in 1935. This development is even more striking when the change in the position of Japan *vis-a-vis* other countries in Manchoukuo's trade is taken into account. In 1932 Japan bought from Manchuria goods valued at 26 million *yuan* more than it sold to Manchuria; while in 1936 Japan sold to Manchuria goods worth 270 million *yuan* more than it bought. During this period the rest of the

[18] Evidence by the author.

world continued to buy more from Manchuria than it sold, although this amount fell from 277 million *yuan* in 1932 to 180 million *yuan* in 1936. Manchoukuo's excess of exports to third countries thus goes to cover increased purchases from Japan. In other words, Manchoukuo's role has become that of helping to rectify the adverse balance of Japan's total foreign trade.

These figures also serve to pose the issue of Manchuria's industrialization in concrete terms. In 1936 Manchoukuo showed a favorable balance of 180 million *yuan* in its trade with third countries, and an adverse balance of 270 million *yuan* in its trade with Japan. The difference, or 90 million *yuan,* can be taken to represent at least part of Japan's investment in Manchoukuo for that year. Such investment in Manchuria's industrial development, it is argued, necessarily contributes to the welfare of the local population. But this does not follow automatically. It is necessary to ask several questions. What sort of investment? For what industries? In whose benefit? These questions can be answered only by breaking down the trade figures into the various categories of export and import commodities, and tracing the resulting effects on the different classes of the population.[19]

With respect to exports, the statistics show no signs of increasing industrialization. Contrary to the trend from 1928 to 1931, under the former Chinese administration, the value of industrial exports from Manchuria declined steadily from 1932 to 1934—a loss which was only slightly redressed in 1935. This occurred during a period when the value of Manchuria's agricultural exports was reduced by approximately one-third. The net result is measured

[19] This exacting task has been competently performed by A. J. Grajdanzev, and the results of his analysis have been summarized in what follows. See "The External Trade of Manchuria, 1928-1935," *Nankai Social and Economic Quarterly,* Tientsin, January 1936, p. 853-894.

in the Manchurian population's reduced consumption of cereals and beans, amounting to a decline of from 445 kilograms *per capita* in 1931 to 378 kilograms in 1934, and to an estimated 340 kilograms in 1935.[20] That is, the living standards of the mass of the Manchurian people had seriously deteriorated since 1931. It may be granted that this result was due to a combination of factors, not all of which were within Japan's control. Nevertheless, there was no sign that the situation was being remedied by greater industrial development. The immediate need was for a revival of Manchuria's export trade. In this respect, Japanese policy had cut Manchoukuo off from its formerly large China market, while Japan itself was buying even less than before from Manchuria.

In the case of import commodities, it is necessary to examine both goods for production and goods for consumption. Manchoukuo's import of production goods showed an absolute and relative increase. While such goods already constituted from 29 to 33 per cent of total imports in the 1928-1931 period, they rose to 40 per cent in 1934 and 1935. The significant fact, however, is that from 70 to 80 per cent of these production goods went solely to railway and allied construction. In so far as earning power is concerned, many of these new railway lines may be considered doubtful ventures. The Kwantung Army built them primarily with an eye to strategic considerations, and not to industrial development. After this item for railway construction is eliminated, little remains for "industrialization" purposes. And this conclusion is borne out by the fact that virtually no general industrial development has occurred in Manchoukuo. Such an attempt would, in any case, meet with the decided opposition of Japan's vested interests at home. The

[20] A. J. Grajdanzev, cited, p. 866.

only exception to this rule is a few heavy industries serving military needs, and such industries in Manchoukuo have been preempted by the government, latterly assisted by Yoshisuke Aikawa—one of Japan's leading industrial capitalists. As for the Chinese population, it will have the privilege of contributing its labor power—at low wages— to these few industries. No all-round industrial development of Manchuria will take place under Japan's auspices.

With regard to imports of consumption goods, the analysis also contributes certain interesting results. The value of these imports, surprisingly enough, remained on a stable level of roughly 280 million *yuan* from 1931 to 1934, after which it slightly increased. When this category is further divided into luxury goods and goods for general consumption, it becomes evident who consumes the bulk of these commodities. Especially after 1933, and in contrast to 1928-1929, the value of imported goods for general consumption exhibits a marked decline. The privation of the mass of the people is rendered even more obvious when it is noted that the population of Manchuria increased by some five millions, or approximately 15 per cent, between 1928 and 1935. Even within this classification, moreover, most of the so-called goods for general consumption were quite beyond reach of the purchasing power of the bulk of the population. They were consumed mainly by the middle class and the well-to-do, including the large influx of Japanese since 1931.

In the case of luxury goods, the picture is even clearer. As compared with 1928 and 1929, the index of luxury imports rose from 100 and 101 to 142 in 1933, 200 in 1934, and 268 in the first seven months of 1935. There can be no question as to what class of the population buys musical instruments, jewelry, radios, laces, perfume and cosmetics, and toilet equipment—all of which show large increases. In this connection, the growth in imports of *tatami* (Japanese mats), rice, trunks, and sporting requisites calls attention to another significant factor. Japanese residents in Manchuria, most of whom are of the middle class or above, now total more than half a million, having doubled their numbers since 1931. The consumption of this group has an important effect on the composition of Manchoukuo's imports, but does little to ameliorate the living conditions of the local Chinese population.

A mass of direct evidence substantiates the conclusions reached by this analysis of Manchoukuo's foreign trade. All classes of Chinese society in Manchuria, upper as well as lower, have suffered from the Japanese irruption. The added 250,000 or more Japanese in Manchoukuo have to a large extent supplanted an equivalent number of middle and upper class Chinese, thousands of whom fled from Manchuria in 1931-1932. In official life, from the lowest ranks up, and in business and professional life, these Japanese now supply the characteristic upper class atmosphere of Manchoukuo. A trip on the afternoon express from Hsinking to Mukden is a revealing experience. Among dozens of Japanese there is only an occasional Chinese, and these have obviously made their peace with the new régime; the fact that the train conductor speaks Japanese supplies an added note of finality to the general impression. This change is equally evident in social life. Amusement resorts are patronized almost exclusively by Japanese; to such an extent is this true, indeed, that the night life of Manchoukuo is more typical of Japan than of China. Luxury and fashionable display are conspicuously absent among the Chinese, who are no longer the patrons of high-class trade.

Similar direct evidence may be adduced with respect to the deterioration of living standards among the Chinese lower classes in Manchoukuo. It is these elements, constituting the great majority of the population, which have suffered most severely. In Eastern countries generally, the condition of rural credit represents one of the surest indices of the economic status of the farmer. The bulk of credit supplied to the farmer in Manchoukuo is advanced through an extensive system of pawnshops. On the security of his tools, clothing and personal possessions, the farmer obtains seeds and fertilizer; after the harvest, he redeems the pledged articles. Approximately three-quarters of such business is handled by the Ta Hsing Company, a Manchoukuo government enterprise. Statistics of this concern showed a large increase of forfeitures in 1936, as well as a marked decline in the value and quality of mortgaged articles. The countryside of Manchuria, in other words, has been denuded of ready cash, even after the harvest has been gathered. Outside of the Ta Hsing Company, some thirty per cent or so of the credit supplied to the Manchurian farmer is advanced by private usurers. It may be taken for granted that the credit terms exacted by these private usurers are even worse than those of the government concern. Apprehension over the existing situation was expressed in the enactment of new chattel loan regulations by the Manchoukuo authorities in November 1936. Among other measures to protect the borrower, this law sought to prohibit rates of interest which exceeded 4 per cent a month—in itself a reflection of prevailing conditions with respect to rural credit.

Beginning in 1936, when a new and more drastic approach toward "pacification" of disturbed areas was adopted, the Manchurian peasantry was forced to shoulder much more onerous burdens. The rapid building of additional military highways, mostly dirt roads surfaced by crushed rock, was encouraged by wholesale resort to forced peasant labor. Nearly 15,000 kilometers of such roads were constructed in Fengtien province alone during the closing months of 1936. This road-building campaign, including also repair of old highways, was inaugurated at the time of the fall harvest, but was nonetheless rigorously pursued. In some regions, only one member of a family was impressed for road service, but in others virtually all men and women between the ages of fifteen and sixty were forced to work on the roads. Young girls and old women engaged in this work. Not only was no remuneration given; those prevented from undertaking road work were forced to supply a monetary contribution calculated on a daily rate which exceeded the average wages of a Manchurian laborer. On the whole, the new roads were designed for military use in disaffected areas, but in some cases, where bus routes were instituted, they were speedily adapted to profitable commercial use. Yet it is difficult to see how, on balance, this type of "economic development" was of any benefit to the Manchurian farmer.

Forced labor on roads constituted one of the minor disabilities of the peasantry, incurred as a result of the revised program of the Japanese military authorities in dealing with so-called "banditry." Other concomitants of this program were far more burdensome. Five years of campaigning against the armed Manchurian volunteers had convinced the Kwantung Army that much more thoroughgoing measures had to be applied if the "bandit" menace was to be eradicated. The heart of the problem was seen to be the support accorded the armed volunteers by millions of the Manchurian farmers. In 1936 the army authorities tackled this aspect of the pacification campaign in characteristically ruthless fashion. The population of whole areas was concentrated in "protected villages"; outlying farm houses were burned to the ground, and in some districts the standing grain was fired. Around each of these villages the farmers were compelled to build high mud walls. The villagers themselves were registered, in order to control the entrance of outsiders; and the headman was made responsible, on pain of death, that no "bandit" received asylum in his village. Periodic check-ups were made. Those villagers unable to produce their residence certificates were summarily executed; at times such executions occurred in some districts at the rate of ten a day. By the middle of 1937 well over 2,000 of these "protected villages" had been established; the total population in areas affected by this program was estimated to range between five and six million. The results of this combination of measures, in regions where they were most rigorously applied, were devastating. Tens of thousands of Chinese farmers in Manchuria's eastern marches, under the spur of impoverishment and the reign of terror, were migrating to north Manchuria and moving south of the Wall in the winter of 1936-1937.[21] This pacification program throws additional light on the general issue of Japan's ability to foster the economic development of conquered Chinese territories.

Another characteristic aspect of Japanese policy should also be carefully noted in this connection. Japan has always lacked adequate capital resources; to compensate for this scarcity, it has been compelled to levy excessive burdens on its colonial populations. The fiscal problem becomes even more acute when serious armed resistance

[21] At three different times in March 1937, the author witnessed hundreds of these refugees, carrying their few belongings on their backs, crowded into the Mukden railway station.

and general disaffection exist in an occupied territory. In
the case of Manchoukuo, the *corvée* duties exacted from
the peasantry constitute but one example of the penny-
squeezing policy to which the Japanese authorities are
forced to resort. A conversation with a Chinese farmer,
who lived in one of the "protected villages" of Manchoukuo, illustrated this point even more circumstantially.[22]
His village lay some miles off the macadamized motor
highway, at the foot of a range of mountains which offered
excellent cover for the operations of the armed volunteers. It was reached by a dirt road hastily built by the
local villagers during the previous autumn. The Chinese
farmer pointed to the piles of crushed rock scattered at
intervals along the road. Although the time for planting
was nearly at hand, he and his fellow villagers would
soon have to start surfacing the road with this material
which they had obtained from the near-by hills. Several
burned farmhouses, lying some distance off the road,
were clearly discernible in the early afternoon sunlight.
One of these, partially hidden by the bluff of a hill,
invited closer observation. The roof had disappeared, and
but two mud walls were left standing; these latter were
half torn down, with a few broken reed laths projecting
from their tops. In what had been the court-yard, there
was a stone mortar that had once been used for grinding
grain; inside the walls, occupying the space of the former
ground floor, were the remains of a mud-brick oven. The
Chinese farmer said that of approximately 150 families in
his village, some 30 or 40 had been forcibly moved in
from the outlying districts, after their homes had been
thus fired and gutted. They had built temporary huts
inside the village, for which no monetary assistance had
been provided by the authorities. In answer to a question

[22] Evidence by author during visit to a "protected village."

as to how the cost had been met, he said simply: *"pang mang"*, i.e., mutual self-help among the villagers.[23]

In further conversation, this Chinese farmer supplied a brief outline of the actual conditions of life in these "protected villages". The details are illustrative of the multiform types of petty tribute exacted from the Manchoukuo peasantry. Taxes ranged from three to five dollars in local currency for every 10 *mou*, that is, for somewhat less than one and one-half acres. Prior to 1931, the equivalent tax had been only one dollar and a half. Each household contributed from four to eight dollars a year to the village headman, making up a sum used for purposes of "military protection." About once a week, a detachment of 40 or 50 Japanese troops visited the village. These had to be welcomed by a reception committee, and quartered and fed for the night at the expense of the villagers. Each household had to join the local branch of the Concordia Society; membership dues per household were collected semi-annually—one dollar in the spring, and one dollar and a half in the fall. In addition, the Society levied occasional contributions to meet emergency needs, such as flood, drought, et cetera. During the fall of 1936, when Japanese-sponsored Chinese and Mongol troops invaded Suiyuan, the Concordia Society exacted a contribution of fifty cents from each household in his village for the "Inner Mongolian independence" campaign. Meetings of the Society's local branch were held about twice a month, when a representative would lecture the villagers on the principle of Wang Tao, racial harmony, and other allied subjects. This phase of his life was summed up in one comprehensive phrase: *"szu hsiang shih tsui"*, that is, "to think is a crime".

[23] In some regions where the "protected village" campaign has been enforced, the new huts were not finished for months, leaving whole families exposed to the wintry weather.

Over the center of this "protected village," when it was finally reached, a Manchoukuo flag was flying bravely in the stiff breeze. The front gate was a new heavy cross-beamed affair of wood. A mud wall some eight feet high completely surrounded the village, with a deep ditch below it. From the top of the mud wall projected a series of newly cut stakes, along which six strands of barbed wire were strung about a foot apart. It was now made clear where some of the money collected for "military protection" went. This fund had been drawn upon to pay for the barbed wire supplied by the Japanese authorities. A freshly dug trench ran up one side of the hill. At its top corner was a little mud block-house, with a galvanized iron roof; gun-holes commanded the trench and its approaches. In all, there were five such block-houses on the wall, so placed as to permit an enfilading fire. All the work had been done by the villagers without pay. Despite the impressive show made by the walls, trenches, barbed wire and block-houses, the Chinese farmer said that the village was not really protected. None of the villagers had any guns; they were given cudgels, but nothing more. He pointed to the new telephone line, strung on thin light poles, which crossed the line of hills into the village. In case of attack, the villagers had to telephone to the nearest Japanese detachment, which could not arrive before some time had elapsed. A near-by village, he said, had been recently attacked; food and other supplies had been taken before the troops arrived on the scene.

Before leaving the village and its friendly Chinese representative, a last determined effort was made to shake the testimony which he had so freely volunteered. Is it not true, he was asked, that the currency of Manchoukuo has been stabilized, thus removing the blight of the old depreciated *feng-p'iao*. Grudgingly he admitted that this was so, and that it represented an improvement. More important, he thought, was the fact that prices of agricultural products were higher in 1937 than they had been for some time past. He stoutly maintained, however, that conditions in general were much worse than *"shih pien i ch'ien"*, i.e., than "before the change in circumstances", or before the incident of September 18, 1931. The increase in taxes bulked largest in his mind. It was no use to ask him whether the Japanese program of "economic development" had not contributed to the welfare of the Manchurian people.

In official and unofficial statements, the Manchoukuo authorities make every effort to minimize the extent of "banditry" in the new state. The subject is usually treated in smooth generalities. A typical example of this approach may be seen in the following quotation: "As a result of a series of intensive campaigns against the bandits, the major outlaw groups have been completely wiped out. Moreover, with the establishment of the peace preservation organizations among the civilians throughout the country, and closer co-operation between the military and the police, the normal state of peace and order has been practically restored." [24] In other cases, it is apparently recognized that somewhat more concrete evidence should be offered to substantiate such general claims. The result is usually a statement in good round figures of the reduced numbers of "bandits" operating in Manchoukuo, illustrated by the following: "As a result of strenuous efforts exerted by the national army and police forces and assisted by the Japanese troops, . . . the number of outlaws became exceedingly small. It is reported that, as against some 200,000 bandit hordes in 1932, there are to-day about 20,000. This number continues to decrease with

[24] *General Survey of Conditions in Manchoukuo*, cited, p. 5.

the progress of campaigns." [25] In reply to a Diet interpellator, the Japanese Vice-Minister of War, Lieutenant-General Yoshijiro Umezu, was not quite so categorical: "There has been a marked restoration of peace and order in Manchoukuo, but we cannot tell just yet when banditry will be completely eliminated." [26]

There are several means of checking up on the validity of these statements. The newly applied pacification program, which seeks to concentrate millions of the Manchurian farmers into "protected villages", does not seem to bear out the contention that the campaign against the insurgents is progressing favorably. It is, in fact, a measure of desperation on the part of the Kwantung Army. No such wholesale suppression and terrorism would be required if the insurgents had been reduced to a negligible factor. The "protected village" campaign further embitters the mass of the Manchurian population, militates seriously against the assiduous efforts of the Concordia Society to win the allegiance of the people to the new régime, and adversely affects agricultural productivity over wide areas of the interior. These grave liabilities would not be incurred without good and sufficient reason. Incidentally, the nature of this pacification program throws considerable light on the term "bandits" universally applied by the Japanese authorities to their military opponents. The so-called "bandits" are clearly supported by the great majority of the Manchurian population. They are the spear-head of the general disaffection which exists in Manchoukuo, the armed section of the people which resists alien domination. They may be more appropriately termed insurgents or, in the phrase most commonly used by the Chinese, "armed volunteers".

[25] *Fifth Report on Progress in Manchuria to 1936,* cited, p. 12.
[26] *The Japan Advertiser,* February 27, 1937.

The stringent precautions adopted to protect lines of communication, far more extensive than was necessary in the pre-1931 era, afford additional evidence as to the actual progress of pacification. The trunk lines of the South Manchuria Railway have been forced to institute an elaborate system of protective devices. Except in the larger cities, such as Mukden, every railway station has been turned into a miniature fortress. A pill-box of steel and concrete guards every bridge-head, and stands at the entrance to every tunnel. At night the smaller stations are blacked out; lights are turned on only to mark the arrival or passage of trains. In some districts armored cars pilot passenger trains at night; crack express trains are sometimes darkened in regions thought to be unsafe. Many stations have been abandoned, and steel shutters placed over doors and windows. High brick walls surround isolated Japanese communities in railway shops or round-house centers. Into the corner of these walls are built pill-boxes, along the top of which are strung barbed wire—partially electrified, as indicated by a porcelain insulator. Gangs of railway laborers work under the protection of detachments of Japanese troops in many areas. These precautions all apply to the South Manchuria Railway lines, which run through the more populous centers of the country. In the case of the state railways, which traverse less settled sections of the interior, even more stringent protective measures are enforced. In addition to the usual railway guards, many of the trains on these lines are manned by machine-gun units.

Fiscal expenditures supply another avenue of approach toward gauging the extent of insurgency in Manchoukuo. The state budget for 1937 appropriated 80,170,141 *yuan* for the Department of Defense, or 40 per cent of total budgetary expenditure. Of this amount at least one-half or 40 million *yuan,* including a sum of 19,500,000 *yuan* listed as a "contribution to share of national defense," may be set down as the sum directly applied to anti-insurgent operations and protective measures. To this figure must be added an appropriate share of the sums annually allotted by the Japanese budget to "Manchuria Incident Expenditures", which jumped from 198 to 268 million yen in 1937. Half this latter amount may be safely charged to the various items of expense incurred by the Kwantung Army's pacification operations in Manchoukuo. On the most conservative basis, therefore, nearly 175 million *yuan* was spent in campaigning against the Manchurian insurgents during 1937. This would seem to be an excessive bill for the curbing of 20,000 "bandits."

The evidence thus far adduced is corroborated by all unbiased reports of the real state of affairs in the Manchurian countryside. Persons with extensive knowledge of interior conditions assert that disorder and insecurity were never so widespread in the Northeastern provinces as during recent years. It is true that banditry existed in Manchuria prior to the Japanese occupation; quite possibly, the outlaws of that period outnumbered the present insurgent forces. Many factors serve to indicate, however, that the banditry formerly existing never constituted the problem that the insurgents now present. Before 1931 the settlement and reclamation of extensive areas were rapidly taking place. There were no such elaborate means of protection and defense as have recently been developed. Towns and villages were not as a rule protected by walls. Isolated families lived on the land in many districts. One notable difference is that the former settlers often had their own weapons, which they could use in self-defense. The possession of such weapons to-day involves the danger that they might be turned against the Japanese.

GATE AND WALL OF A "PROTECTED VILLAGE" IN MANCHOUKUO.

The activities of the armed volunteers, moreover, are not limited to outlying regions, as in the former period. During the summer and early fall, when the standing grain affords excellent cover, the insurgents carry their operations right up to the outskirts of the larger cities. Raids and kidnapings have occurred on the fringes of Mukden and in the neighborhood of Fushun, as well as not far from Harbin and Hsinking. In the summer of 1935 the authorities found it necessary to move a group of Korean rice farmers, who were located near Fushun, and re-settle them within sight of Mukden. This is the season when the Manchurian volunteers take the offensive, choosing at will their points of attack. Never certain where the insurgents will strike, the government forces are placed on the defensive, with little chance to coordinate their superior numerical and mechanical strength. At such a time much of the Kwantung Army, which numbered approximately 125,000 before the start of the China war, is forced to take the field. In addition, it has to call on the assistance of the Kwantung Bureau police, the consular police, and the Manchoukuo gendarmerie. The so-called Manchoukuo Army, of about 130,000 troops officered mainly by Japanese, is also called out to ward off the guerrilla attacks. The actual amount of assistance rendered by this force is problematic. Defections are reported from time to time; in the fall of 1937 a serious mutiny cost the lives of several score Japanese officers. In the autumn, the whole aspect of the campaign changes. With the grain cut, the volunteers are forced to merge with the local population or retire into the most inaccessible regions of the mountains. Japanese punitive expeditions take the offensive, seeking to discover the insurgent hide-outs and raze their bases. Some of the fiercest struggles of the year's campaigning take place during these punitive expeditions in the winter months.

The prolonged struggle with the Japanese troops, equipped with every weapon of modern military science, has exerted a marked effect on the evolution of the insurgent forces. In the early years of the Japanese occupation, the Manchurian armed opposition consisted mainly of former Chinese troops and professional bandits. Their numbers dwindled as the pressure increased; their character also changed, until finally the present insurgent forces emerged. Hardened by an incessant guerrilla warfare, the Manchurian volunteers are now in many respects analogous to the Chinese Communist armies south of the Wall. The names of the various insurgent units, such as the "National Salvation Army," the "People's Revolutionary Army," and the "Korean National Army," are indicative of their nationalist outlook and aims. At first more or less independent of each other, the bands of volunteers have lately tended to coalesce into larger units, with effective military organization and staff work. The movements of widely separated detachments, for example, are now coordinated by means of portable radio transmitters. Their original stock of munitions was derived from the Chinese armies which were broken up during the conquest of Manchuria in 1931-1932. To this have since been added the supplies gained from successful engagements with their Japanese or Manchoukuo opponents, or from raids on Manchoukuo arms depots. Munitions are also smuggled in from China. Virtually no military supplies seem to come in from the Soviet Union, as the Japanese military authorities readily admit in private conversation. Finally, the insurgents themselves operate arsenals for small arms ammunition in their hidden bases. Careful estimates placed their total number at somewhere between 50,000 and 75,000 in 1937. Their forces appeared to be increasing during 1937, and probably approximated the latter figure at the end of the year.

Like the Red armies south of the Wall, the Manchurian volunteers draw their main strength and sustenance from close and friendly relations with the local population. In certain districts they have maintained stable organized governments, embracing considerable numbers of people, for long periods of time. Uniforms, clothing and other equipment are produced for them by the local peasantry, and food supplies are gathered and stored at their headquarters. In the summer, when the volunteers range over wide areas, a fixed policy—enforced by strict discipline—is carefully maintained. The poorer elements of the population are protected from despoliation, receiving adequate pay for food supplies or other requisitions. Wealthy individuals are occasionally kidnapped and held for ransom, but even in these cases the ransom has been known to be set as low as 10 *yuan*. Special anti-Japanese leaflets are prepared, and such propaganda is spread throughout the countryside. This propaganda does not stop with the Chinese population or with the local Koreans; efforts, reported successful in some cases, are made to win over the rank-and-file of the Japanese troops, and induce them to mutiny against their officers. In rapid marches covering long distances, the volunteers are materially aided by the generally sympathetic attitude of the peasantry and townspeople. They are apprised by the people of the approach of Japanese forces long before these latter appear, and conversely, are enabled to strike at the enemy with full the Kwantung Army officers have been amazed to discover knowledge of his disposition and numbers. In some cases,

that the volunteers were in possession of the Japanese
code ciphers, and were making effective use of the information thus derived.

These are some of the factors which give rise to the
great difficulty experienced by the Kwantung Army in
eradicating "banditry" in Manchoukuo. Despite the
added handicaps imposed on the volunteers by institution of the "protected village" system, there is no sign
that their military effectiveness has been seriously impaired. The struggle is virtually continuous, summer and
winter. Over a period of three months, a total of 250
engagements by a single Japanese garrison headquarters
is not unusual. The serious nature of some of these engagements is suggested by the reported description of an
attack on one of the insurgent bases in the winter of
1936-1937. A Japanese punitive expedition had engaged
a volunteer force which had taken its stand on a steep
hill deep in the mountains. The volunteers operated in
alternate lines of rifle-men and machine-gunners, one line
retiring through the other to reload after its ammunition
was fired. Against this steady, murderous fire, the Japanese unit was forced to charge the hill. The cost of such
an operation is obvious.

Evidence from many sources indicates that Japanese
casualties over the course of a year mount into large
figures. An official announcement by the Tokyo War
Office, one of the last made in recent years, listed 138
killed and 330 wounded in the September-November
quarter of 1935. Hundreds of casualties, invalided home
as unfit for further service, may be counted in the reports
of the "white robed heroes" traveling on special trains
through Manchuria to Dairen. Most of these have been
incapacitated by serious wounds; some are either tubercu-
lar or affected by other diseases. In 1936, during the

month of September, 215 of these permanently disabled soldiers were transported to Japan. Similar evidence is supplied by the item of 11,610 *yuan* for "cremation" in the 1937 Manchoukuo budget, allotted to the Department of Defense. Since cremation is not a Chinese custom, it may be supposed that this sum applied chiefly to the Japanese officers and subalterns serving in the Manchoukuo Army. Unless special ceremony is involved, the cost of an individual cremation does not exceed five *yuan;* it should not be more in the case of an army man. Calculated at the normal rate, this budgetary item evidently anticipated the deaths of some 2,300 Japanese in the Manchoukuo Army alone for the year 1937. The pacification of Manchoukuo takes a heavy toll of Japanese lives.

The military struggle waged by the Manchurian volunteers is no longer an isolated affair. It constitutes the northernmost front of a united war of liberation by the Chinese people. Behind the lines in Manchoukuo, the Japanese military are still engaged in the task of consolidating their position against a determined armed resistance. They now seek to enforce their rule over a great portion of China south of the Wall. If they would, they might read an omen in the stubborn resistance of the Manchurian population to the Japanese yoke. Such resistance will be multiplied ten-fold in the wide reaches of China to the south. In the end it will turn the tide, and win for China the unchallenged right to a free and unfettered national development. It will also gain freedom for the Japanese people, who are to-day equally at the mercy of their militarist masters.

INDEX

A

Abe, Dr., 264
Abe, General, 221
Abo, Kiyotane, 319, 320
Adachi, Kenzo, 208, 217
Aggression, Japanese, 2, 63, 79, 191; diplomatic pressure at Nanking, 49-50; in North China, 40; reasons for 1937 onslaught, 185-191; secures revision of Chinese tariff, 53; see also Jehol invasion, Tangku Truce, Ho-Umetsu agreement, Chin-Doihara agreement, *New Life Weekly* incident. Lukouchiao incident, Chang Chun-Kawagoe negotiations, Autonomy movement in North China
Aikawa, Yoshisuke, 238, 346, 348, 349, 350, 351, 352, 353
Aikyojuku, 210
Akamatsu, Katsumaro, 207
Akita, Kiyoshi, 320
All-China Federation of National Salvation Unions, 136, 138, 139, 152, 177; arrest and trial of leaders, 152, 178, 181; release of leaders, 278
All-China Students' Union, 136
All-Japan Council of Labor and Farmer Unions, 333
Amau doctrine, 87
Ando, Seijun, 262
Anfu clique, 107, 135, 314
Araki, Sadao, 207, 209, 211, 212, 214, 220, 221, 222, 238, 319, 320, 332
Arrest of Chiang Kai-shek at Sian, 154; attitude of officials at Nanking, 168-169; Chang Hsueh-liang's attitude toward the Communists, 158-159; Chiang's ulti-

matum, 166-167; collapse of northwestern front, 175; commitments by Chiang, 173-174; eight-point program of rebels, 168; nationalist movement at Sian, 159-160; negotiations for Chiang's release, 171-173; other leaders arrested, 167; preliminaries to, 160-161; revolutionary movement in northwest, 170-171; role of Communists, 169-170, 173, 174
Arita, Hachiro, 128, 231
Ariyoshi, Akira, 50, 65, 76, 100, 124, 127
Asahi, 201, 222, 310, 317, 320
Aso, Hisashi, 223, 319
Augusta, 282
Autonomy movement in North China, 109; Ariyoshi deplores "unsettled conditions" in north, 76-77; arrests by Japanese military, 88-89; climax and collapse of, 94; conferences by Japan's officials in China, 72-74; demands at Tientsin by Kawagoe, 74, 75-76, 87-88, 143; Doihara confers with North China officials, 101; Doihara disavowed, 95-96; Doihara-Hsiao Chen-ying negotiations, 91-92; Kwantung Army divisions mobilized, 91; Nanking's attitude and policy, 92, 93, 94, 95, 98, 99, 100, 101, 102, 103-104; Peiping educators' manifesto, 99; preliminary Japanese moves, 69-70; riots at Hsiangho, 74; statement by Tokyo War Office spokesman, 72; Sung Che-yuan's telegram, 90; Tada statement, 70-71; temporary occupation of Fengtai, 101; Tokyo Ministries formulate "new China policy," 71-72, 74, 215

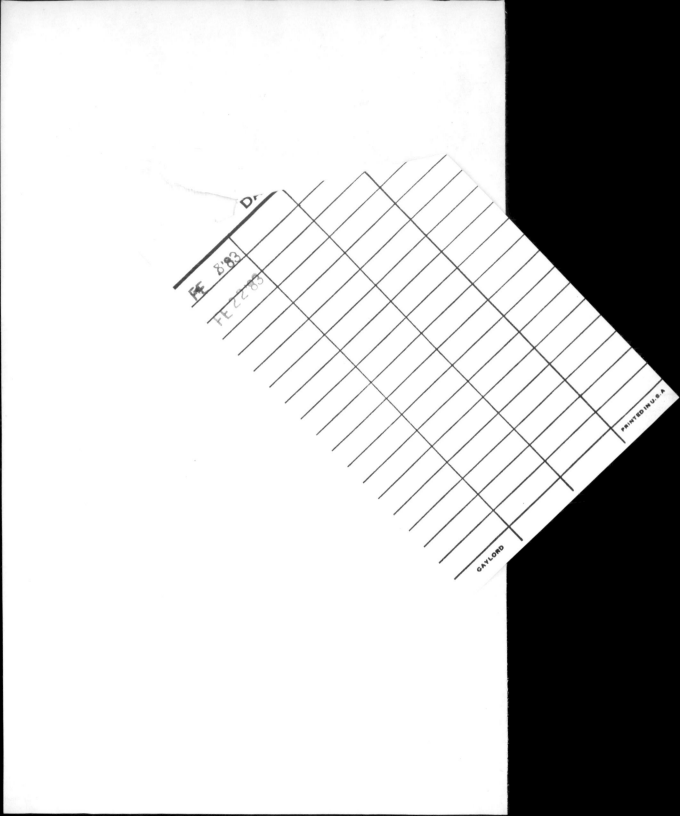